PAUL JENKINS'

SIDEKICK ™

VOLUME 1

12-GAUGE

12 GAUGE COMICS, LLC
KEVEN GARDNER - PRESIDENT
DOUG WAGNER - MANAGING EDITOR
BRIAN STELFREEZE - ART DIRECTOR
JASON PEARSON - DIRECTOR OF DEVELOPMENT
CULLY HAMNER - CREATIVE CONSULTANT
RANDY MARTIN - PUBLICATION DESIGNER

IMAGE COMICS, INC.
Erik Larsen - *Publisher*
Todd McFarlane - *President*
Marc Silvestri - *CEO*
Jim Valentino - *Vice-President*

Eric Stephenson - *Executive Director*
Joe Keatinge - *PR & Marketing Coordinator*
Thao Le - *Accounts Manager*
Rosemary Cao - *Accounting Assistant*
Traci Hui - *Traffic Manager*
Allen Hui - *Production Manager*
Jonathan Chan - *Production Artist*
Drew Gill - *Production Artist*
Chris Giarrusso - *Production Artist*
www.imagecomics.com

PAUL JENKINS' SIDEKICK, Vol. 1. 2007. First Printing. Published by Image Comics, Inc., Office of publication: 1942 University Avenue, Suite 305, Berkeley, California 94704. Originally published in single magazine format as PAUL JENKINS' SIDEKICK #1-5.

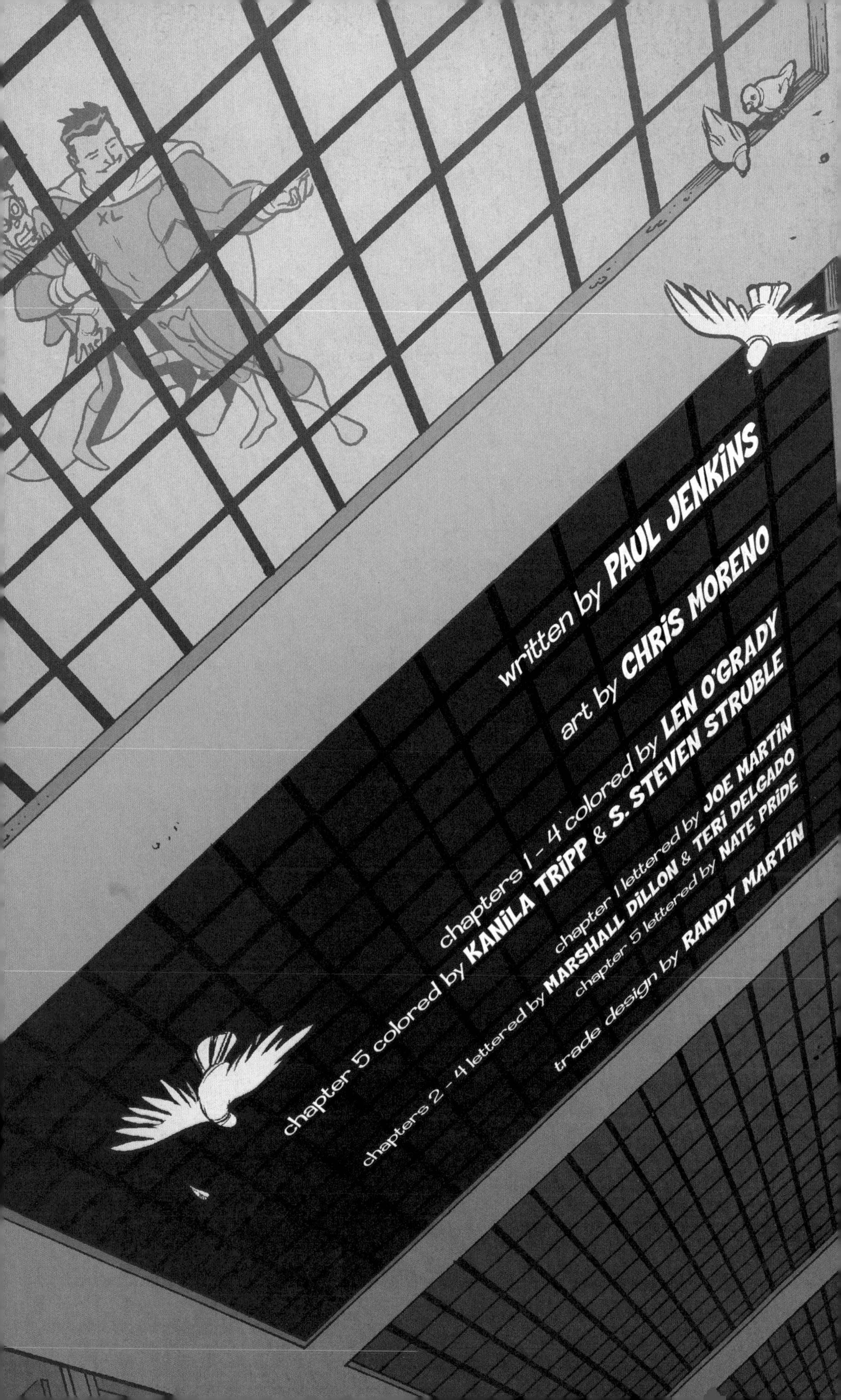
written by PAUL JENKINS
art by CHRIS MORENO
chapters 1 - 4 colored by LEN O'GRADY
chapter 5 colored by KANILA TRIPP & S. STEVEN STRUBLE
chapter 1 lettered by JOE MARTIN
chapters 2 - 4 lettered by MARSHALL DILLON & TERI DELGADO
chapter 5 lettered by NATE PRIDE
trade design by RANDY MARTIN
XL

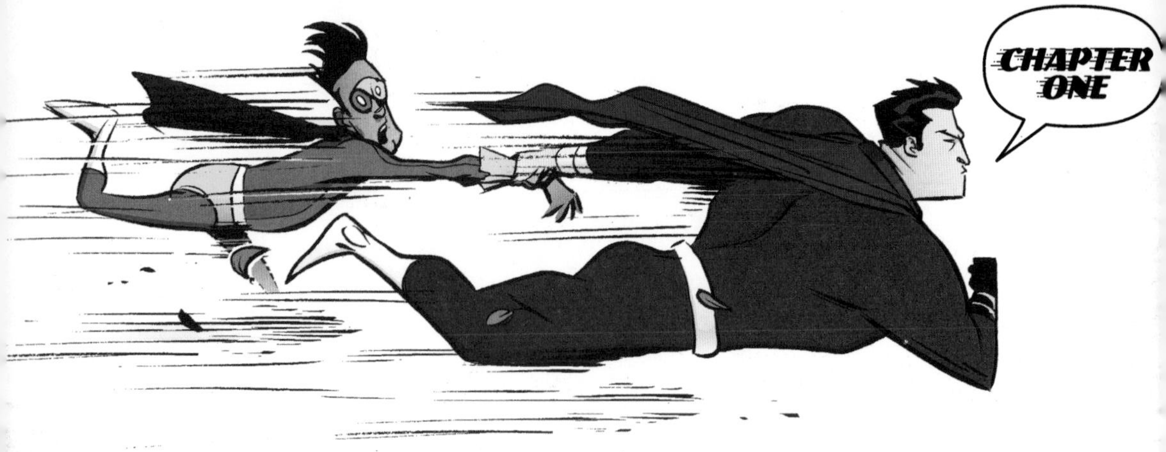
CHAPTER ONE

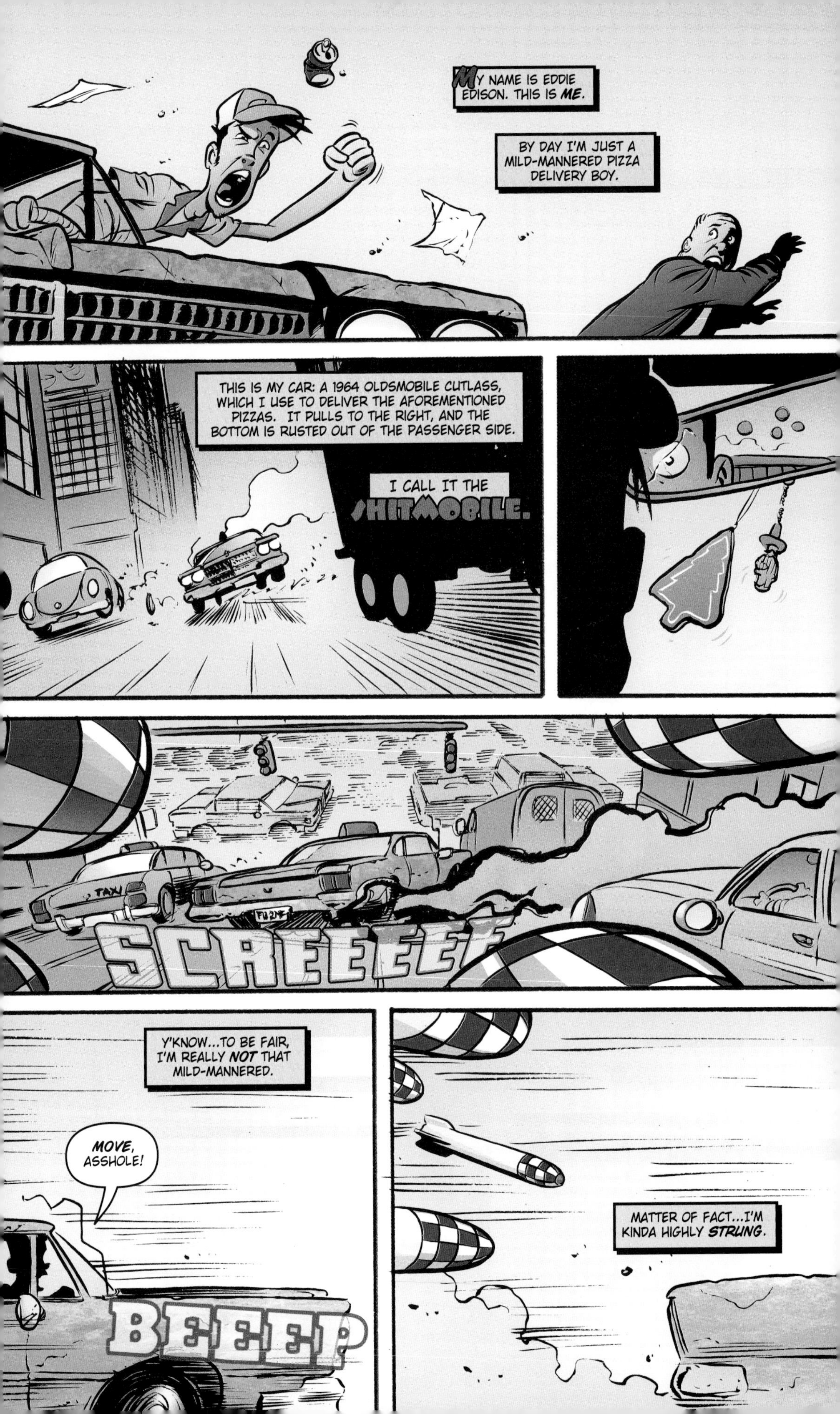

MY NAME IS EDDIE EDISON. THIS IS ***ME***.
BY DAY I'M JUST A MILD-MANNERED PIZZA DELIVERY BOY.
THIS IS MY CAR: A 1964 OLDSMOBILE CUTLASS, WHICH I USE TO DELIVER THE AFOREMENTIONED PIZZAS. IT PULLS TO THE RIGHT, AND THE BOTTOM IS RUSTED OUT OF THE PASSENGER SIDE.
I CALL IT THE
SHITMOBILE.
TAXI
SCREEEEE
Y'KNOW...TO BE FAIR, I'M REALLY ***NOT*** THAT MILD-MANNERED.
MOVE, ASSHOLE!
BEEEP
MATTER OF FACT...I'M KINDA HIGHLY ***STRUNG***.

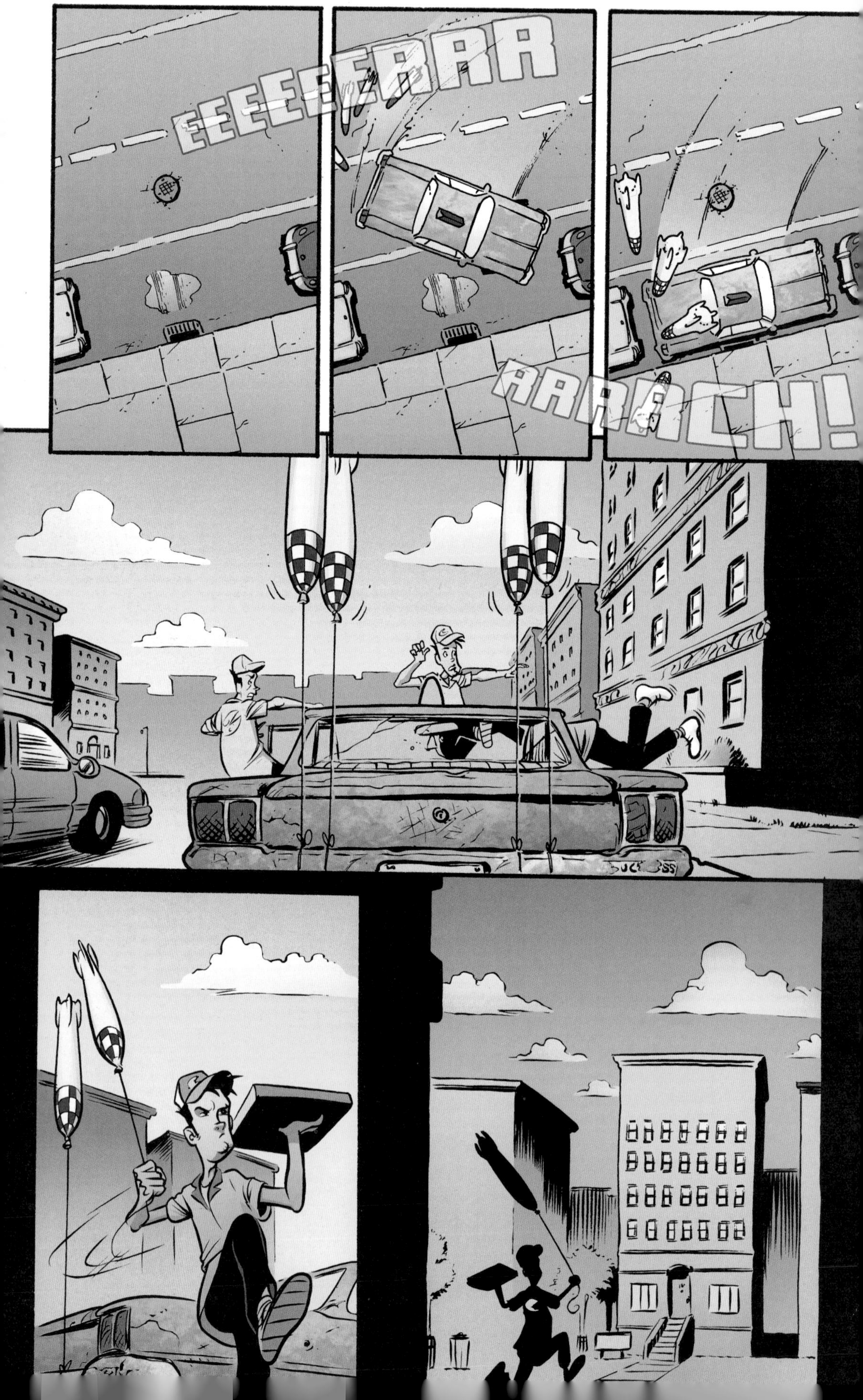
EEEEEERRR
RRRRCH!

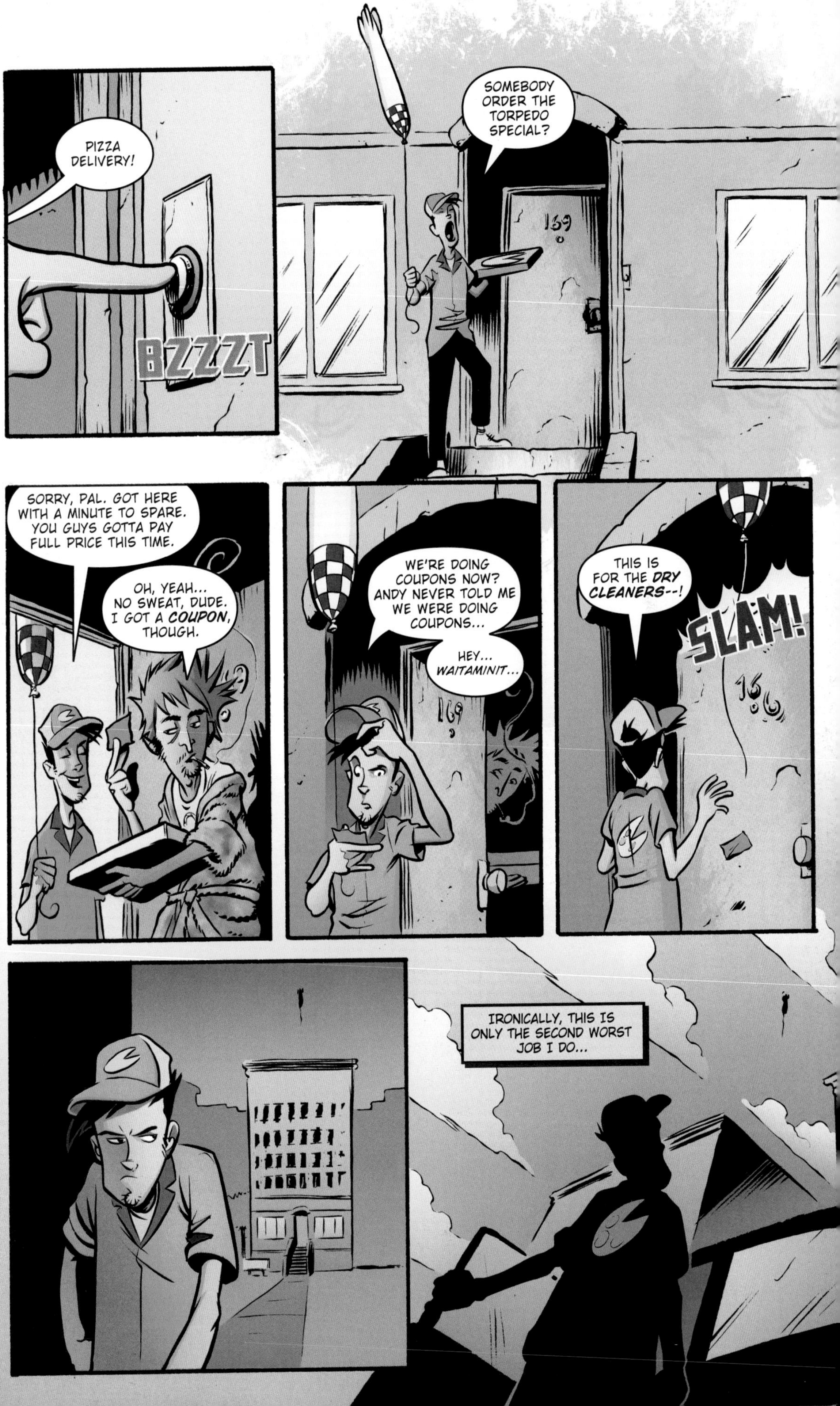
PIZZA DELIVERY!
BZZZT
SOMEBODY ORDER THE TORPEDO SPECIAL?
169
SORRY, PAL. GOT HERE WITH A MINUTE TO SPARE. YOU GUYS GOTTA PAY FULL PRICE THIS TIME.
OH, YEAH... NO SWEAT, DUDE. I GOT A *COUPON*, THOUGH.
WE'RE DOING COUPONS NOW? ANDY NEVER TOLD ME WE WERE DOING COUPONS...
HEY... *WAITAMINIT*...
169
THIS IS FOR THE *DRY CLEANERS*--!
SLAM!
IRONICALLY, THIS IS ONLY THE SECOND WORST JOB I DO...

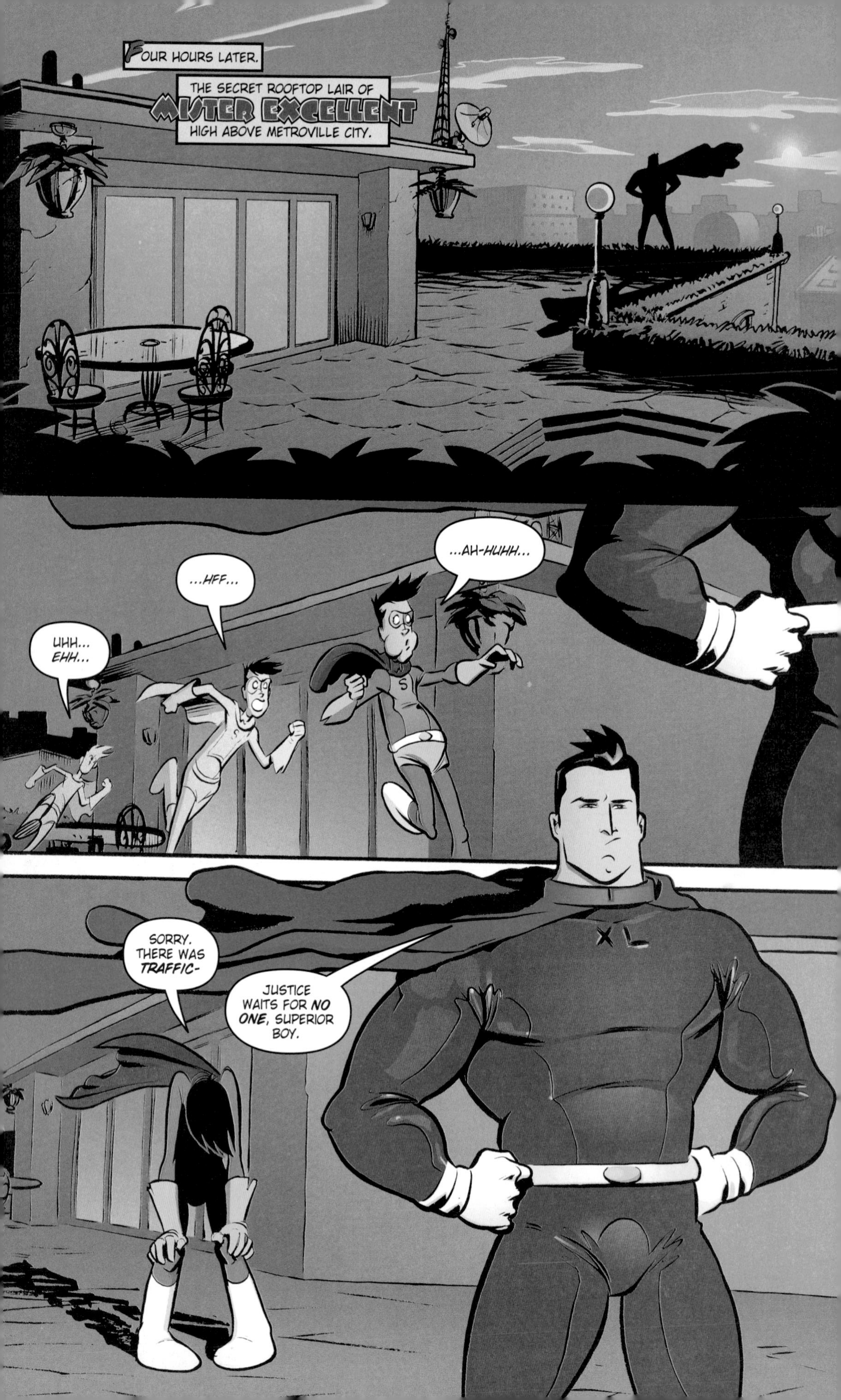
FOUR HOURS LATER.
THE SECRET ROOFTOP LAIR OF
MISTER EXCELLENT
HIGH ABOVE METROVILLE CITY.
UHH... EHH...
...HFF...
...AH-HUHH...
SORRY. THERE WAS TRAFFIC-
JUSTICE WAITS FOR NO ONE, SUPERIOR BOY.

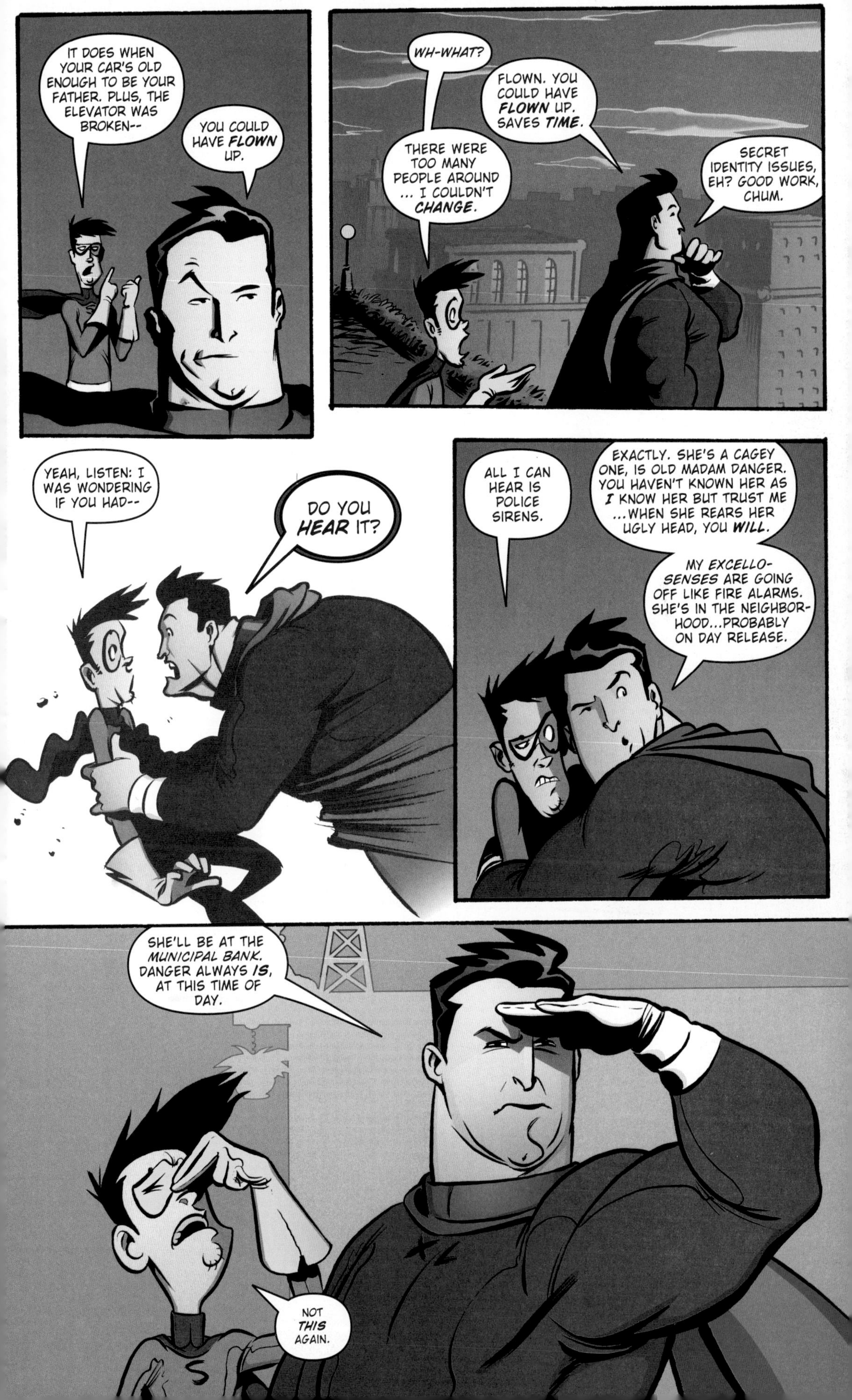
IT DOES WHEN YOUR CAR'S OLD ENOUGH TO BE YOUR FATHER. PLUS, THE ELEVATOR WAS BROKEN--
YOU COULD HAVE FLOWN UP.
WH-WHAT?
FLOWN. YOU COULD HAVE FLOWN UP. SAVES TIME.
THERE WERE TOO MANY PEOPLE AROUND ... I COULDN'T CHANGE.
SECRET IDENTITY ISSUES, EH? GOOD WORK, CHUM.
YEAH, LISTEN: I WAS WONDERING IF YOU HAD--
DO YOU HEAR IT?
ALL I CAN HEAR IS POLICE SIRENS.
EXACTLY. SHE'S A CAGEY ONE, IS OLD MADAM DANGER. YOU HAVEN'T KNOWN HER AS I KNOW HER BUT TRUST ME ...WHEN SHE REARS HER UGLY HEAD, YOU WILL.
MY EXCELLO-SENSES ARE GOING OFF LIKE FIRE ALARMS. SHE'S IN THE NEIGHBOR-HOOD...PROBABLY ON DAY RELEASE.
SHE'LL BE AT THE MUNICIPAL BANK. DANGER ALWAYS IS, AT THIS TIME OF DAY.
NOT THIS AGAIN.

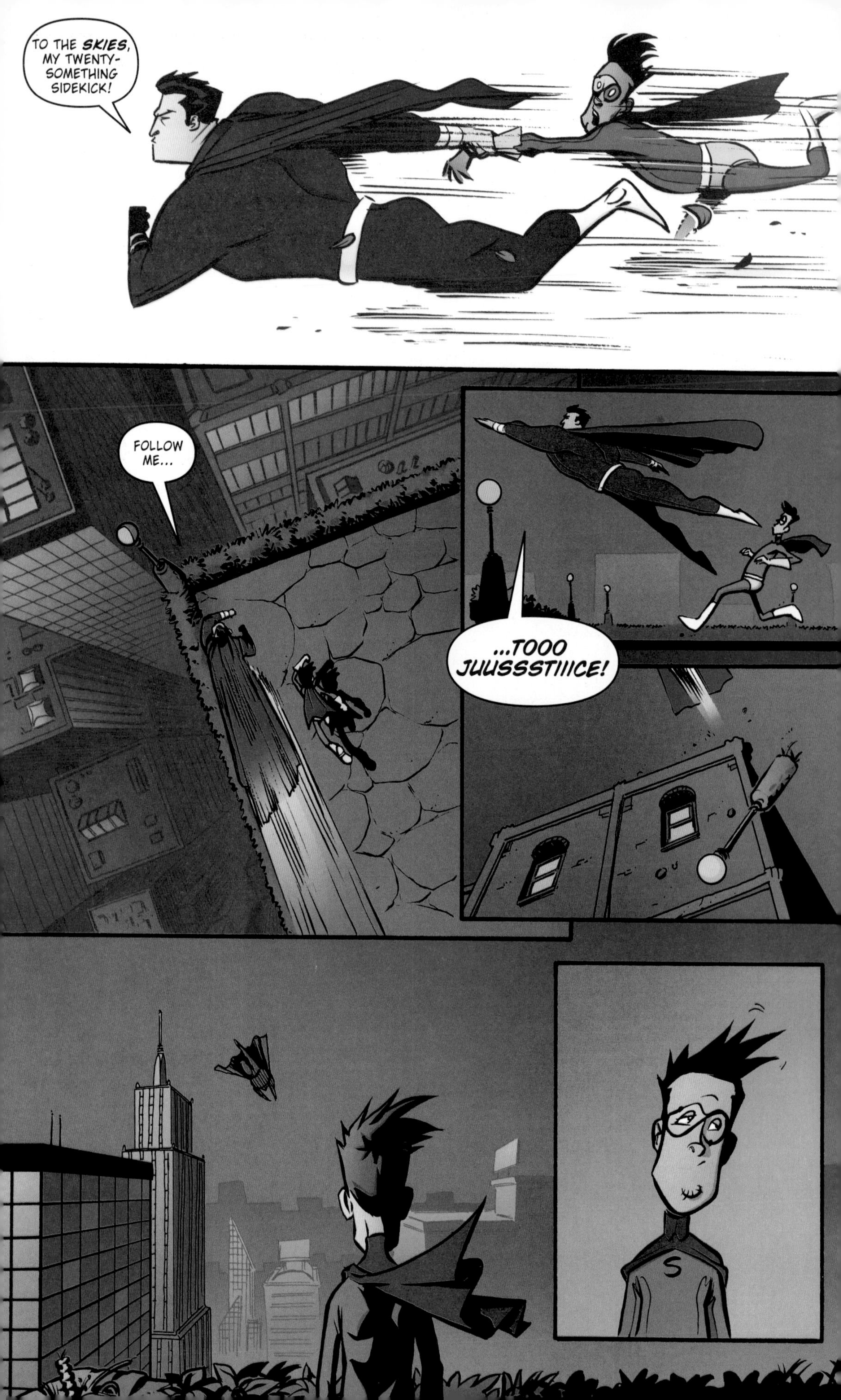
TO THE SKIES, MY TWENTY-SOMETHING SIDEKICK!
FOLLOW ME...
...TOOO JUUSSSTIIICE!

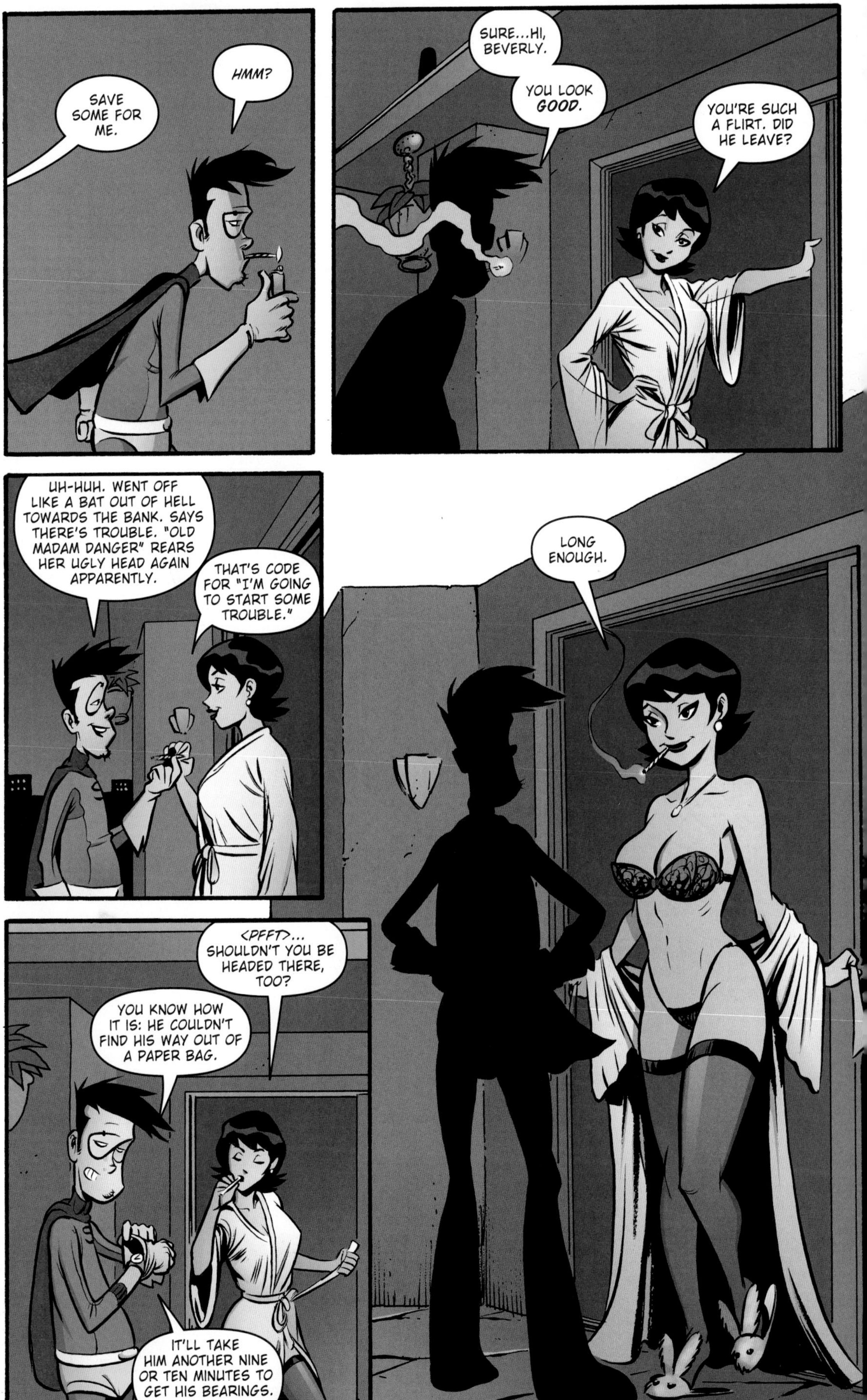
SAVE SOME FOR ME.
HMM?
SURE...HI, BEVERLY.
YOU LOOK GOOD.
YOU'RE SUCH A FLIRT. DID HE LEAVE?
UH-HUH. WENT OFF LIKE A BAT OUT OF HELL TOWARDS THE BANK. SAYS THERE'S TROUBLE. "OLD MADAM DANGER" REARS HER UGLY HEAD AGAIN APPARENTLY.
THAT'S CODE FOR "I'M GOING TO START SOME TROUBLE."
<PFFT>... SHOULDN'T YOU BE HEADED THERE, TOO?
YOU KNOW HOW IT IS: HE COULDN'T FIND HIS WAY OUT OF A PAPER BAG.
IT'LL TAKE HIM ANOTHER NINE OR TEN MINUTES TO GET HIS BEARINGS.
LONG ENOUGH.

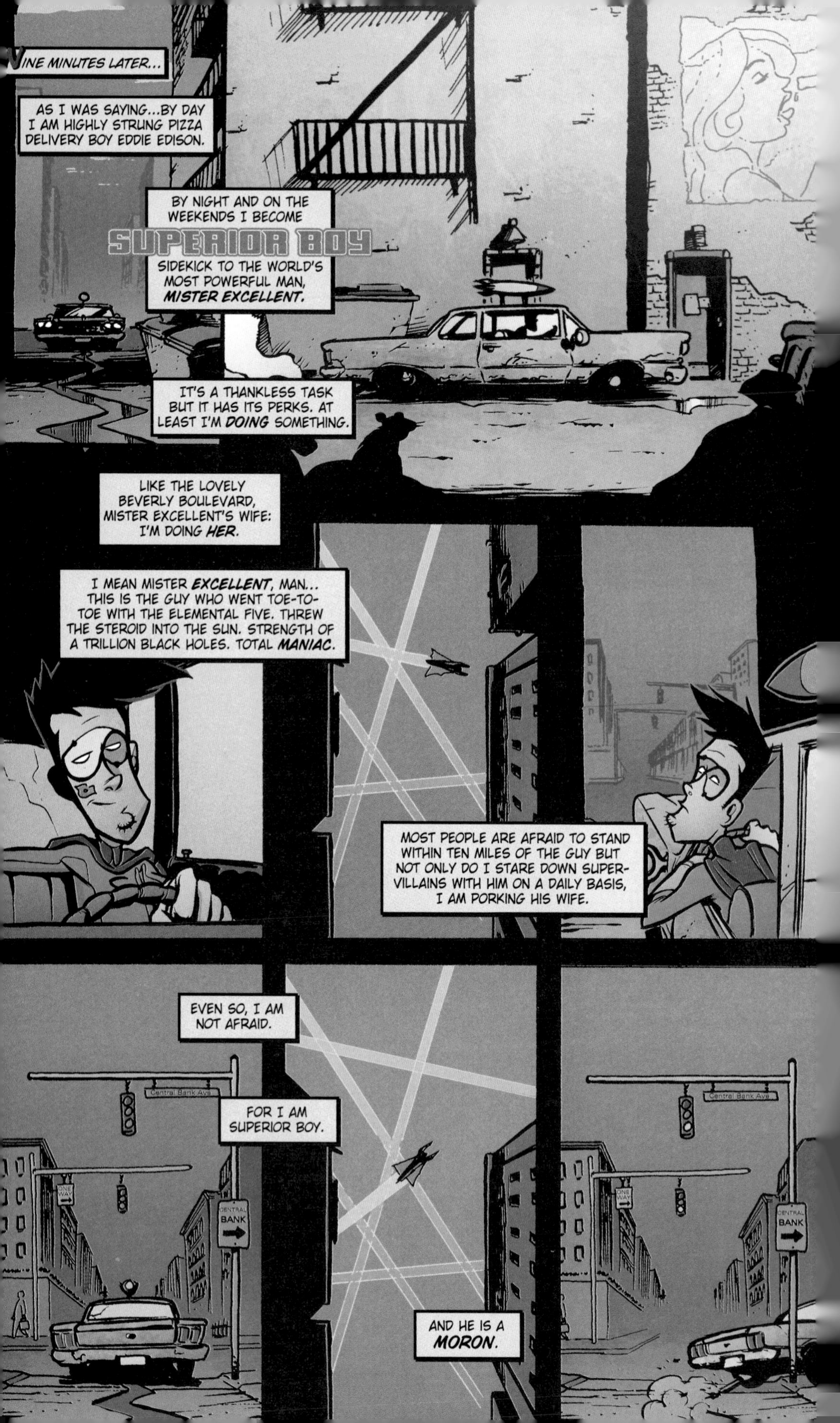
NINE MINUTES LATER...
AS I WAS SAYING...BY DAY I AM HIGHLY STRUNG PIZZA DELIVERY BOY EDDIE EDISON.
BY NIGHT AND ON THE WEEKENDS I BECOME SUPERIOR BOY SIDEKICK TO THE WORLD'S MOST POWERFUL MAN, MISTER EXCELLENT.
IT'S A THANKLESS TASK BUT IT HAS ITS PERKS. AT LEAST I'M DOING SOMETHING.
LIKE THE LOVELY BEVERLY BOULEVARD, MISTER EXCELLENT'S WIFE: I'M DOING HER.
I MEAN MISTER EXCELLENT, MAN... THIS IS THE GUY WHO WENT TOE-TO-TOE WITH THE ELEMENTAL FIVE. THREW THE STEROID INTO THE SUN. STRENGTH OF A TRILLION BLACK HOLES. TOTAL MANIAC.
MOST PEOPLE ARE AFRAID TO STAND WITHIN TEN MILES OF THE GUY BUT NOT ONLY DO I STARE DOWN SUPER-VILLAINS WITH HIM ON A DAILY BASIS, I AM PORKING HIS WIFE.
EVEN SO, I AM NOT AFRAID.
Central Bank Ave
FOR I AM SUPERIOR BOY.
ONE WAY
CENTRAL BANK
AND HE IS A MORON.
Central Bank Ave
ONE WAY
CENTRAL BANK

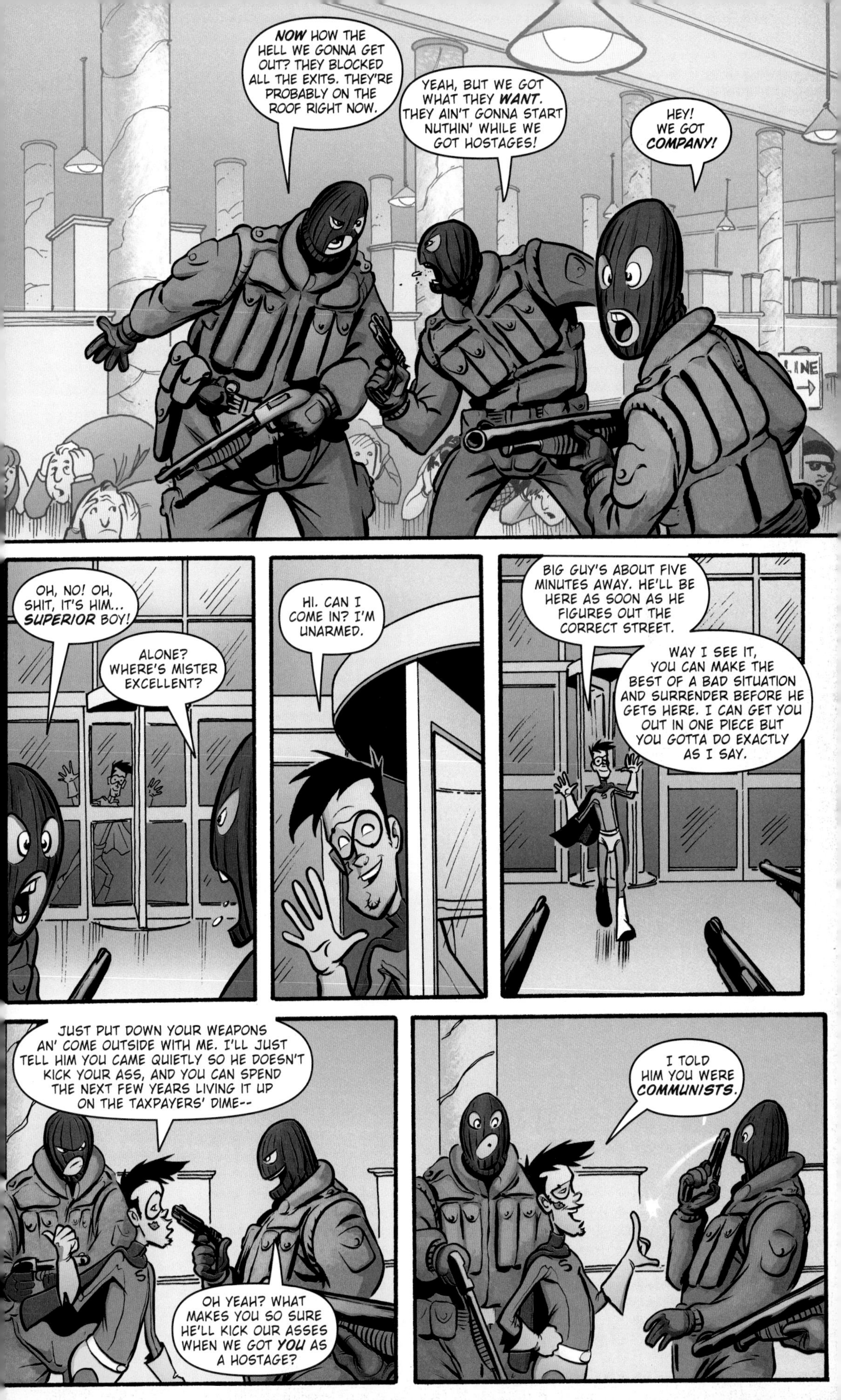
NOW HOW THE HELL WE GONNA GET OUT? THEY BLOCKED ALL THE EXITS. THEY'RE PROBABLY ON THE ROOF RIGHT NOW.
YEAH, BUT WE GOT WHAT THEY WANT. THEY AIN'T GONNA START NUTHIN' WHILE WE GOT HOSTAGES!
HEY! WE GOT COMPANY!
LINE
OH, NO! OH, SHIT, IT'S HIM... SUPERIOR BOY!
ALONE? WHERE'S MISTER EXCELLENT?
HI. CAN I COME IN? I'M UNARMED.
BIG GUY'S ABOUT FIVE MINUTES AWAY. HE'LL BE HERE AS SOON AS HE FIGURES OUT THE CORRECT STREET.
WAY I SEE IT, YOU CAN MAKE THE BEST OF A BAD SITUATION AND SURRENDER BEFORE HE GETS HERE. I CAN GET YOU OUT IN ONE PIECE BUT YOU GOTTA DO EXACTLY AS I SAY.
JUST PUT DOWN YOUR WEAPONS AN' COME OUTSIDE WITH ME. I'LL JUST TELL HIM YOU CAME QUIETLY SO HE DOESN'T KICK YOUR ASS, AND YOU CAN SPEND THE NEXT FEW YEARS LIVING IT UP ON THE TAXPAYERS' DIME--
OH YEAH? WHAT MAKES YOU SO SURE HE'LL KICK OUR ASSES WHEN WE GOT YOU AS A HOSTAGE?
I TOLD HIM YOU WERE COMMUNISTS.

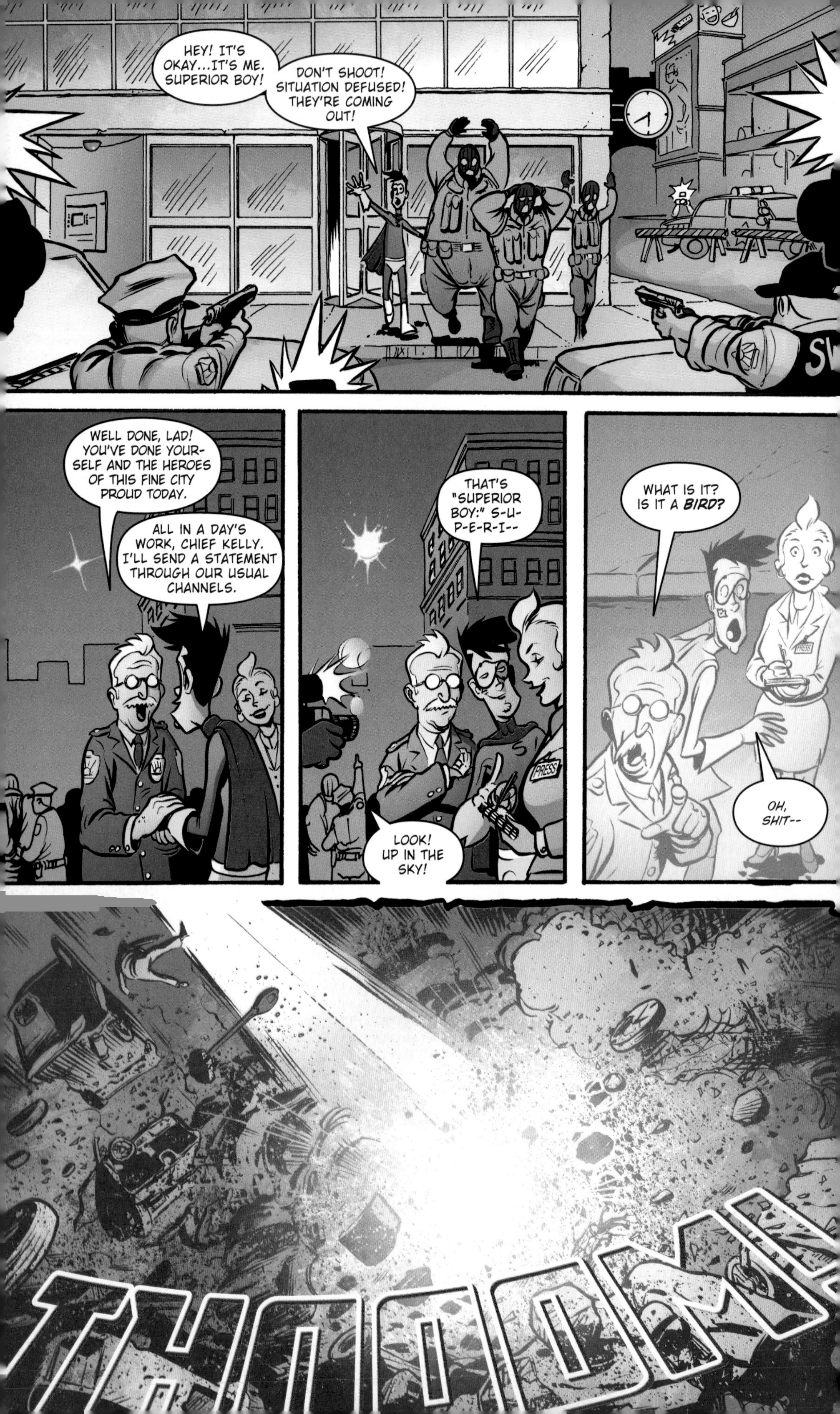
HEY! IT'S OKAY...IT'S ME. SUPERIOR BOY!
DON'T SHOOT! SITUATION DEFUSED! THEY'RE COMING OUT!
WELL DONE, LAD! YOU'VE DONE YOUR-SELF AND THE HEROES OF THIS FINE CITY PROUD TODAY.
ALL IN A DAY'S WORK, CHIEF KELLY. I'LL SEND A STATEMENT THROUGH OUR USUAL CHANNELS.
THAT'S "SUPERIOR BOY:" S-U-P-E-R-I--
LOOK! UP IN THE SKY!
WHAT IS IT? IS IT A *BIRD?*
OH, SHIT--
THOOOM!

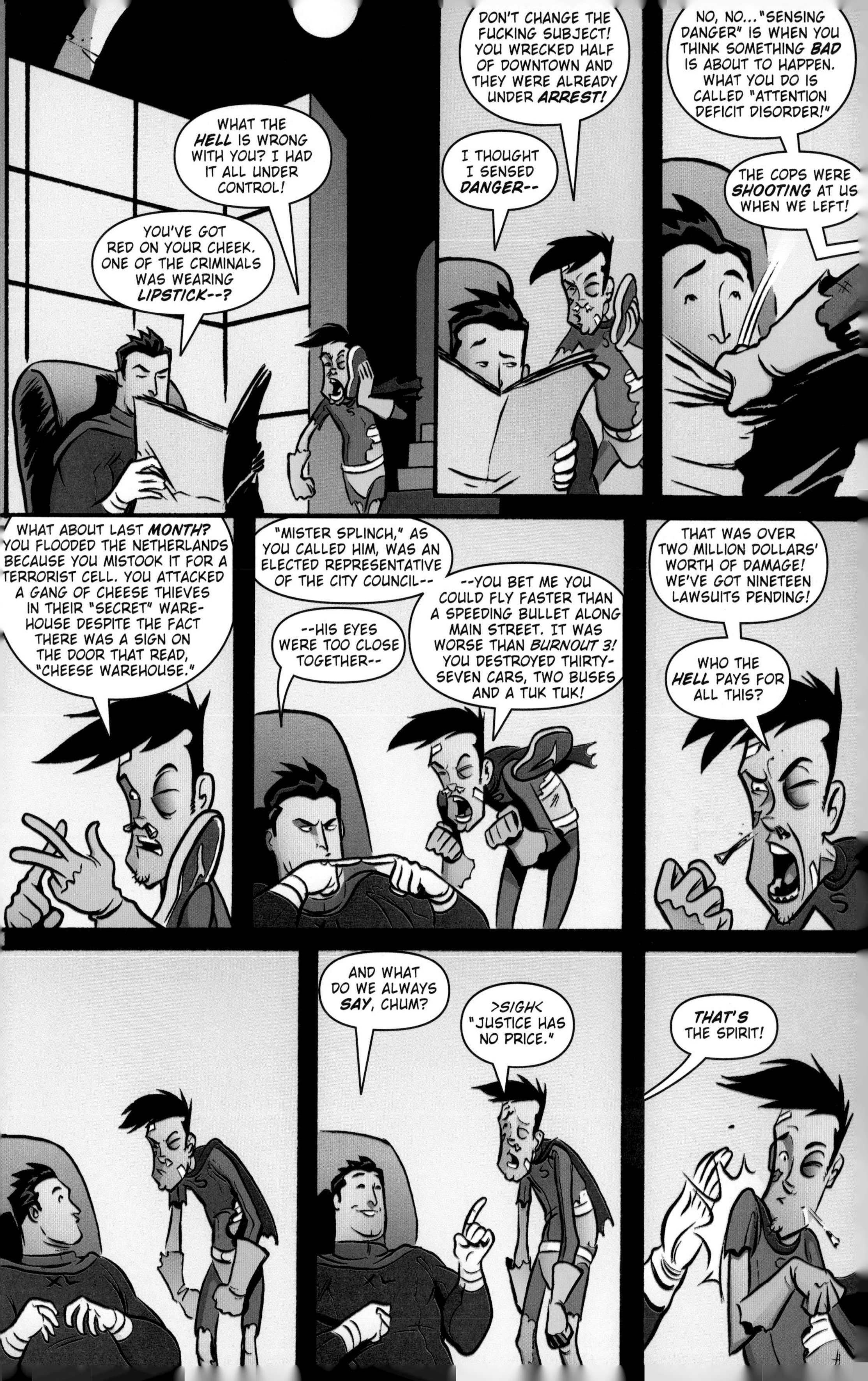
WHAT THE HELL IS WRONG WITH YOU? I HAD IT ALL UNDER CONTROL!
YOU'VE GOT RED ON YOUR CHEEK. ONE OF THE CRIMINALS WAS WEARING LIPSTICK--?
DON'T CHANGE THE FUCKING SUBJECT! YOU WRECKED HALF OF DOWNTOWN AND THEY WERE ALREADY UNDER ARREST!
I THOUGHT I SENSED DANGER--
NO, NO..."SENSING DANGER" IS WHEN YOU THINK SOMETHING BAD IS ABOUT TO HAPPEN. WHAT YOU DO IS CALLED "ATTENTION DEFICIT DISORDER!"
THE COPS WERE SHOOTING AT US WHEN WE LEFT!
WHAT ABOUT LAST MONTH? YOU FLOODED THE NETHERLANDS BECAUSE YOU MISTOOK IT FOR A TERRORIST CELL. YOU ATTACKED A GANG OF CHEESE THIEVES IN THEIR "SECRET" WAREHOUSE DESPITE THE FACT THERE WAS A SIGN ON THE DOOR THAT READ, "CHEESE WAREHOUSE."
"MISTER SPLINCH," AS YOU CALLED HIM, WAS AN ELECTED REPRESENTATIVE OF THE CITY COUNCIL--
--HIS EYES WERE TOO CLOSE TOGETHER--
--YOU BET ME YOU COULD FLY FASTER THAN A SPEEDING BULLET ALONG MAIN STREET. IT WAS WORSE THAN BURNOUT 3! YOU DESTROYED THIRTY-SEVEN CARS, TWO BUSES AND A TUK TUK!
THAT WAS OVER TWO MILLION DOLLARS' WORTH OF DAMAGE! WE'VE GOT NINETEEN LAWSUITS PENDING!
WHO THE HELL PAYS FOR ALL THIS?
AND WHAT DO WE ALWAYS SAY, CHUM?
>SIGH< "JUSTICE HAS NO PRICE."
THAT'S THE SPIRIT!

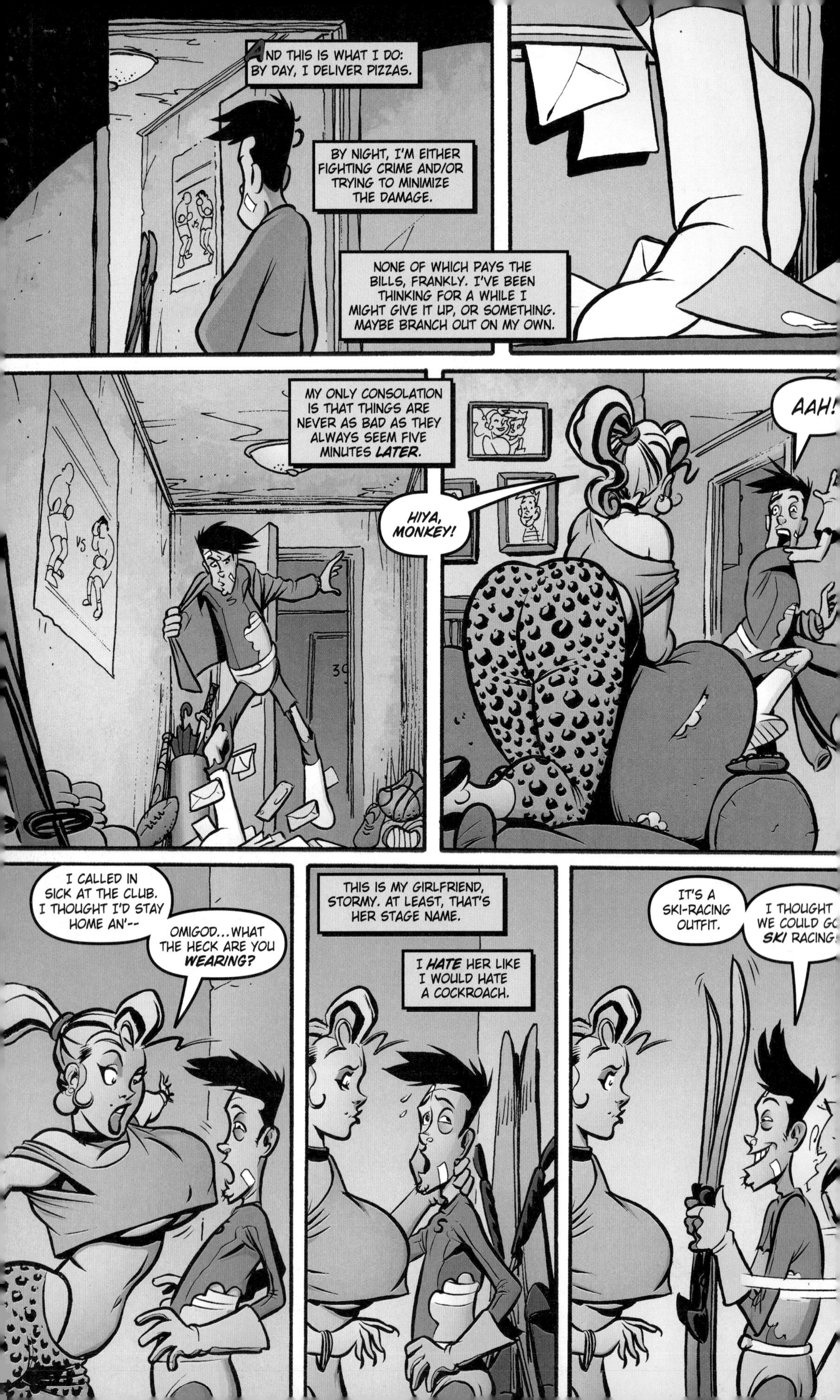
AND THIS IS WHAT I DO: BY DAY, I DELIVER PIZZAS.
BY NIGHT, I'M EITHER FIGHTING CRIME AND/OR TRYING TO MINIMIZE THE DAMAGE.
NONE OF WHICH PAYS THE BILLS, FRANKLY. I'VE BEEN THINKING FOR A WHILE I MIGHT GIVE IT UP, OR SOMETHING. MAYBE BRANCH OUT ON MY OWN.
MY ONLY CONSOLATION IS THAT THINGS ARE NEVER AS BAD AS THEY ALWAYS SEEM FIVE MINUTES LATER.
HIYA, MONKEY!
AAH!
I CALLED IN SICK AT THE CLUB. I THOUGHT I'D STAY HOME AN'--
OMIGOD...WHAT THE HECK ARE YOU WEARING?
THIS IS MY GIRLFRIEND, STORMY. AT LEAST, THAT'S HER STAGE NAME.
I HATE HER LIKE I WOULD HATE A COCKROACH.
IT'S A SKI-RACING OUTFIT.
I THOUGHT WE COULD GO SKI RACING!

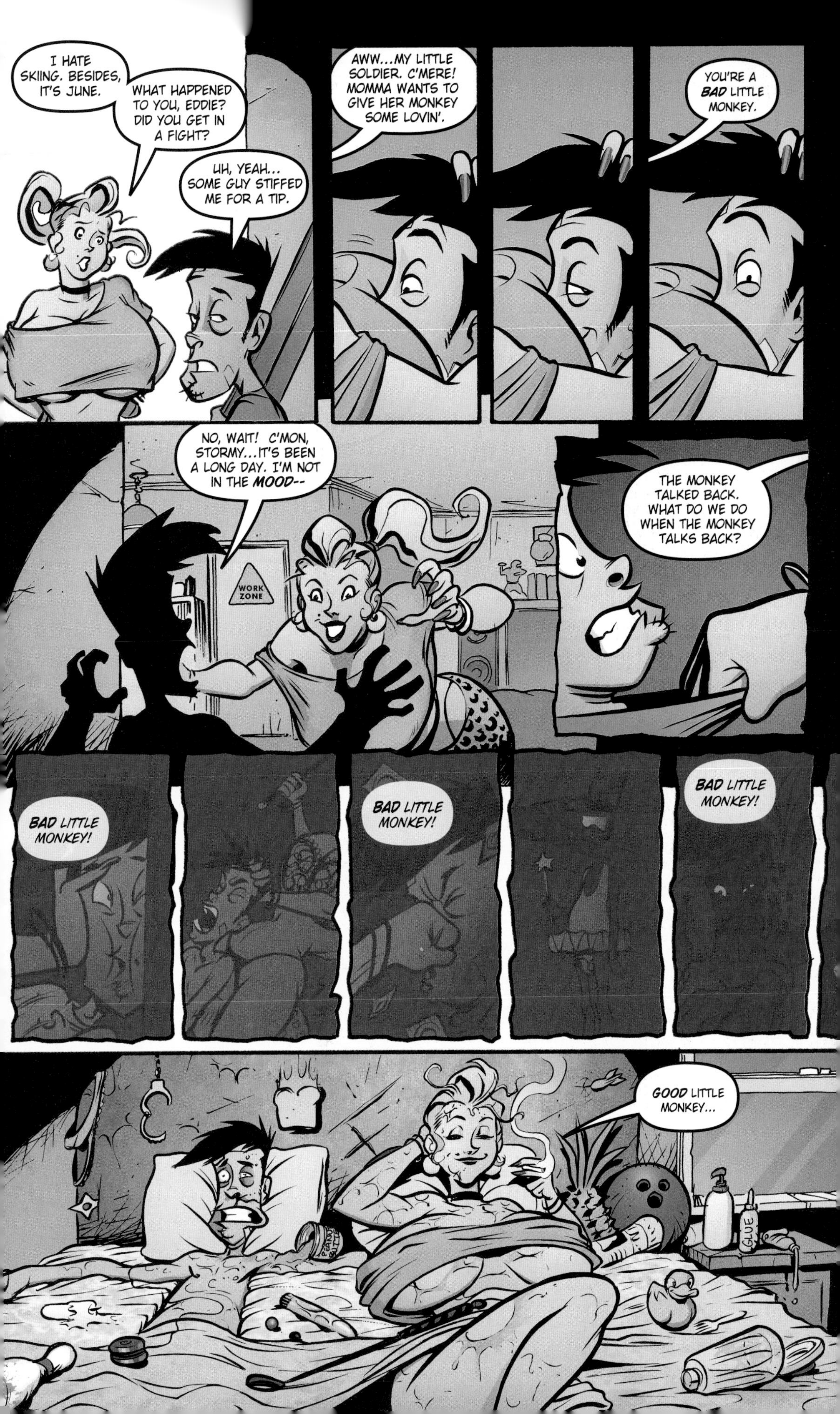
I HATE SKIING. BESIDES, IT'S JUNE.
WHAT HAPPENED TO YOU, EDDIE? DID YOU GET IN A FIGHT?
UH, YEAH... SOME GUY STIFFED ME FOR A TIP.
AWW...MY LITTLE SOLDIER. C'MERE! MOMMA WANTS TO GIVE HER MONKEY SOME LOVIN'.
YOU'RE A BAD LITTLE MONKEY.
NO, WAIT! C'MON, STORMY...IT'S BEEN A LONG DAY. I'M NOT IN THE MOOD--
WORK ZONE
THE MONKEY TALKED BACK. WHAT DO WE DO WHEN THE MONKEY TALKS BACK?
BAD LITTLE MONKEY!
BAD LITTLE MONKEY!
BAD LITTLE MONKEY!
GOOD LITTLE MONKEY...
PEANUT BUTTER
GLUE

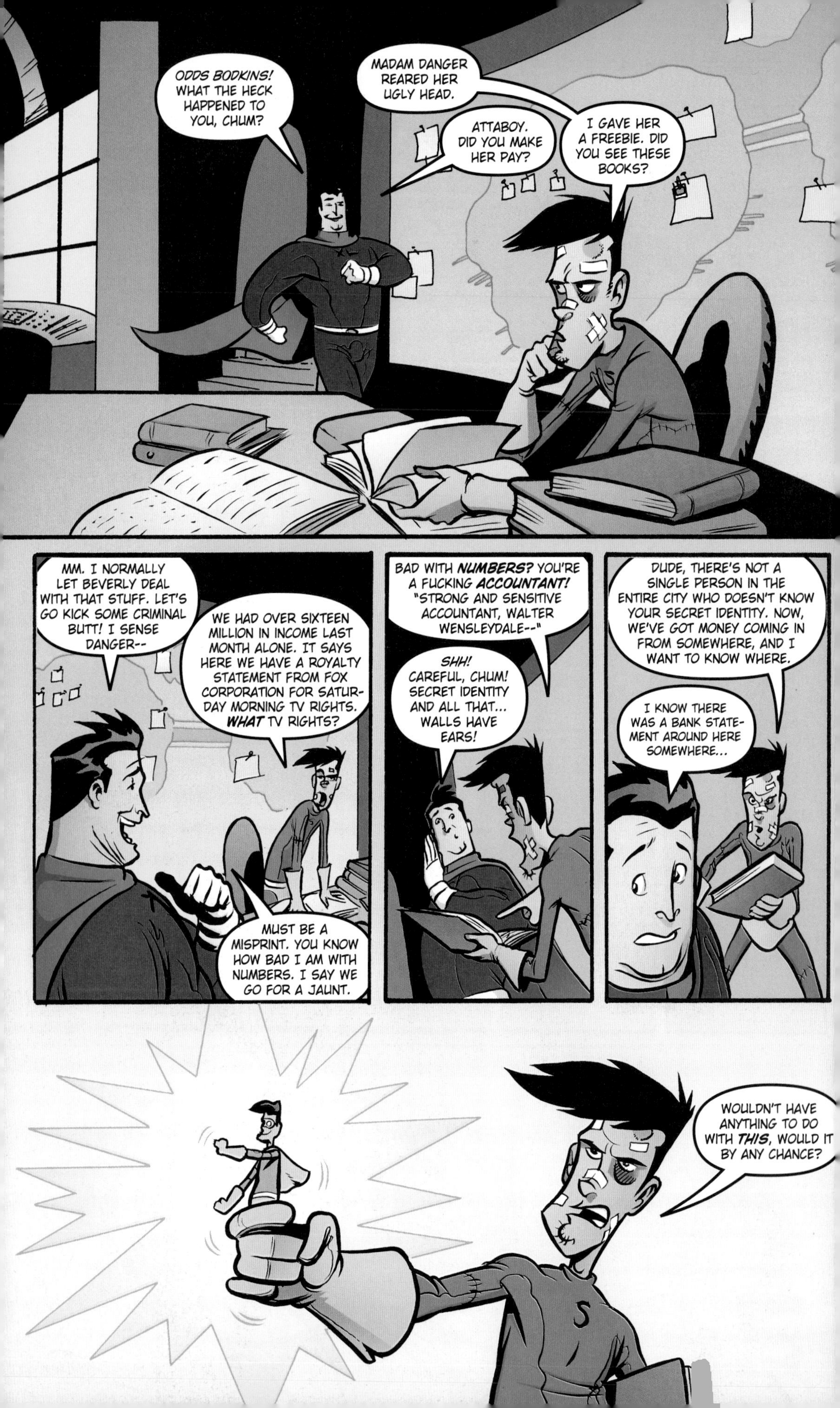
ODDS BODKINS! WHAT THE HECK HAPPENED TO YOU, CHUM?
MADAM DANGER REARED HER UGLY HEAD.
ATTABOY. DID YOU MAKE HER PAY?
I GAVE HER A FREEBIE. DID YOU SEE THESE BOOKS?
MM. I NORMALLY LET BEVERLY DEAL WITH THAT STUFF. LET'S GO KICK SOME CRIMINAL BUTT! I SENSE DANGER--
WE HAD OVER SIXTEEN MILLION IN INCOME LAST MONTH ALONE. IT SAYS HERE WE HAVE A ROYALTY STATEMENT FROM FOX CORPORATION FOR SATURDAY MORNING TV RIGHTS. WHAT TV RIGHTS?
MUST BE A MISPRINT. YOU KNOW HOW BAD I AM WITH NUMBERS. I SAY WE GO FOR A JAUNT.
BAD WITH NUMBERS? YOU'RE A FUCKING ACCOUNTANT! "STRONG AND SENSITIVE ACCOUNTANT, WALTER WENSLEYDALE--"
SHH! CAREFUL, CHUM! SECRET IDENTITY AND ALL THAT... WALLS HAVE EARS!
DUDE, THERE'S NOT A SINGLE PERSON IN THE ENTIRE CITY WHO DOESN'T KNOW YOUR SECRET IDENTITY. NOW, WE'VE GOT MONEY COMING IN FROM SOMEWHERE, AND I WANT TO KNOW WHERE.
I KNOW THERE WAS A BANK STATEMENT AROUND HERE SOMEWHERE...
WOULDN'T HAVE ANYTHING TO DO WITH THIS, WOULD IT BY ANY CHANCE?

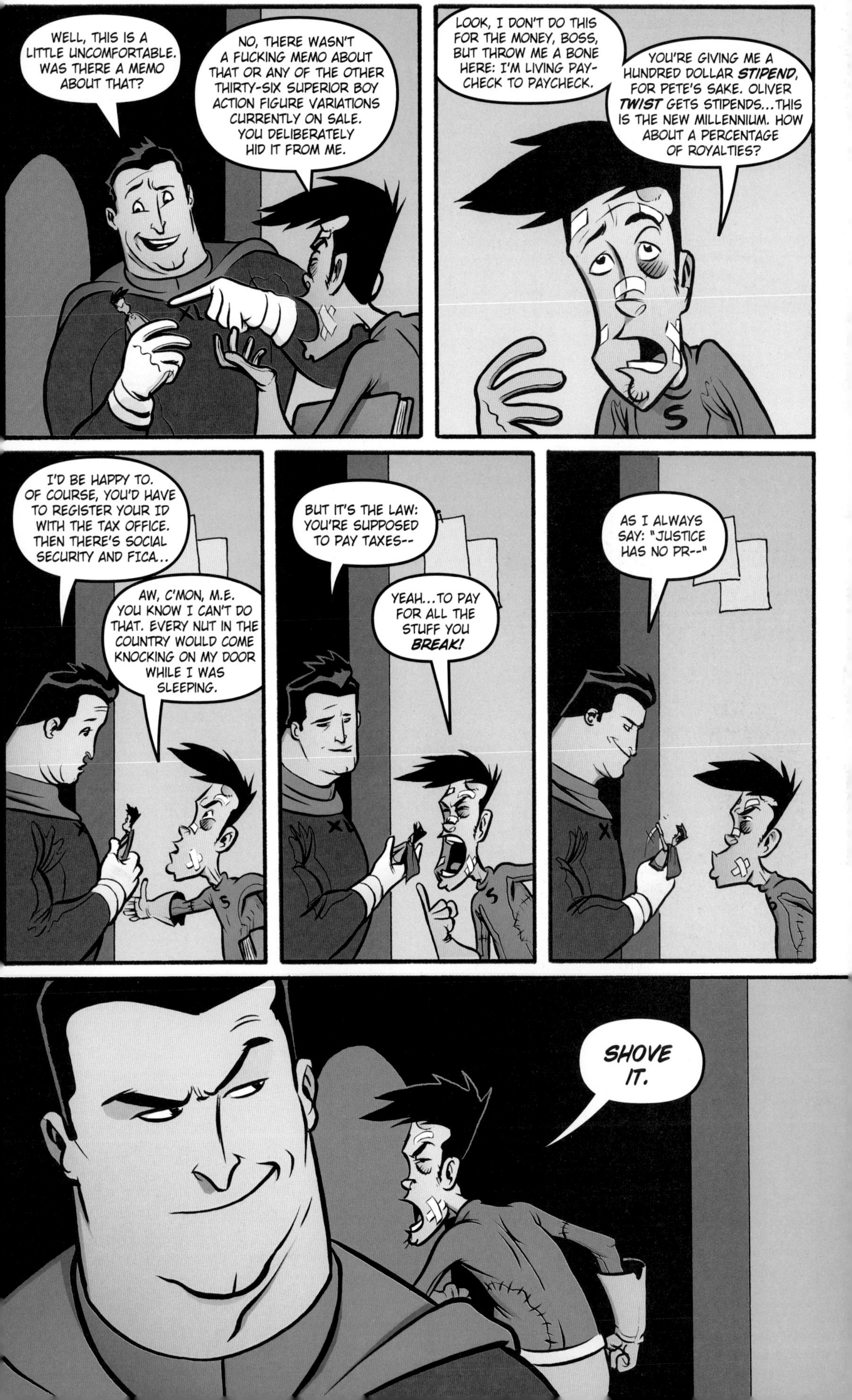
WELL, THIS IS A LITTLE UNCOMFORTABLE. WAS THERE A MEMO ABOUT THAT?
NO, THERE WASN'T A FUCKING MEMO ABOUT THAT OR ANY OF THE OTHER THIRTY-SIX SUPERIOR BOY ACTION FIGURE VARIATIONS CURRENTLY ON SALE. YOU DELIBERATELY HID IT FROM ME.
LOOK, I DON'T DO THIS FOR THE MONEY, BOSS, BUT THROW ME A BONE HERE: I'M LIVING PAY-CHECK TO PAYCHECK.
YOU'RE GIVING ME A HUNDRED DOLLAR *STIPEND*, FOR PETE'S SAKE. OLIVER *TWIST* GETS STIPENDS... THIS IS THE NEW MILLENNIUM. HOW ABOUT A PERCENTAGE OF ROYALTIES?
I'D BE HAPPY TO. OF COURSE, YOU'D HAVE TO REGISTER YOUR ID WITH THE TAX OFFICE. THEN THERE'S SOCIAL SECURITY AND FICA...
AW, C'MON, M.E. YOU KNOW I CAN'T DO THAT. EVERY NUT IN THE COUNTRY WOULD COME KNOCKING ON MY DOOR WHILE I WAS SLEEPING.
BUT IT'S THE LAW: YOU'RE SUPPOSED TO PAY TAXES--
YEAH... TO PAY FOR ALL THE STUFF YOU *BREAK!*
AS I ALWAYS SAY: "JUSTICE HAS NO PR--"
SHOVE IT.

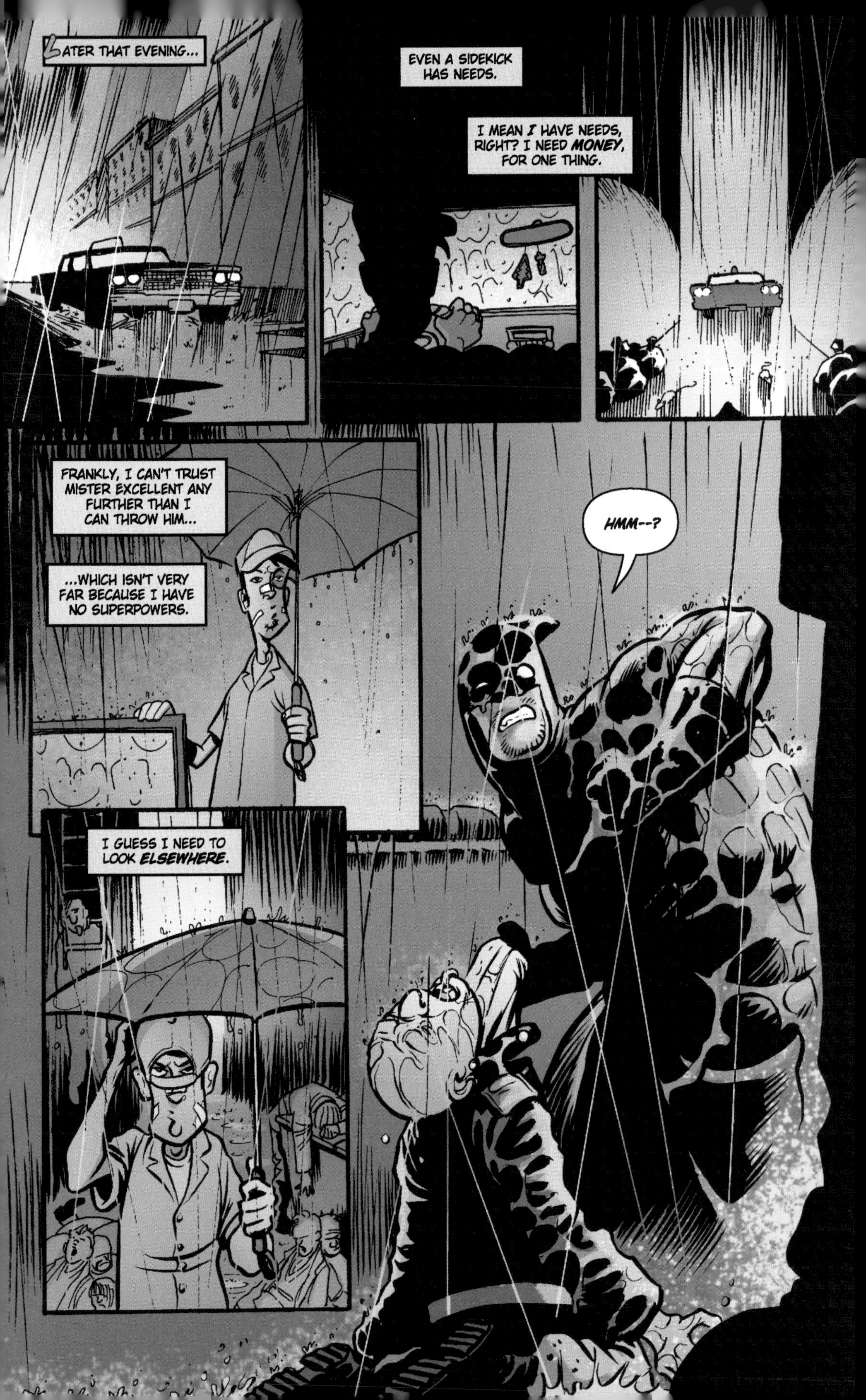
LATER THAT EVENING...
EVEN A SIDEKICK HAS NEEDS.
I MEAN I HAVE NEEDS, RIGHT? I NEED MONEY, FOR ONE THING.
FRANKLY, I CAN'T TRUST MISTER EXCELLENT ANY FURTHER THAN I CAN THROW HIM...
...WHICH ISN'T VERY FAR BECAUSE I HAVE NO SUPERPOWERS.
HMM--?
I GUESS I NEED TO LOOK ELSEWHERE.

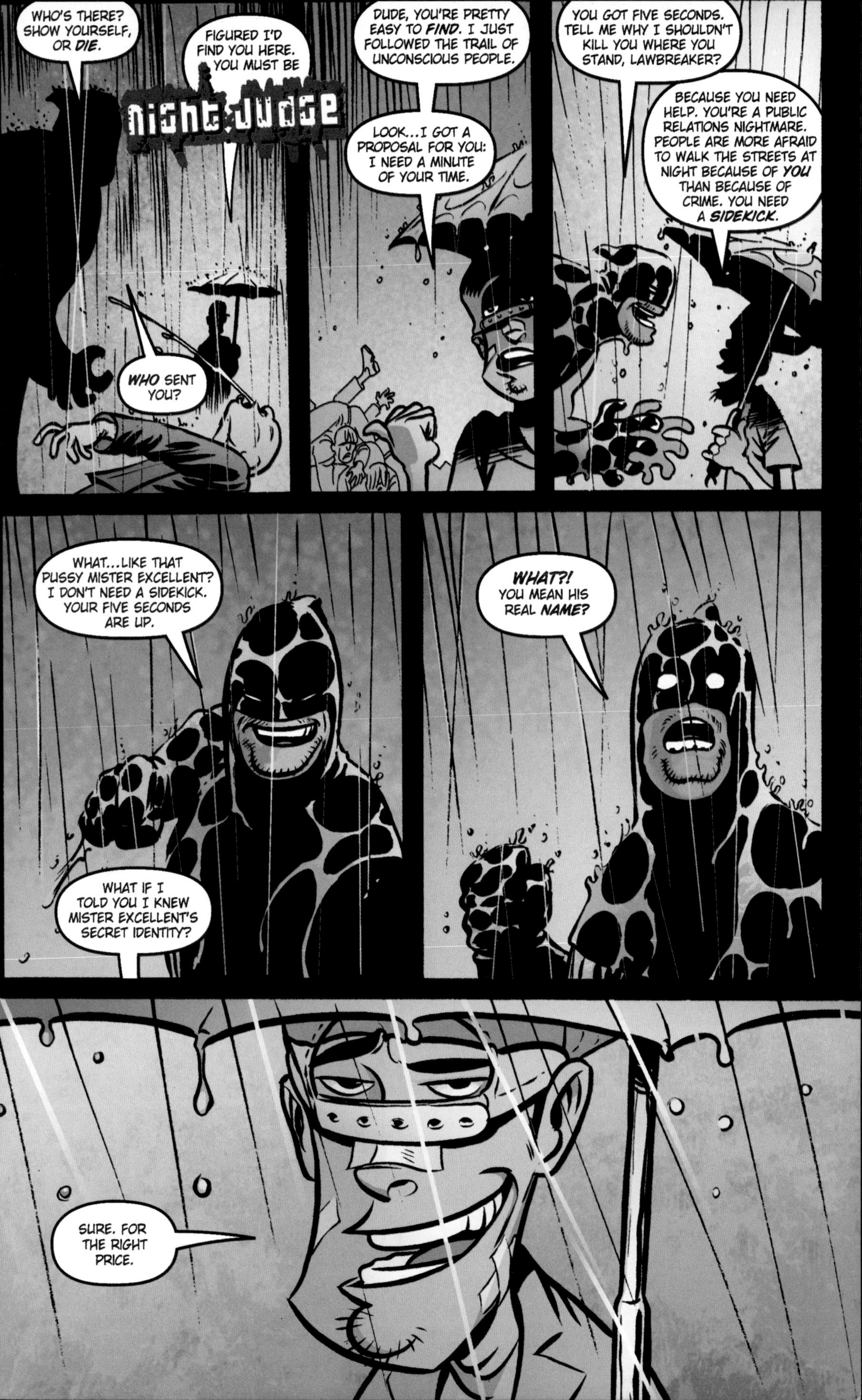
WHO'S THERE? SHOW YOURSELF, OR DIE.
FIGURED I'D FIND YOU HERE. YOU MUST BE
NIGHT JUDGE
WHO SENT YOU?
DUDE, YOU'RE PRETTY EASY TO FIND. I JUST FOLLOWED THE TRAIL OF UNCONSCIOUS PEOPLE.
LOOK...I GOT A PROPOSAL FOR YOU: I NEED A MINUTE OF YOUR TIME.
YOU GOT FIVE SECONDS. TELL ME WHY I SHOULDN'T KILL YOU WHERE YOU STAND, LAWBREAKER?
BECAUSE YOU NEED HELP. YOU'RE A PUBLIC RELATIONS NIGHTMARE. PEOPLE ARE MORE AFRAID TO WALK THE STREETS AT NIGHT BECAUSE OF YOU THAN BECAUSE OF CRIME. YOU NEED A SIDEKICK.
WHAT...LIKE THAT PUSSY MISTER EXCELLENT? I DON'T NEED A SIDEKICK. YOUR FIVE SECONDS ARE UP.
WHAT IF I TOLD YOU I KNEW MISTER EXCELLENT'S SECRET IDENTITY?
WHAT?! YOU MEAN HIS REAL NAME?
SURE. FOR THE RIGHT PRICE.

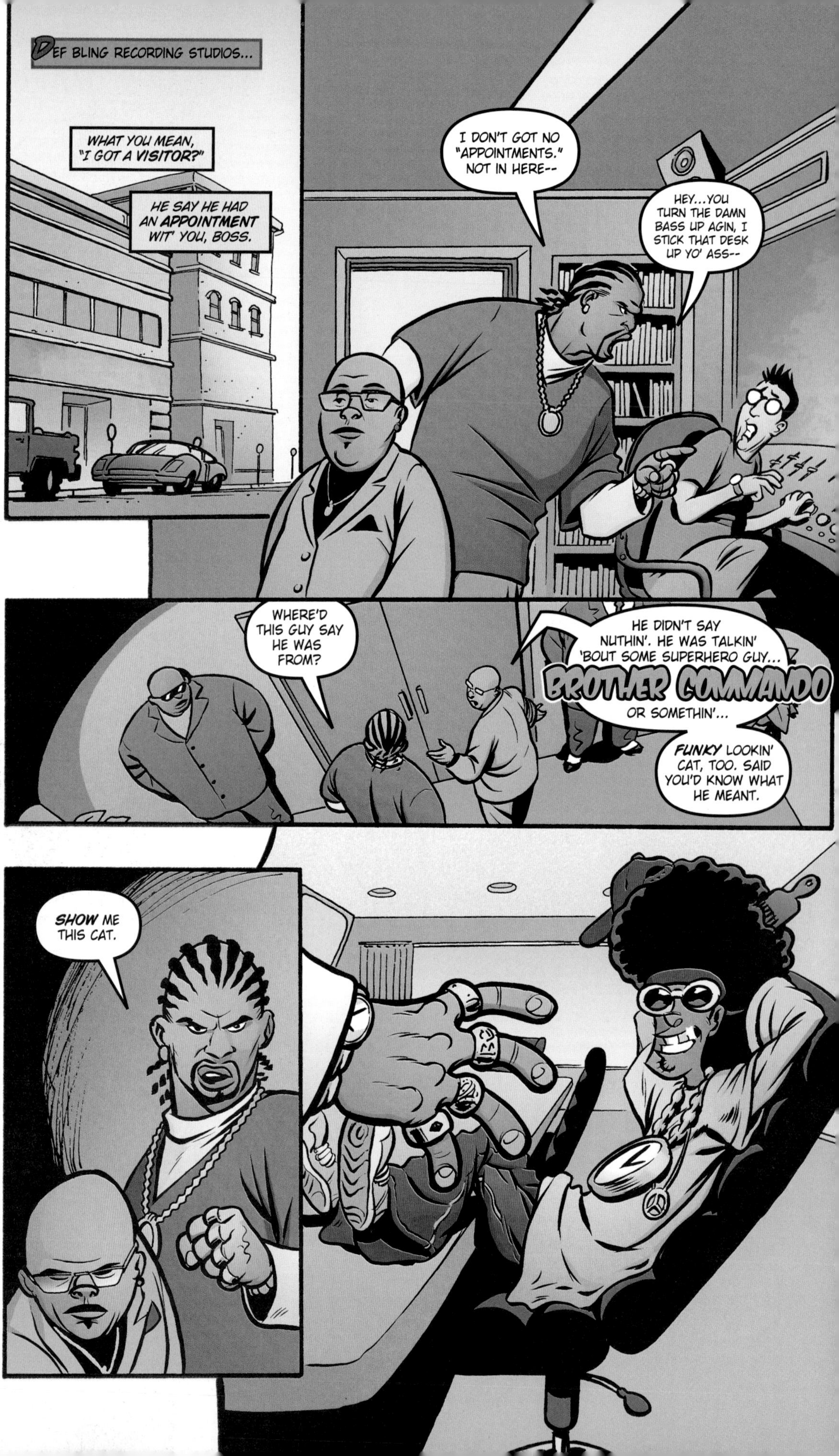
DEF BLING RECORDING STUDIOS...
WHAT YOU MEAN, "I GOT A VISITOR?"
HE SAY HE HAD AN APPOINTMENT WIT' YOU, BOSS.
I DON'T GOT NO "APPOINTMENTS." NOT IN HERE--
HEY...YOU TURN THE DAMN BASS UP AGIN, I STICK THAT DESK UP YO' ASS--
WHERE'D THIS GUY SAY HE WAS FROM?
HE DIDN'T SAY NUTHIN'. HE WAS TALKIN' 'BOUT SOME SUPERHERO GUY... BROTHER COMMANDO OR SOMETHIN'...
FUNKY LOOKIN' CAT, TOO. SAID YOU'D KNOW WHAT HE MEANT.
SHOW ME THIS CAT.

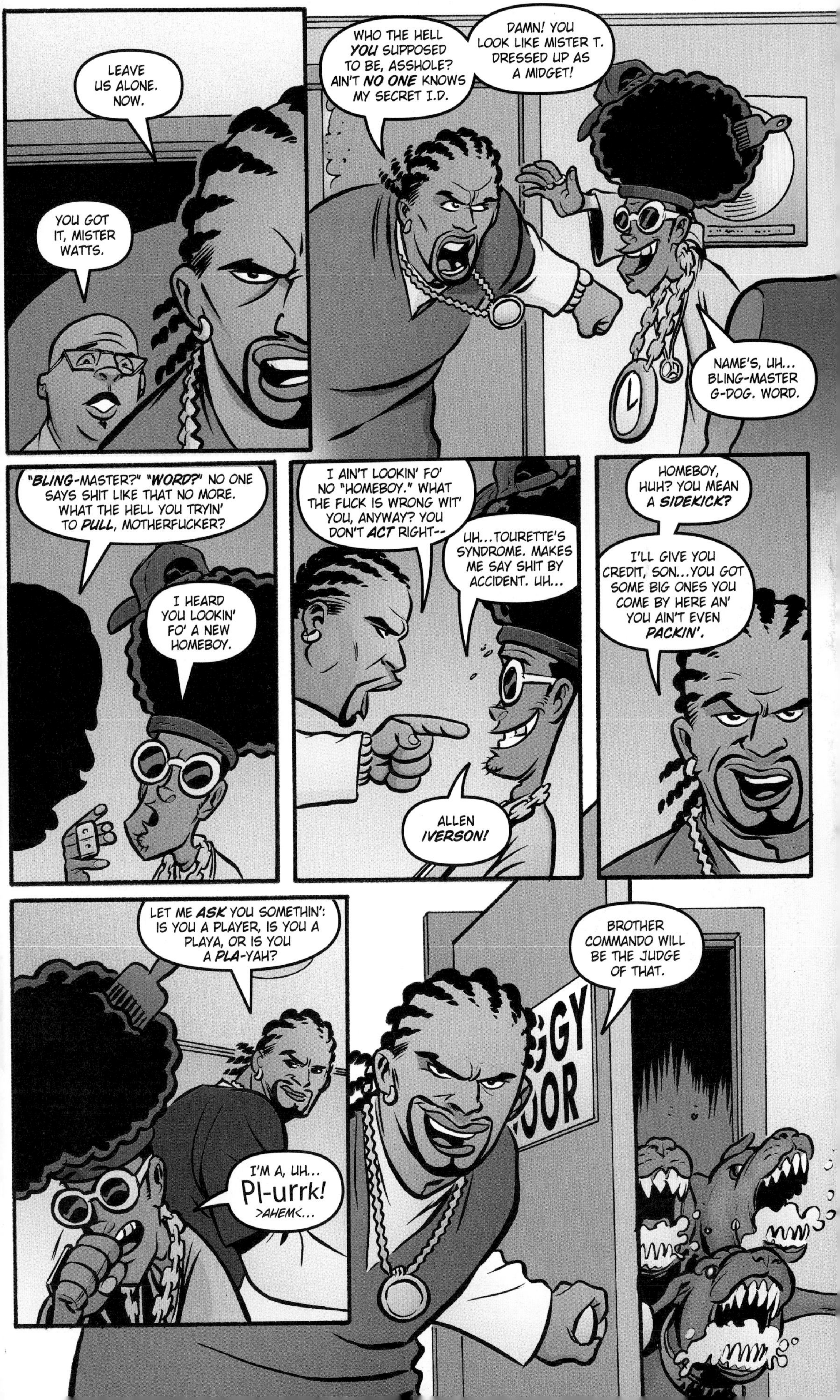
LEAVE US ALONE. NOW.
YOU GOT IT, MISTER WATTS.
WHO THE HELL **YOU** SUPPOSED TO BE, ASSHOLE? AIN'T **NO ONE** KNOWS MY SECRET I.D.
DAMN! YOU LOOK LIKE MISTER T. DRESSED UP AS A MIDGET!
NAME'S, UH... BLING-MASTER G-DOG. WORD.
"**BLING**-MASTER?" "**WORD?**" NO ONE SAYS SHIT LIKE THAT NO MORE. WHAT THE HELL YOU TRYIN' TO **PULL**, MOTHERFUCKER?
I HEARD YOU LOOKIN' FO' A NEW HOMEBOY.
I AIN'T LOOKIN' FO' NO "HOMEBOY." WHAT THE FUCK IS WRONG WIT' YOU, ANYWAY? YOU DON'T **ACT** RIGHT--
UH...TOURETTE'S SYNDROME. MAKES ME SAY SHIT BY ACCIDENT. UH...
ALLEN **IVERSON!**
HOMEBOY, HUH? YOU MEAN A **SIDEKICK?**
I'LL GIVE YOU CREDIT, SON...YOU GOT SOME BIG ONES YOU COME BY HERE AN' YOU AIN'T EVEN **PACKIN'.**
LET ME **ASK** YOU SOMETHIN': IS YOU A PLAYER, IS YOU A PLAYA, OR IS YOU A **PLA**-YAH?
I'M A, UH... Pl-urrk! >AHEM<...
BROTHER COMMANDO WILL BE THE JUDGE OF THAT.

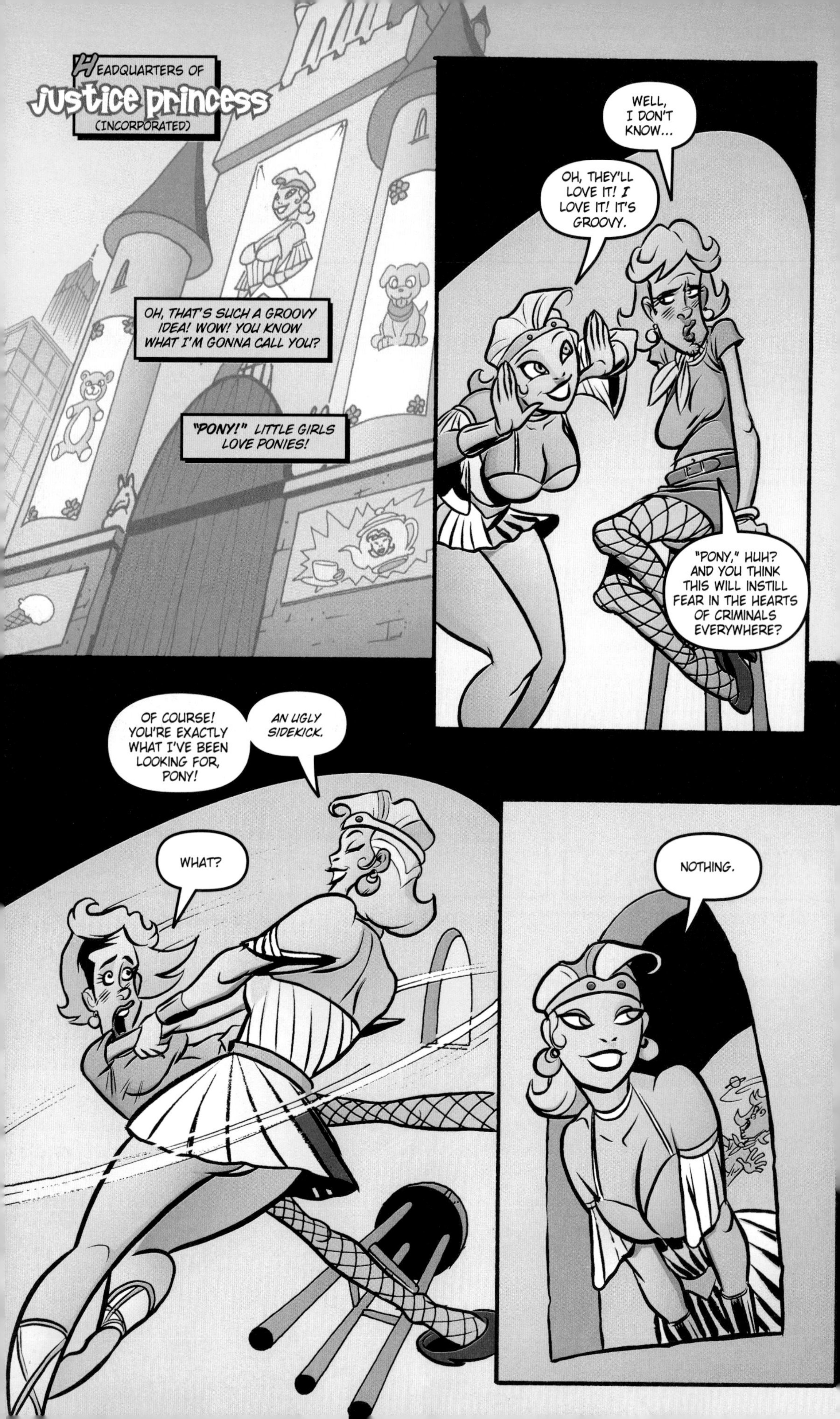
HEADQUARTERS OF
JUSTICE PRINCESS
(INCORPORATED)
OH, THAT'S SUCH A GROOVY IDEA! WOW! YOU KNOW WHAT I'M GONNA CALL YOU?
"PONY!" LITTLE GIRLS LOVE PONIES!
WELL, I DON'T KNOW...
OH, THEY'LL LOVE IT! I LOVE IT! IT'S GROOVY.
"PONY," HUH? AND YOU THINK THIS WILL INSTILL FEAR IN THE HEARTS OF CRIMINALS EVERYWHERE?
OF COURSE! YOU'RE EXACTLY WHAT I'VE BEEN LOOKING FOR, PONY!
AN UGLY SIDEKICK.
WHAT?
NOTHING.

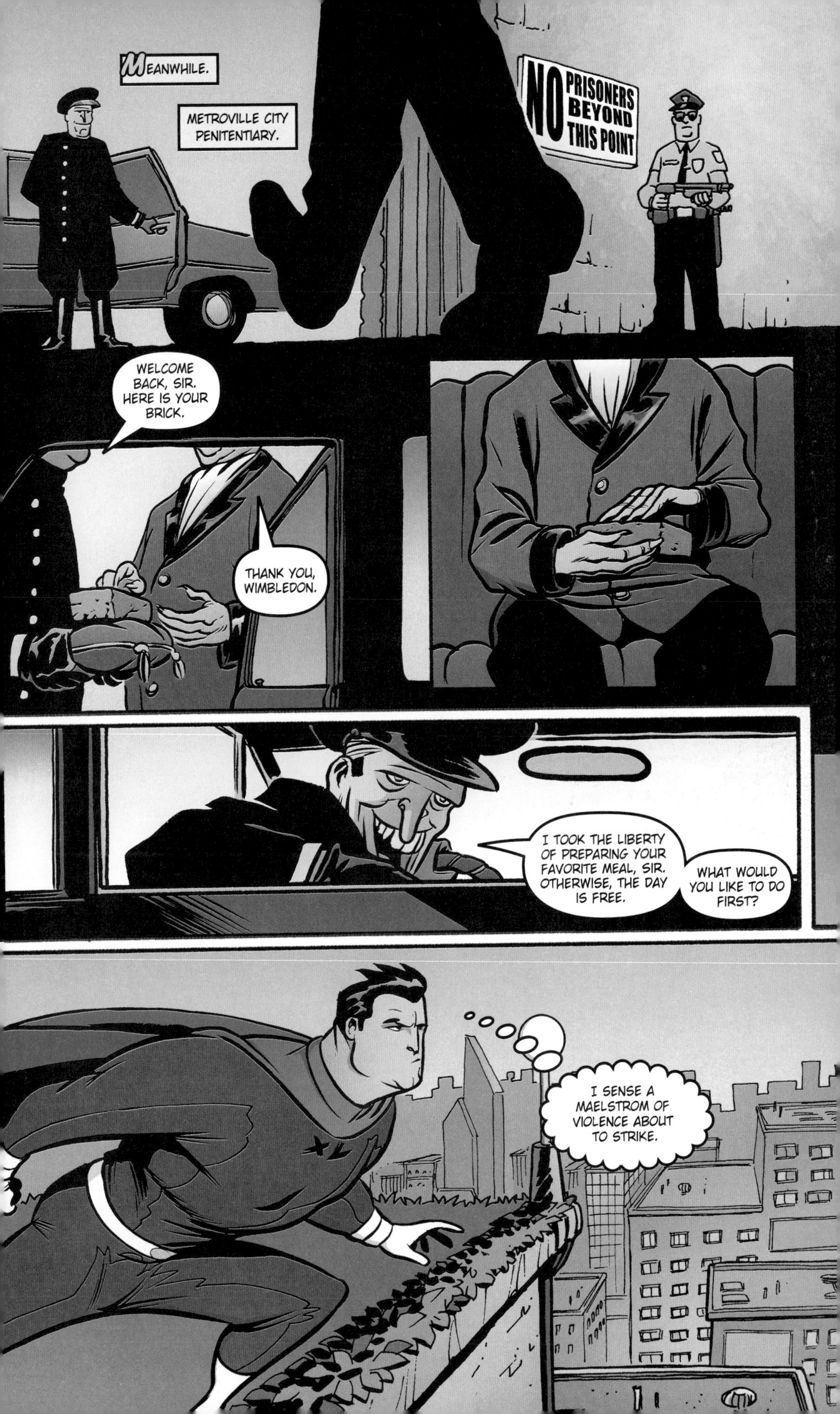
MEANWHILE.
METROVILLE CITY PENITENTIARY.
NO PRISONERS BEYOND THIS POINT
WELCOME BACK, SIR. HERE IS YOUR BRICK.
THANK YOU, WIMBLEDON.
I TOOK THE LIBERTY OF PREPARING YOUR FAVORITE MEAL, SIR. OTHERWISE, THE DAY IS FREE.
WHAT WOULD YOU LIKE TO DO FIRST?
I SENSE A MAELSTROM OF VIOLENCE ABOUT TO STRIKE.

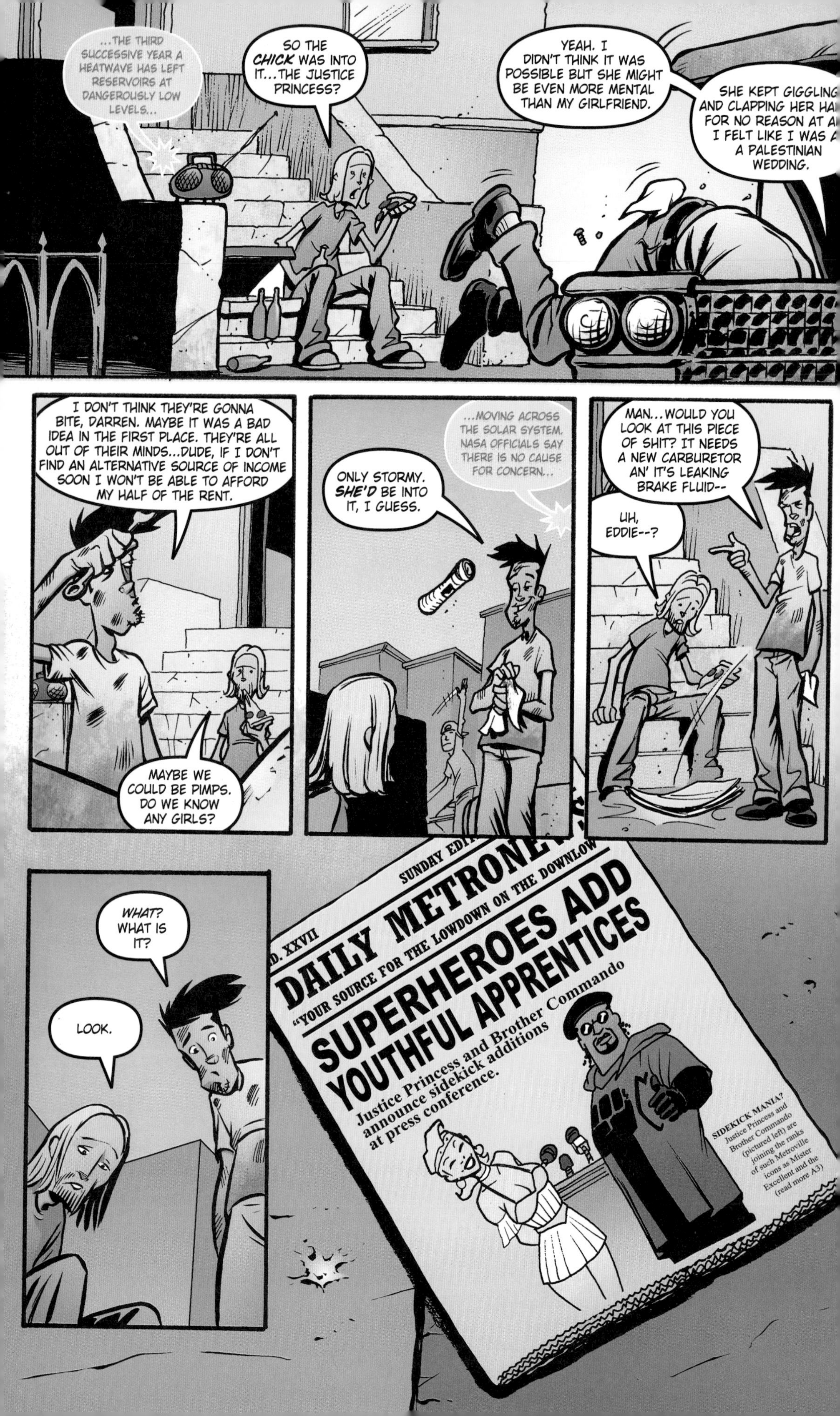

...THE THIRD SUCCESSIVE YEAR A HEATWAVE HAS LEFT RESERVOIRS AT DANGEROUSLY LOW LEVELS...
SO THE CHICK WAS INTO IT...THE JUSTICE PRINCESS?
YEAH. I DIDN'T THINK IT WAS POSSIBLE BUT SHE MIGHT BE EVEN MORE MENTAL THAN MY GIRLFRIEND.
SHE KEPT GIGGLING AND CLAPPING HER HA FOR NO REASON AT A I FELT LIKE I WAS A A PALESTINIAN WEDDING.
I DON'T THINK THEY'RE GONNA BITE, DARREN. MAYBE IT WAS A BAD IDEA IN THE FIRST PLACE. THEY'RE ALL OUT OF THEIR MINDS...DUDE, IF I DON'T FIND AN ALTERNATIVE SOURCE OF INCOME SOON I WON'T BE ABLE TO AFFORD MY HALF OF THE RENT.
MAYBE WE COULD BE PIMPS. DO WE KNOW ANY GIRLS?
ONLY STORMY. SHE'D BE INTO IT, I GUESS.
...MOVING ACROSS THE SOLAR SYSTEM. NASA OFFICIALS SAY THERE IS NO CAUSE FOR CONCERN...
MAN...WOULD YOU LOOK AT THIS PIECE OF SHIT? IT NEEDS A NEW CARBURETOR AN' IT'S LEAKING BRAKE FLUID--
UH, EDDIE--?
WHAT? WHAT IS IT?
LOOK.
SUNDAY EDI
DAILY METRONEW
D. XXVII
"YOUR SOURCE FOR THE LOWDOWN ON THE DOWNLOW
SUPERHEROES ADD YOUTHFUL APPRENTICES
Justice Princess and Brother Commando announce sidekick additions at press conference.
SIDEKICK MANIA? Justice Princess and Brother Commando (pictured left) are joining the ranks of such Metroville icons as Mister Excellent and the (read more A3)

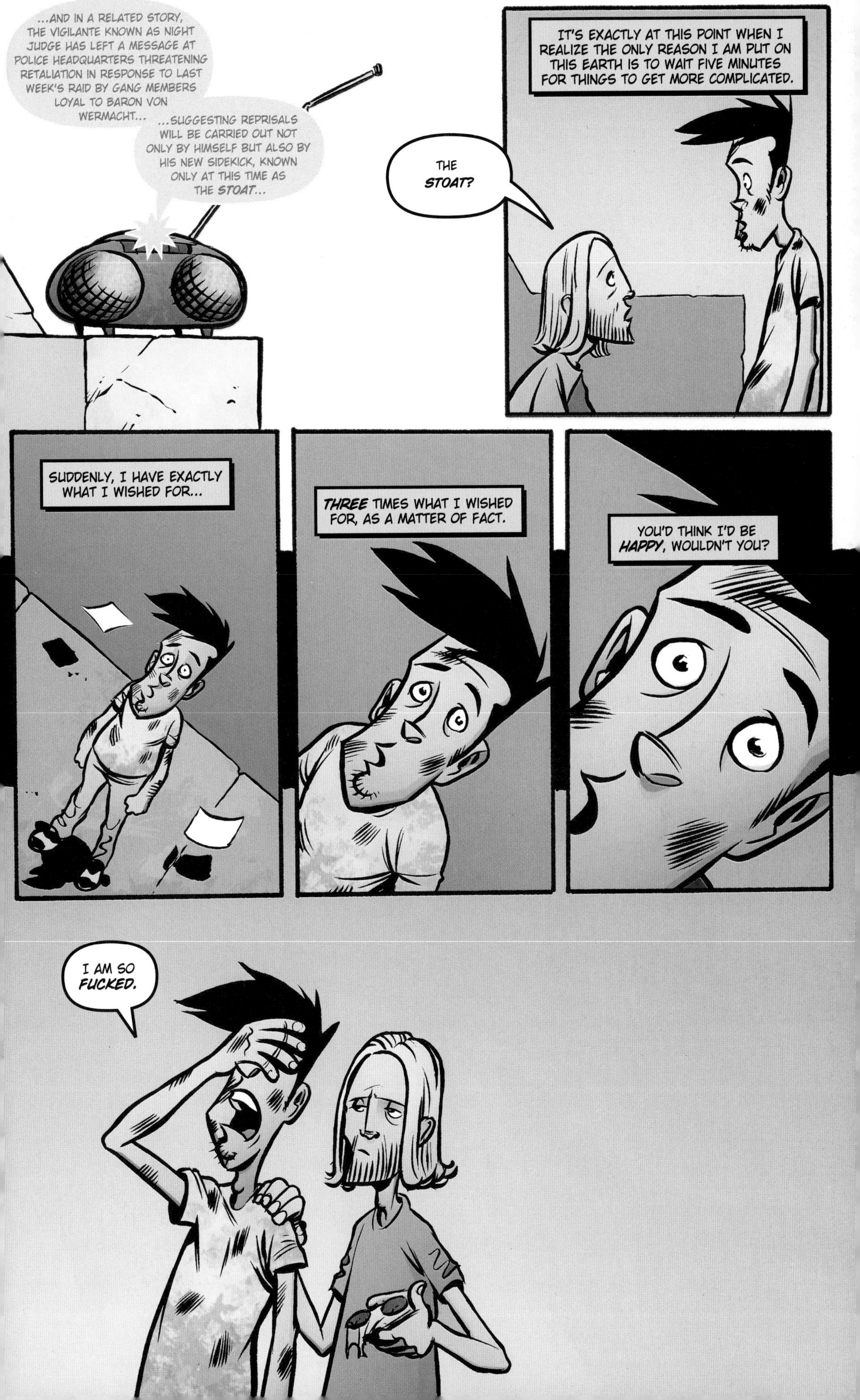
...AND IN A RELATED STORY, THE VIGILANTE KNOWN AS NIGHT JUDGE HAS LEFT A MESSAGE AT POLICE HEADQUARTERS THREATENING RETALIATION IN RESPONSE TO LAST WEEK'S RAID BY GANG MEMBERS LOYAL TO BARON VON WERMACHT...
...SUGGESTING REPRISALS WILL BE CARRIED OUT NOT ONLY BY HIMSELF BUT ALSO BY HIS NEW SIDEKICK, KNOWN ONLY AT THIS TIME AS THE *STOAT*...
IT'S EXACTLY AT THIS POINT WHEN I REALIZE THE ONLY REASON I AM PUT ON THIS EARTH IS TO WAIT FIVE MINUTES FOR THINGS TO GET MORE COMPLICATED.
THE *STOAT?*
SUDDENLY, I HAVE EXACTLY WHAT I WISHED FOR...
THREE TIMES WHAT I WISHED FOR, AS A MATTER OF FACT.
YOU'D THINK I'D BE *HAPPY*, WOULDN'T YOU?
I AM SO *FUCKED.*

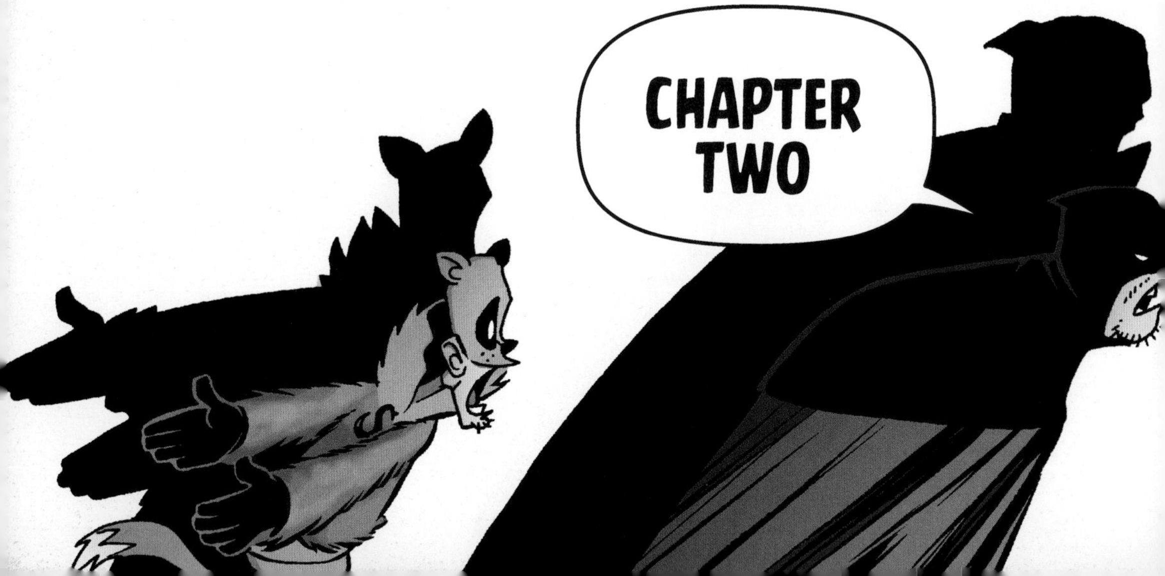
CHAPTER TWO

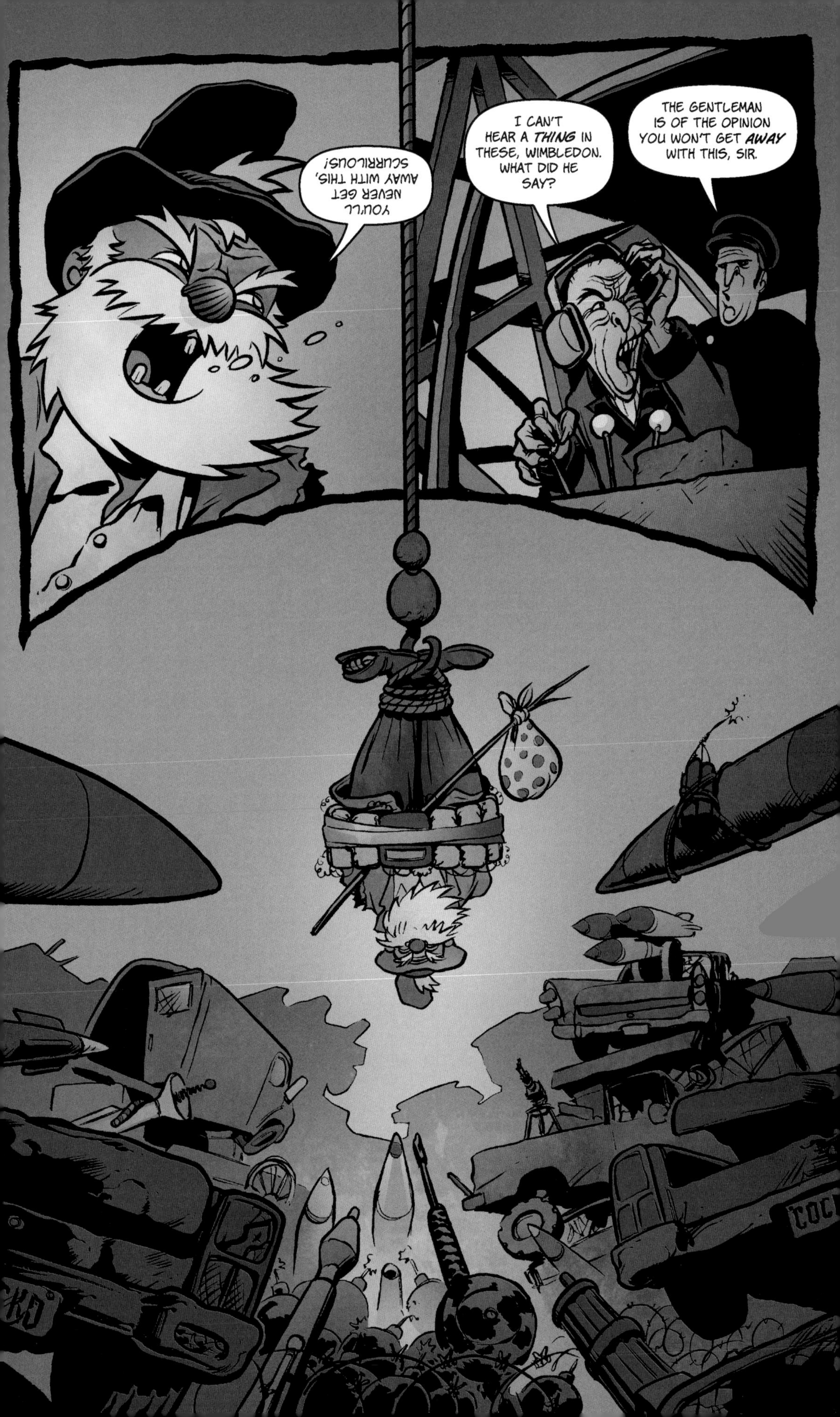
YOU'LL NEVER GET AWAY WITH THIS, SCURRILOUS!
I CAN'T HEAR A *THING* IN THESE, WIMBLEDON. WHAT DID HE SAY?
THE GENTLEMAN IS OF THE OPINION YOU WON'T GET ***AWAY*** WITH THIS, SIR.

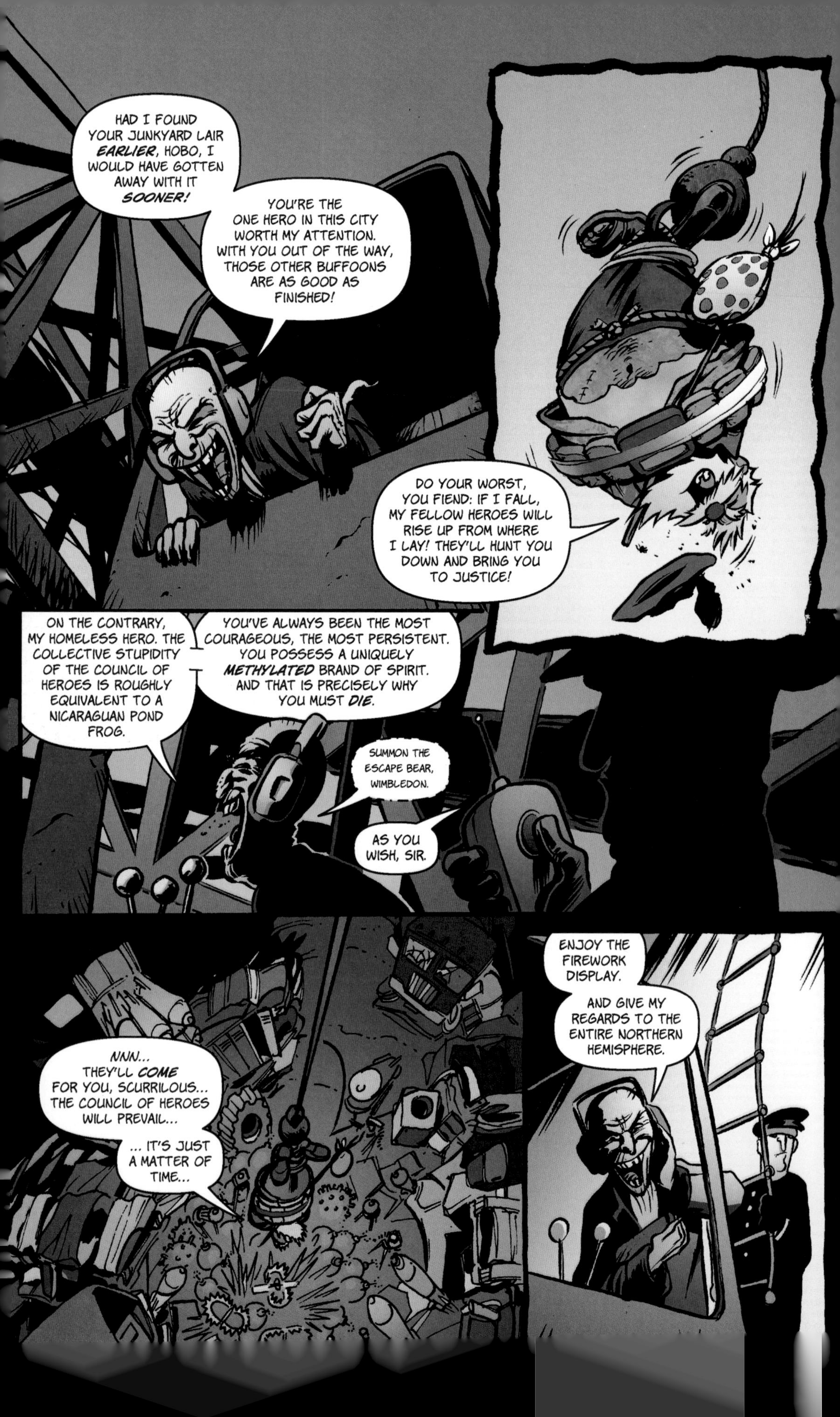

HAD I FOUND YOUR JUNKYARD LAIR EARLIER, HOBO, I WOULD HAVE GOTTEN AWAY WITH IT SOONER!
YOU'RE THE ONE HERO IN THIS CITY WORTH MY ATTENTION. WITH YOU OUT OF THE WAY, THOSE OTHER BUFFOONS ARE AS GOOD AS FINISHED!
DO YOUR WORST, YOU FIEND: IF I FALL, MY FELLOW HEROES WILL RISE UP FROM WHERE I LAY! THEY'LL HUNT YOU DOWN AND BRING YOU TO JUSTICE!
ON THE CONTRARY, MY HOMELESS HERO. THE COLLECTIVE STUPIDITY OF THE COUNCIL OF HEROES IS ROUGHLY EQUIVALENT TO A NICARAGUAN POND FROG.
YOU'VE ALWAYS BEEN THE MOST COURAGEOUS, THE MOST PERSISTENT. YOU POSSESS A UNIQUELY METHYLATED BRAND OF SPIRIT. AND THAT IS PRECISELY WHY YOU MUST DIE.
SUMMON THE ESCAPE BEAR, WIMBLEDON.
AS YOU WISH, SIR.
NNN... THEY'LL COME FOR YOU, SCURRILOUS... THE COUNCIL OF HEROES WILL PREVAIL...
... IT'S JUST A MATTER OF TIME...
ENJOY THE FIREWORK DISPLAY.
AND GIVE MY REGARDS TO THE ENTIRE NORTHERN HEMISPHERE.

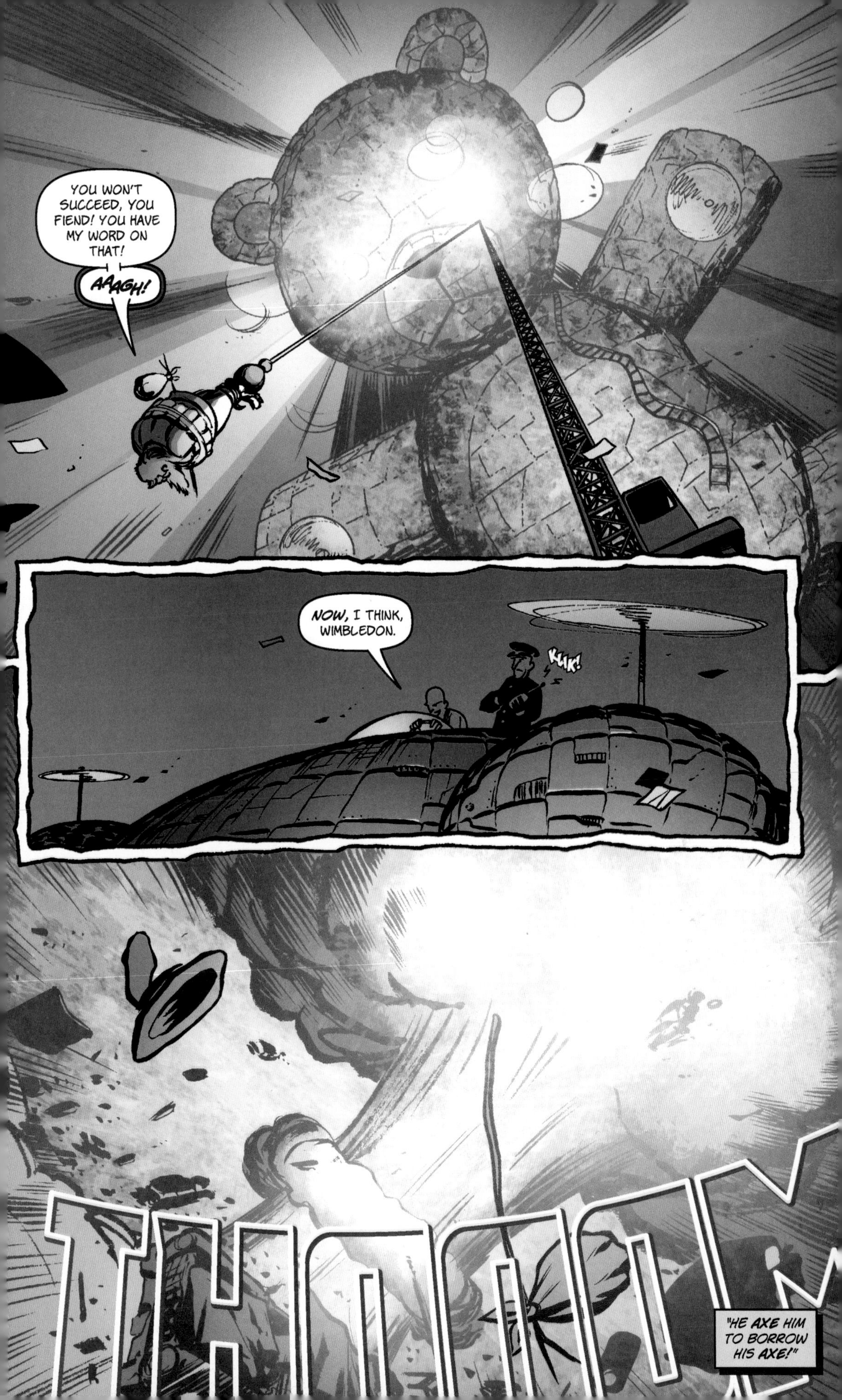

YOU WON'T SUCCEED, YOU FIEND! YOU HAVE MY WORD ON THAT!
AAAGH!
NOW, I THINK, WIMBLEDON.
KLIK!
"HE AXE HIM TO BORROW HIS AXE!"

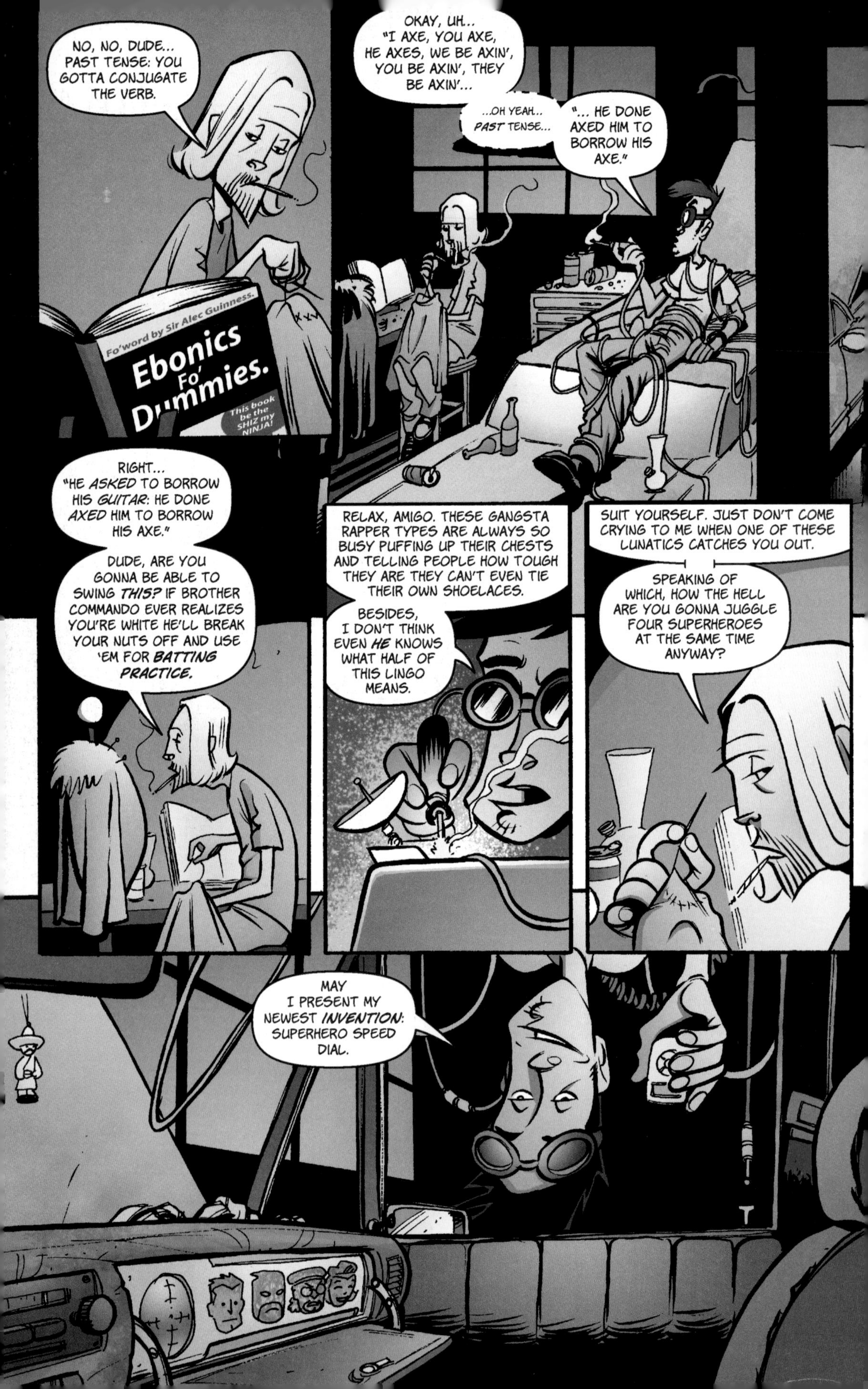
NO, NO, DUDE... PAST TENSE: YOU GOTTA CONJUGATE THE VERB.
Fo'word by Sir Alec Guinness.
Ebonics Fo' Dummies.
This book be the SHIZ my NINJA!
OKAY, UH... "I AXE, YOU AXE, HE AXES, WE BE AXIN', YOU BE AXIN', THEY BE AXIN'...
...OH YEAH... PAST TENSE...
"... HE DONE AXED HIM TO BORROW HIS AXE."
RIGHT... "HE ASKED TO BORROW HIS GUITAR: HE DONE AXED HIM TO BORROW HIS AXE."
DUDE, ARE YOU GONNA BE ABLE TO SWING THIS? IF BROTHER COMMANDO EVER REALIZES YOU'RE WHITE HE'LL BREAK YOUR NUTS OFF AND USE 'EM FOR BATTING PRACTICE.
RELAX, AMIGO. THESE GANGSTA RAPPER TYPES ARE ALWAYS SO BUSY PUFFING UP THEIR CHESTS AND TELLING PEOPLE HOW TOUGH THEY ARE THEY CAN'T EVEN TIE THEIR OWN SHOELACES.
BESIDES, I DON'T THINK EVEN HE KNOWS WHAT HALF OF THIS LINGO MEANS.
SUIT YOURSELF. JUST DON'T COME CRYING TO ME WHEN ONE OF THESE LUNATICS CATCHES YOU OUT.
SPEAKING OF WHICH, HOW THE HELL ARE YOU GONNA JUGGLE FOUR SUPERHEROES AT THE SAME TIME ANYWAY?
MAY I PRESENT MY NEWEST INVENTION: SUPERHERO SPEED DIAL.

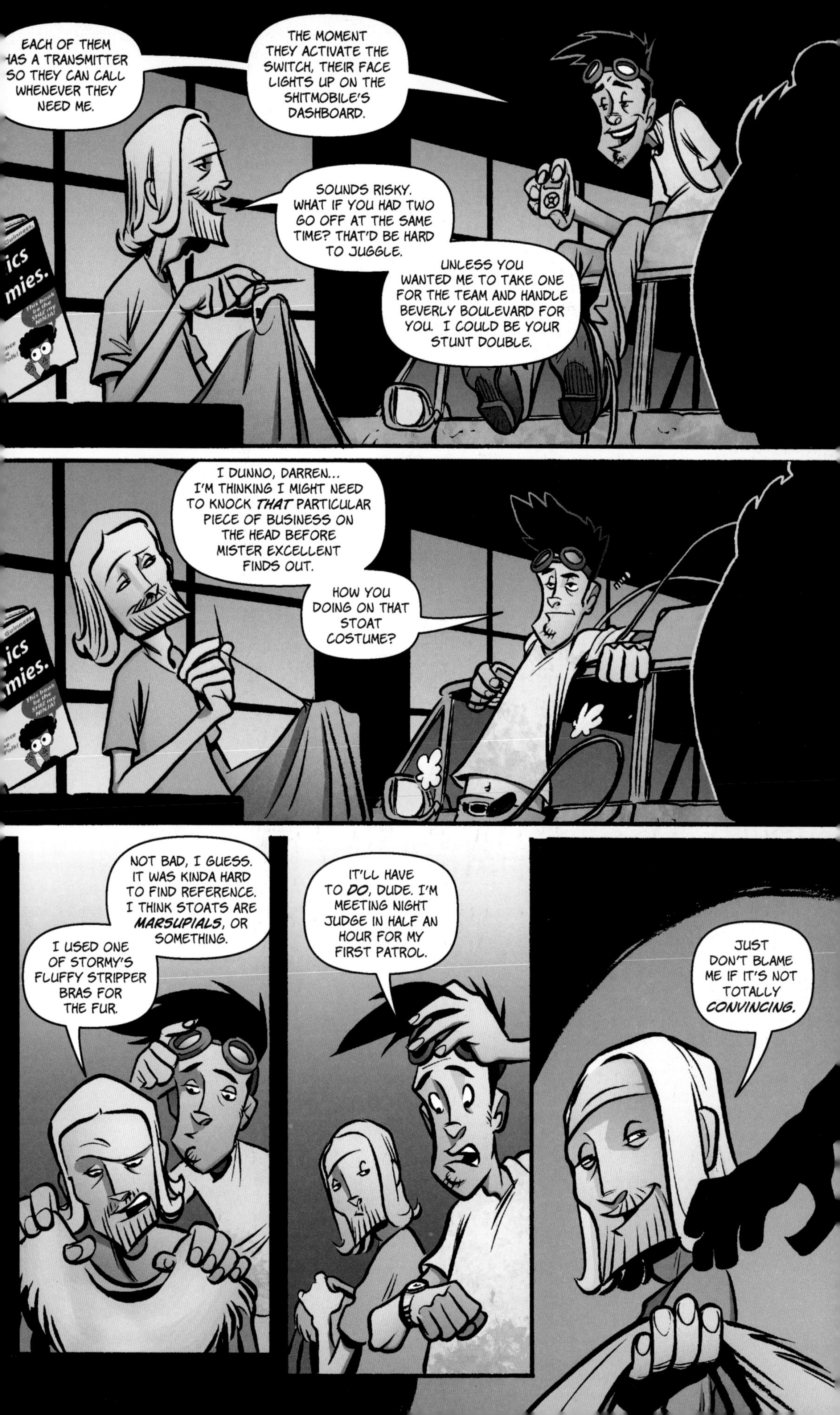
EACH OF THEM HAS A TRANSMITTER SO THEY CAN CALL WHENEVER THEY NEED ME.
THE MOMENT THEY ACTIVATE THE SWITCH, THEIR FACE LIGHTS UP ON THE SHITMOBILE'S DASHBOARD.
SOUNDS RISKY. WHAT IF YOU HAD TWO GO OFF AT THE SAME TIME? THAT'D BE HARD TO JUGGLE.
UNLESS YOU WANTED ME TO TAKE ONE FOR THE TEAM AND HANDLE BEVERLY BOULEVARD FOR YOU. I COULD BE YOUR STUNT DOUBLE.
I DUNNO, DARREN... I'M THINKING I MIGHT NEED TO KNOCK *THAT* PARTICULAR PIECE OF BUSINESS ON THE HEAD BEFORE MISTER EXCELLENT FINDS OUT.
HOW YOU DOING ON THAT STOAT COSTUME?
NOT BAD, I GUESS. IT WAS KINDA HARD TO FIND REFERENCE. I THINK STOATS ARE *MARSUPIALS*, OR SOMETHING.
I USED ONE OF STORMY'S FLUFFY STRIPPER BRAS FOR THE FUR.
IT'LL HAVE TO *DO*, DUDE. I'M MEETING NIGHT JUDGE IN HALF AN HOUR FOR MY FIRST PATROL.
JUST DON'T BLAME ME IF IT'S NOT TOTALLY *CONVINCING.*

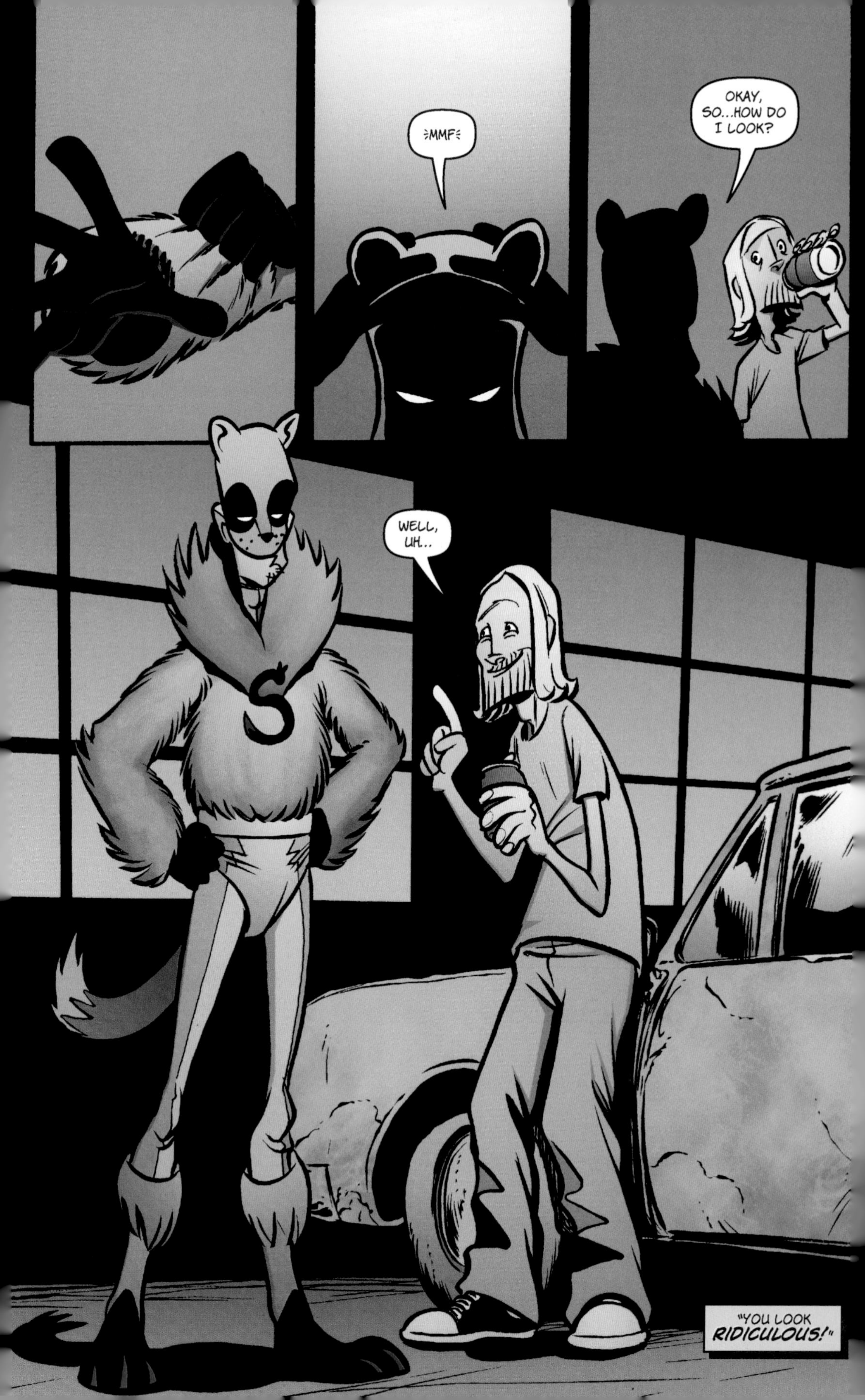
MMF
OKAY, SO...HOW DO I LOOK?
WELL, UH...
"YOU LOOK RIDICULOUS!"

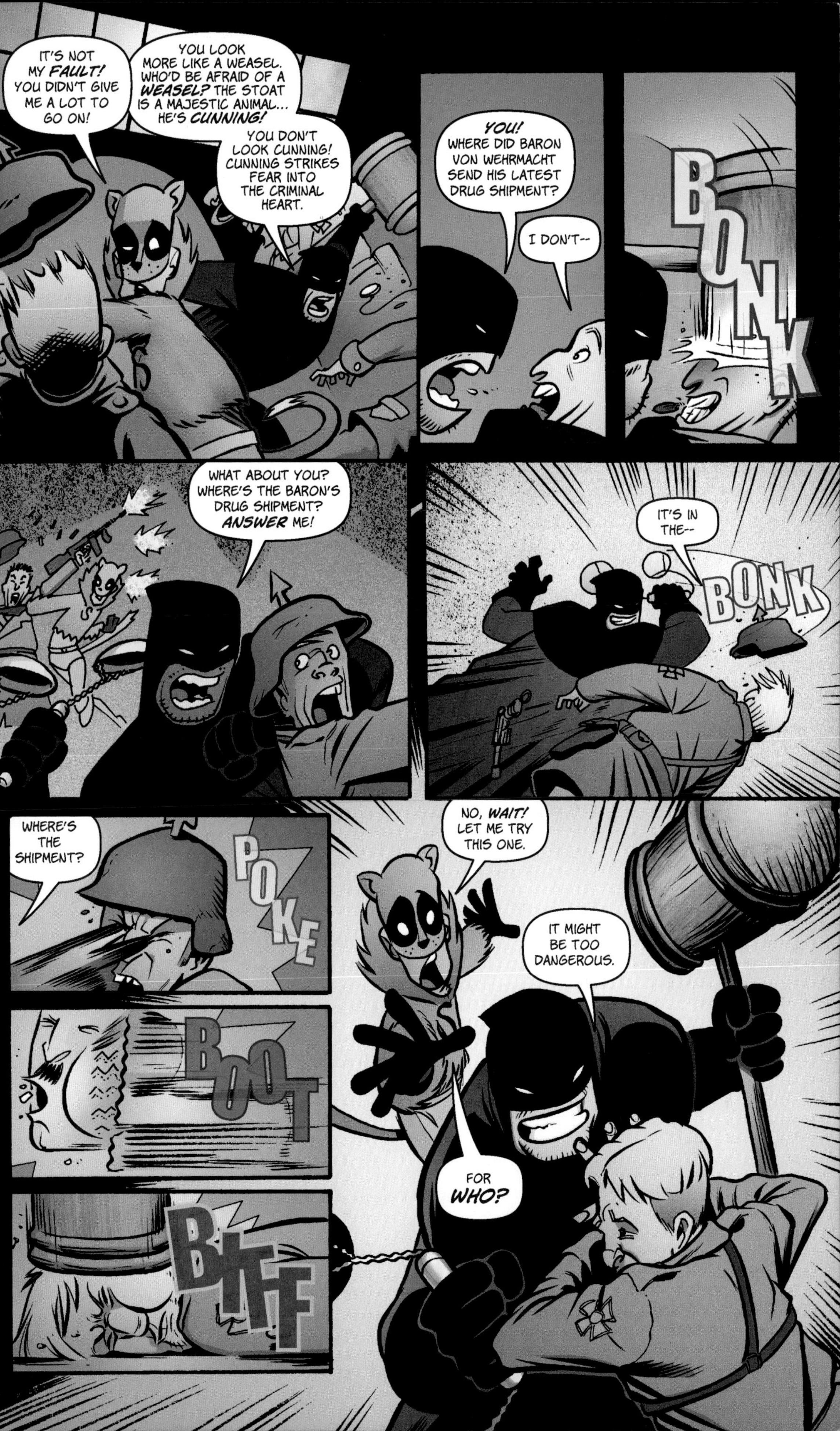
IT'S NOT MY FAULT! YOU DIDN'T GIVE ME A LOT TO GO ON!
YOU LOOK MORE LIKE A WEASEL. WHO'D BE AFRAID OF A WEASEL? THE STOAT IS A MAJESTIC ANIMAL... HE'S CUNNING!
YOU DON'T LOOK CUNNING! CUNNING STRIKES FEAR INTO THE CRIMINAL HEART.
YOU! WHERE DID BARON VON WEHRMACHT SEND HIS LATEST DRUG SHIPMENT?
I DON'T--
BONK
WHAT ABOUT YOU? WHERE'S THE BARON'S DRUG SHIPMENT? ANSWER ME!
IT'S IN THE--
BONK
WHERE'S THE SHIPMENT?
POKE
BOOT
BIFF
NO, WAIT! LET ME TRY THIS ONE.
IT MIGHT BE TOO DANGEROUS.
FOR WHO?

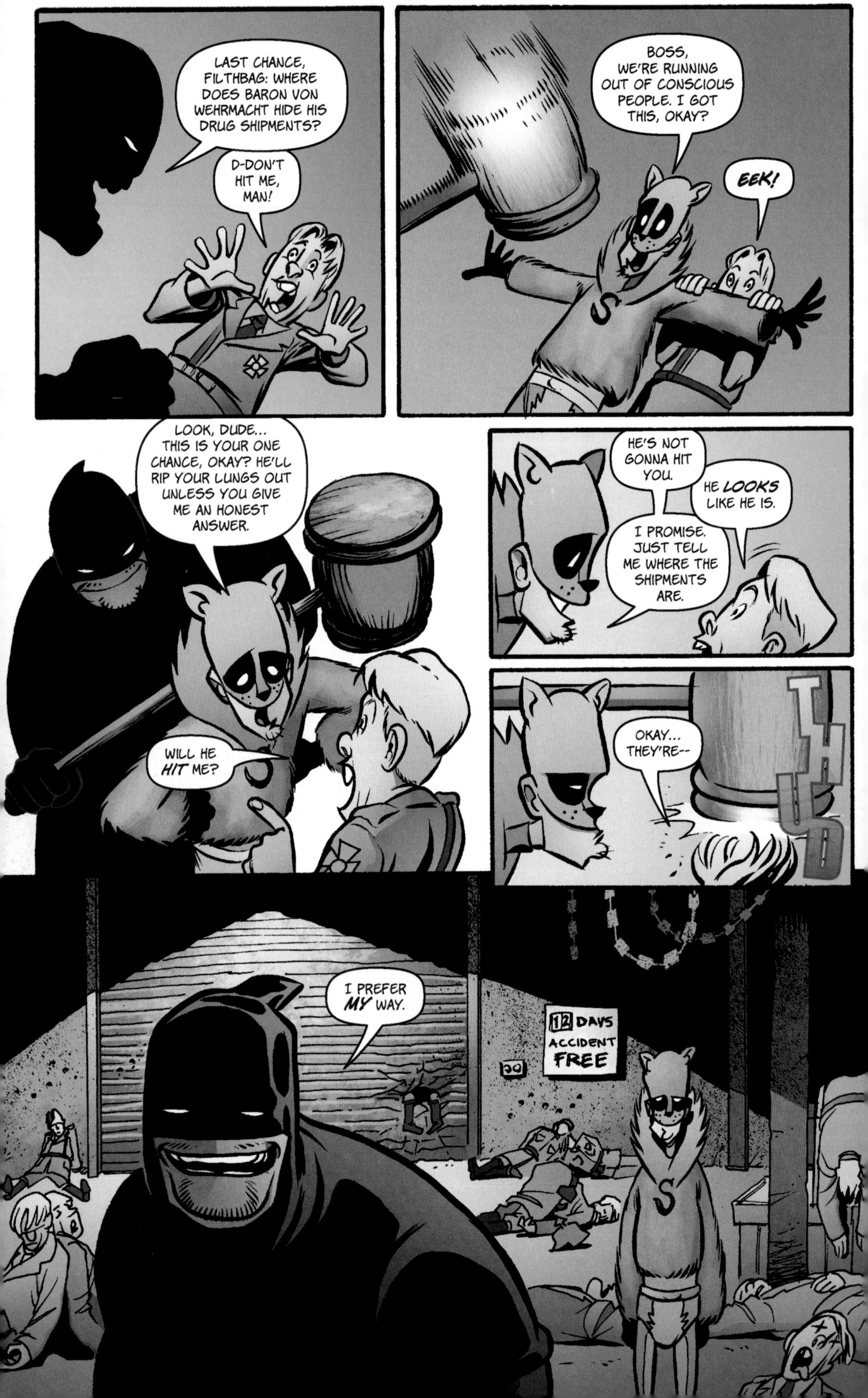
LAST CHANCE, FILTHBAG: WHERE DOES BARON VON WEHRMACHT HIDE HIS DRUG SHIPMENTS?
D-DON'T HIT ME, MAN!
BOSS, WE'RE RUNNING OUT OF CONSCIOUS PEOPLE. I GOT THIS, OKAY?
EEK!
LOOK, DUDE... THIS IS YOUR ONE CHANCE, OKAY? HE'LL RIP YOUR LUNGS OUT UNLESS YOU GIVE ME AN HONEST ANSWER.
WILL HE HIT ME?
HE'S NOT GONNA HIT YOU.
HE LOOKS LIKE HE IS.
I PROMISE. JUST TELL ME WHERE THE SHIPMENTS ARE.
OKAY... THEY'RE--
THUD
I PREFER MY WAY.
12 DAYS ACCIDENT FREE

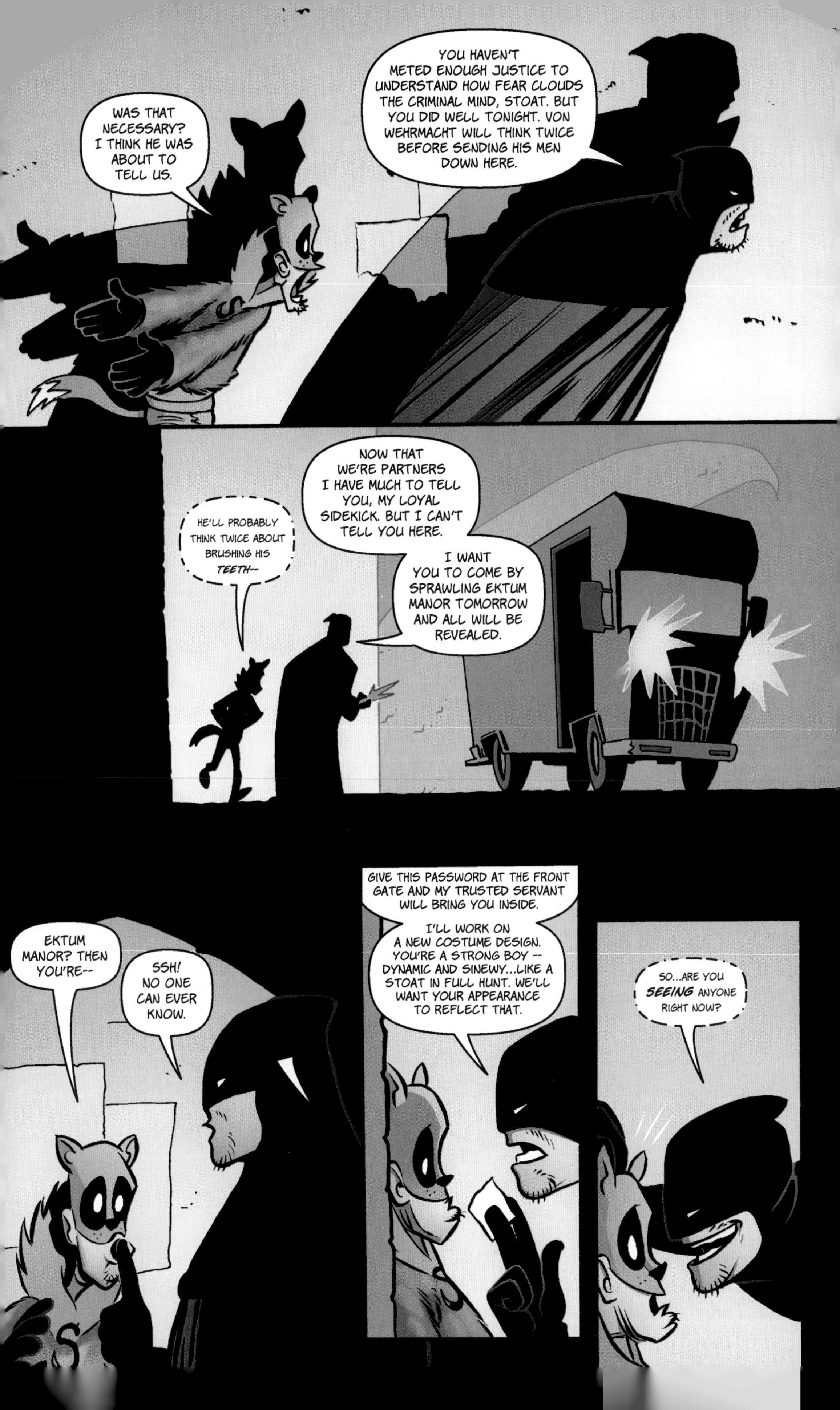
WAS THAT NECESSARY? I THINK HE WAS ABOUT TO TELL US.
YOU HAVEN'T METED ENOUGH JUSTICE TO UNDERSTAND HOW FEAR CLOUDS THE CRIMINAL MIND, STOAT. BUT YOU DID WELL TONIGHT. VON WEHRMACHT WILL THINK TWICE BEFORE SENDING HIS MEN DOWN HERE.
HE'LL PROBABLY THINK TWICE ABOUT BRUSHING HIS *TEETH*--
NOW THAT WE'RE PARTNERS I HAVE MUCH TO TELL YOU, MY LOYAL SIDEKICK. BUT I CAN'T TELL YOU HERE.
I WANT YOU TO COME BY SPRAWLING EKTUM MANOR TOMORROW AND ALL WILL BE REVEALED.
EKTUM MANOR? THEN YOU'RE--
SSH! NO ONE CAN EVER KNOW.
GIVE THIS PASSWORD AT THE FRONT GATE AND MY TRUSTED SERVANT WILL BRING YOU INSIDE.
I'LL WORK ON A NEW COSTUME DESIGN. YOU'RE A STRONG BOY -- DYNAMIC AND SINEWY...LIKE A STOAT IN FULL HUNT. WE'LL WANT YOUR APPEARANCE TO REFLECT THAT.
SO...ARE YOU *SEEING* ANYONE RIGHT NOW?

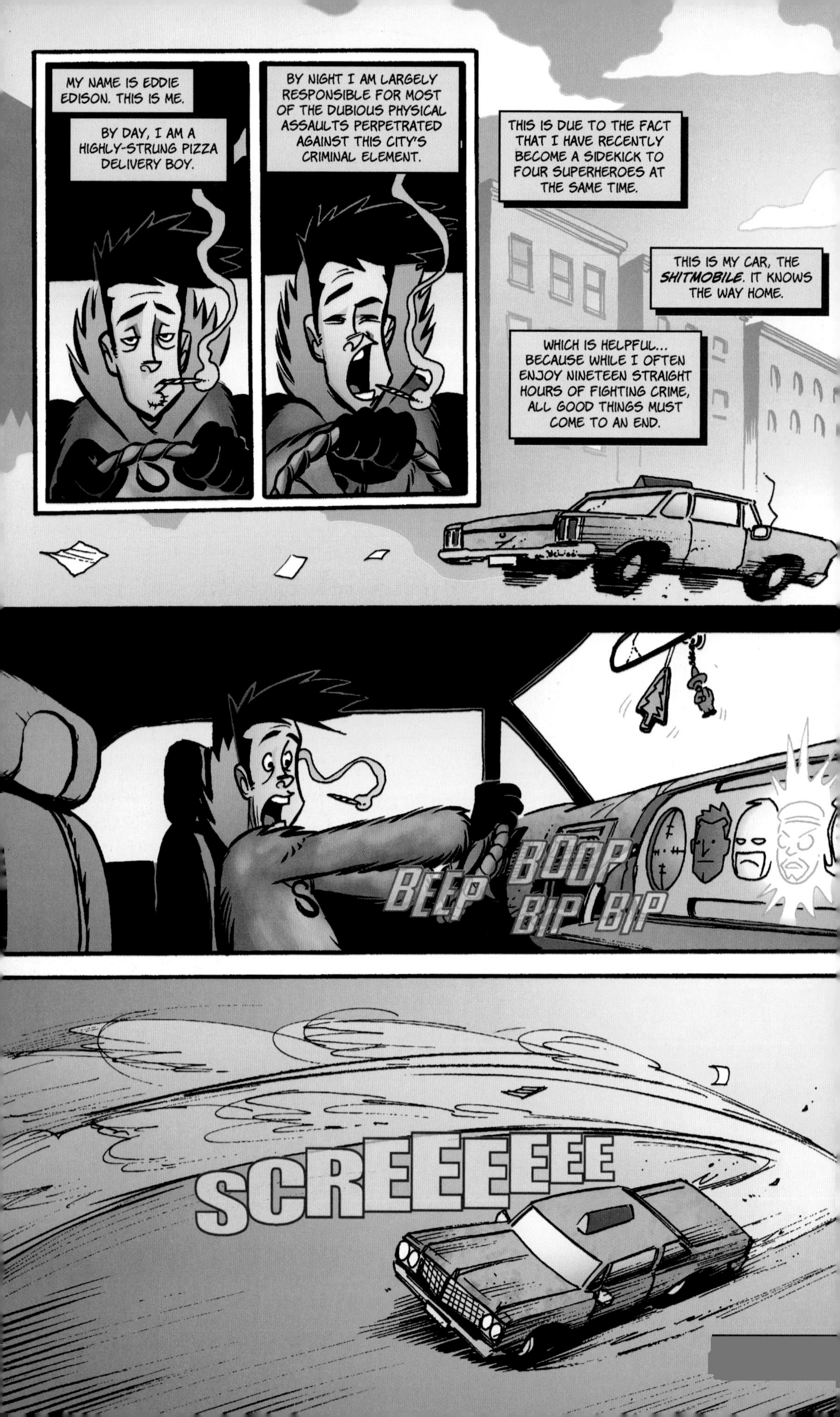

MY NAME IS EDDIE EDISON. THIS IS ME.
BY DAY, I AM A HIGHLY-STRUNG PIZZA DELIVERY BOY.
BY NIGHT I AM LARGELY RESPONSIBLE FOR MOST OF THE DUBIOUS PHYSICAL ASSAULTS PERPETRATED AGAINST THIS CITY'S CRIMINAL ELEMENT.
THIS IS DUE TO THE FACT THAT I HAVE RECENTLY BECOME A SIDEKICK TO FOUR SUPERHEROES AT THE SAME TIME.
THIS IS MY CAR, THE *SHITMOBILE*. IT KNOWS THE WAY HOME.
WHICH IS HELPFUL... BECAUSE WHILE I OFTEN ENJOY NINETEEN STRAIGHT HOURS OF FIGHTING CRIME, ALL GOOD THINGS MUST COME TO AN END.
BEEP BOOP
BIP BIP
SCREEEEEE

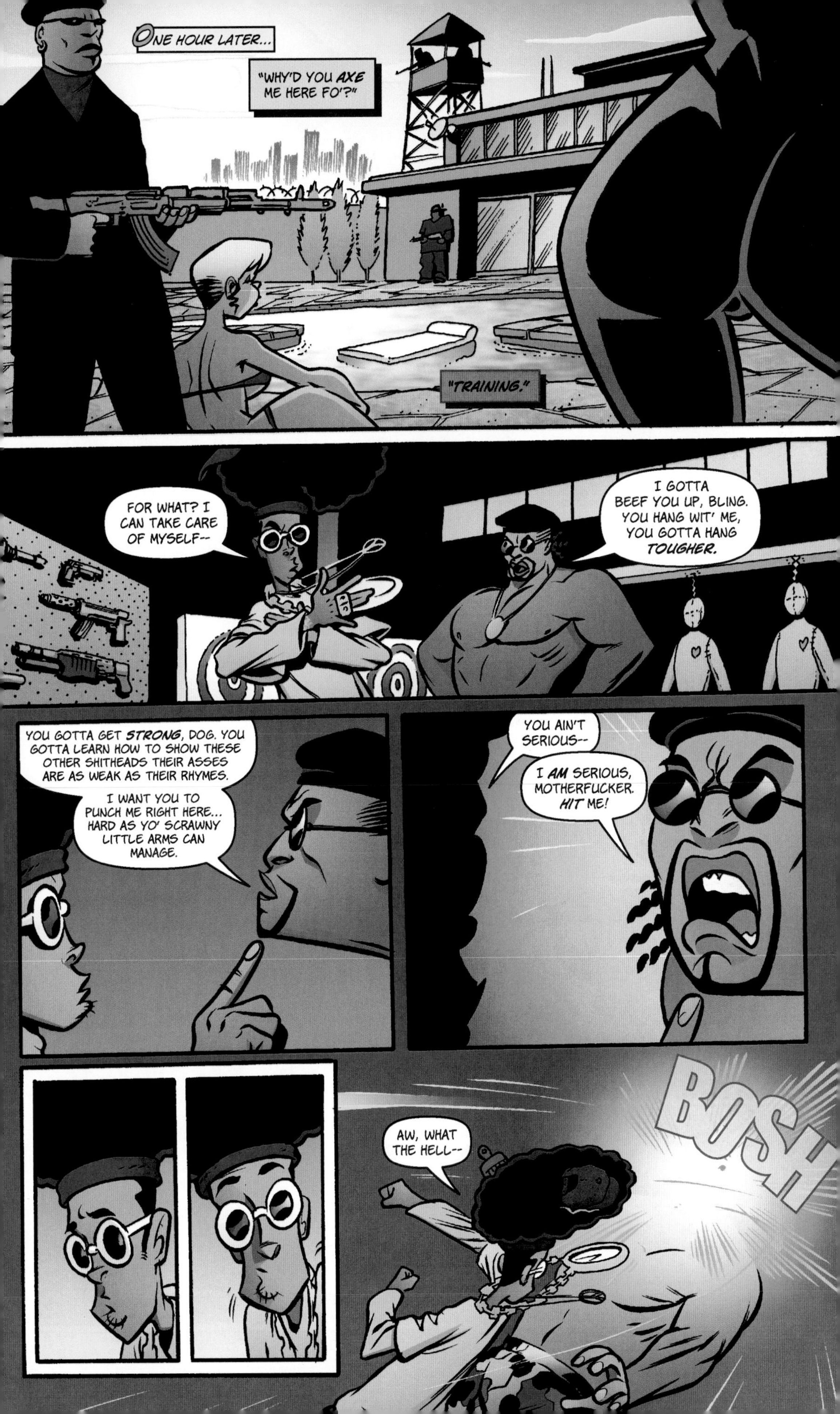
ONE HOUR LATER...
"WHY'D YOU AXE ME HERE FO'?"
"TRAINING."
FOR WHAT? I CAN TAKE CARE OF MYSELF--
I GOTTA BEEF YOU UP, BLING. YOU HANG WIT' ME, YOU GOTTA HANG TOUGHER.
YOU GOTTA GET STRONG, DOG. YOU GOTTA LEARN HOW TO SHOW THESE OTHER SHITHEADS THEIR ASSES ARE AS WEAK AS THEIR RHYMES.
I WANT YOU TO PUNCH ME RIGHT HERE... HARD AS YO' SCRAWNY LITTLE ARMS CAN MANAGE.
YOU AIN'T SERIOUS--
I AM SERIOUS, MOTHERFUCKER. HIT ME!
AW, WHAT THE HELL--
BOSH

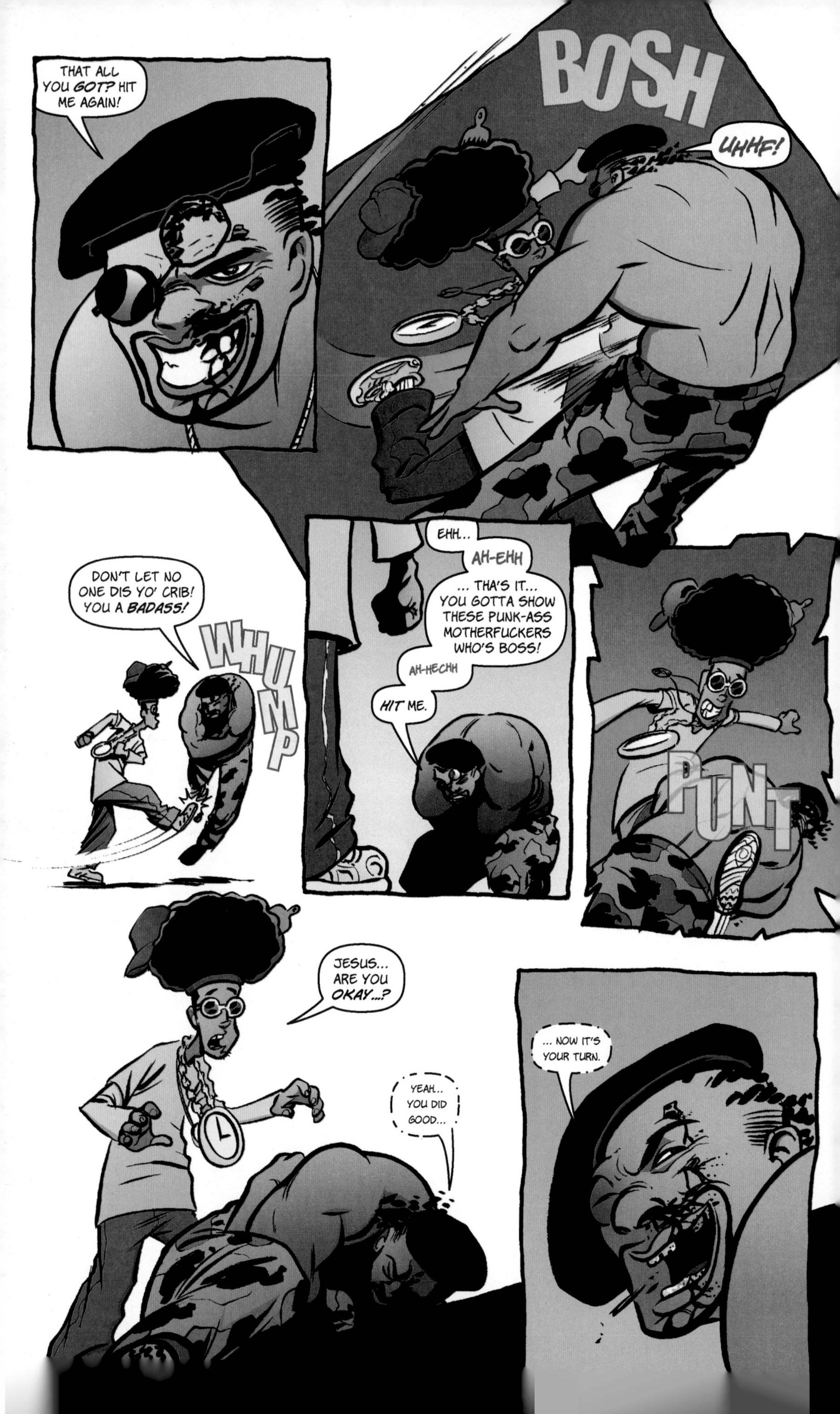
THAT ALL YOU GOT? HIT ME AGAIN!
BOSH
UHHF!
DON'T LET NO ONE DIS YO' CRIB! YOU A BADASS!
WHUMP
EHH...
AH-EHH
... THA'S IT... YOU GOTTA SHOW THESE PUNK-ASS MOTHERFUCKERS WHO'S BOSS!
AH-HECHH
HIT ME.
PUNT
JESUS... ARE YOU OKAY...?
YEAH.. YOU DID GOOD...
... NOW IT'S YOUR TURN.

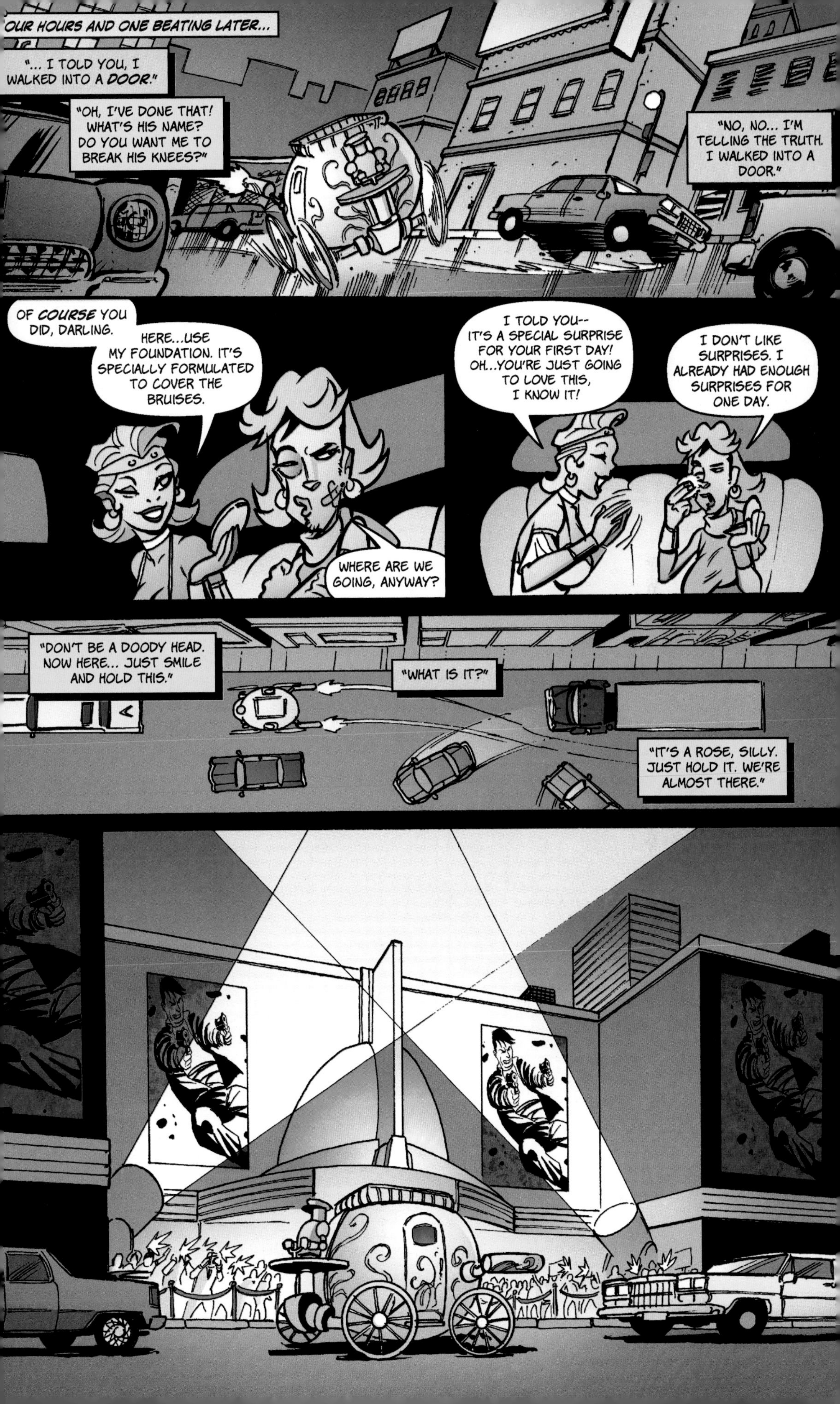
OUR HOURS AND ONE BEATING LATER...
"... I TOLD YOU, I WALKED INTO A DOOR."
"OH, I'VE DONE THAT! WHAT'S HIS NAME? DO YOU WANT ME TO BREAK HIS KNEES?"
"NO, NO... I'M TELLING THE TRUTH. I WALKED INTO A DOOR."
OF COURSE YOU DID, DARLING.
HERE...USE MY FOUNDATION. IT'S SPECIALLY FORMULATED TO COVER THE BRUISES.
WHERE ARE WE GOING, ANYWAY?
I TOLD YOU-- IT'S A SPECIAL SURPRISE FOR YOUR FIRST DAY! OH...YOU'RE JUST GOING TO LOVE THIS, I KNOW IT!
I DON'T LIKE SURPRISES. I ALREADY HAD ENOUGH SURPRISES FOR ONE DAY.
"DON'T BE A DOODY HEAD. NOW HERE... JUST SMILE AND HOLD THIS."
"WHAT IS IT?"
"IT'S A ROSE, SILLY. JUST HOLD IT. WE'RE ALMOST THERE."

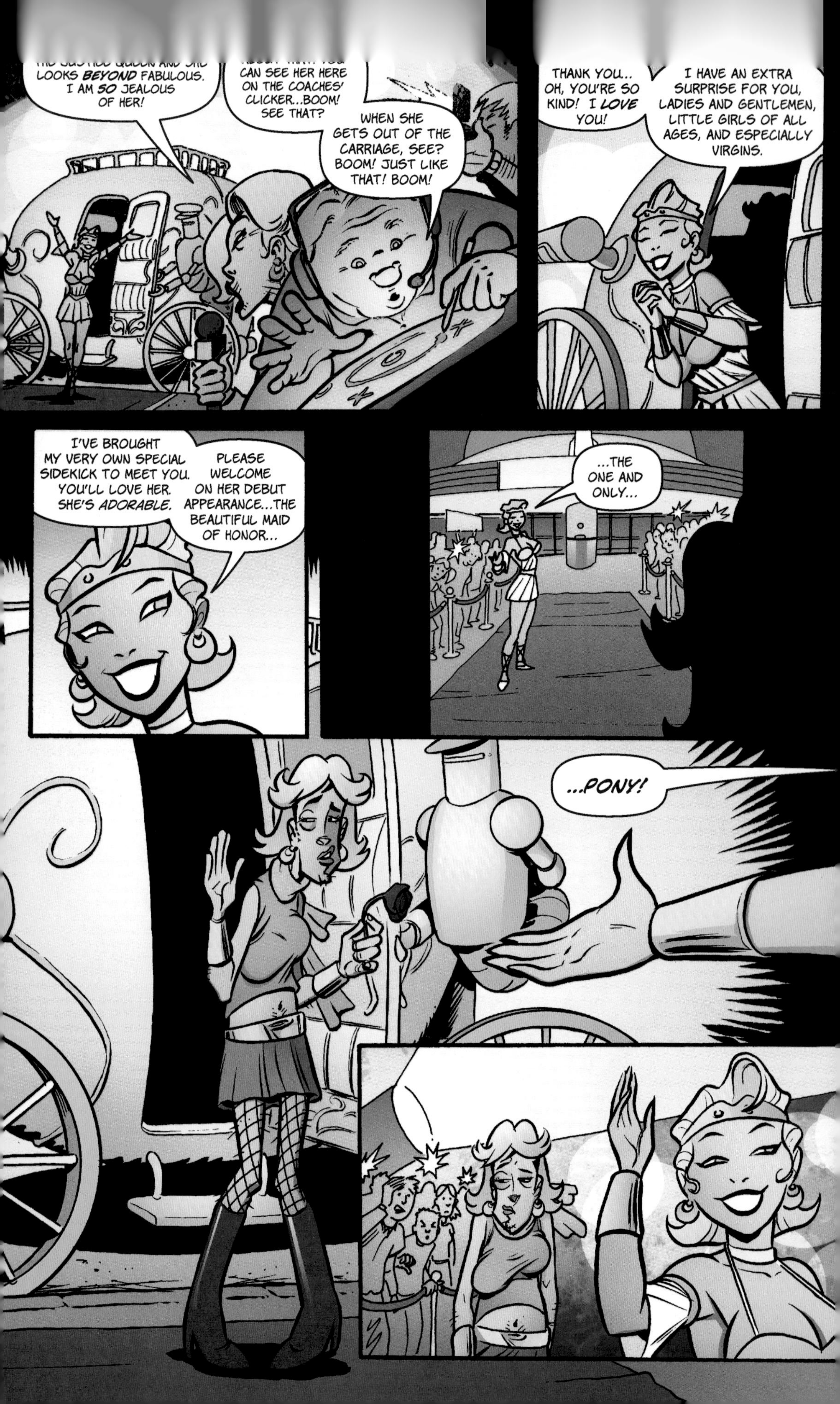
LOOKS BEYOND FABULOUS. I AM SO JEALOUS OF HER!
CAN SEE HER HERE ON THE COACHES' CLICKER...BOOM! SEE THAT?
WHEN SHE GETS OUT OF THE CARRIAGE, SEE? BOOM! JUST LIKE THAT! BOOM!
THANK YOU... OH, YOU'RE SO KIND! I LOVE YOU!
I HAVE AN EXTRA SURPRISE FOR YOU, LADIES AND GENTLEMEN, LITTLE GIRLS OF ALL AGES, AND ESPECIALLY VIRGINS.
I'VE BROUGHT MY VERY OWN SPECIAL SIDEKICK TO MEET YOU. YOU'LL LOVE HER. SHE'S ADORABLE.
PLEASE WELCOME ON HER DEBUT APPEARANCE...THE BEAUTIFUL MAID OF HONOR...
...THE ONE AND ONLY...
...PONY!

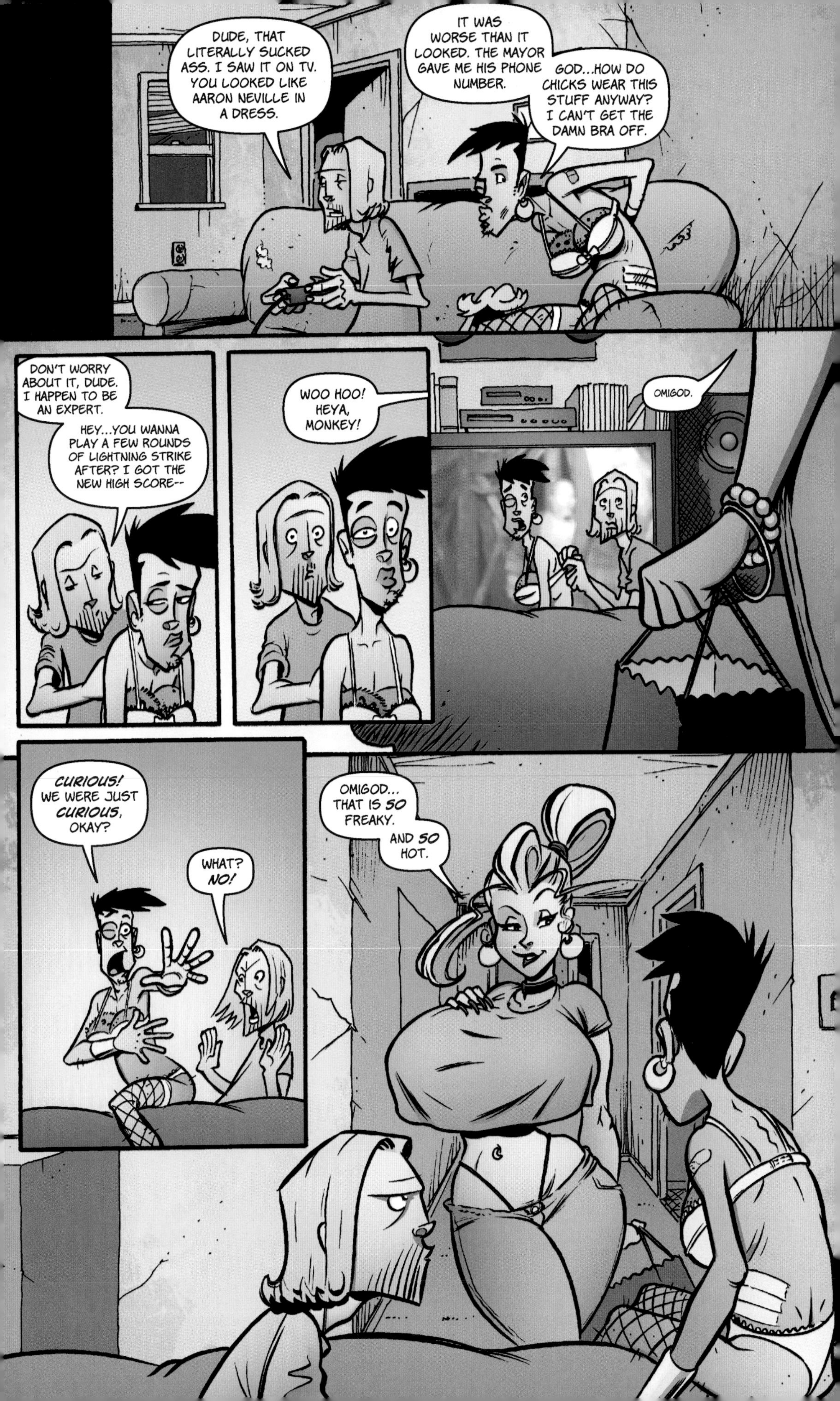
DUDE, THAT LITERALLY SUCKED ASS. I SAW IT ON TV. YOU LOOKED LIKE AARON NEVILLE IN A DRESS.
IT WAS WORSE THAN IT LOOKED. THE MAYOR GAVE ME HIS PHONE NUMBER.
GOD...HOW DO CHICKS WEAR THIS STUFF ANYWAY? I CAN'T GET THE DAMN BRA OFF.
DON'T WORRY ABOUT IT, DUDE. I HAPPEN TO BE AN EXPERT.
HEY...YOU WANNA PLAY A FEW ROUNDS OF LIGHTNING STRIKE AFTER? I GOT THE NEW HIGH SCORE--
WOO HOO! HEYA, MONKEY!
OMIGOD.
CURIOUS! WE WERE JUST CURIOUS, OKAY?
WHAT? NO!
OMIGOD... THAT IS SO FREAKY.
AND SO HOT.

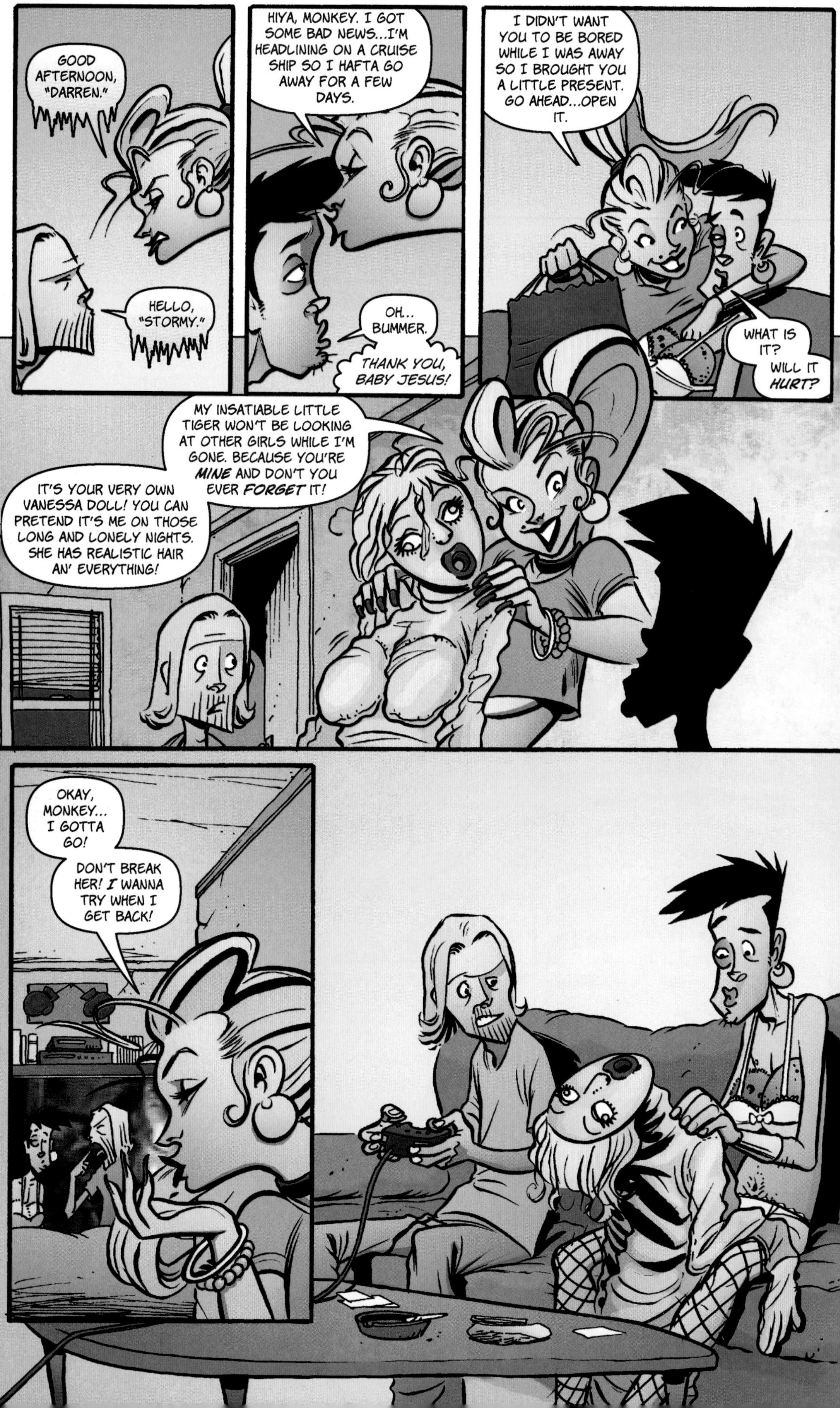
GOOD AFTERNOON, "DARREN."
HELLO, "STORMY."
HIYA, MONKEY. I GOT SOME BAD NEWS...I'M HEADLINING ON A CRUISE SHIP SO I HAFTA GO AWAY FOR A FEW DAYS.
OH... BUMMER.
THANK YOU, BABY JESUS!
I DIDN'T WANT YOU TO BE BORED WHILE I WAS AWAY SO I BROUGHT YOU A LITTLE PRESENT. GO AHEAD...OPEN IT.
WHAT IS IT?
WILL IT HURT?
IT'S YOUR VERY OWN VANESSA DOLL! YOU CAN PRETEND IT'S ME ON THOSE LONG AND LONELY NIGHTS. SHE HAS REALISTIC HAIR AN' EVERYTHING!
MY INSATIABLE LITTLE TIGER WON'T BE LOOKING AT OTHER GIRLS WHILE I'M GONE. BECAUSE YOU'RE MINE AND DON'T YOU EVER FORGET IT!
OKAY, MONKEY... I GOTTA GO!
DON'T BREAK HER! I WANNA TRY WHEN I GET BACK!

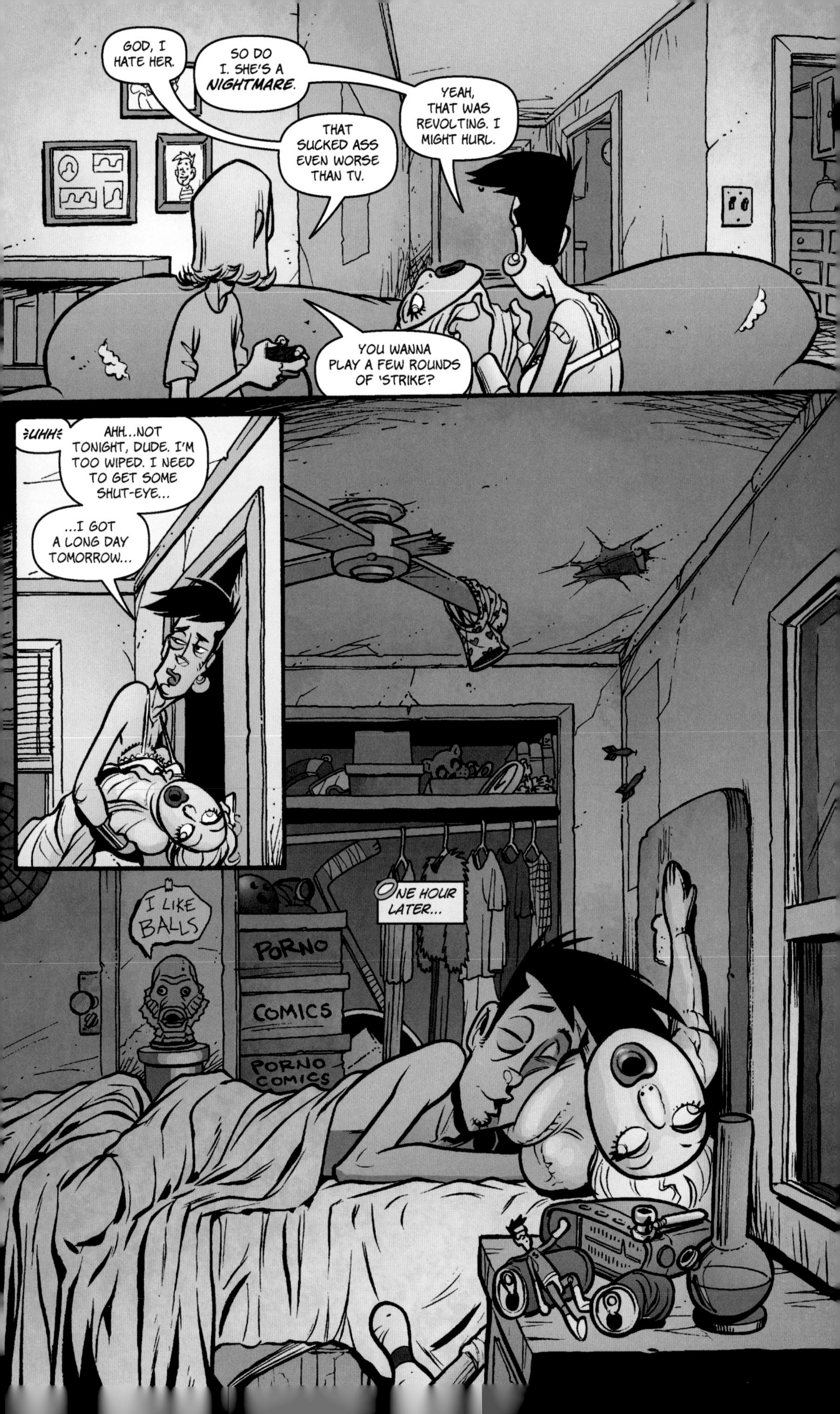

GOD, I HATE HER.
SO DO I. SHE'S A NIGHTMARE.
THAT SUCKED ASS EVEN WORSE THAN TV.
YEAH, THAT WAS REVOLTING. I MIGHT HURL.
YOU WANNA PLAY A FEW ROUNDS OF 'STRIKE?
UHH
AHH...NOT TONIGHT, DUDE. I'M TOO WIPED. I NEED TO GET SOME SHUT-EYE...
...I GOT A LONG DAY TOMORROW...
I LIKE BALLS
PORNO
COMICS
PORNO COMICS
ONE HOUR LATER...

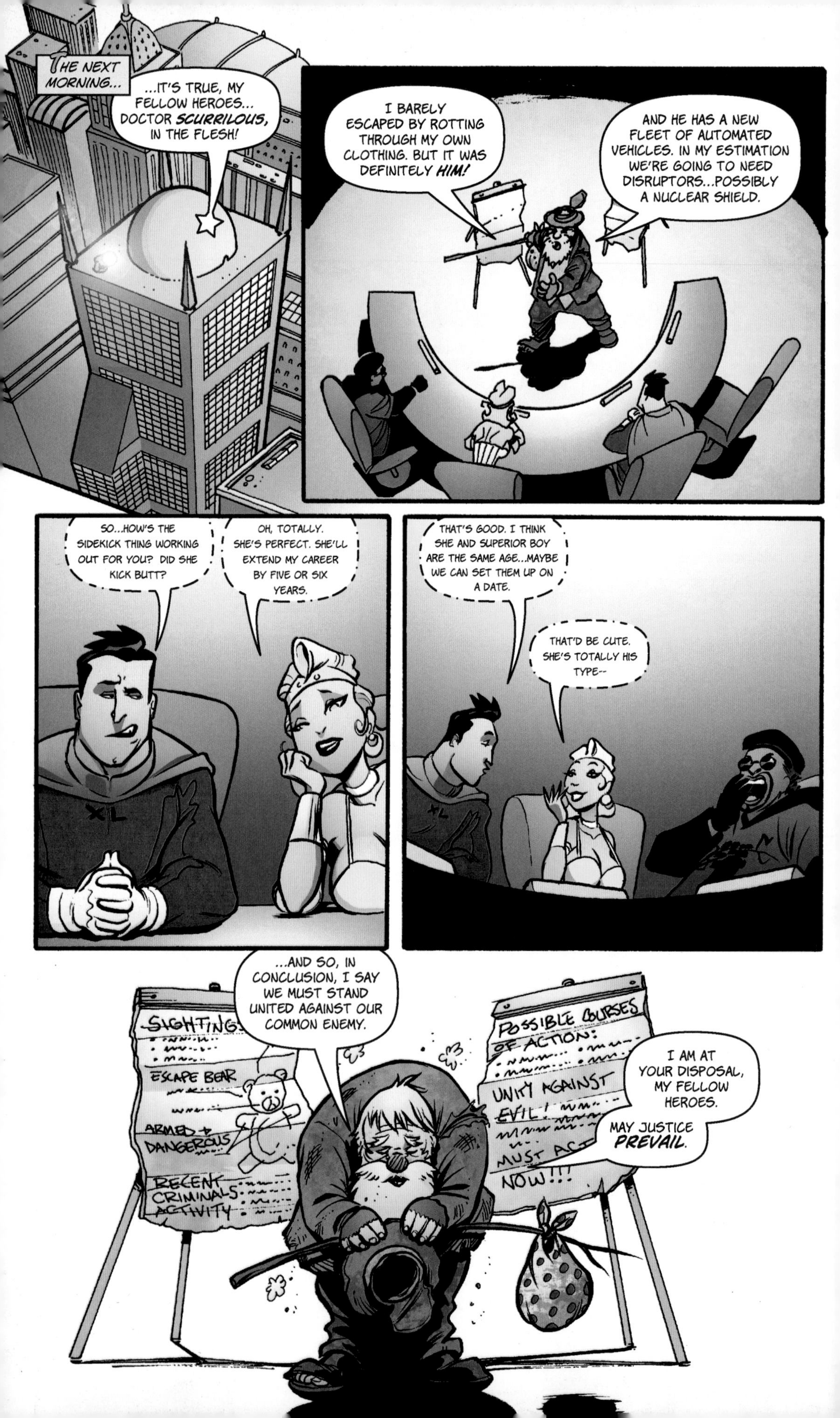
THE NEXT MORNING...
...IT'S TRUE, MY FELLOW HEROES... DOCTOR SCURRILOUS, IN THE FLESH!
I BARELY ESCAPED BY ROTTING THROUGH MY OWN CLOTHING. BUT IT WAS DEFINITELY HIM!
AND HE HAS A NEW FLEET OF AUTOMATED VEHICLES. IN MY ESTIMATION WE'RE GOING TO NEED DISRUPTORS...POSSIBLY A NUCLEAR SHIELD.
SO...HOW'S THE SIDEKICK THING WORKING OUT FOR YOU? DID SHE KICK BUTT?
OH, TOTALLY. SHE'S PERFECT. SHE'LL EXTEND MY CAREER BY FIVE OR SIX YEARS.
THAT'S GOOD. I THINK SHE AND SUPERIOR BOY ARE THE SAME AGE...MAYBE WE CAN SET THEM UP ON A DATE.
THAT'D BE CUTE. SHE'S TOTALLY HIS TYPE--
...AND SO, IN CONCLUSION, I SAY WE MUST STAND UNITED AGAINST OUR COMMON ENEMY.
SIGHTINGS
ESCAPE BEAR
ARMED + DANGEROUS
RECENT CRIMINALS ACTIVITY
POSSIBLE COURSES OF ACTION:
UNITY AGAINST EVIL!
MUST ACT NOW!!!
I AM AT YOUR DISPOSAL, MY FELLOW HEROES.
MAY JUSTICE PREVAIL.

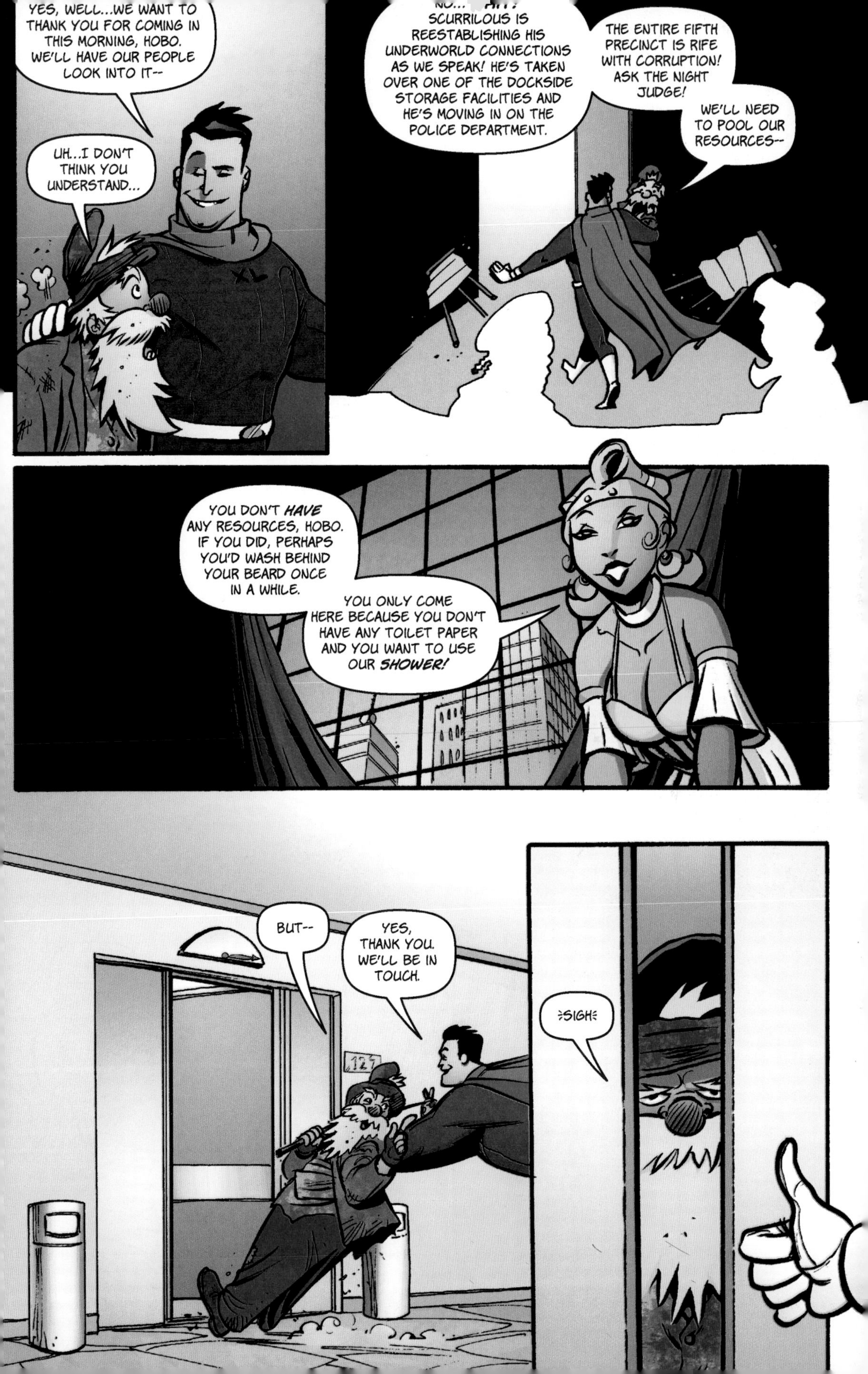
YES, WELL...WE WANT TO THANK YOU FOR COMING IN THIS MORNING, HOBO. WE'LL HAVE OUR PEOPLE LOOK INTO IT--
UH...I DON'T THINK YOU UNDERSTAND...
SCURRILOUS IS REESTABLISHING HIS UNDERWORLD CONNECTIONS AS WE SPEAK! HE'S TAKEN OVER ONE OF THE DOCKSIDE STORAGE FACILITIES AND HE'S MOVING IN ON THE POLICE DEPARTMENT.
THE ENTIRE FIFTH PRECINCT IS RIFE WITH CORRUPTION! ASK THE NIGHT JUDGE!
WE'LL NEED TO POOL OUR RESOURCES--
YOU DON'T HAVE ANY RESOURCES, HOBO. IF YOU DID, PERHAPS YOU'D WASH BEHIND YOUR BEARD ONCE IN A WHILE.
YOU ONLY COME HERE BECAUSE YOU DON'T HAVE ANY TOILET PAPER AND YOU WANT TO USE OUR SHOWER!
BUT--
YES, THANK YOU. WE'LL BE IN TOUCH.
SIGH

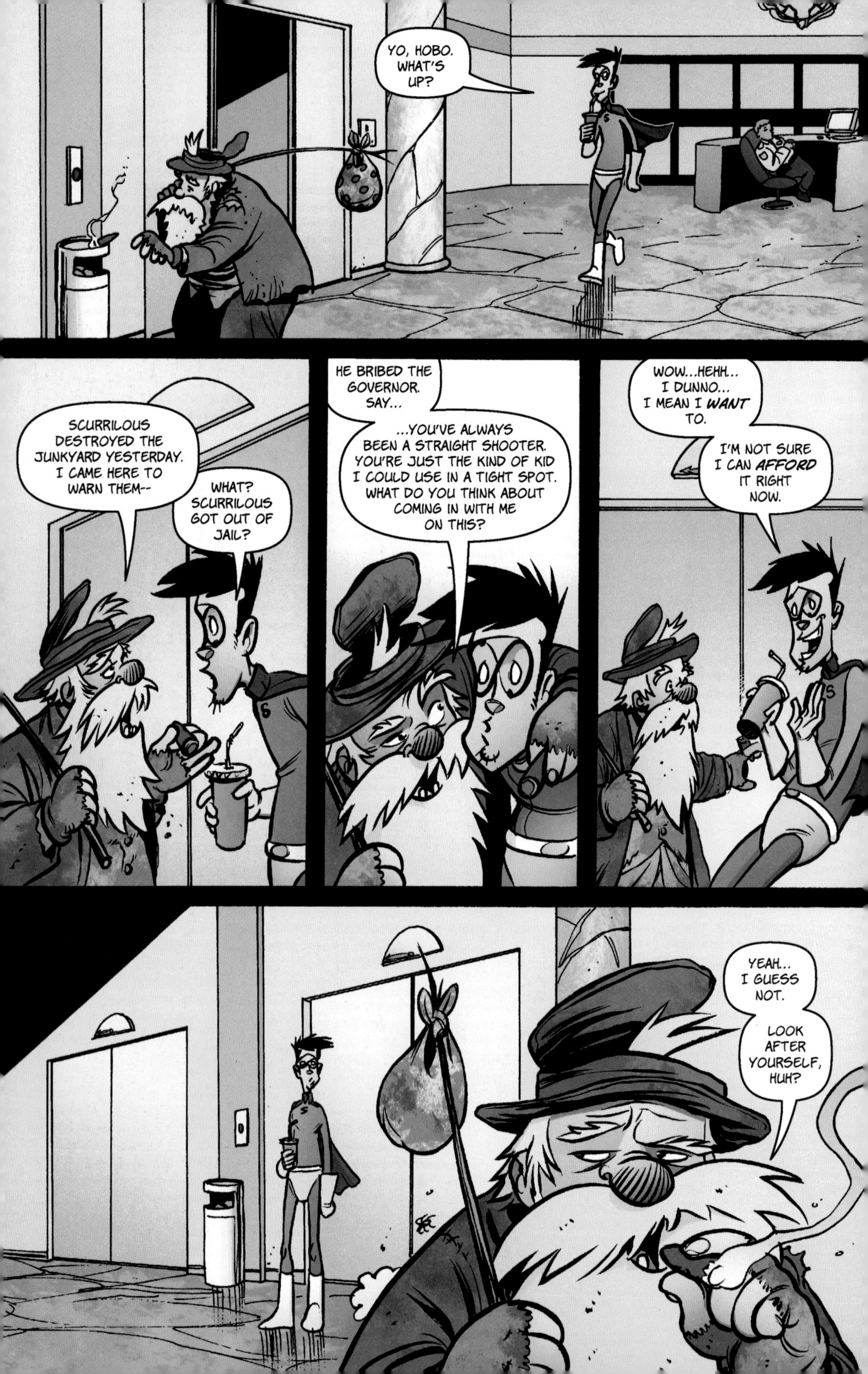
YO, HOBO. WHAT'S UP?
SCURRILOUS DESTROYED THE JUNKYARD YESTERDAY. I CAME HERE TO WARN THEM--
WHAT? SCURRILOUS GOT OUT OF JAIL?
HE BRIBED THE GOVERNOR. SAY...
...YOU'VE ALWAYS BEEN A STRAIGHT SHOOTER. YOU'RE JUST THE KIND OF KID I COULD USE IN A TIGHT SPOT. WHAT DO YOU THINK ABOUT COMING IN WITH ME ON THIS?
WOW...HEHH... I DUNNO... I MEAN I *WANT* TO.
I'M NOT SURE I CAN *AFFORD* IT RIGHT NOW.
YEAH... I GUESS NOT.
LOOK AFTER YOURSELF, HUH?

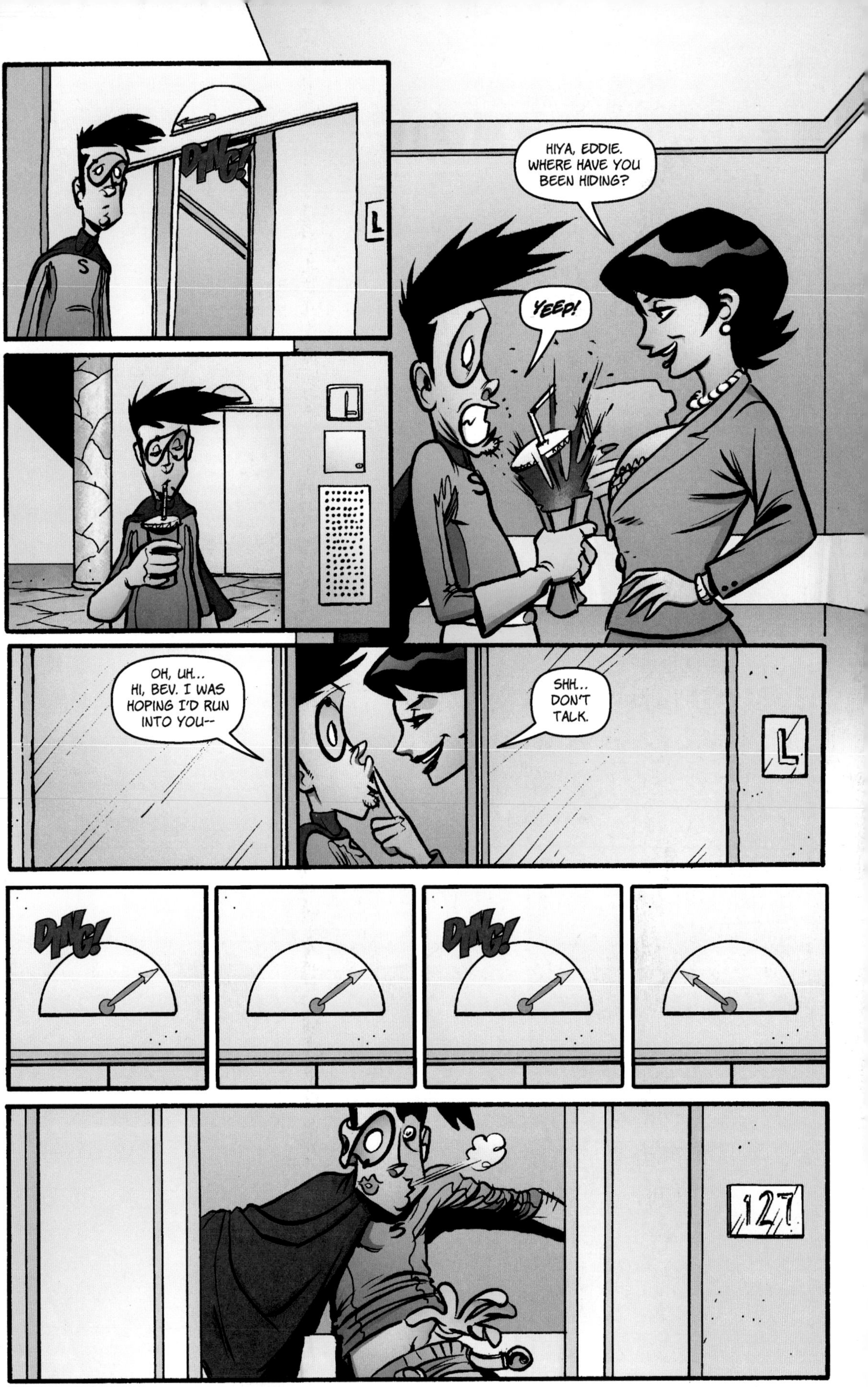
DING!
HIYA, EDDIE. WHERE HAVE YOU BEEN HIDING?
YEEP!
OH, UH... HI, BEV. I WAS HOPING I'D RUN INTO YOU--
SHH... DON'T TALK.
DING!
DING!
127

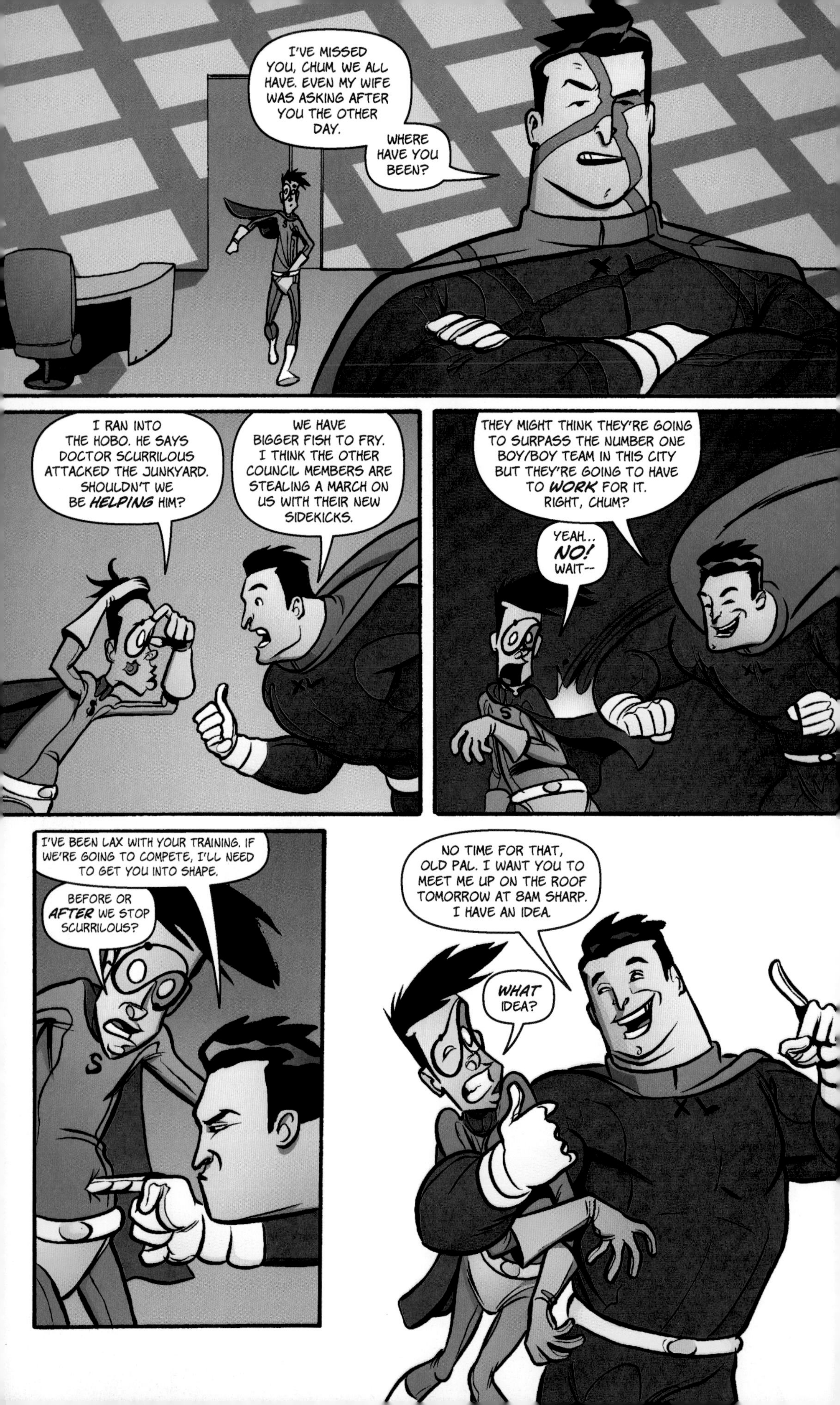
I'VE MISSED YOU, CHUM. WE ALL HAVE. EVEN MY WIFE WAS ASKING AFTER YOU THE OTHER DAY.
WHERE HAVE YOU BEEN?
I RAN INTO THE HOBO. HE SAYS DOCTOR SCURRILOUS ATTACKED THE JUNKYARD. SHOULDN'T WE BE *HELPING* HIM?
WE HAVE BIGGER FISH TO FRY. I THINK THE OTHER COUNCIL MEMBERS ARE STEALING A MARCH ON US WITH THEIR NEW SIDEKICKS.
THEY MIGHT THINK THEY'RE GOING TO SURPASS THE NUMBER ONE BOY/BOY TEAM IN THIS CITY BUT THEY'RE GOING TO HAVE TO *WORK* FOR IT. RIGHT, CHUM?
YEAH... *NO!* WAIT--
I'VE BEEN LAX WITH YOUR TRAINING. IF WE'RE GOING TO COMPETE, I'LL NEED TO GET YOU INTO SHAPE.
BEFORE OR *AFTER* WE STOP SCURRILOUS?
NO TIME FOR THAT, OLD PAL. I WANT YOU TO MEET ME UP ON THE ROOF TOMORROW AT 8AM SHARP. I HAVE AN IDEA.
WHAT IDEA?

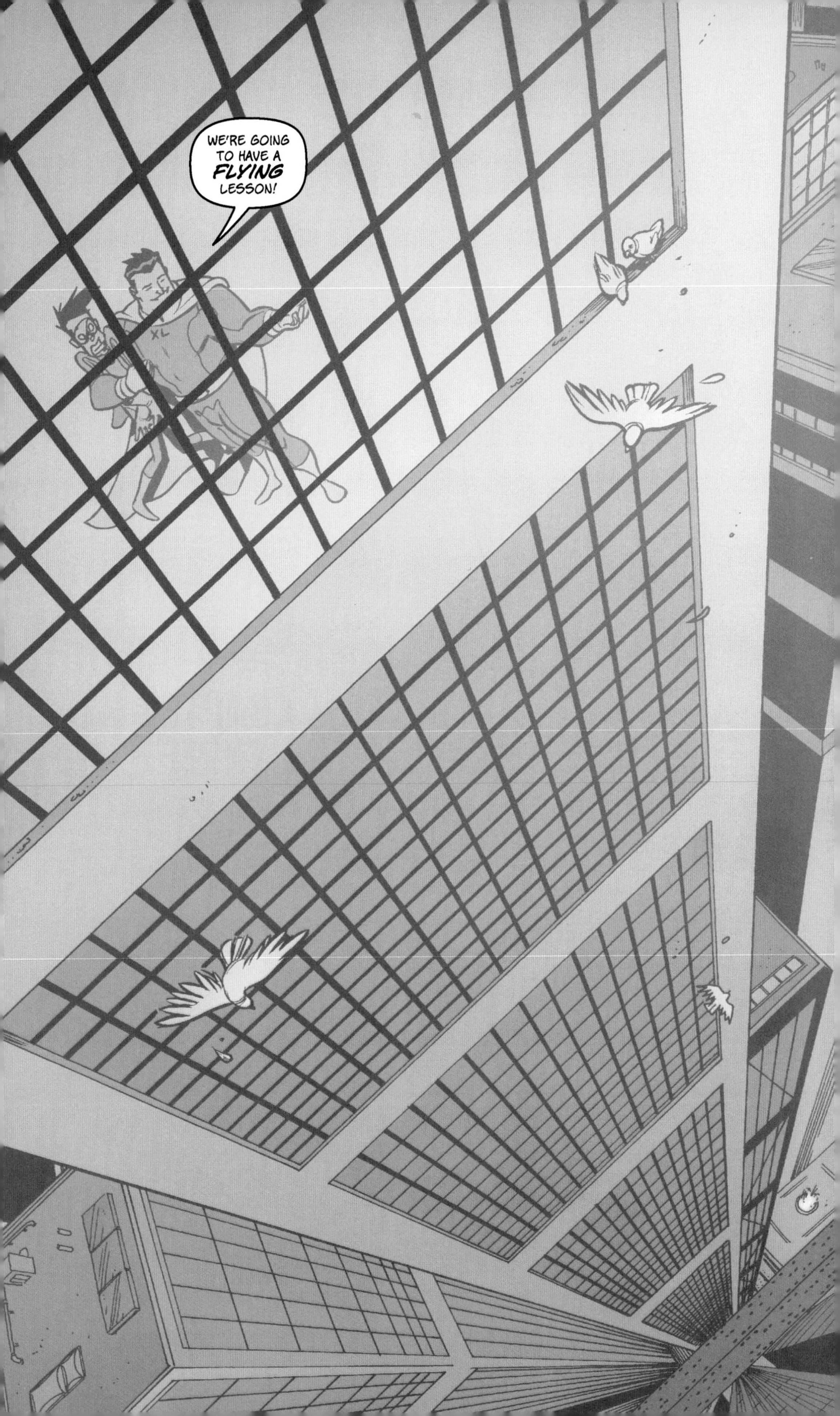
WE'RE GOING TO HAVE A FLYING LESSON!

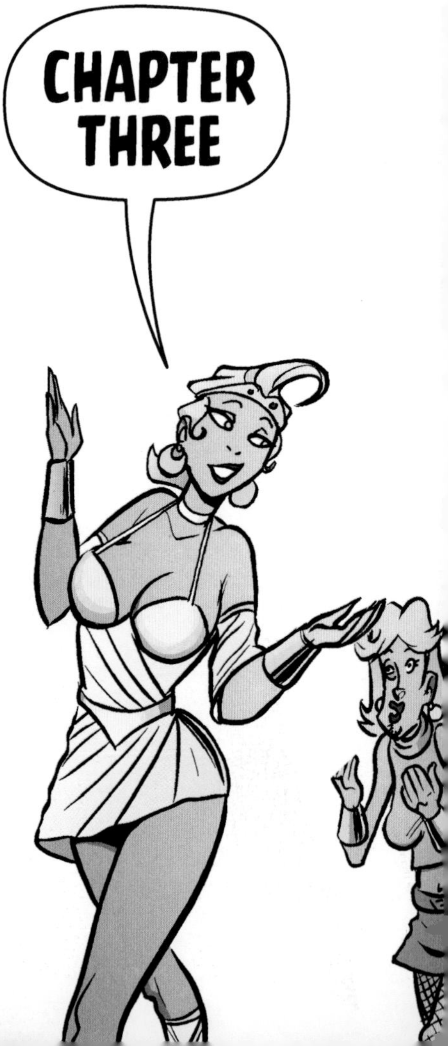
CHAPTER THREE

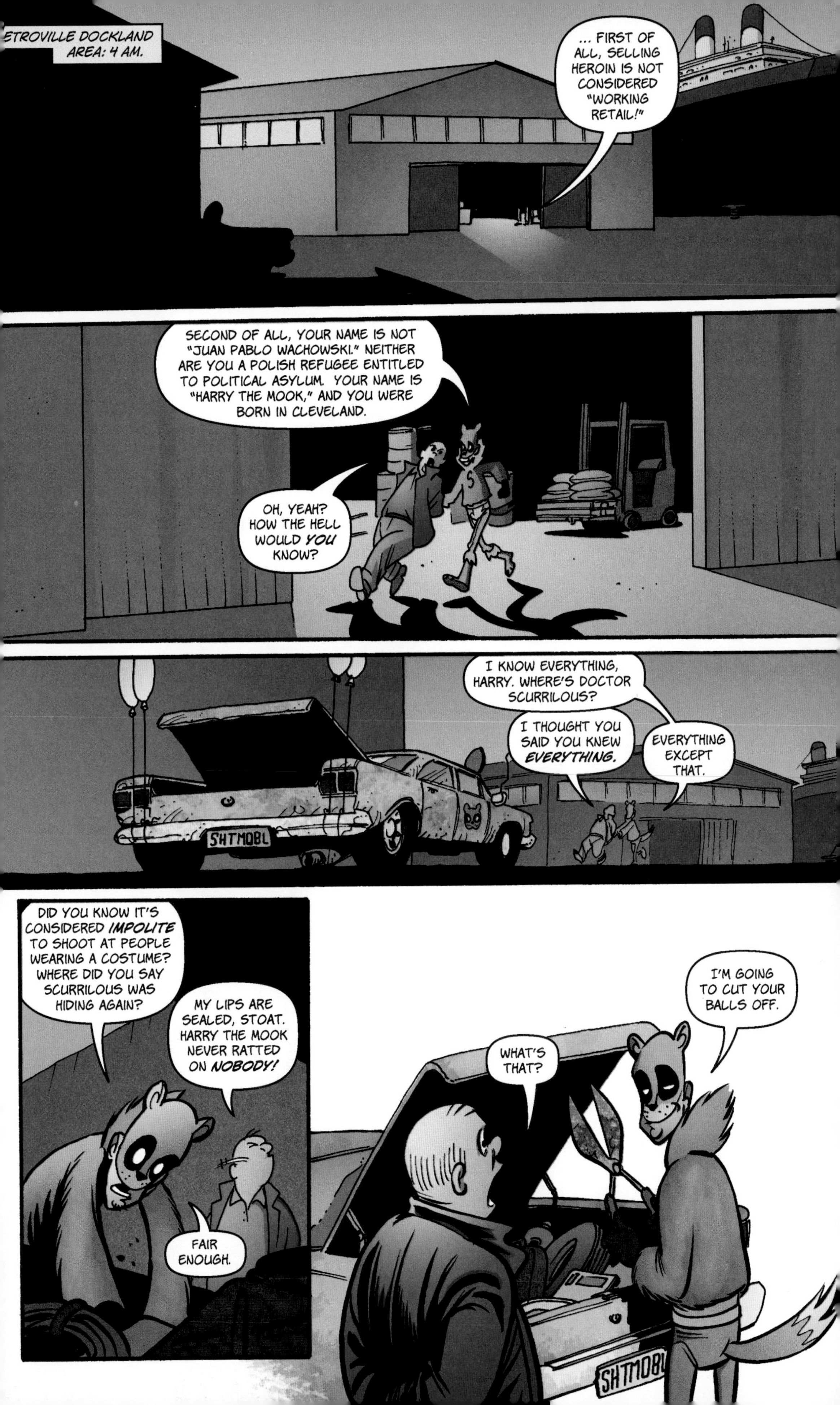
ETROVILLE DOCKLAND AREA: 4 AM.
... FIRST OF ALL, SELLING HEROIN IS NOT CONSIDERED "WORKING RETAIL!"
SECOND OF ALL, YOUR NAME IS NOT "JUAN PABLO WACHOWSKI." NEITHER ARE YOU A POLISH REFUGEE ENTITLED TO POLITICAL ASYLUM. YOUR NAME IS "HARRY THE MOOK," AND YOU WERE BORN IN CLEVELAND.
OH, YEAH? HOW THE HELL WOULD YOU KNOW?
I KNOW EVERYTHING, HARRY. WHERE'S DOCTOR SCURRILOUS?
I THOUGHT YOU SAID YOU KNEW EVERYTHING.
EVERYTHING EXCEPT THAT.
SHTMOBL
DID YOU KNOW IT'S CONSIDERED IMPOLITE TO SHOOT AT PEOPLE WEARING A COSTUME? WHERE DID YOU SAY SCURRILOUS WAS HIDING AGAIN?
MY LIPS ARE SEALED, STOAT. HARRY THE MOOK NEVER RATTED ON NOBODY!
FAIR ENOUGH.
WHAT'S THAT?
I'M GOING TO CUT YOUR BALLS OFF.
SHTMOBL

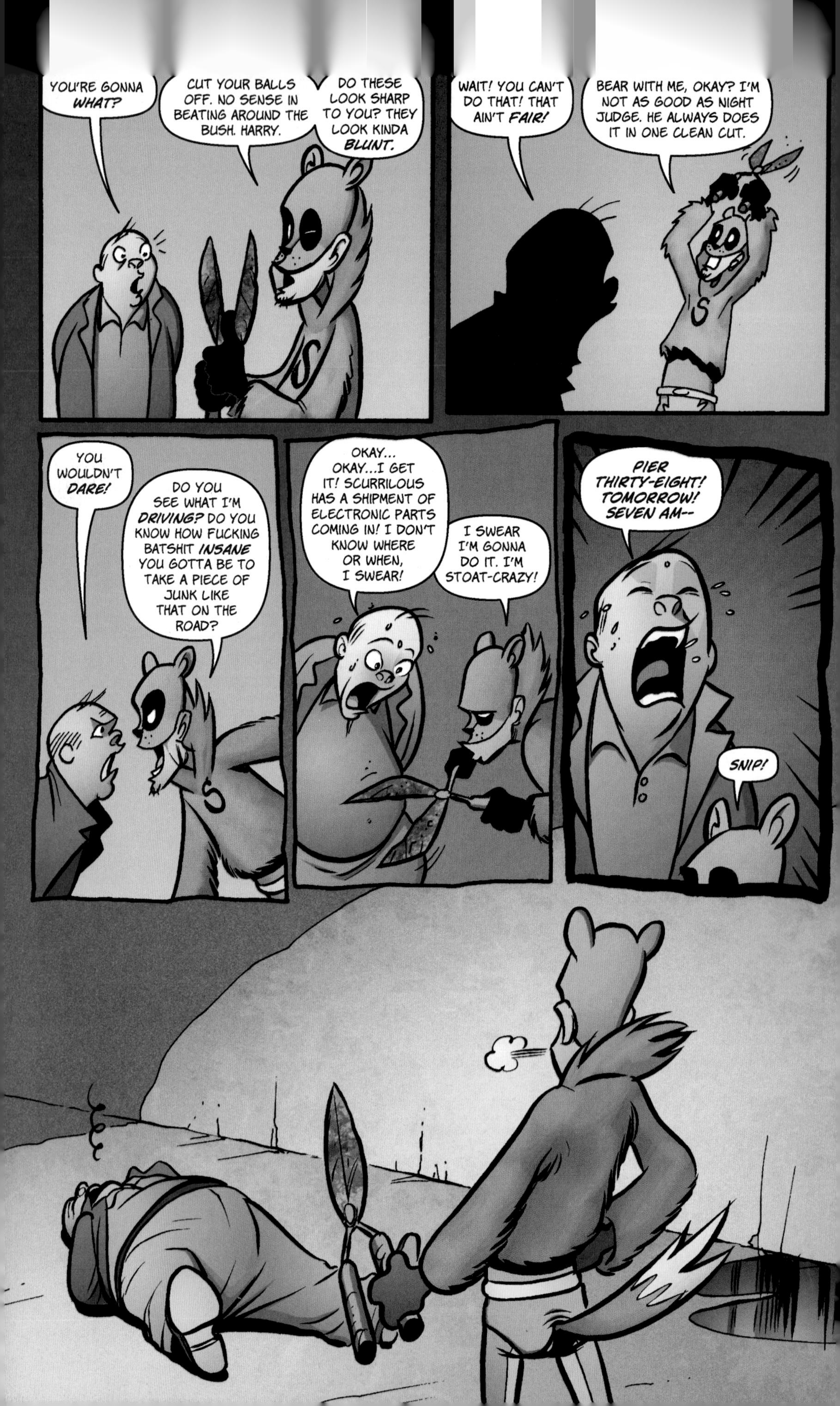

YOU'RE GONNA WHAT?
CUT YOUR BALLS OFF. NO SENSE IN BEATING AROUND THE BUSH. HARRY.
DO THESE LOOK SHARP TO YOU? THEY LOOK KINDA BLUNT.
WAIT! YOU CAN'T DO THAT! THAT AIN'T FAIR!
BEAR WITH ME, OKAY? I'M NOT AS GOOD AS NIGHT JUDGE. HE ALWAYS DOES IT IN ONE CLEAN CUT.
YOU WOULDN'T DARE!
DO YOU SEE WHAT I'M DRIVING? DO YOU KNOW HOW FUCKING BATSHIT INSANE YOU GOTTA BE TO TAKE A PIECE OF JUNK LIKE THAT ON THE ROAD?
OKAY... OKAY...I GET IT! SCURRILOUS HAS A SHIPMENT OF ELECTRONIC PARTS COMING IN! I DON'T KNOW WHERE OR WHEN, I SWEAR!
I SWEAR I'M GONNA DO IT. I'M STOAT-CRAZY!
PIER THIRTY-EIGHT! TOMORROW! SEVEN AM--
SNIP!

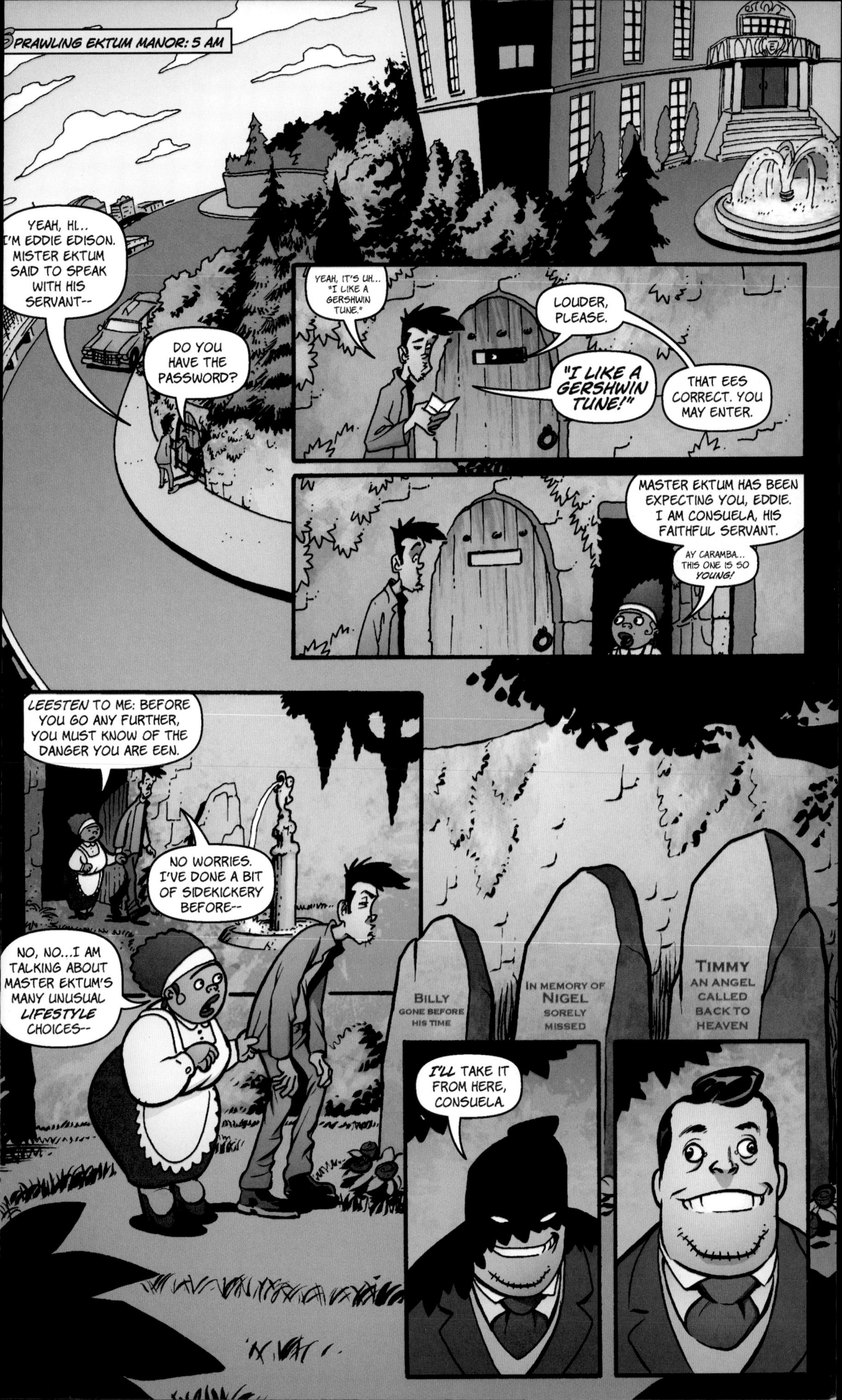
SPRAWLING EKTUM MANOR: 5 AM
YEAH, HI.. I'M EDDIE EDISON. MISTER EKTUM SAID TO SPEAK WITH HIS SERVANT--
DO YOU HAVE THE PASSWORD?
YEAH, IT'S UH.. "I LIKE A GERSHWIN TUNE."
LOUDER, PLEASE.
"I LIKE A GERSHWIN TUNE!"
THAT EES CORRECT. YOU MAY ENTER.
MASTER EKTUM HAS BEEN EXPECTING YOU, EDDIE. I AM CONSUELA, HIS FAITHFUL SERVANT.
AY CARAMBA... THIS ONE IS SO YOUNG!
LEESTEN TO ME: BEFORE YOU GO ANY FURTHER, YOU MUST KNOW OF THE DANGER YOU ARE EEN.
NO WORRIES. I'VE DONE A BIT OF SIDEKICKERY BEFORE--
NO, NO...I AM TALKING ABOUT MASTER EKTUM'S MANY UNUSUAL LIFESTYLE CHOICES--
BILLY GONE BEFORE HIS TIME
IN MEMORY OF NIGEL SORELY MISSED
TIMMY AN ANGEL CALLED BACK TO HEAVEN
I'LL TAKE IT FROM HERE, CONSUELA

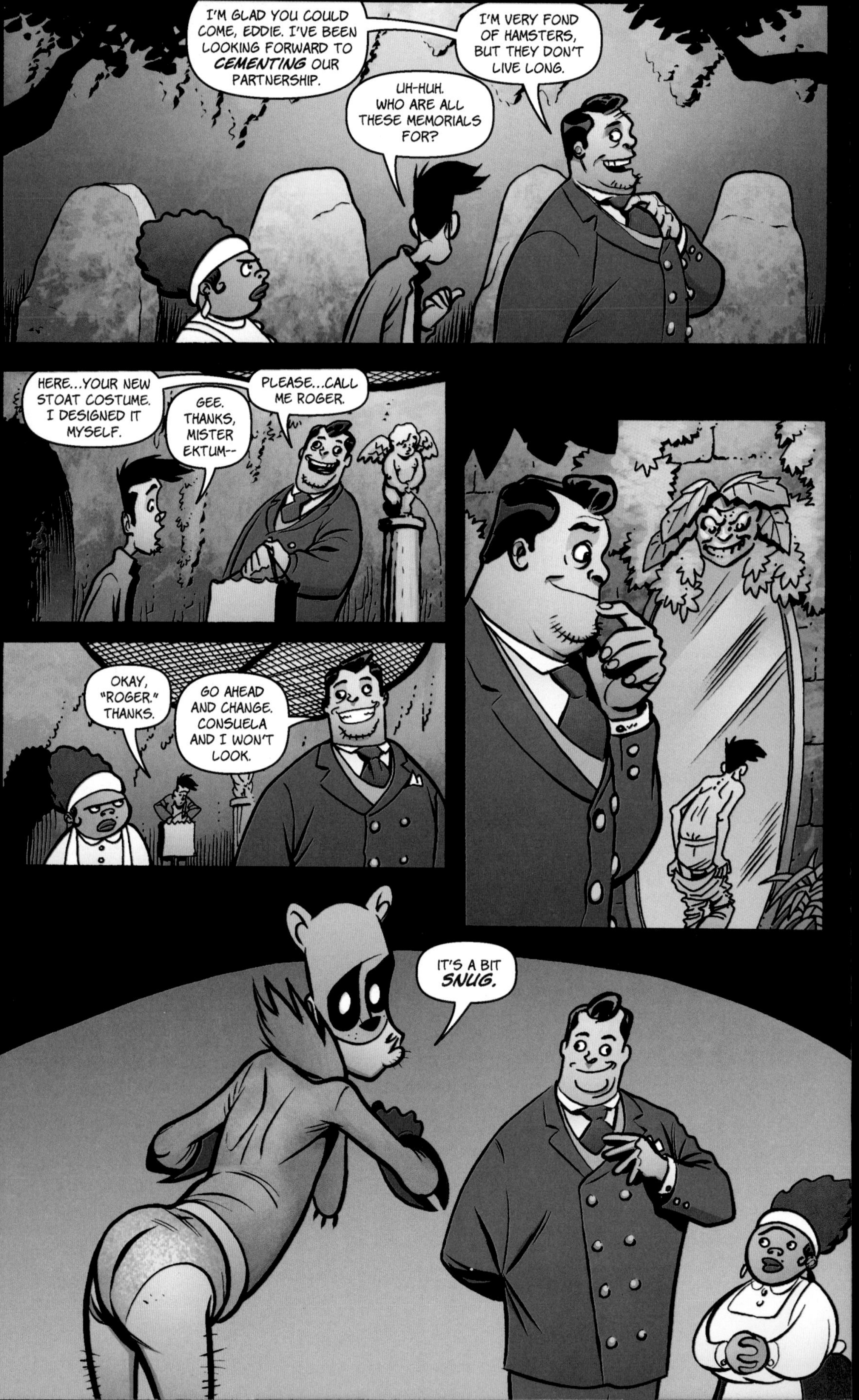
I'M GLAD YOU COULD COME, EDDIE. I'VE BEEN LOOKING FORWARD TO **CEMENTING** OUR PARTNERSHIP.
UH-HUH. WHO ARE ALL THESE MEMORIALS FOR?
I'M VERY FOND OF HAMSTERS, BUT THEY DON'T LIVE LONG.
HERE...YOUR NEW STOAT COSTUME. I DESIGNED IT MYSELF.
GEE. THANKS, MISTER EKTUM--
PLEASE...CALL ME ROGER.
OKAY, "ROGER." THANKS.
GO AHEAD AND CHANGE. CONSUELA AND I WON'T LOOK.
IT'S A BIT **SNUG.**

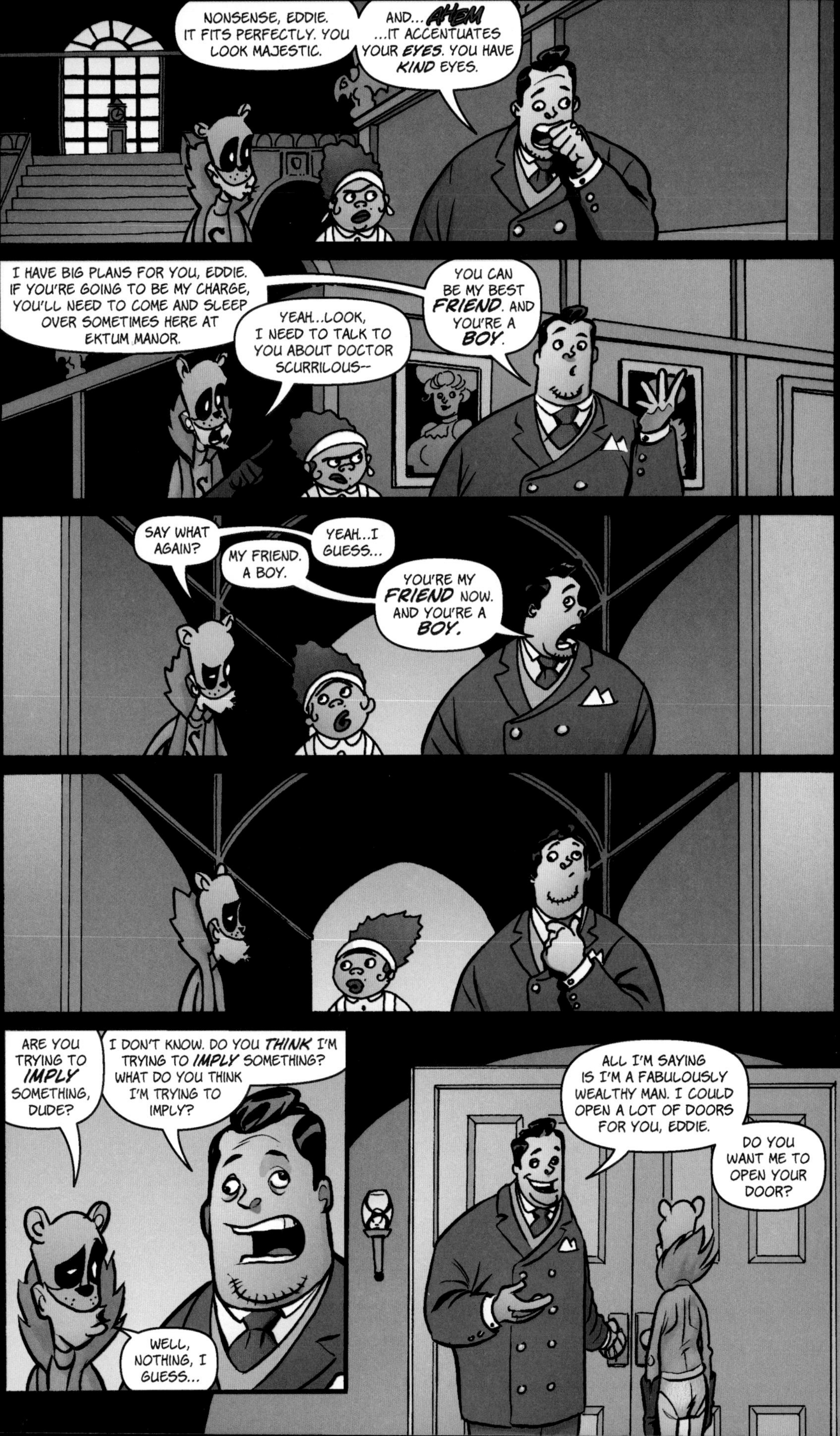
NONSENSE, EDDIE. IT FITS PERFECTLY. YOU LOOK MAJESTIC.
AND... AHEM ...IT ACCENTUATES YOUR EYES. YOU HAVE KIND EYES.
I HAVE BIG PLANS FOR YOU, EDDIE. IF YOU'RE GOING TO BE MY CHARGE, YOU'LL NEED TO COME AND SLEEP OVER SOMETIMES HERE AT EKTUM MANOR.
YEAH...LOOK, I NEED TO TALK TO YOU ABOUT DOCTOR SCURRILOUS--
YOU CAN BE MY BEST FRIEND. AND YOU'RE A BOY.
SAY WHAT AGAIN?
MY FRIEND. A BOY.
YEAH...I GUESS...
YOU'RE MY FRIEND NOW. AND YOU'RE A BOY.
ARE YOU TRYING TO IMPLY SOMETHING, DUDE?
I DON'T KNOW. DO YOU THINK I'M TRYING TO IMPLY SOMETHING? WHAT DO YOU THINK I'M TRYING TO IMPLY?
WELL, NOTHING, I GUESS...
ALL I'M SAYING IS I'M A FABULOUSLY WEALTHY MAN. I COULD OPEN A LOT OF DOORS FOR YOU, EDDIE.
DO YOU WANT ME TO OPEN YOUR DOOR?

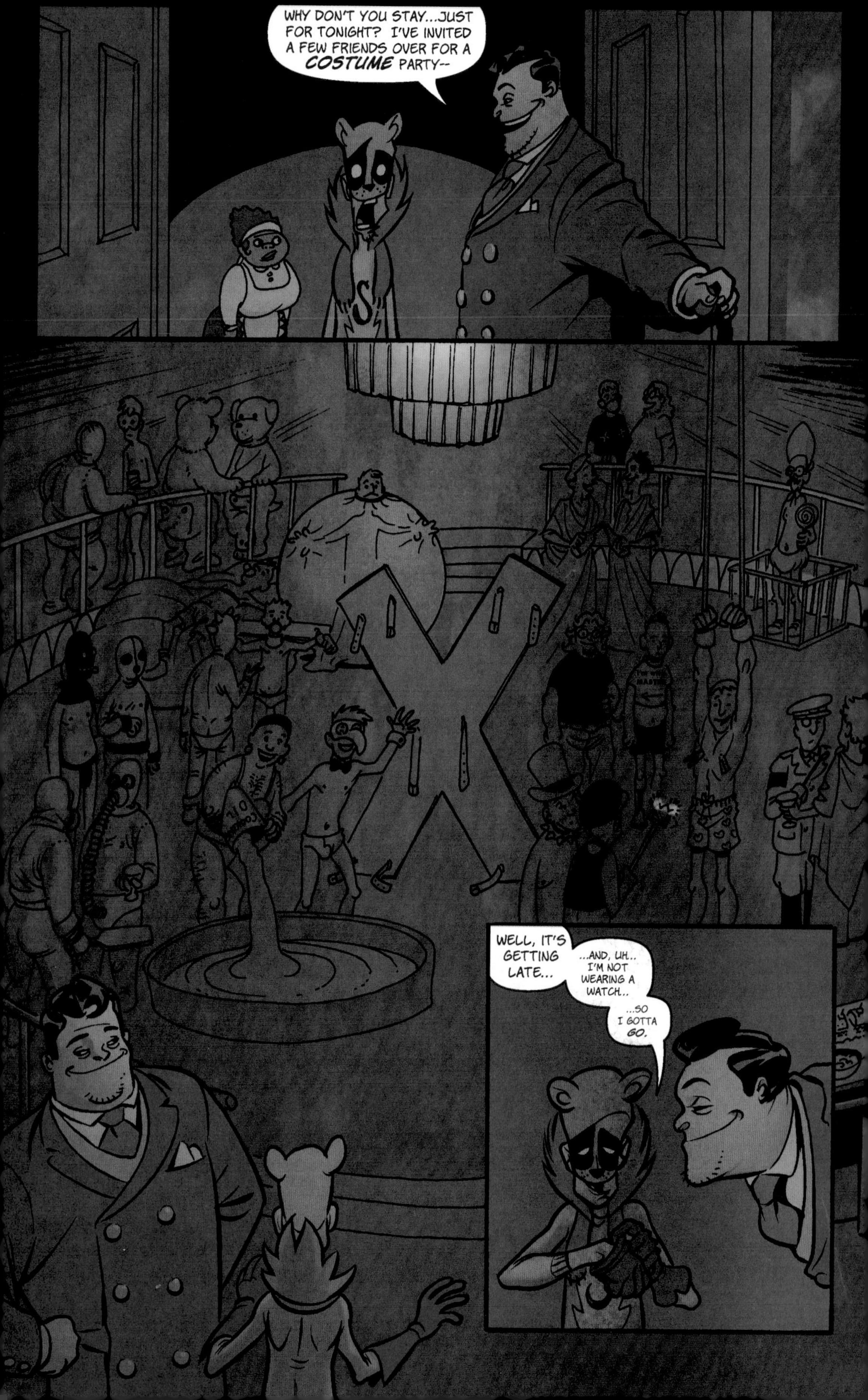
WHY DON'T YOU STAY...JUST FOR TONIGHT? I'VE INVITED A FEW FRIENDS OVER FOR A COSTUME PARTY--
WELL, IT'S GETTING LATE...
...AND, UH.. I'M NOT WEARING A WATCH..
...SO I GOTTA GO.

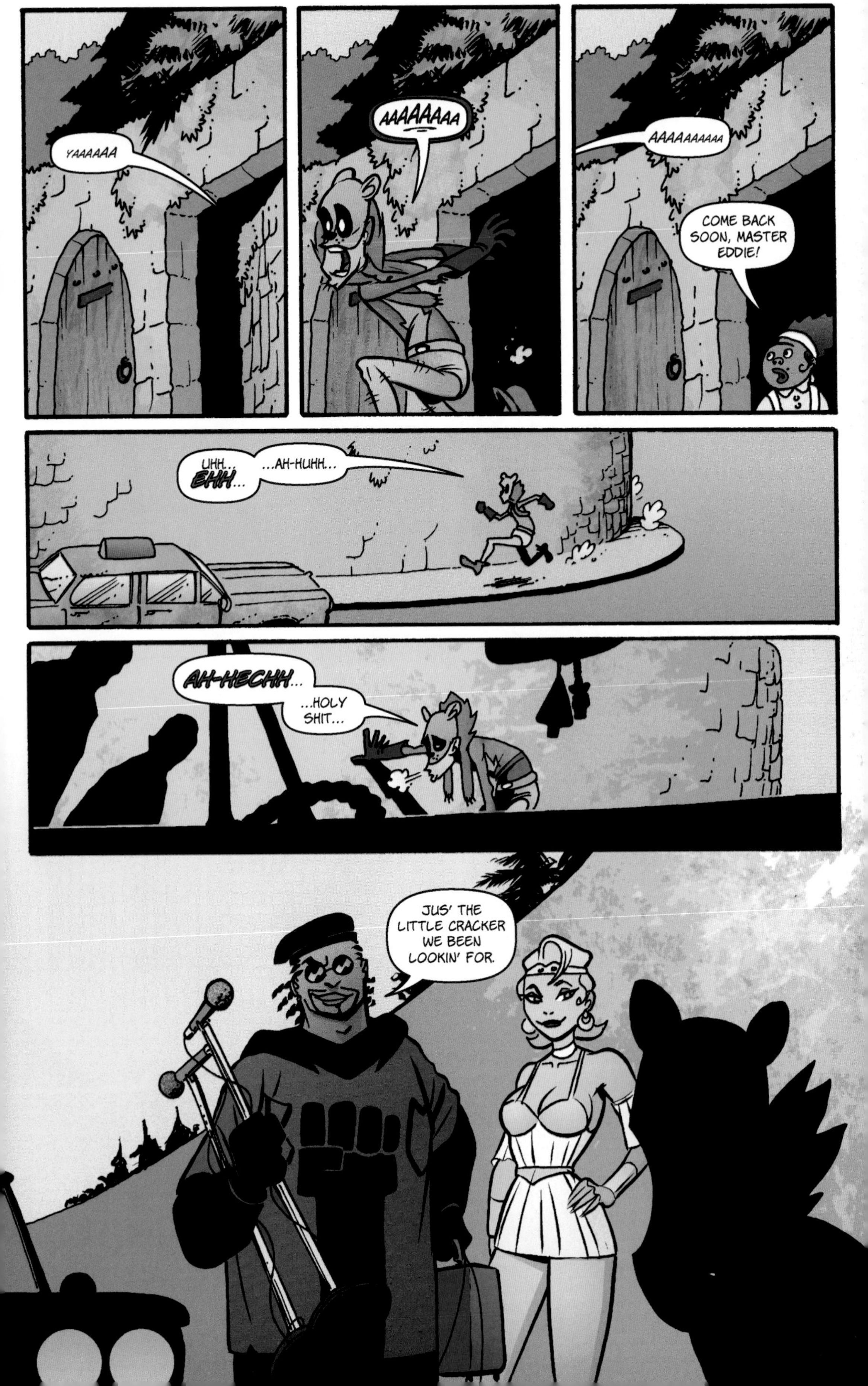
YAAAAAA
AAAAAAAA
AAAAAAAAAA
COME BACK SOON, MASTER EDDIE!
UHH... EHH...
...AH-HUHH...
AH-HECHH...
...HOLY SHIT...
JUS' THE LITTLE CRACKER WE BEEN LOOKIN' FOR.

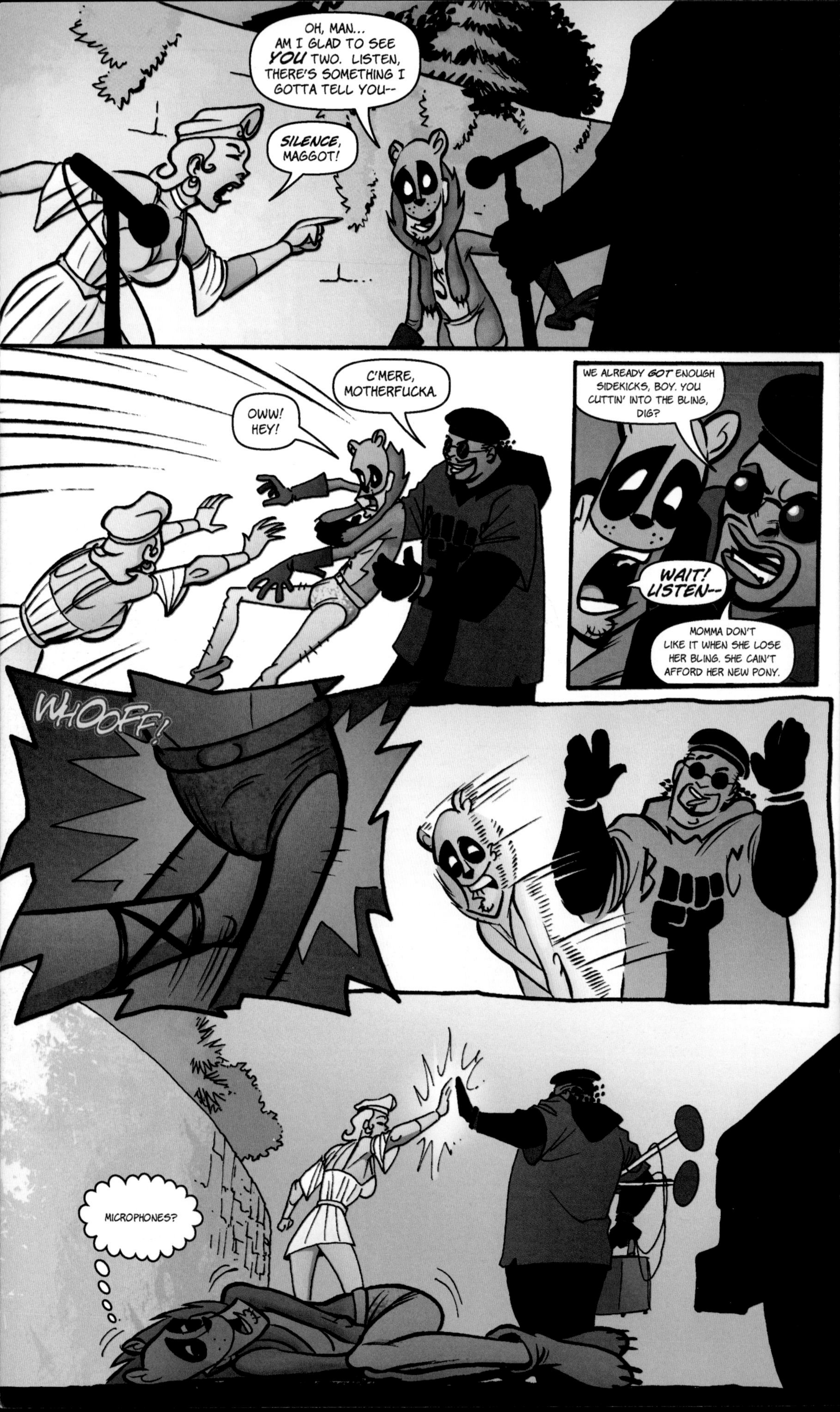
OH, MAN... AM I GLAD TO SEE YOU TWO. LISTEN, THERE'S SOMETHING I GOTTA TELL YOU--
SILENCE, MAGGOT!
C'MERE, MOTHERFUCKA.
OWW! HEY!
WE ALREADY GOT ENOUGH SIDEKICKS, BOY. YOU CUTTIN' INTO THE BLING, DIG?
WAIT! LISTEN--
MOMMA DON'T LIKE IT WHEN SHE LOSE HER BLING. SHE CAIN'T AFFORD HER NEW PONY.
WHOOFF!
MICROPHONES?

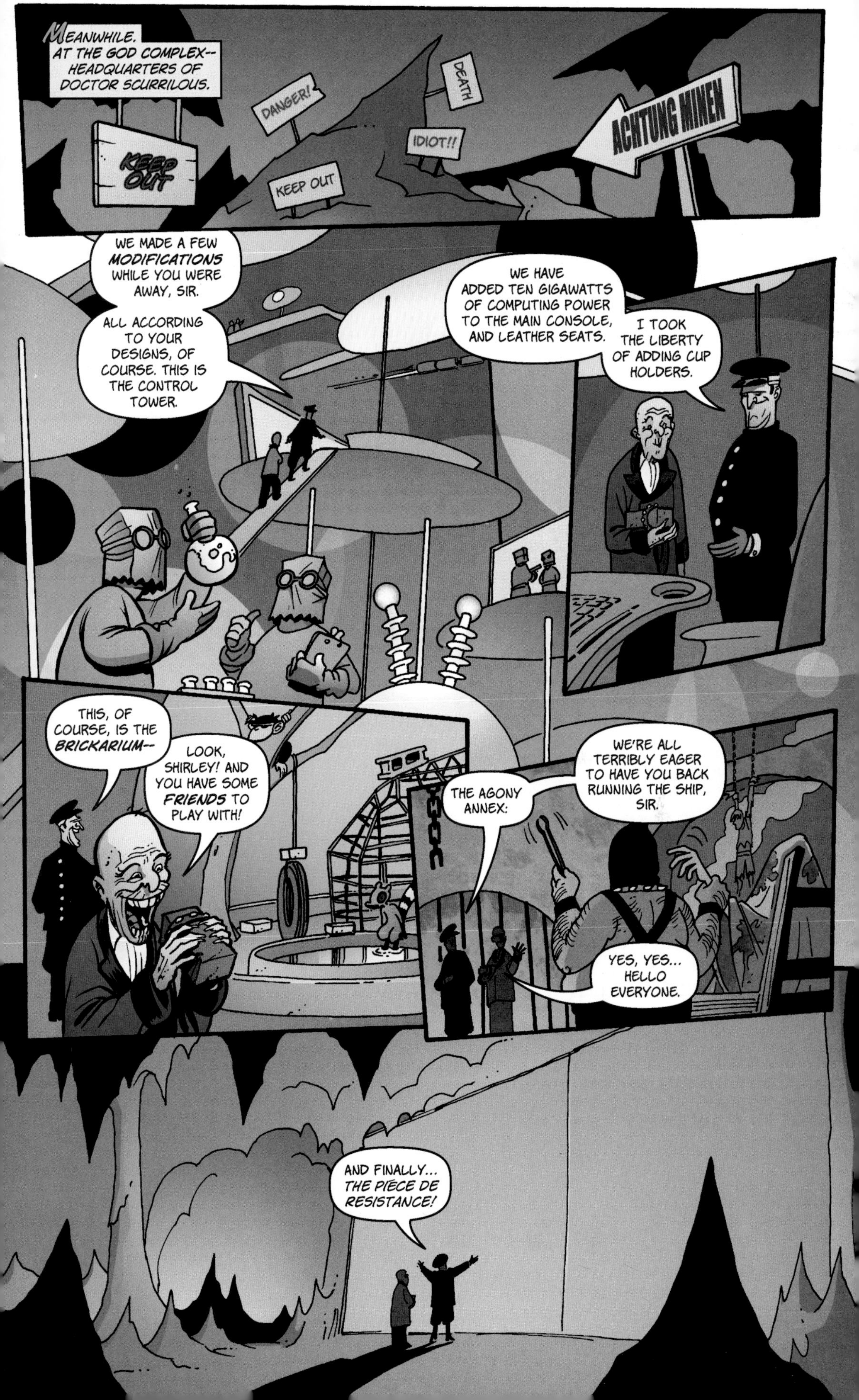
MEANWHILE. AT THE GOD COMPLEX-- HEADQUARTERS OF DOCTOR SCURRILOUS.
KEEP OUT
DANGER!
KEEP OUT
DEATH
IDIOT!!
ACHTUNG MINEN
WE MADE A FEW *MODIFICATIONS* WHILE YOU WERE AWAY, SIR.
ALL ACCORDING TO YOUR DESIGNS, OF COURSE. THIS IS THE CONTROL TOWER.
WE HAVE ADDED TEN GIGAWATTS OF COMPUTING POWER TO THE MAIN CONSOLE, AND LEATHER SEATS.
I TOOK THE LIBERTY OF ADDING CUP HOLDERS.
THIS, OF COURSE, IS THE *BRICKARIUM*--
LOOK, SHIRLEY! AND YOU HAVE SOME *FRIENDS* TO PLAY WITH!
THE AGONY ANNEX:
WE'RE ALL TERRIBLY EAGER TO HAVE YOU BACK RUNNING THE SHIP, SIR.
YES, YES... HELLO EVERYONE.
AND FINALLY... *THE PIÉCE DE RESISTANCE!*

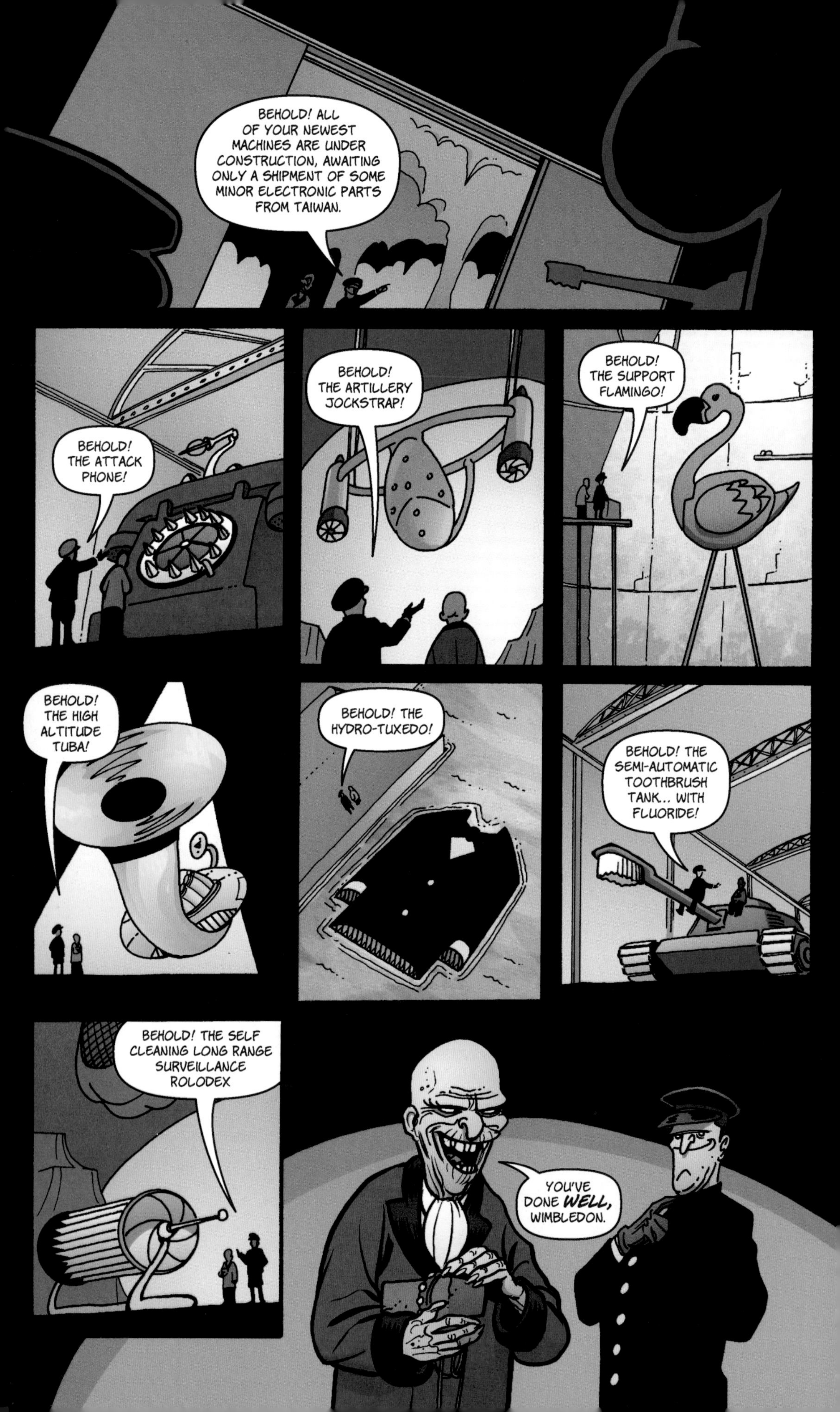
BEHOLD! ALL OF YOUR NEWEST MACHINES ARE UNDER CONSTRUCTION, AWAITING ONLY A SHIPMENT OF SOME MINOR ELECTRONIC PARTS FROM TAIWAN.
BEHOLD! THE ATTACK PHONE!
BEHOLD! THE ARTILLERY JOCKSTRAP!
BEHOLD! THE SUPPORT FLAMINGO!
BEHOLD! THE HIGH ALTITUDE TUBA!
BEHOLD! THE HYDRO-TUXEDO!
BEHOLD! THE SEMI-AUTOMATIC TOOTHBRUSH TANK... WITH FLUORIDE!
BEHOLD! THE SELF CLEANING LONG RANGE SURVEILLANCE ROLODEX
YOU'VE DONE ***WELL,*** WIMBLEDON.

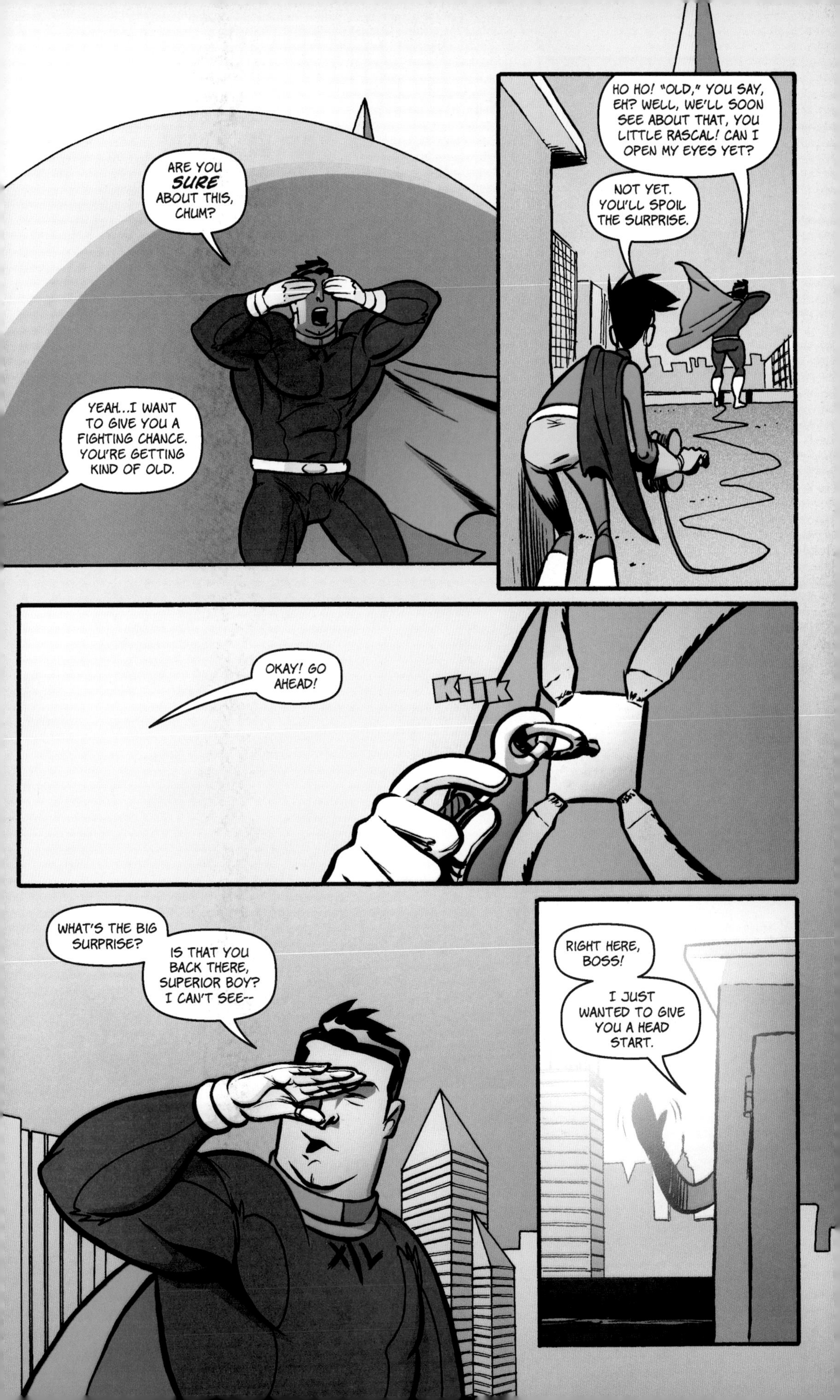

ARE YOU SURE ABOUT THIS, CHUM?
YEAH...I WANT TO GIVE YOU A FIGHTING CHANCE. YOU'RE GETTING KIND OF OLD.
HO HO! "OLD," YOU SAY, EH? WELL, WE'LL SOON SEE ABOUT THAT, YOU LITTLE RASCAL! CAN I OPEN MY EYES YET?
NOT YET. YOU'LL SPOIL THE SURPRISE.
OKAY! GO AHEAD!
KLIK
WHAT'S THE BIG SURPRISE?
IS THAT YOU BACK THERE, SUPERIOR BOY? I CAN'T SEE--
RIGHT HERE, BOSS!
I JUST WANTED TO GIVE YOU A HEAD START.

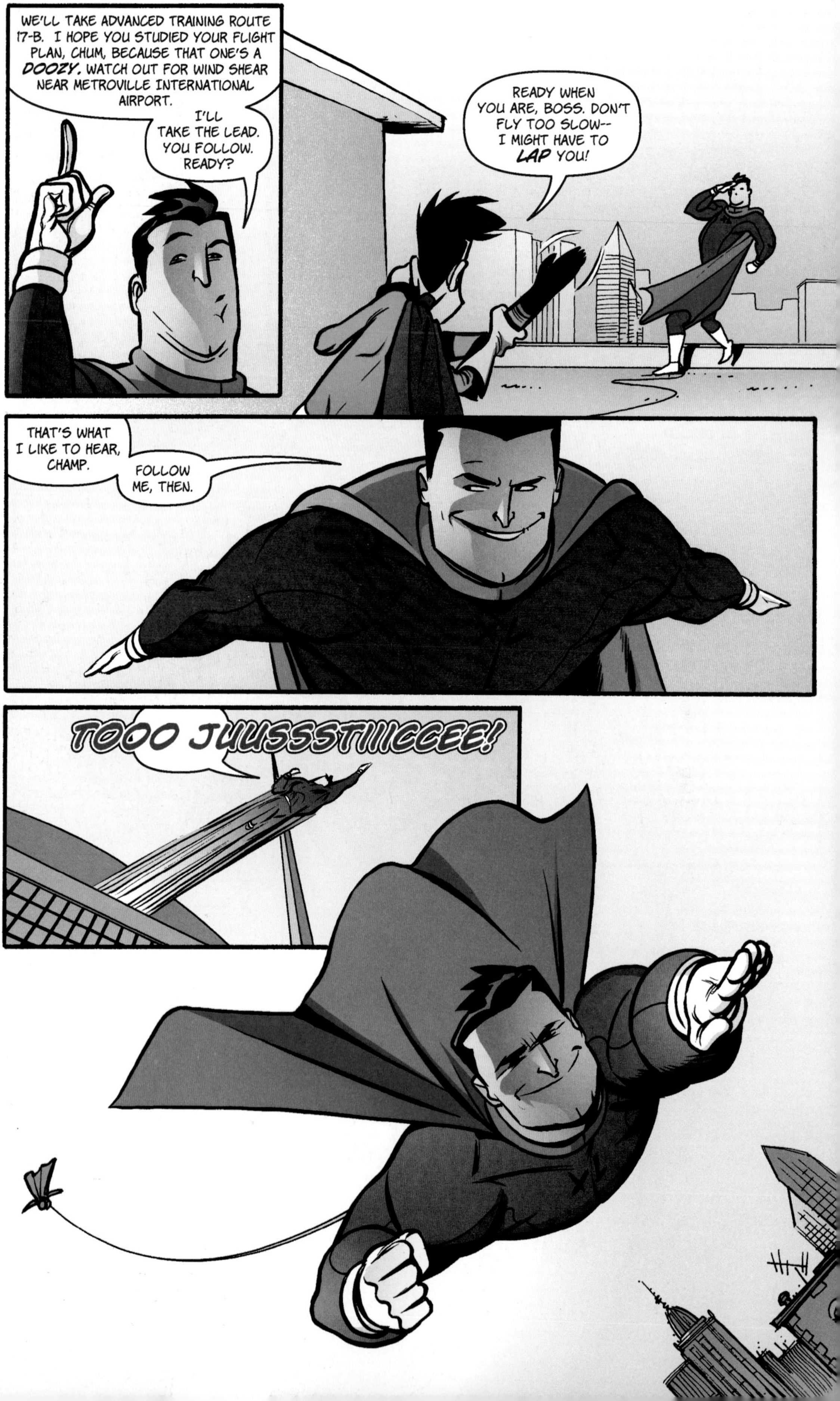
WE'LL TAKE ADVANCED TRAINING ROUTE 17-B. I HOPE YOU STUDIED YOUR FLIGHT PLAN, CHUM, BECAUSE THAT ONE'S A DOOZY. WATCH OUT FOR WIND SHEAR NEAR METROVILLE INTERNATIONAL AIRPORT.
I'LL TAKE THE LEAD. YOU FOLLOW. READY?
READY WHEN YOU ARE, BOSS. DON'T FLY TOO SLOW-- I MIGHT HAVE TO LAP YOU!
THAT'S WHAT I LIKE TO HEAR, CHAMP.
FOLLOW ME, THEN.
TOOO JUUSSSSTIIICCEE!

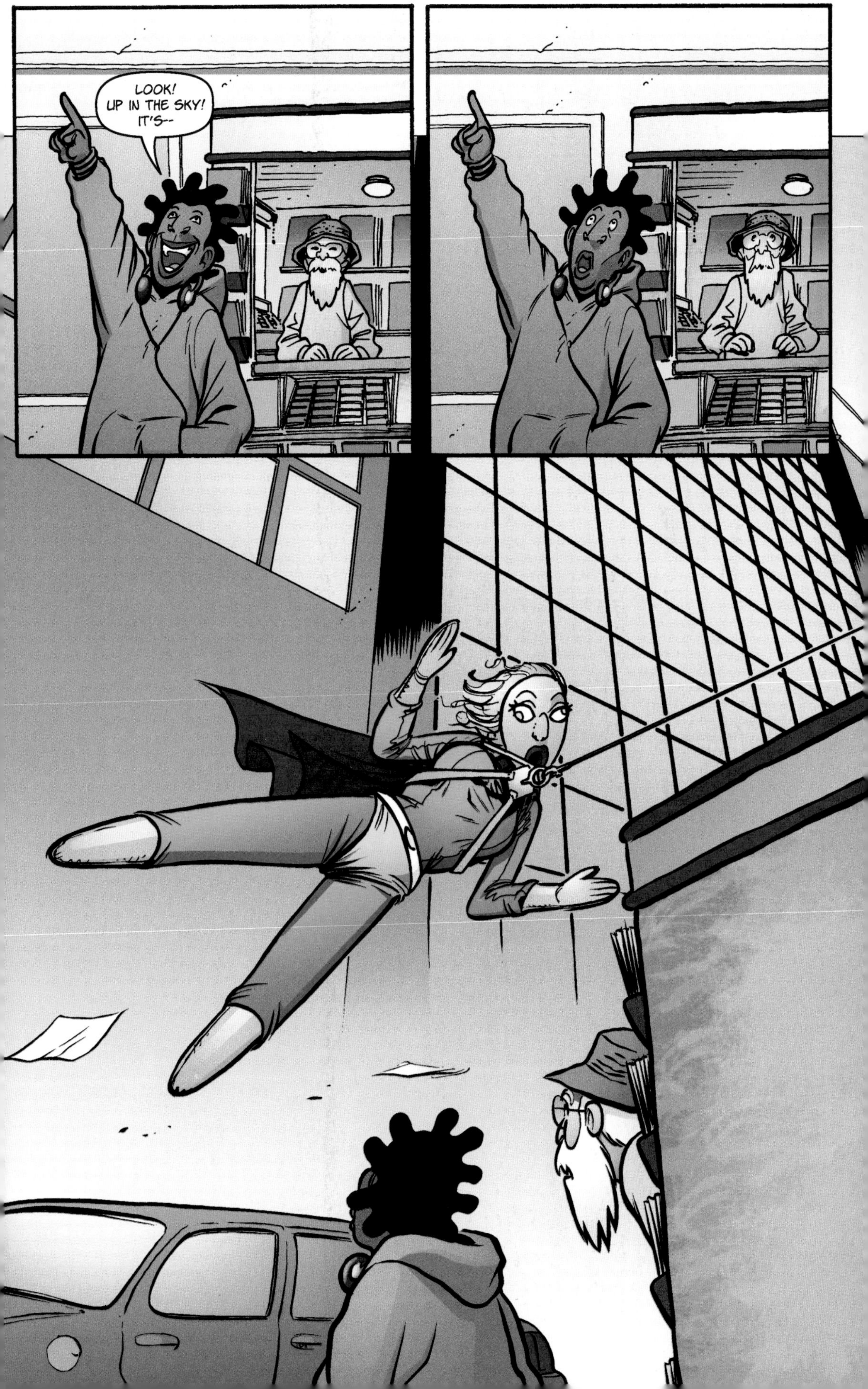
LOOK!
UP IN THE SKY!
IT'S--

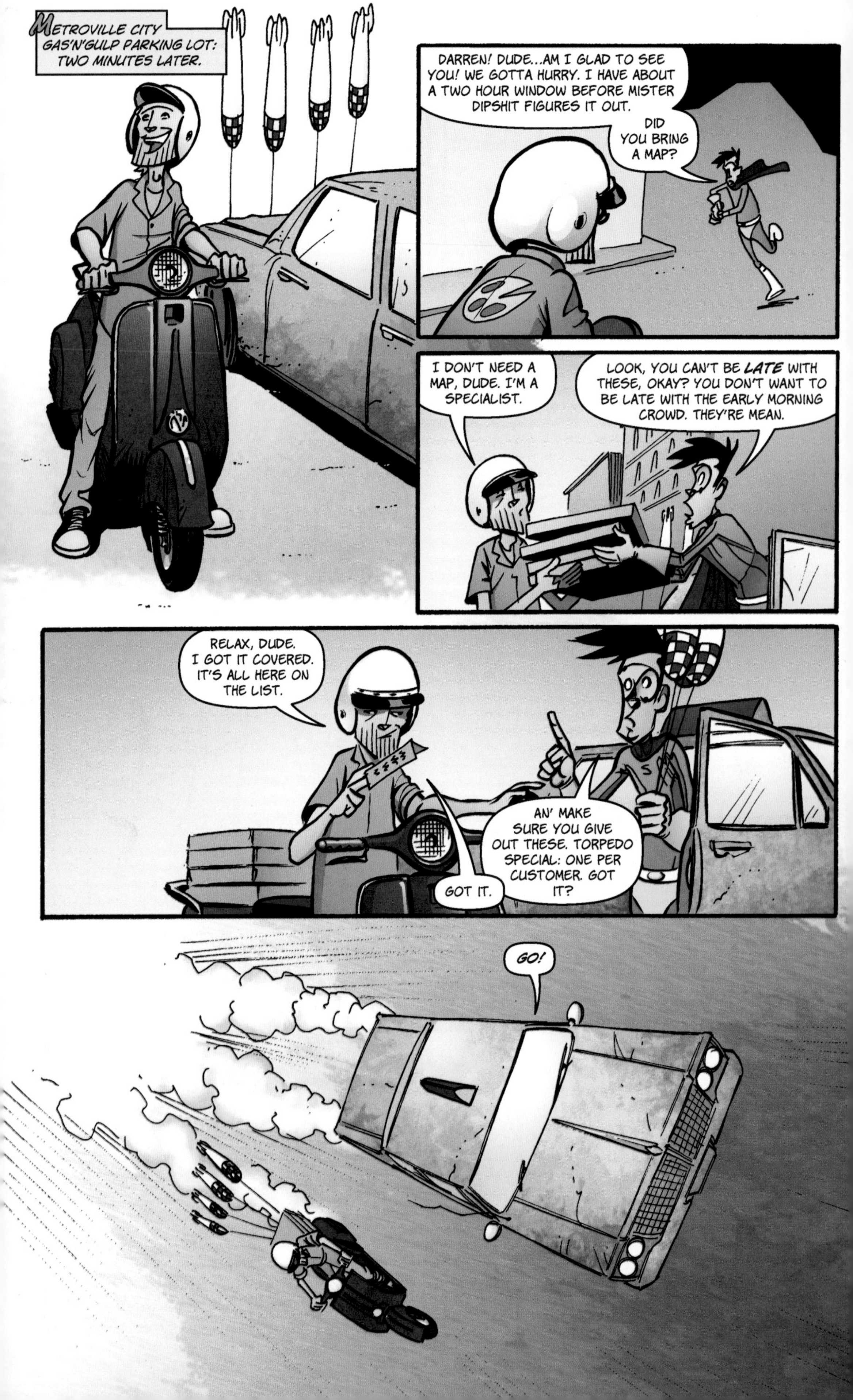
METROVILLE CITY
GAS'N'GULP PARKING LOT: TWO MINUTES LATER.
DARREN! DUDE...AM I GLAD TO SEE YOU! WE GOTTA HURRY. I HAVE ABOUT A TWO HOUR WINDOW BEFORE MISTER DIPSHIT FIGURES IT OUT.
DID YOU BRING A MAP?
I DON'T NEED A MAP, DUDE. I'M A SPECIALIST.
LOOK, YOU CAN'T BE LATE WITH THESE, OKAY? YOU DON'T WANT TO BE LATE WITH THE EARLY MORNING CROWD. THEY'RE MEAN.
RELAX, DUDE. I GOT IT COVERED. IT'S ALL HERE ON THE LIST.
AN' MAKE SURE YOU GIVE OUT THESE. TORPEDO SPECIAL: ONE PER CUSTOMER. GOT IT?
GOT IT.
GO!

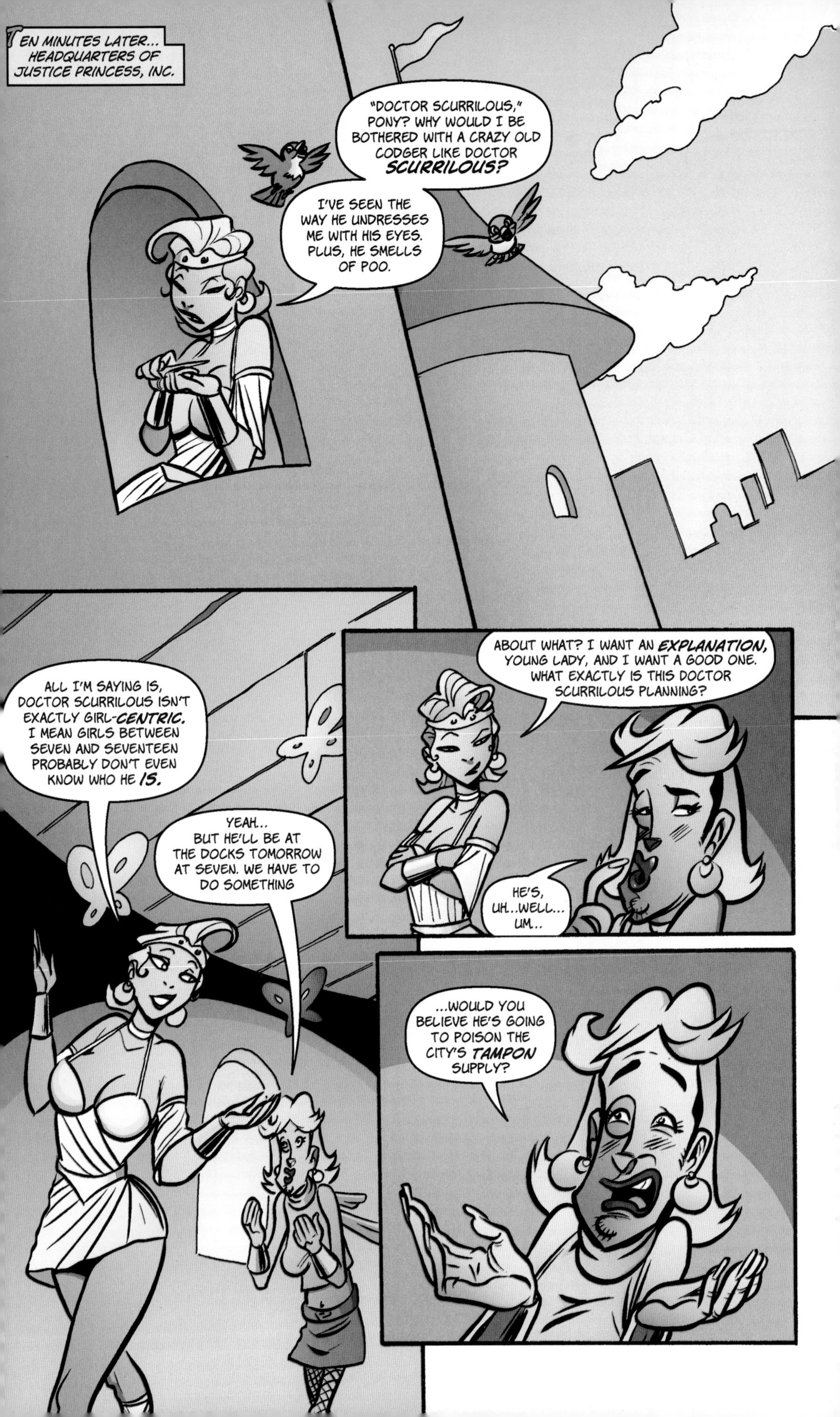
TEN MINUTES LATER... HEADQUARTERS OF JUSTICE PRINCESS, INC.
"DOCTOR SCURRILOUS," PONY? WHY WOULD I BE BOTHERED WITH A CRAZY OLD CODGER LIKE DOCTOR SCURRILOUS?
I'VE SEEN THE WAY HE UNDRESSES ME WITH HIS EYES. PLUS, HE SMELLS OF POO.
ALL I'M SAYING IS, DOCTOR SCURRILOUS ISN'T EXACTLY GIRL-CENTRIC. I MEAN GIRLS BETWEEN SEVEN AND SEVENTEEN PROBABLY DON'T EVEN KNOW WHO HE IS.
YEAH... BUT HE'LL BE AT THE DOCKS TOMORROW AT SEVEN. WE HAVE TO DO SOMETHING
ABOUT WHAT? I WANT AN EXPLANATION, YOUNG LADY, AND I WANT A GOOD ONE. WHAT EXACTLY IS THIS DOCTOR SCURRILOUS PLANNING?
HE'S, UH...WELL... UM..
...WOULD YOU BELIEVE HE'S GOING TO POISON THE CITY'S TAMPON SUPPLY?

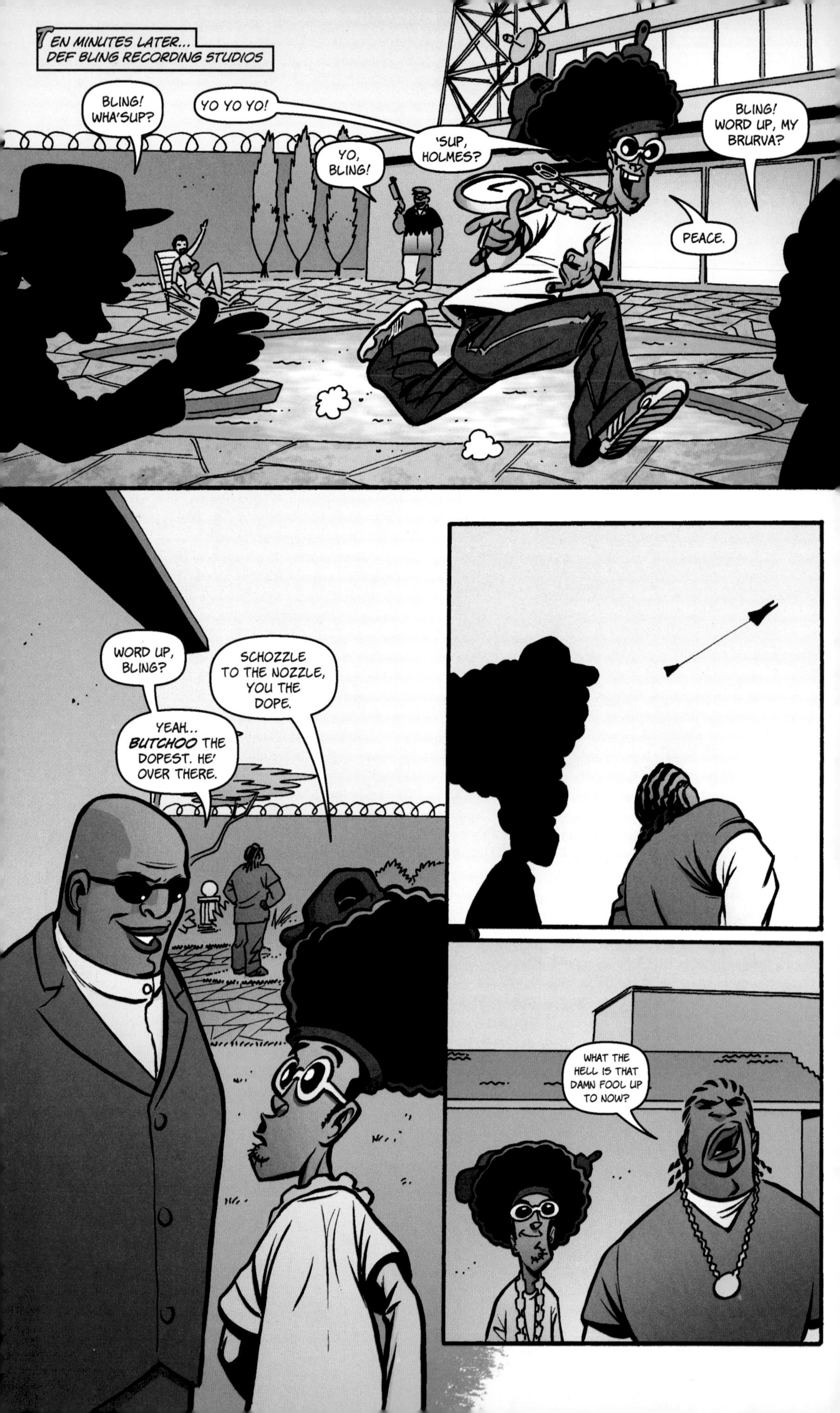
TEN MINUTES LATER... DEF BLING RECORDING STUDIOS
BLING! WHA'SUP?
YO YO YO!
'SUP, HOLMES?
YO, BLING!
BLING! WORD UP, MY BRURVA?
PEACE.
WORD UP, BLING?
YEAH... BUTCHOO THE DOPEST. HE' OVER THERE.
SCHOZZLE TO THE NOZZLE, YOU THE DOPE.
WHAT THE HELL IS THAT DAMN FOOL UP TO NOW?

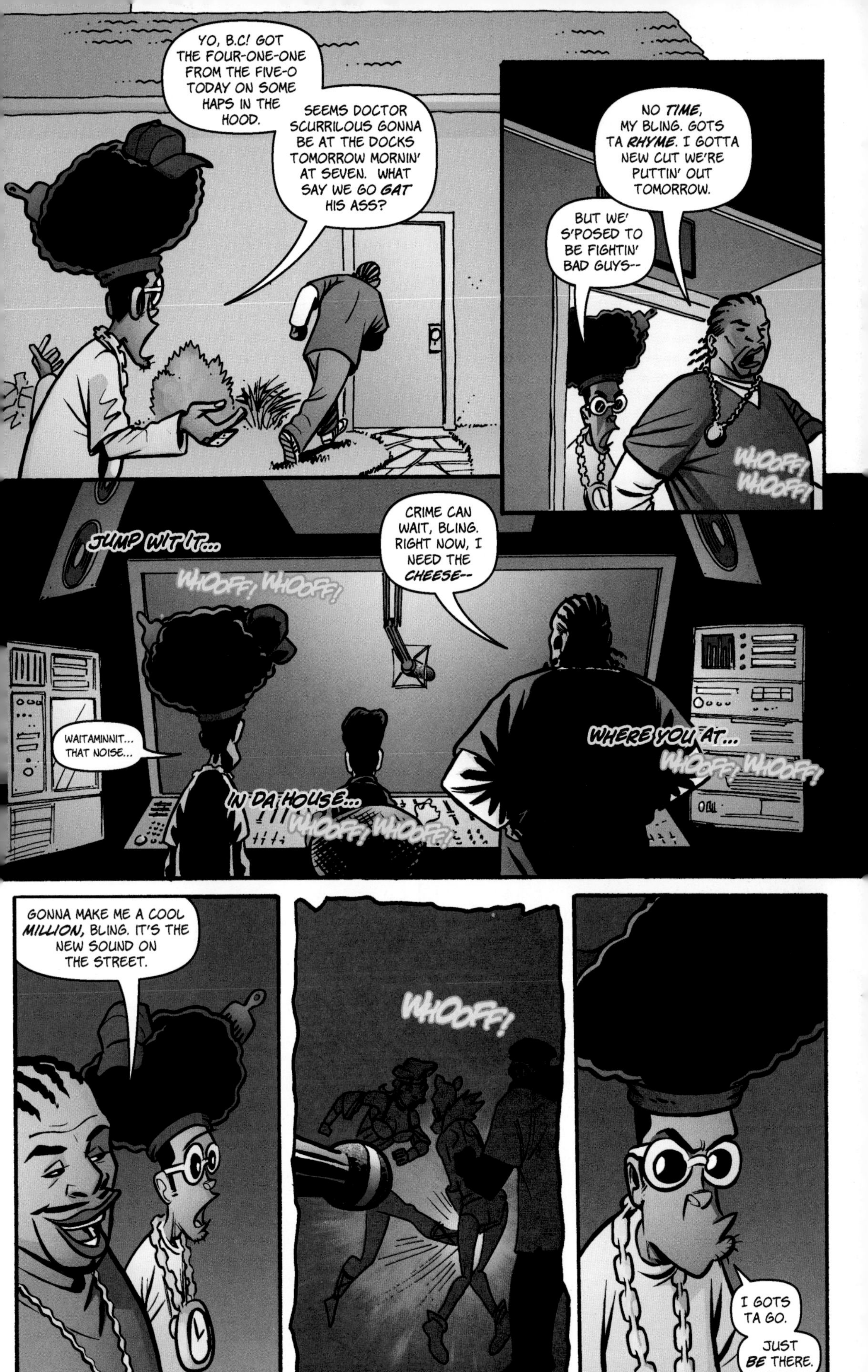

YO, B.C! GOT THE FOUR-ONE-ONE FROM THE FIVE-O TODAY ON SOME HAPS IN THE HOOD.
SEEMS DOCTOR SCURRILOUS GONNA BE AT THE DOCKS TOMORROW MORNIN' AT SEVEN. WHAT SAY WE GO GAT HIS ASS?
NO TIME, MY BLING. GOTS TA RHYME. I GOTTA NEW CUT WE'RE PUTTIN' OUT TOMORROW.
BUT WE' S'POSED TO BE FIGHTIN' BAD GUYS--
WHOOFF! WHOOFF!
JUMP WIT IT...
WHOOFF! WHOOFF!
CRIME CAN WAIT, BLING. RIGHT NOW, I NEED THE CHEESE--
WAITAMINNIT... THAT NOISE...
WHERE YOU AT...
WHOOFF! WHOOFF!
IN DA HOUSE...
WHOOFF! WHOOFF!
GONNA MAKE ME A COOL MILLION, BLING. IT'S THE NEW SOUND ON THE STREET.
WHOOFF!
I GOTS TA GO.
JUST BE THERE.

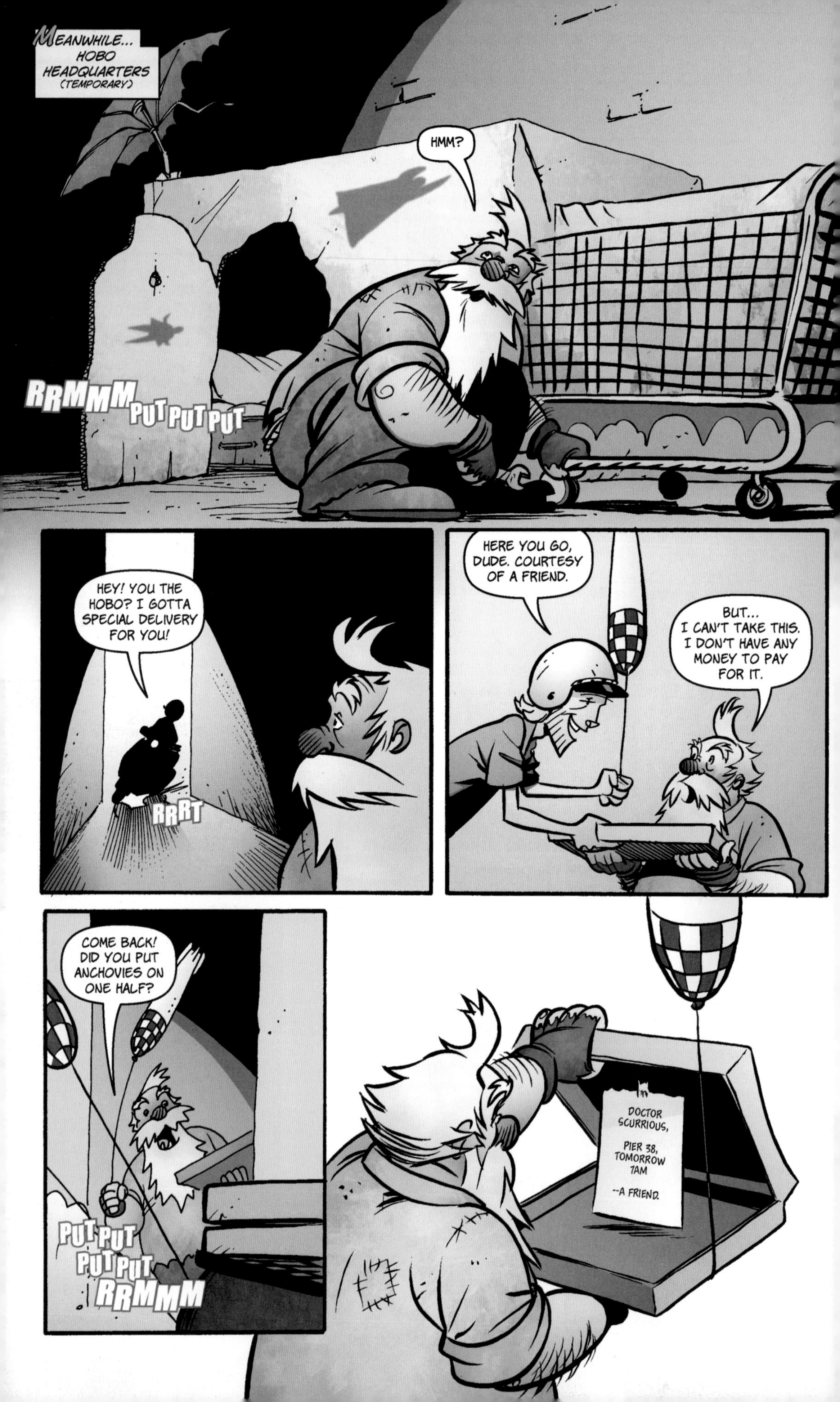
MEANWHILE... HOBO HEADQUARTERS (TEMPORARY)
HMM?
RRMMMM PUT PUT PUT
HEY! YOU THE HOBO? I GOTTA SPECIAL DELIVERY FOR YOU!
RRRT
HERE YOU GO, DUDE. COURTESY OF A FRIEND.
BUT... I CAN'T TAKE THIS. I DON'T HAVE ANY MONEY TO PAY FOR IT.
COME BACK! DID YOU PUT ANCHOVIES ON ONE HALF?
PUT PUT PUT PUT RRMMMM
DOCTOR SCURRIOUS,
PIER 38, TOMORROW 7AM
--A FRIEND.

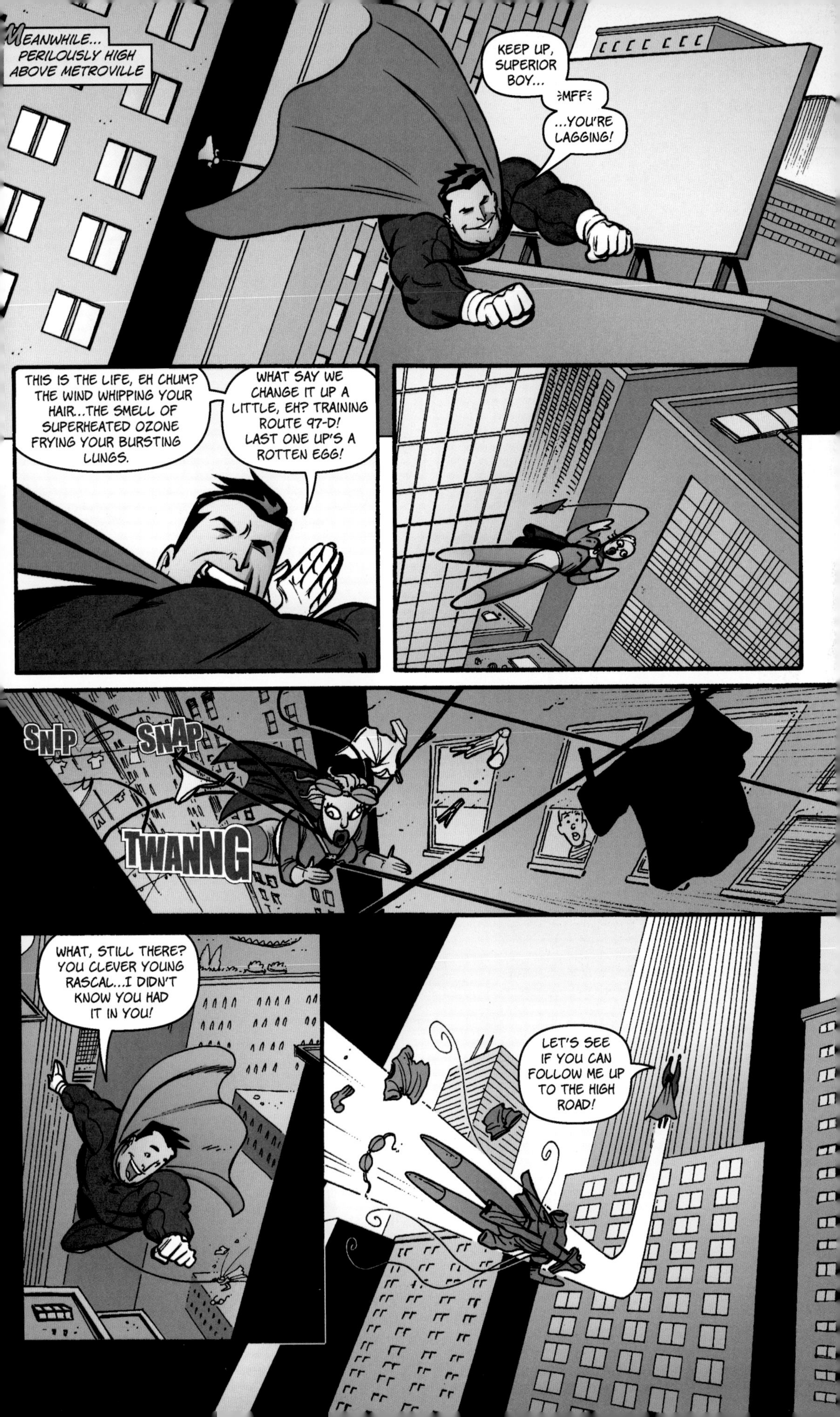
MEANWHILE... PERILOUSLY HIGH ABOVE METROVILLE
KEEP UP, SUPERIOR BOY...
MFF
...YOU'RE LAGGING!
THIS IS THE LIFE, EH CHUM? THE WIND WHIPPING YOUR HAIR...THE SMELL OF SUPERHEATED OZONE FRYING YOUR BURSTING LUNGS.
WHAT SAY WE CHANGE IT UP A LITTLE, EH? TRAINING ROUTE 97-D! LAST ONE UP'S A ROTTEN EGG!
SNIP
SNAP
TWANNG
WHAT, STILL THERE? YOU CLEVER YOUNG RASCAL...I DIDN'T KNOW YOU HAD IT IN YOU!
LET'S SEE IF YOU CAN FOLLOW ME UP TO THE HIGH ROAD!

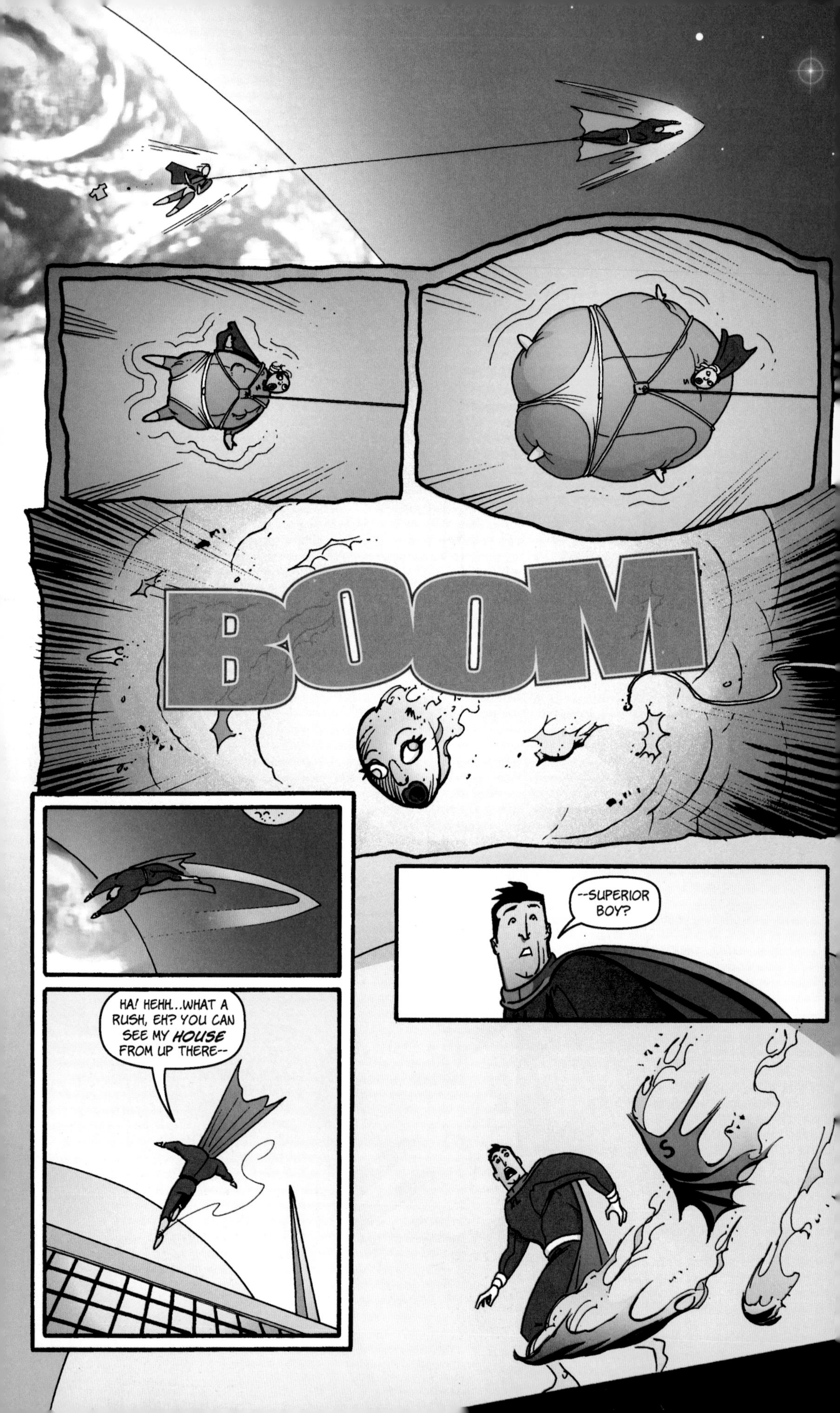
BOOM
--SUPERIOR BOY?
HA! HEHH...WHAT A RUSH, EH? YOU CAN SEE MY *HOUSE* FROM UP THERE--

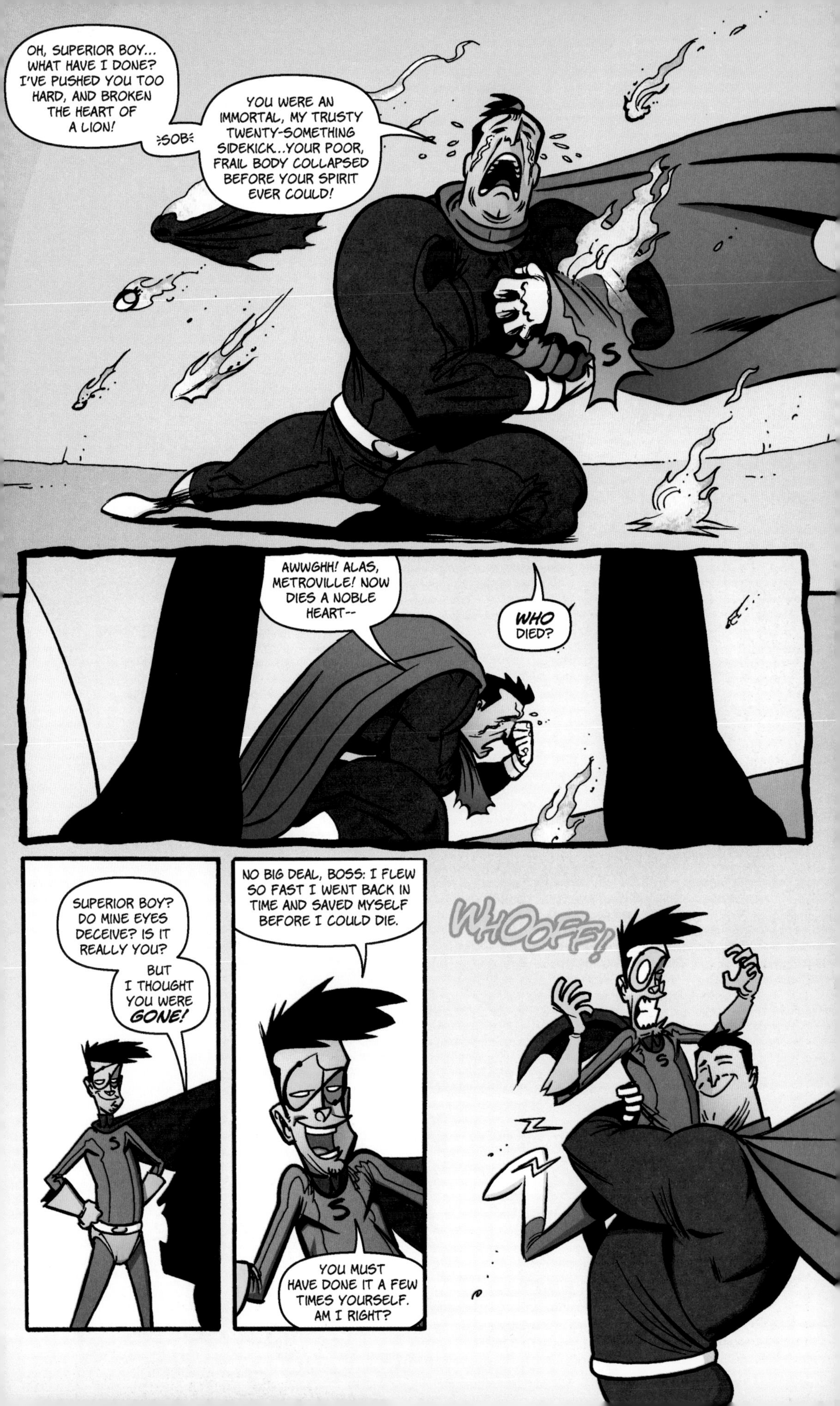

OH, SUPERIOR BOY... WHAT HAVE I DONE? I'VE PUSHED YOU TOO HARD, AND BROKEN THE HEART OF A LION!
SOB
YOU WERE AN IMMORTAL, MY TRUSTY TWENTY-SOMETHING SIDEKICK...YOUR POOR, FRAIL BODY COLLAPSED BEFORE YOUR SPIRIT EVER COULD!
AWWGHH! ALAS, METROVILLE! NOW DIES A NOBLE HEART--
WHO DIED?
SUPERIOR BOY? DO MINE EYES DECEIVE? IS IT REALLY YOU?
BUT I THOUGHT YOU WERE GONE!
NO BIG DEAL, BOSS: I FLEW SO FAST I WENT BACK IN TIME AND SAVED MYSELF BEFORE I COULD DIE.
YOU MUST HAVE DONE IT A FEW TIMES YOURSELF. AM I RIGHT?
WHOOFF!

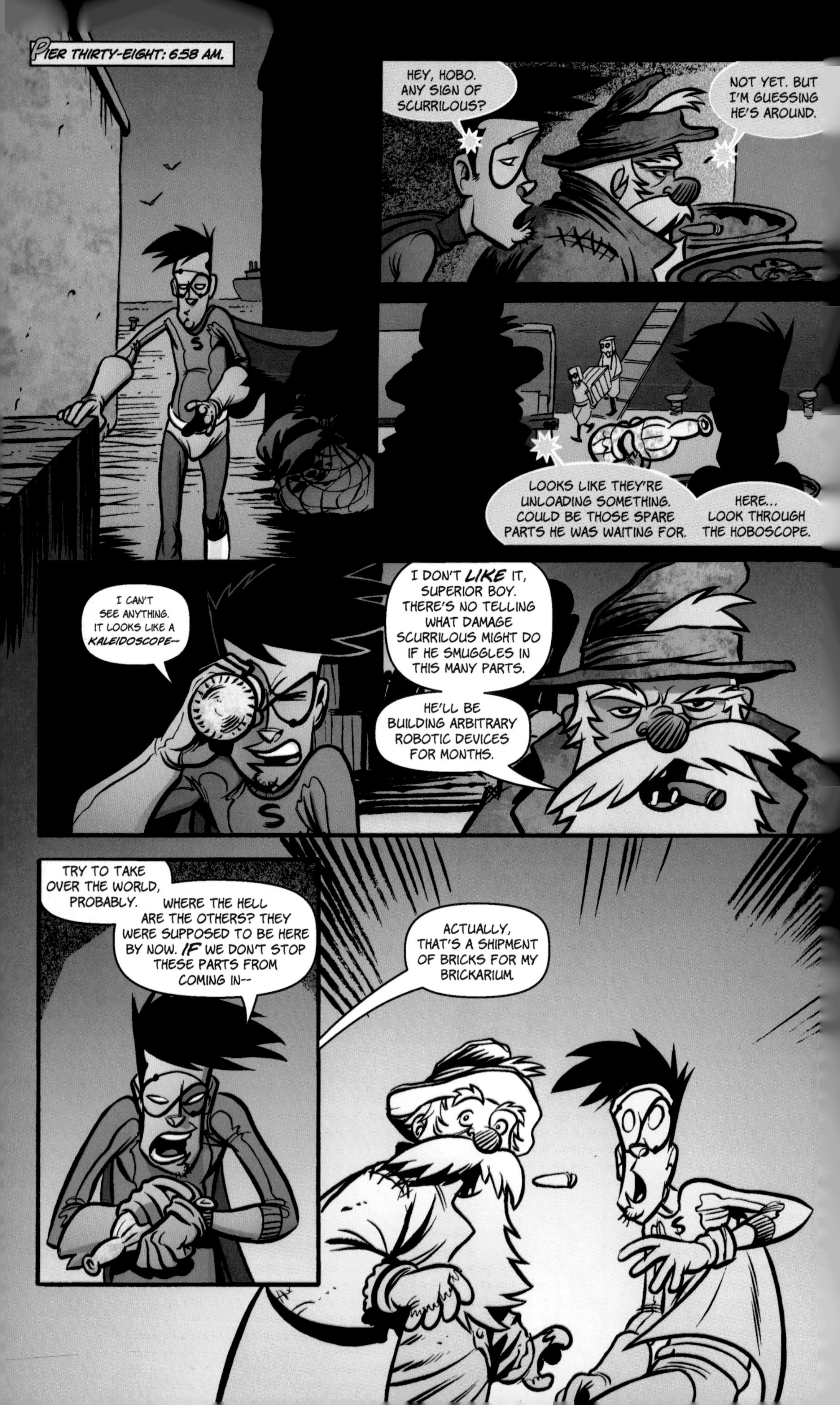
PIER THIRTY-EIGHT: 6:58 AM.
HEY, HOBO. ANY SIGN OF SCURRILOUS?
NOT YET. BUT I'M GUESSING HE'S AROUND.
LOOKS LIKE THEY'RE UNLOADING SOMETHING. COULD BE THOSE SPARE PARTS HE WAS WAITING FOR.
HERE... LOOK THROUGH THE HOBOSCOPE.
I CAN'T SEE ANYTHING. IT LOOKS LIKE A KALEIDOSCOPE--
I DON'T LIKE IT, SUPERIOR BOY. THERE'S NO TELLING WHAT DAMAGE SCURRILOUS MIGHT DO IF HE SMUGGLES IN THIS MANY PARTS.
HE'LL BE BUILDING ARBITRARY ROBOTIC DEVICES FOR MONTHS.
TRY TO TAKE OVER THE WORLD, PROBABLY.
WHERE THE HELL ARE THE OTHERS? THEY WERE SUPPOSED TO BE HERE BY NOW. IF WE DON'T STOP THESE PARTS FROM COMING IN--
ACTUALLY, THAT'S A SHIPMENT OF BRICKS FOR MY BRICKARIUM.

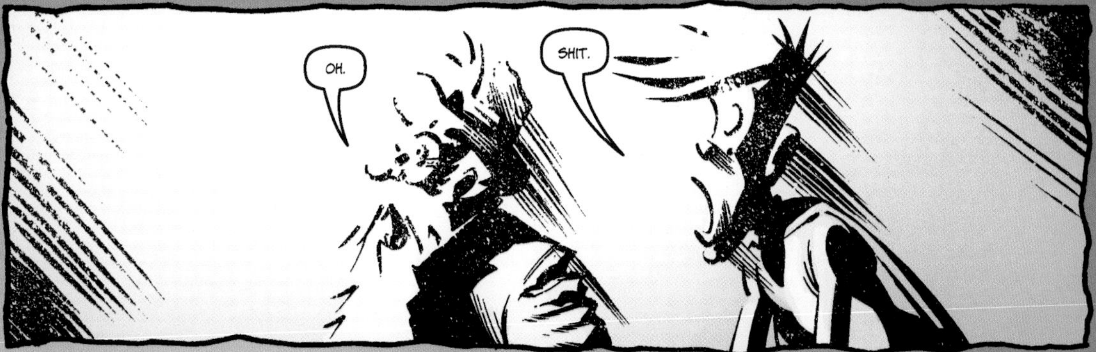
OH.
SHIT.

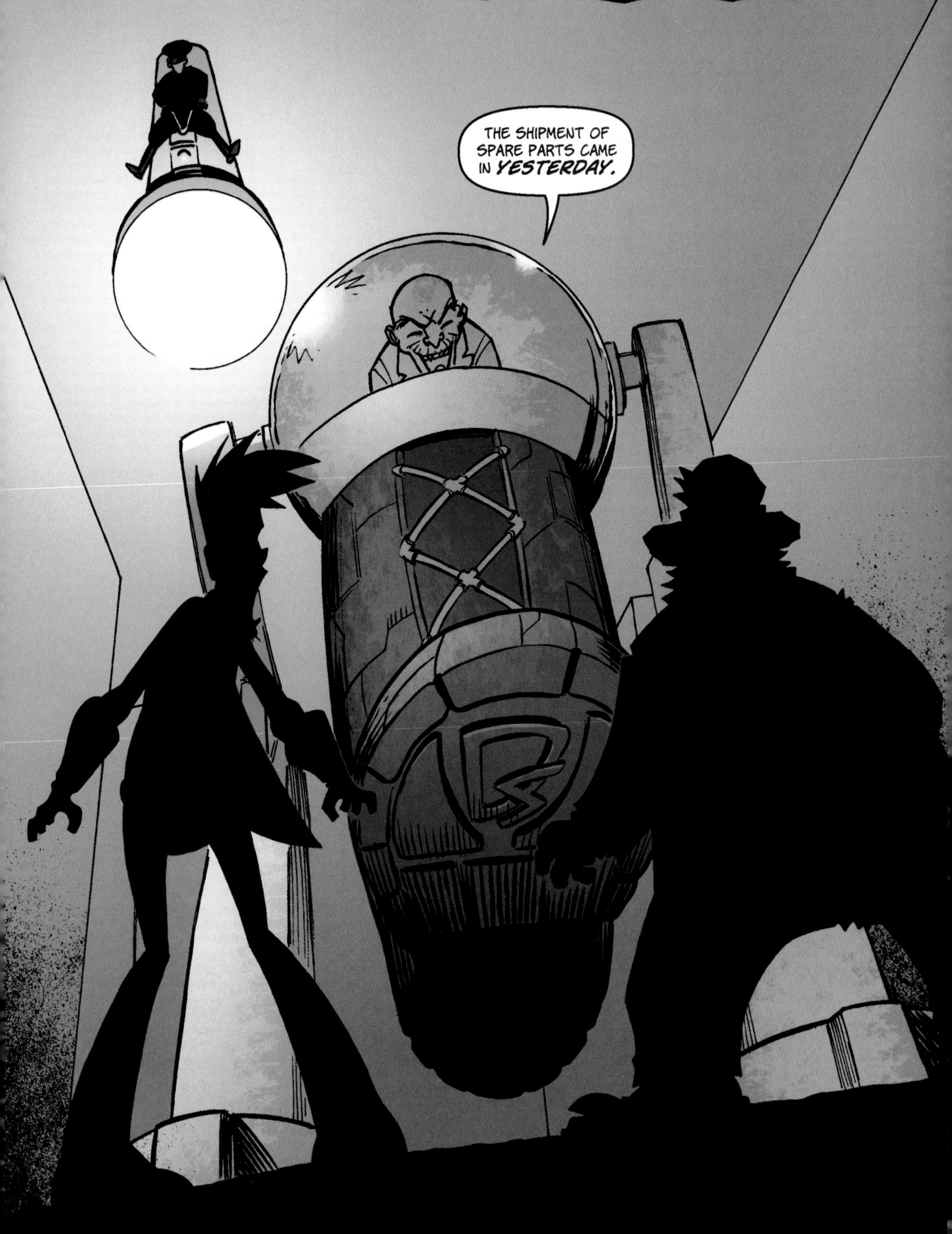
THE SHIPMENT OF SPARE PARTS CAME IN YESTERDAY.

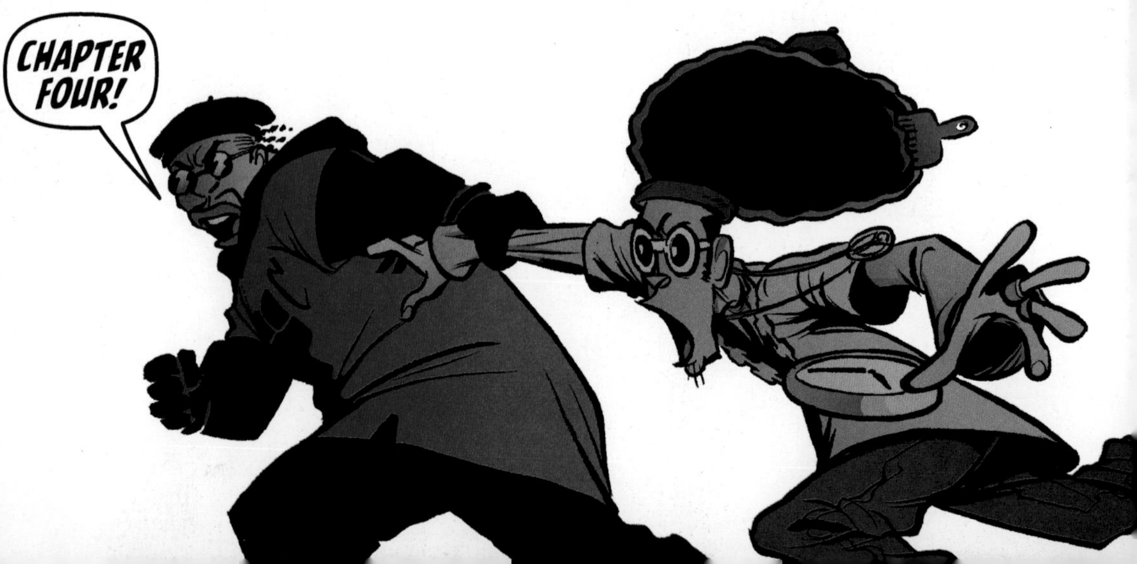
CHAPTER
FOUR!

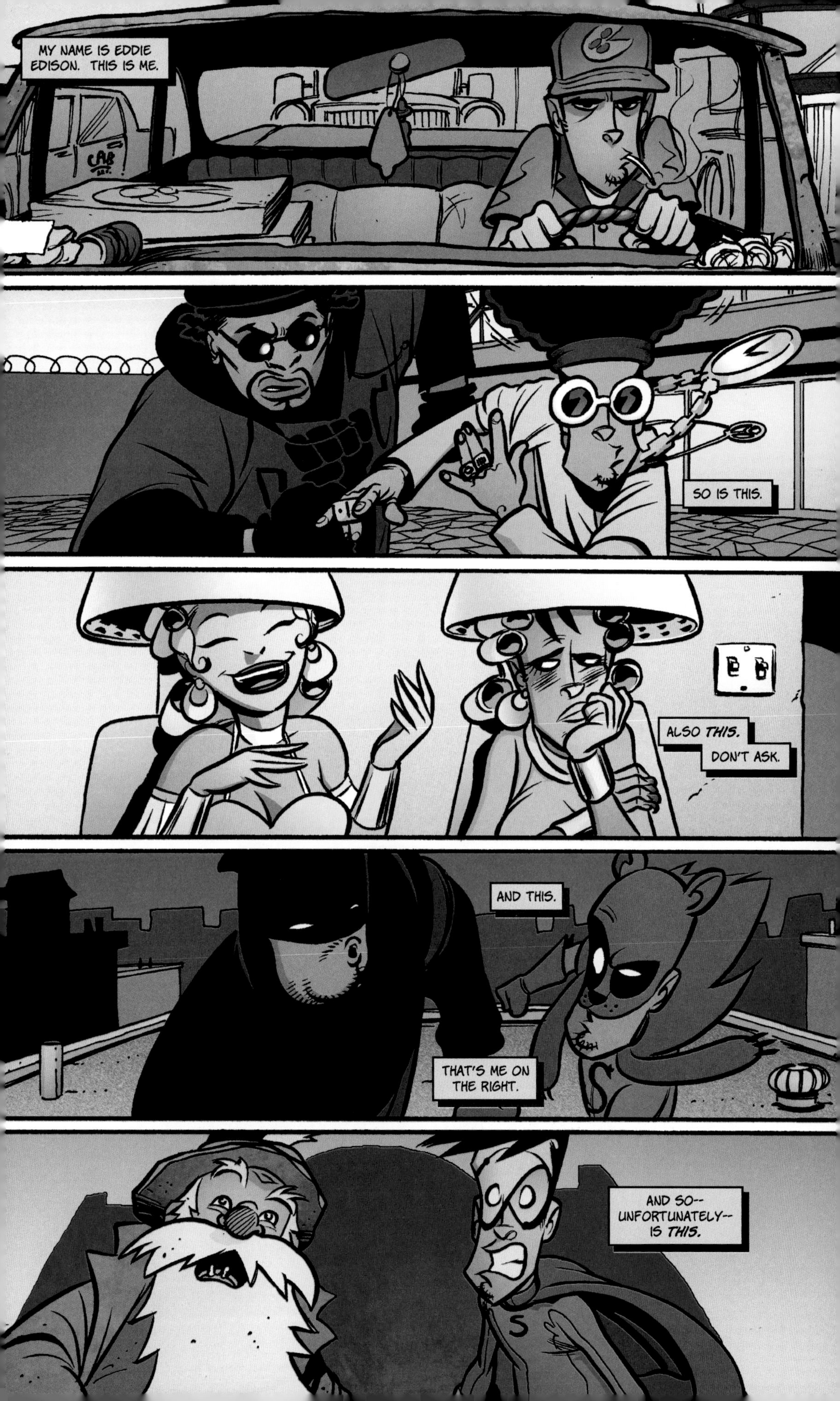
MY NAME IS EDDIE EDISON. THIS IS ME.
SO IS THIS.
ALSO *THIS.*
DON'T ASK.
AND THIS.
THAT'S ME ON THE RIGHT.
AND SO-- UNFORTUNATELY-- IS *THIS.*

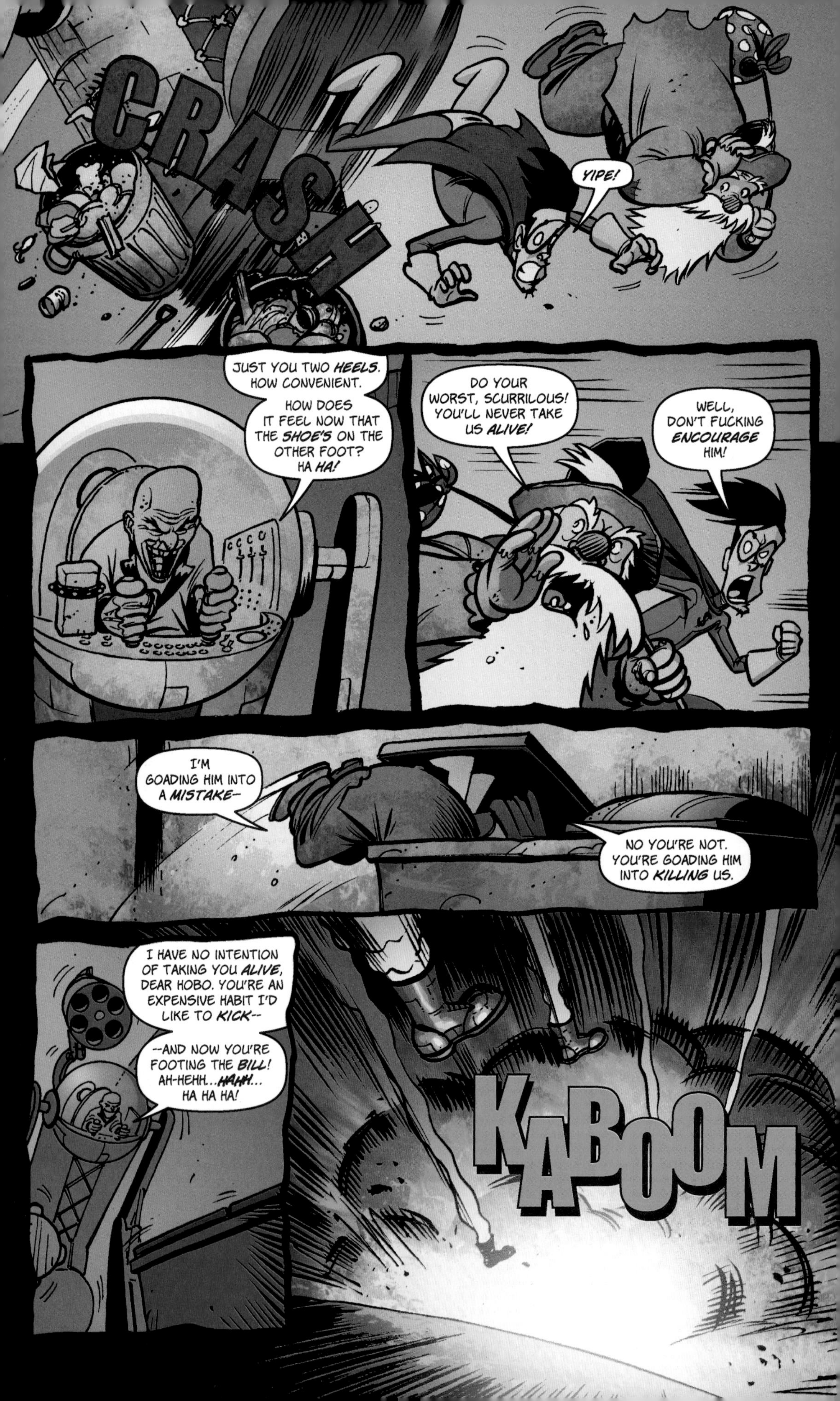
CRASH
YIPE!
JUST YOU TWO HEELS. HOW CONVENIENT.
HOW DOES IT FEEL NOW THAT THE SHOE'S ON THE OTHER FOOT? HA HA!
DO YOUR WORST, SCURRILOUS! YOU'LL NEVER TAKE US ALIVE!
WELL, DON'T FUCKING ENCOURAGE HIM!
I'M GOADING HIM INTO A MISTAKE--
NO YOU'RE NOT. YOU'RE GOADING HIM INTO KILLING US.
I HAVE NO INTENTION OF TAKING YOU ALIVE, DEAR HOBO. YOU'RE AN EXPENSIVE HABIT I'D LIKE TO KICK--
--AND NOW YOU'RE FOOTING THE BILL! AH-HEHH...HAHH... HA HA HA!
KABOOM

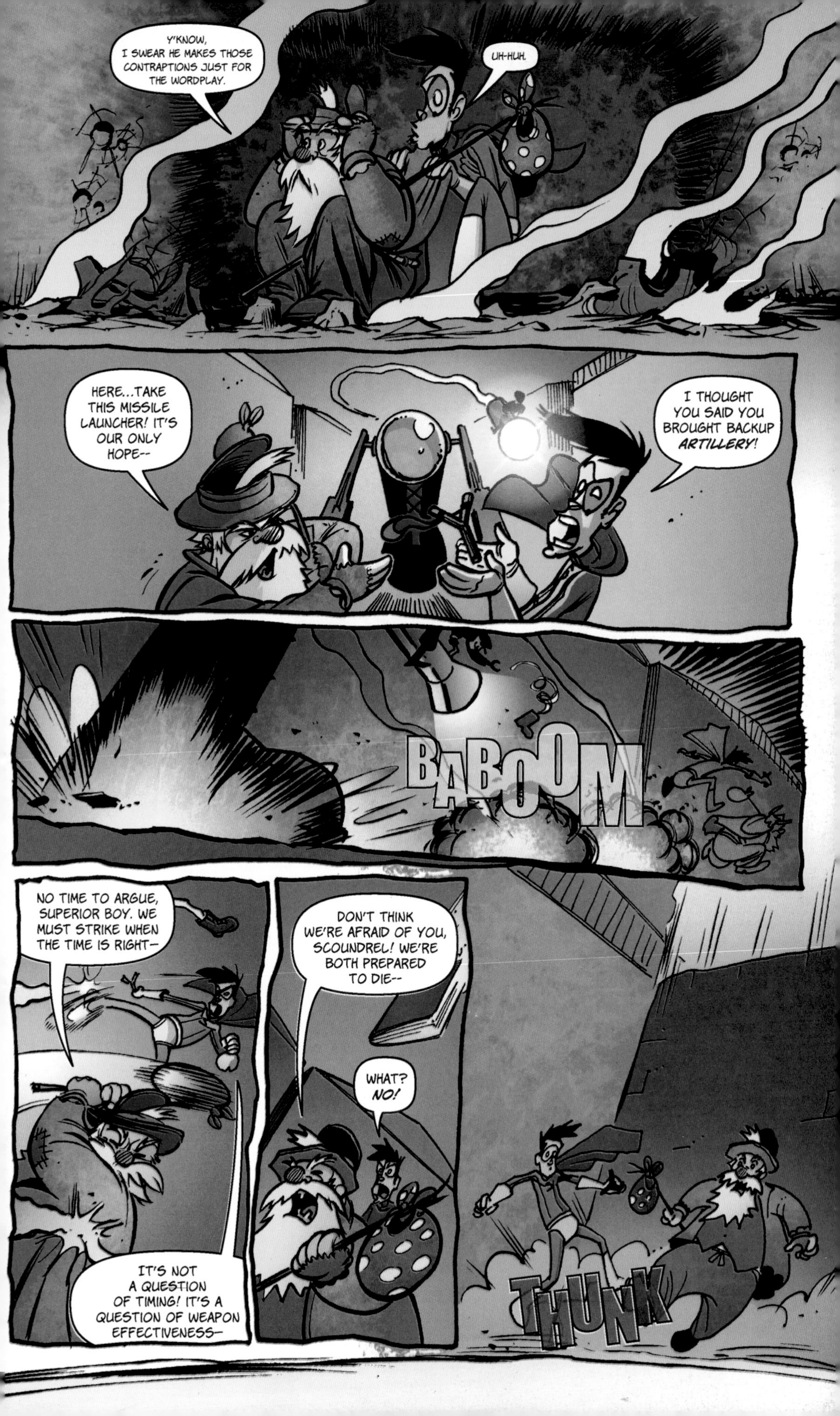
Y'KNOW, I SWEAR HE MAKES THOSE CONTRAPTIONS JUST FOR THE WORDPLAY.
UH-HUH.
HERE...TAKE THIS MISSILE LAUNCHER! IT'S OUR ONLY HOPE--
I THOUGHT YOU SAID YOU BROUGHT BACKUP *ARTILLERY*!
BABOOM
NO TIME TO ARGUE, SUPERIOR BOY. WE MUST STRIKE WHEN THE TIME IS RIGHT--
IT'S NOT A QUESTION OF TIMING! IT'S A QUESTION OF WEAPON EFFECTIVENESS--
DON'T THINK WE'RE AFRAID OF YOU, SCOUNDREL! WE'RE BOTH PREPARED TO DIE--
WHAT? *NO!*
THUNK

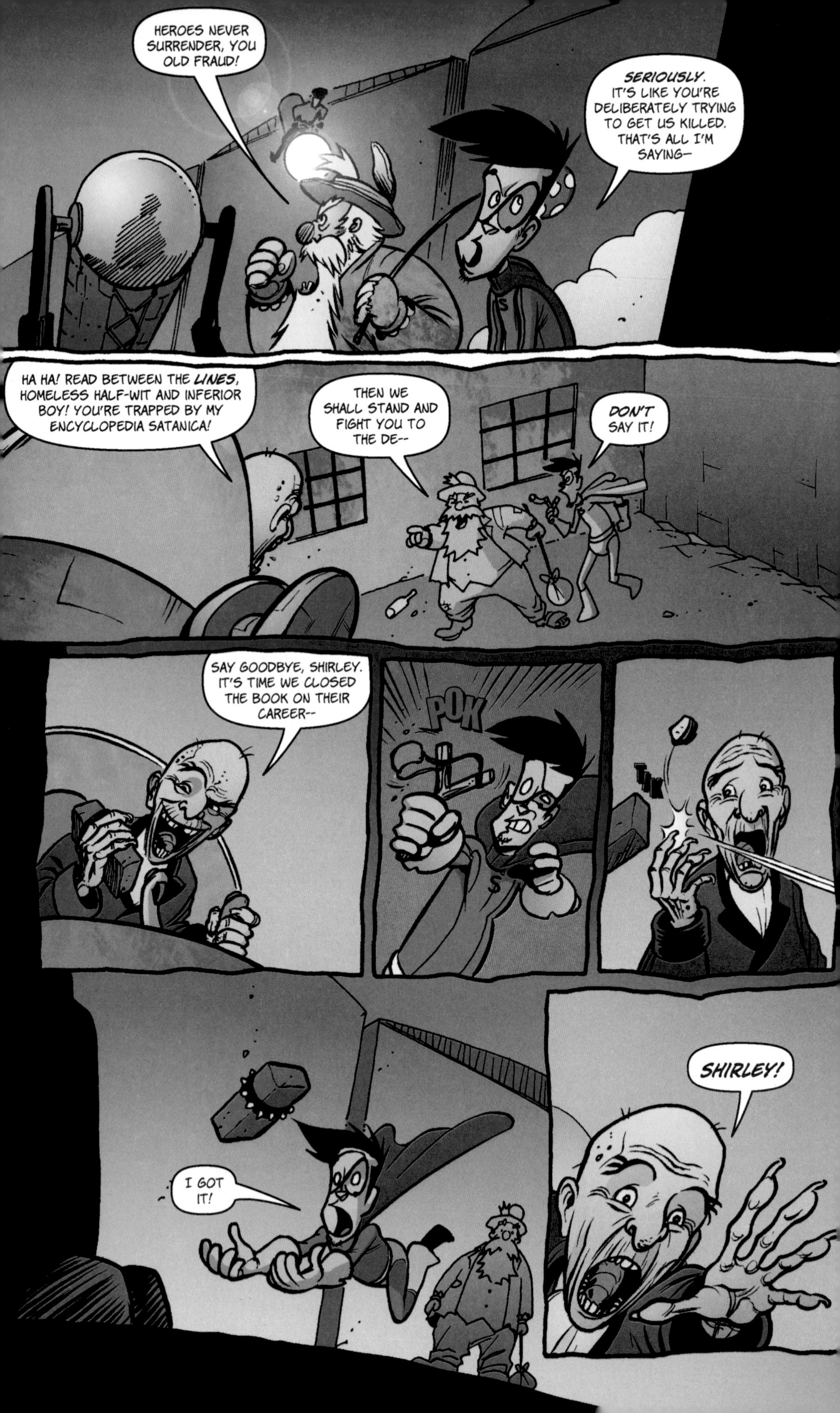
HEROES NEVER SURRENDER, YOU OLD FRAUD!
SERIOUSLY. IT'S LIKE YOU'RE DELIBERATELY TRYING TO GET US KILLED. THAT'S ALL I'M SAYING--
HA HA! READ BETWEEN THE LINES, HOMELESS HALF-WIT AND INFERIOR BOY! YOU'RE TRAPPED BY MY ENCYCLOPEDIA SATANICA!
THEN WE SHALL STAND AND FIGHT YOU TO THE DE--
DON'T SAY IT!
SAY GOODBYE, SHIRLEY. IT'S TIME WE CLOSED THE BOOK ON THEIR CAREER--
POK
TIK
I GOT IT!
SHIRLEY!

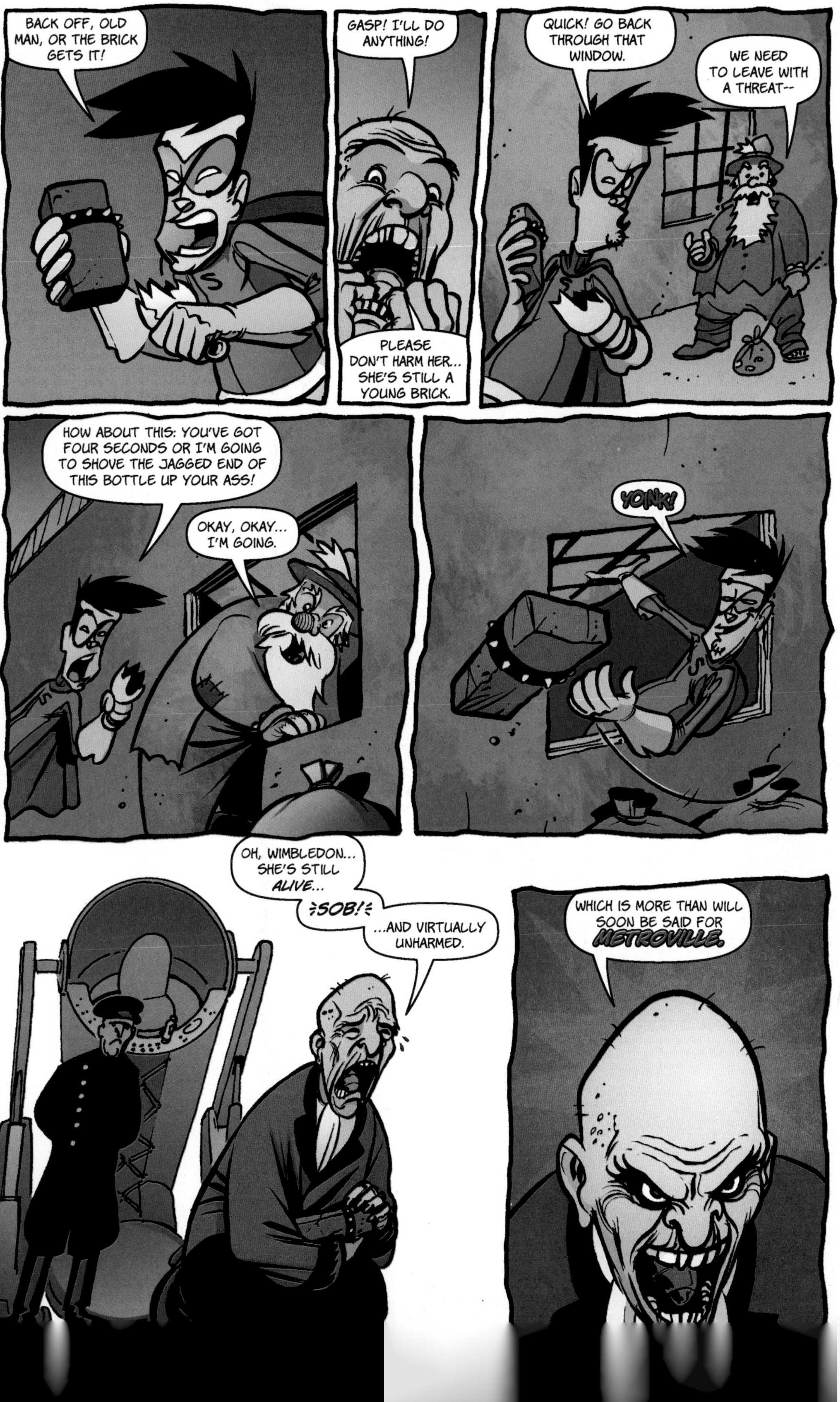

BACK OFF, OLD MAN, OR THE BRICK GETS IT!
GASP! I'LL DO ANYTHING!
PLEASE DON'T HARM HER... SHE'S STILL A YOUNG BRICK.
QUICK! GO BACK THROUGH THAT WINDOW.
WE NEED TO LEAVE WITH A THREAT--
HOW ABOUT THIS: YOU'VE GOT FOUR SECONDS OR I'M GOING TO SHOVE THE JAGGED END OF THIS BOTTLE UP YOUR ASS!
OKAY, OKAY... I'M GOING.
YOINK!
OH, WIMBLEDON... SHE'S STILL ALIVE...
SOB!
...AND VIRTUALLY UNHARMED.
WHICH IS MORE THAN WILL SOON BE SAID FOR METROVILLE.

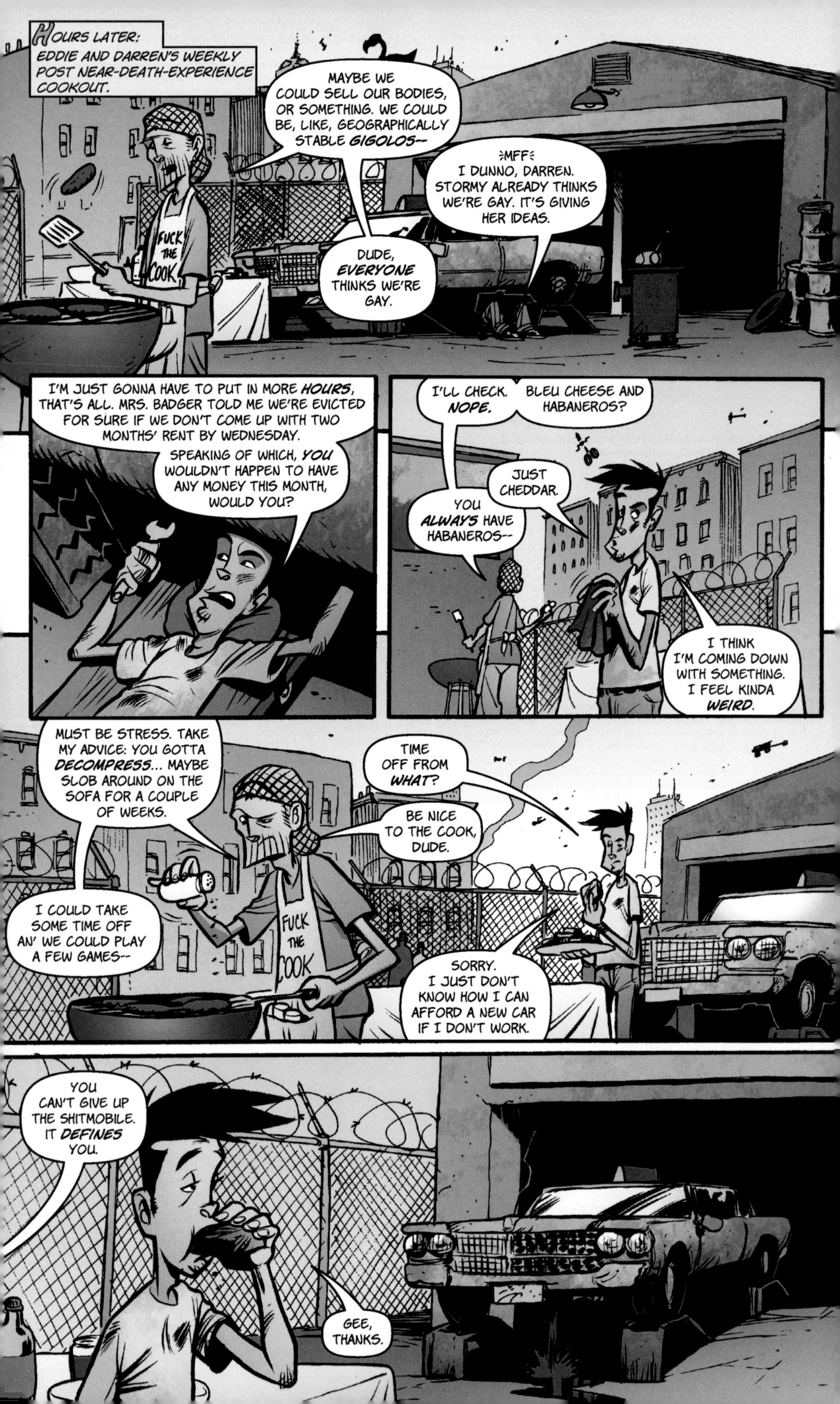
HOURS LATER: EDDIE AND DARREN'S WEEKLY POST NEAR-DEATH-EXPERIENCE COOKOUT.
MAYBE WE COULD SELL OUR BODIES, OR SOMETHING. WE COULD BE, LIKE, GEOGRAPHICALLY STABLE GIGOLOS--
MFF
I DUNNO, DARREN. STORMY ALREADY THINKS WE'RE GAY. IT'S GIVING HER IDEAS.
DUDE, EVERYONE THINKS WE'RE GAY.
FUCK THE COOK
I'M JUST GONNA HAVE TO PUT IN MORE HOURS, THAT'S ALL. MRS. BADGER TOLD ME WE'RE EVICTED FOR SURE IF WE DON'T COME UP WITH TWO MONTHS' RENT BY WEDNESDAY.
SPEAKING OF WHICH, YOU WOULDN'T HAPPEN TO HAVE ANY MONEY THIS MONTH, WOULD YOU?
BLEU CHEESE AND HABANEROS?
I'LL CHECK. NOPE.
JUST CHEDDAR.
YOU ALWAYS HAVE HABANEROS--
I THINK I'M COMING DOWN WITH SOMETHING. I FEEL KINDA WEIRD.
MUST BE STRESS. TAKE MY ADVICE: YOU GOTTA DECOMPRESS... MAYBE SLOB AROUND ON THE SOFA FOR A COUPLE OF WEEKS.
I COULD TAKE SOME TIME OFF AN' WE COULD PLAY A FEW GAMES--
TIME OFF FROM WHAT?
BE NICE TO THE COOK, DUDE.
FUCK THE COOK
SORRY. I JUST DON'T KNOW HOW I CAN AFFORD A NEW CAR IF I DON'T WORK.
YOU CAN'T GIVE UP THE SHITMOBILE. IT DEFINES YOU.
GEE, THANKS.

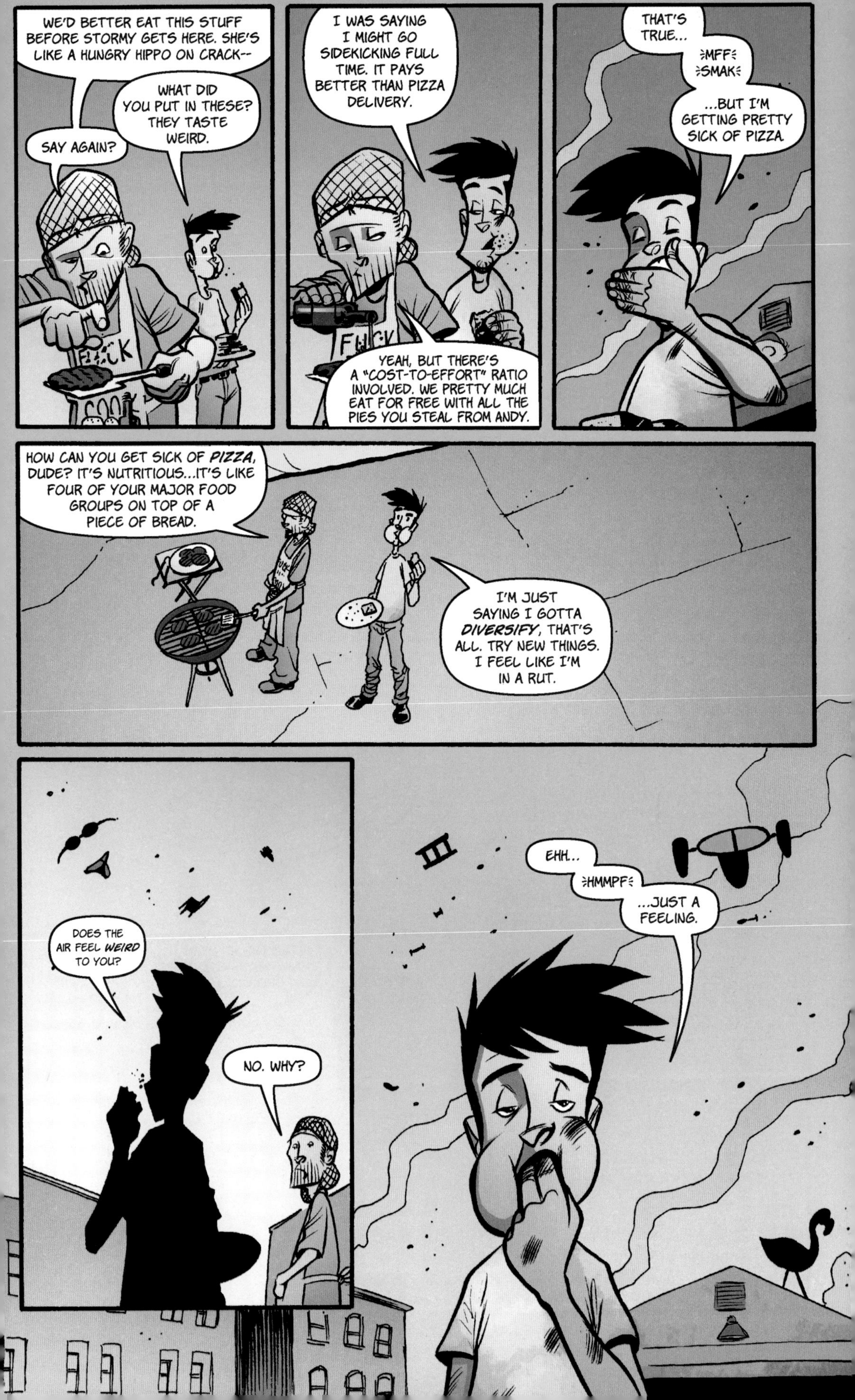
WE'D BETTER EAT THIS STUFF BEFORE STORMY GETS HERE. SHE'S LIKE A HUNGRY HIPPO ON CRACK--
WHAT DID YOU PUT IN THESE? THEY TASTE WEIRD.
SAY AGAIN?
I WAS SAYING I MIGHT GO SIDEKICKING FULL TIME. IT PAYS BETTER THAN PIZZA DELIVERY.
YEAH, BUT THERE'S A "COST-TO-EFFORT" RATIO INVOLVED. WE PRETTY MUCH EAT FOR FREE WITH ALL THE PIES YOU STEAL FROM ANDY.
THAT'S TRUE...
MFF
SMAK
...BUT I'M GETTING PRETTY SICK OF PIZZA
HOW CAN YOU GET SICK OF *PIZZA*, DUDE? IT'S NUTRITIOUS...IT'S LIKE FOUR OF YOUR MAJOR FOOD GROUPS ON TOP OF A PIECE OF BREAD.
I'M JUST SAYING I GOTTA *DIVERSIFY*, THAT'S ALL. TRY NEW THINGS. I FEEL LIKE I'M IN A RUT.
DOES THE AIR FEEL *WEIRD* TO YOU?
NO. WHY?
EHH...
HMMPF
...JUST A FEELING.

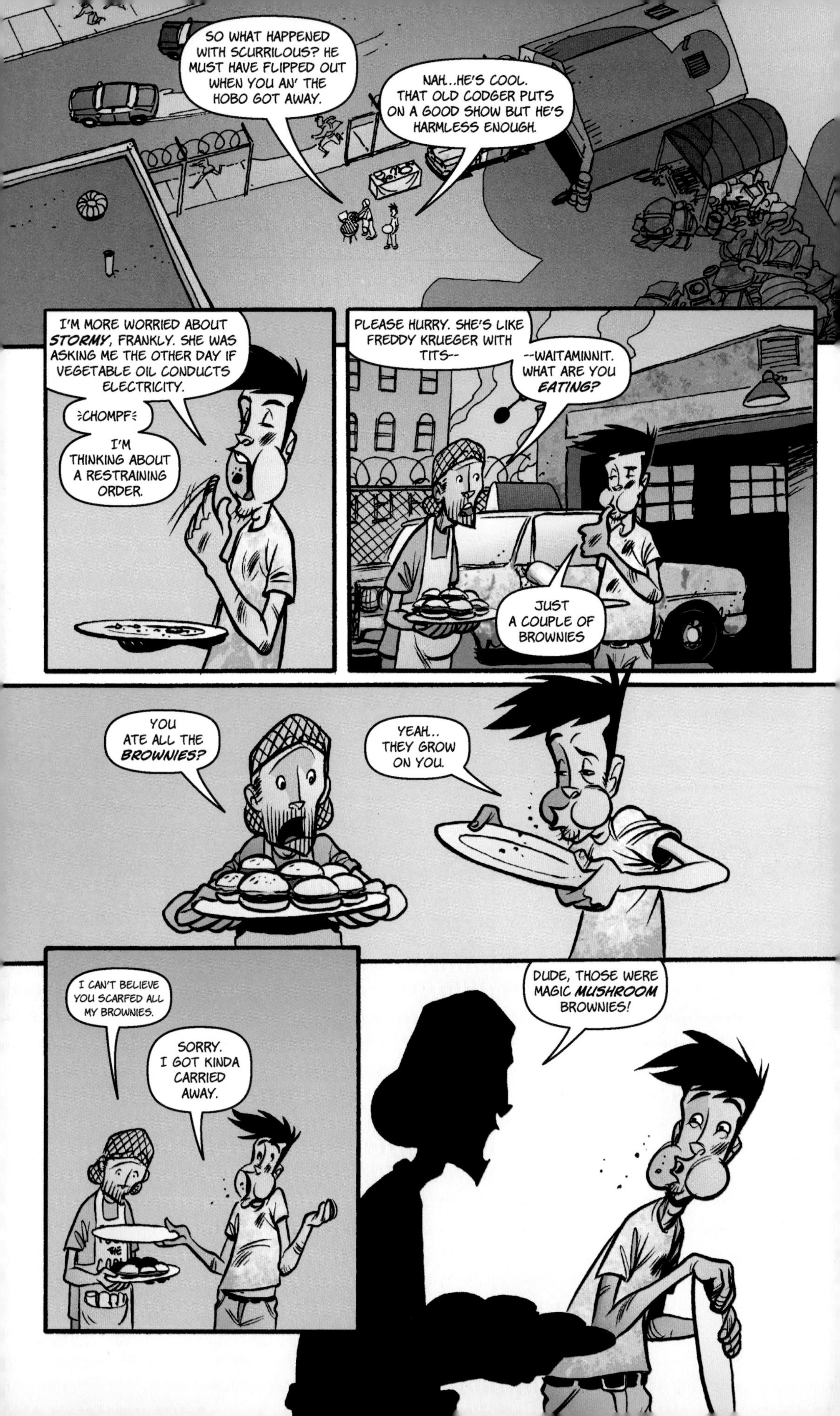

SO WHAT HAPPENED WITH SCURRILOUS? HE MUST HAVE FLIPPED OUT WHEN YOU AN' THE HOBO GOT AWAY.
NAH...HE'S COOL. THAT OLD CODGER PUTS ON A GOOD SHOW BUT HE'S HARMLESS ENOUGH.
I'M MORE WORRIED ABOUT STORMY, FRANKLY. SHE WAS ASKING ME THE OTHER DAY IF VEGETABLE OIL CONDUCTS ELECTRICITY.
CHOMPF
I'M THINKING ABOUT A RESTRAINING ORDER.
PLEASE HURRY. SHE'S LIKE FREDDY KRUEGER WITH TITS--
--WAITAMINNIT. WHAT ARE YOU EATING?
JUST A COUPLE OF BROWNIES
YOU ATE ALL THE BROWNIES?
YEAH.. THEY GROW ON YOU.
I CAN'T BELIEVE YOU SCARFED ALL MY BROWNIES.
SORRY. I GOT KINDA CARRIED AWAY.
DUDE, THOSE WERE MAGIC MUSHROOM BROWNIES!

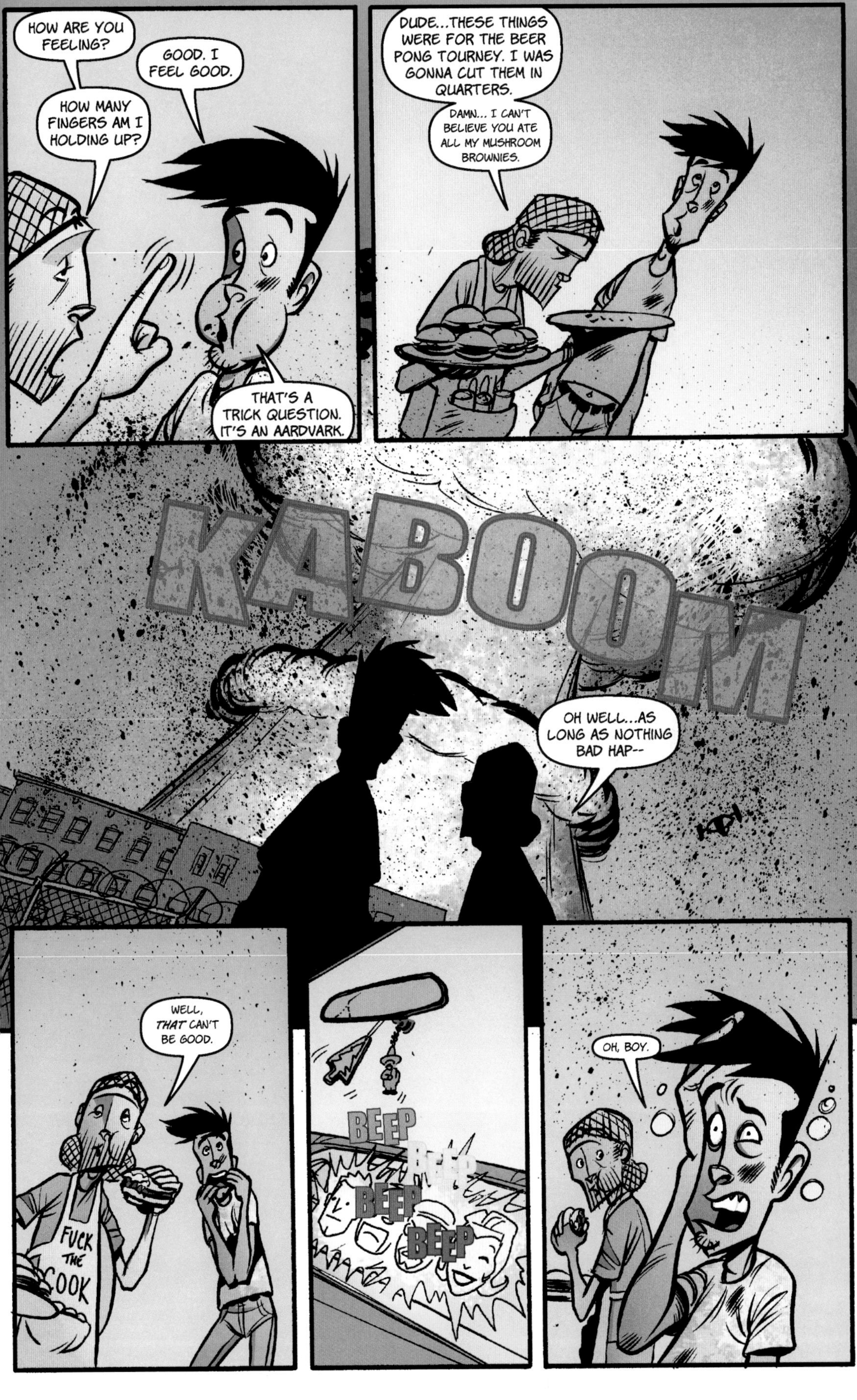

HOW ARE YOU FEELING?
GOOD. I FEEL GOOD.
HOW MANY FINGERS AM I HOLDING UP?
THAT'S A TRICK QUESTION. IT'S AN AARDVARK.
DUDE...THESE THINGS WERE FOR THE BEER PONG TOURNEY. I WAS GONNA CUT THEM IN QUARTERS.
DAMN... I CAN'T BELIEVE YOU ATE ALL MY MUSHROOM BROWNIES.
KABOOM
OH WELL...AS LONG AS NOTHING BAD HAP--
WELL, *THAT* CAN'T BE GOOD.
FUCK THE COOK
BEEP
BEEP
BEEP
BEEP
OH, BOY.

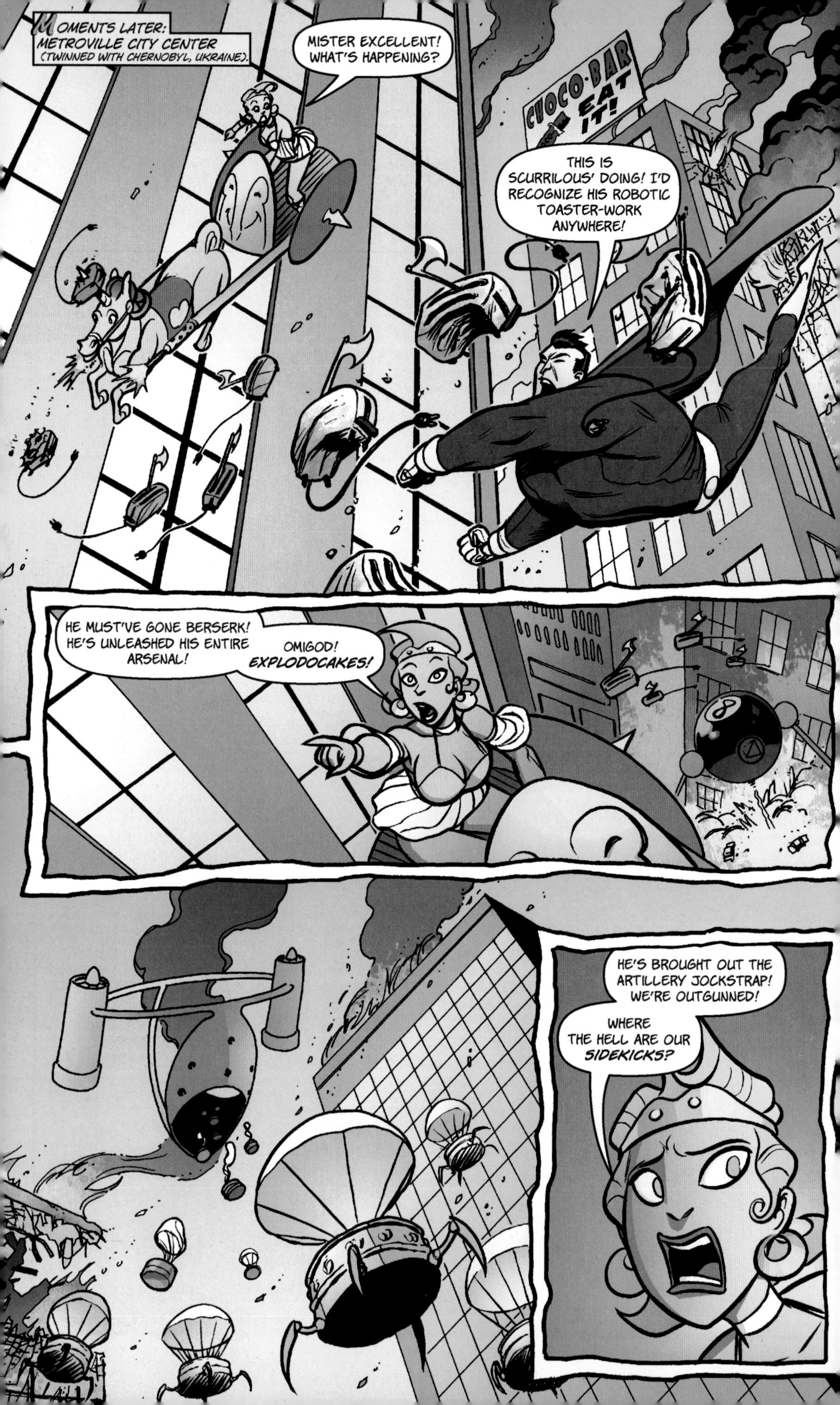
MOMENTS LATER:
METROVILLE CITY CENTER
(TWINNED WITH CHERNOBYL, UKRAINE).
MISTER EXCELLENT! WHAT'S HAPPENING?
CHOCO-BAR
EAT IT!
THIS IS SCURRILOUS' DOING! I'D RECOGNIZE HIS ROBOTIC TOASTER-WORK ANYWHERE!
HE MUST'VE GONE BERSERK! HE'S UNLEASHED HIS ENTIRE ARSENAL!
OMIGOD! EXPLODOCAKES!
HE'S BROUGHT OUT THE ARTILLERY JOCKSTRAP! WE'RE OUTGUNNED!
WHERE THE HELL ARE OUR SIDEKICKS?

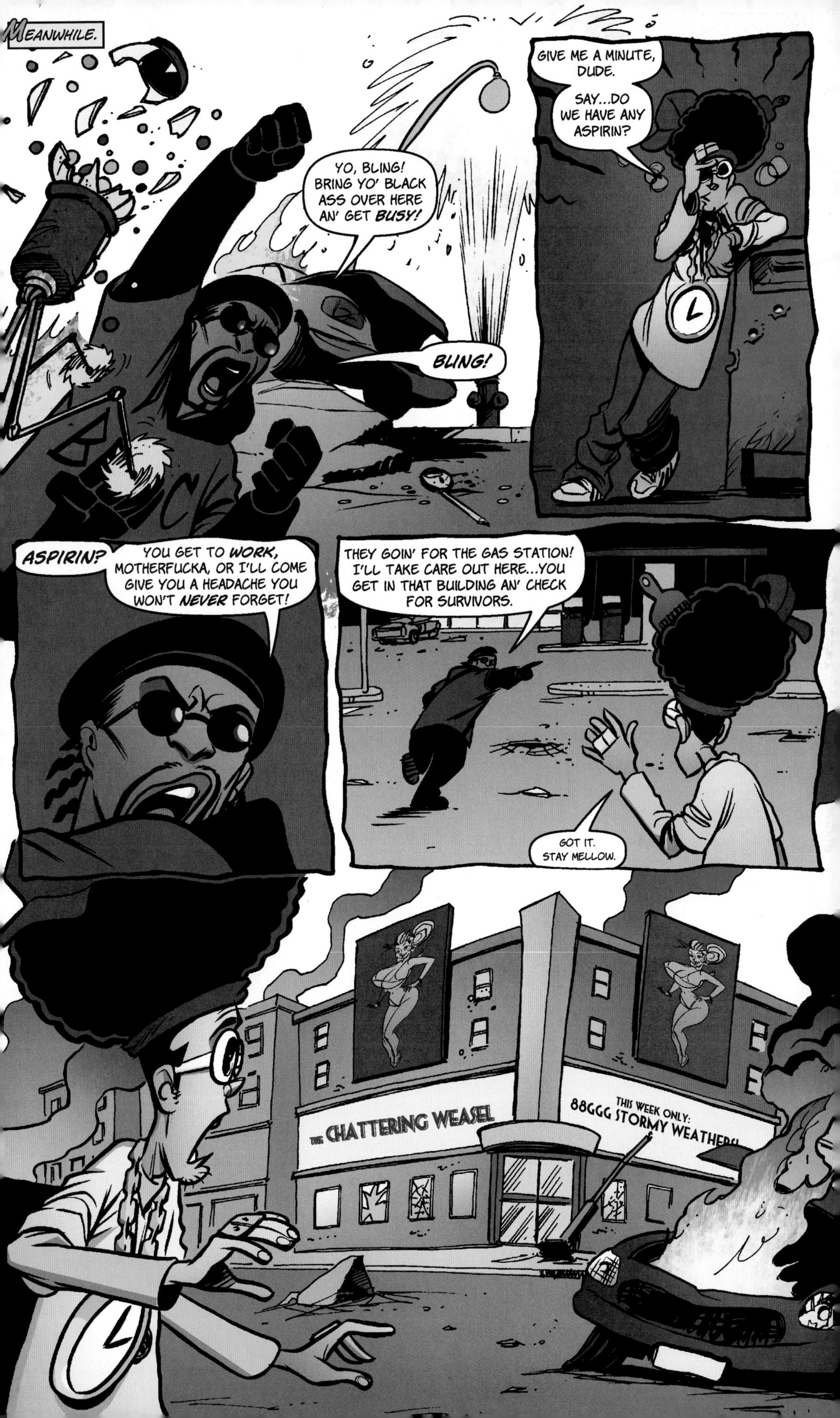
MEANWHILE.
YO, BLING! BRING YO' BLACK ASS OVER HERE AN' GET BUSY!
BLING!
GIVE ME A MINUTE, DUDE.
SAY...DO WE HAVE ANY ASPIRIN?
ASPIRIN?
YOU GET TO WORK, MOTHERFUCKA, OR I'LL COME GIVE YOU A HEADACHE YOU WON'T NEVER FORGET!
THEY GOIN' FOR THE GAS STATION! I'LL TAKE CARE OUT HERE...YOU GET IN THAT BUILDING AN' CHECK FOR SURVIVORS.
GOT IT. STAY MELLOW.
THE CHATTERING WEASEL
THIS WEEK ONLY:
88GGG STORMY WEATHERS!

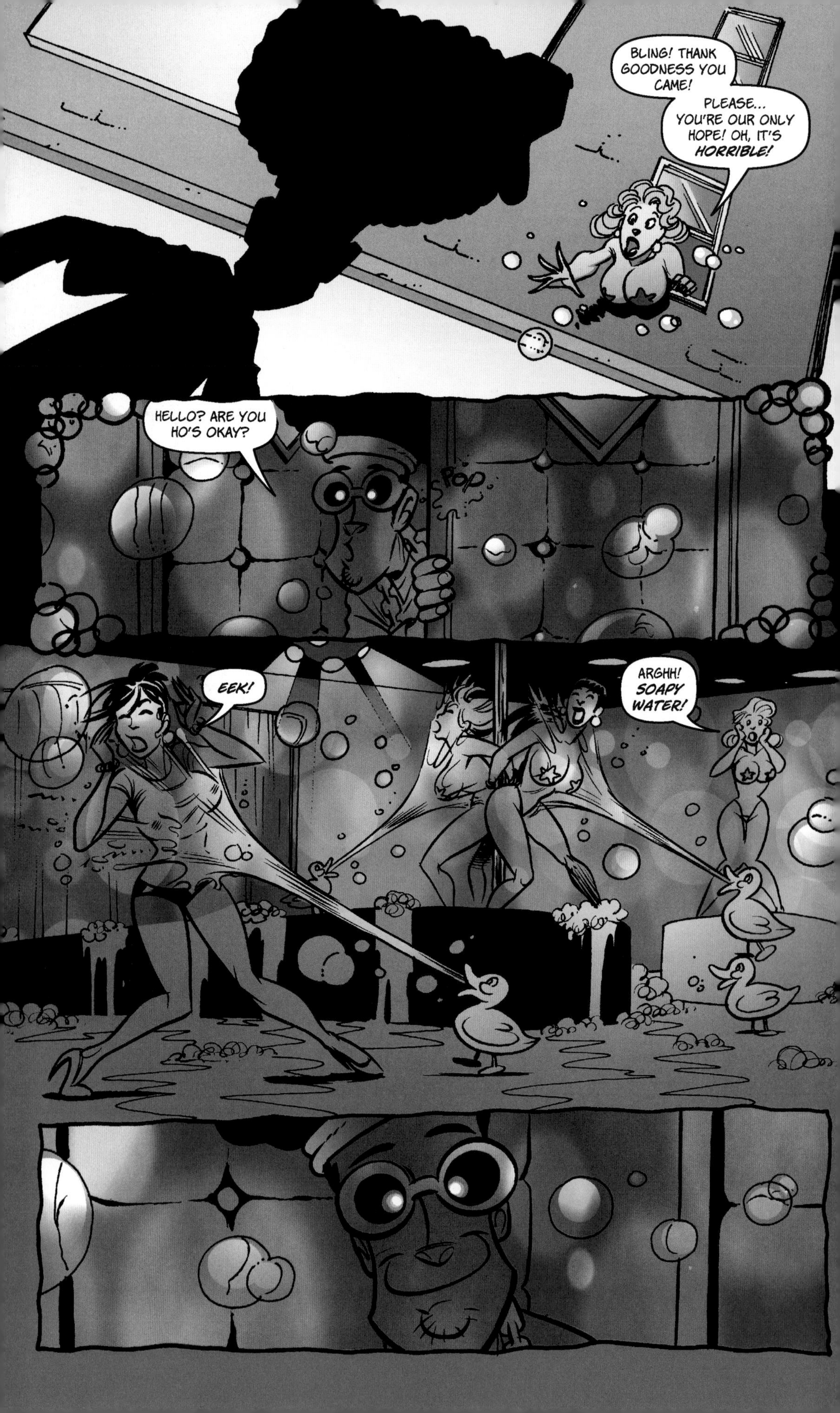
BLING! THANK GOODNESS YOU CAME!
PLEASE... YOU'RE OUR ONLY HOPE! OH, IT'S *HORRIBLE!*
HELLO? ARE YOU HO'S OKAY?
POP
EEK!
ARGHH! *SOAPY WATER!*

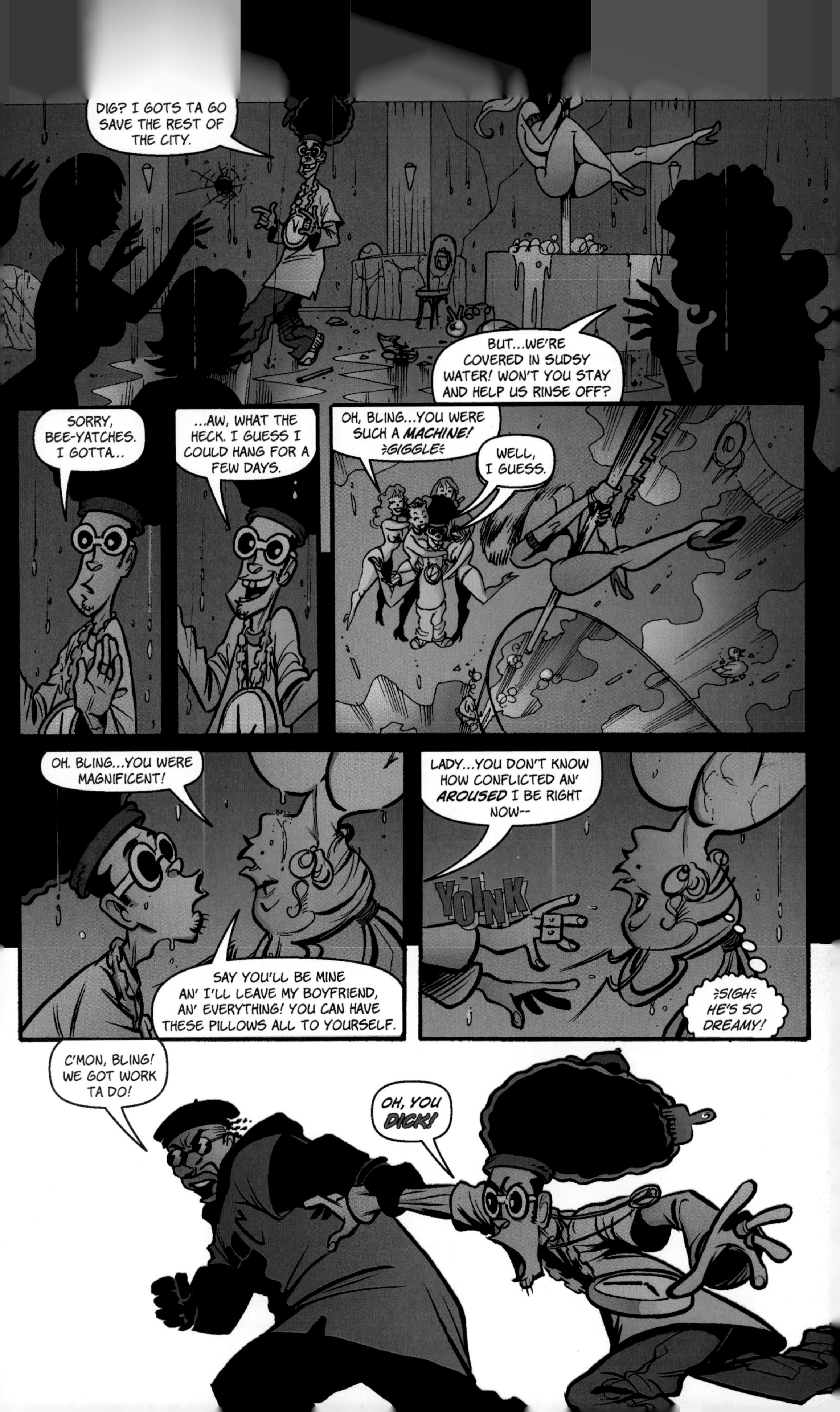
DIG? I GOTS TA GO SAVE THE REST OF THE CITY.
BUT...WE'RE COVERED IN SUDSY WATER! WON'T YOU STAY AND HELP US RINSE OFF?
SORRY, BEE-YATCHES. I GOTTA..
...AW, WHAT THE HECK. I GUESS I COULD HANG FOR A FEW DAYS.
OH, BLING...YOU WERE SUCH A MACHINE! GIGGLE
WELL, I GUESS.
OH. BLING...YOU WERE MAGNIFICENT!
SAY YOU'LL BE MINE AN' I'LL LEAVE MY BOYFRIEND, AN' EVERYTHING! YOU CAN HAVE THESE PILLOWS ALL TO YOURSELF.
LADY...YOU DON'T KNOW HOW CONFLICTED AN' AROUSED I BE RIGHT NOW--
YOINK
SIGH HE'S SO DREAMY!
C'MON, BLING! WE GOT WORK TA DO!
OH, YOU DICK!

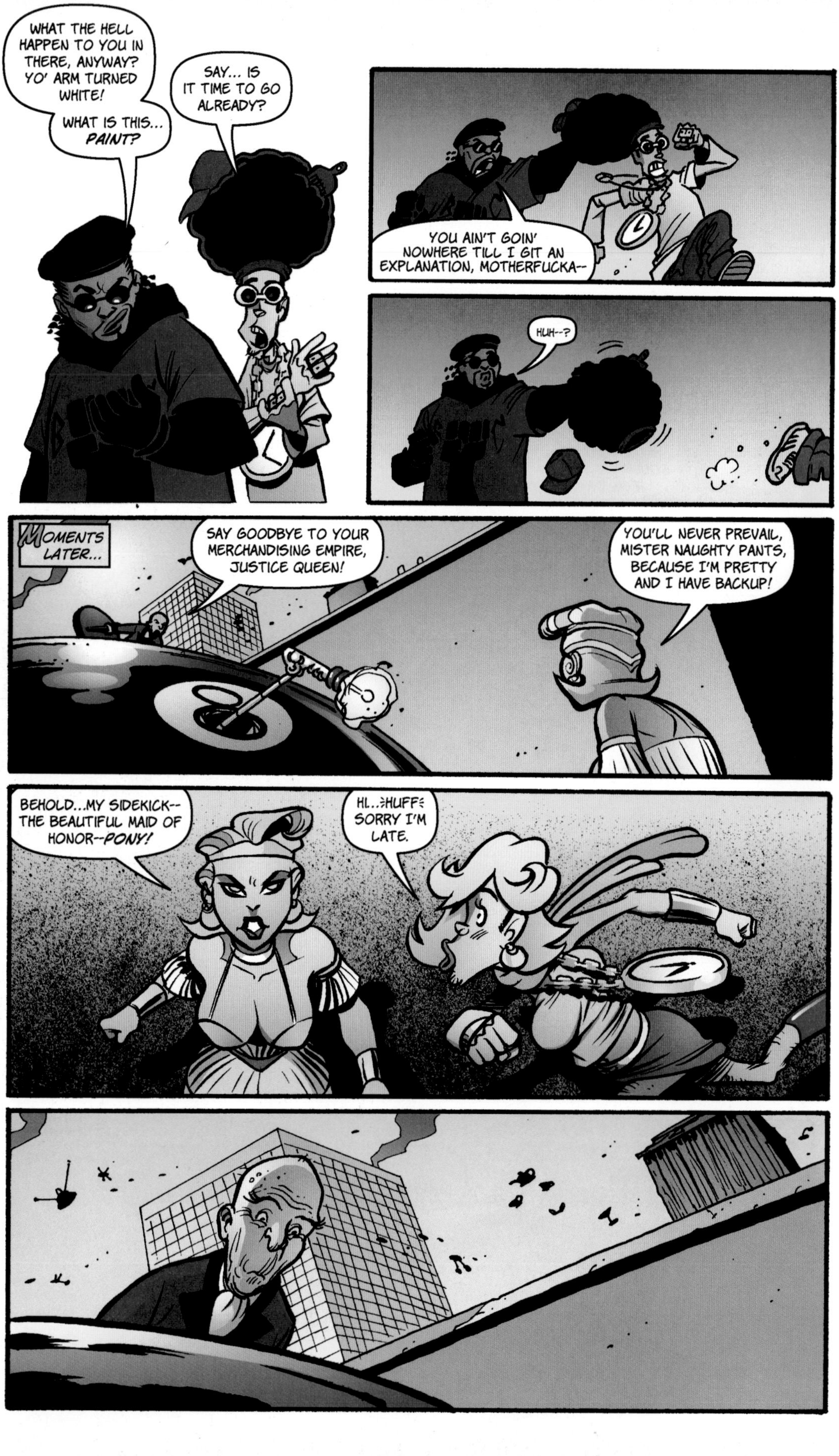
WHAT THE HELL HAPPEN TO YOU IN THERE, ANYWAY? YO' ARM TURNED WHITE!
WHAT IS THIS... PAINT?
SAY... IS IT TIME TO GO ALREADY?
YOU AIN'T GOIN' NOWHERE TILL I GIT AN EXPLANATION, MOTHERFUCKA--
HUH--?
MOMENTS LATER...
SAY GOODBYE TO YOUR MERCHANDISING EMPIRE, JUSTICE QUEEN!
YOU'LL NEVER PREVAIL, MISTER NAUGHTY PANTS, BECAUSE I'M PRETTY AND I HAVE BACKUP!
BEHOLD...MY SIDEKICK-- THE BEAUTIFUL MAID OF HONOR--PONY!
HI...HUFF SORRY I'M LATE.

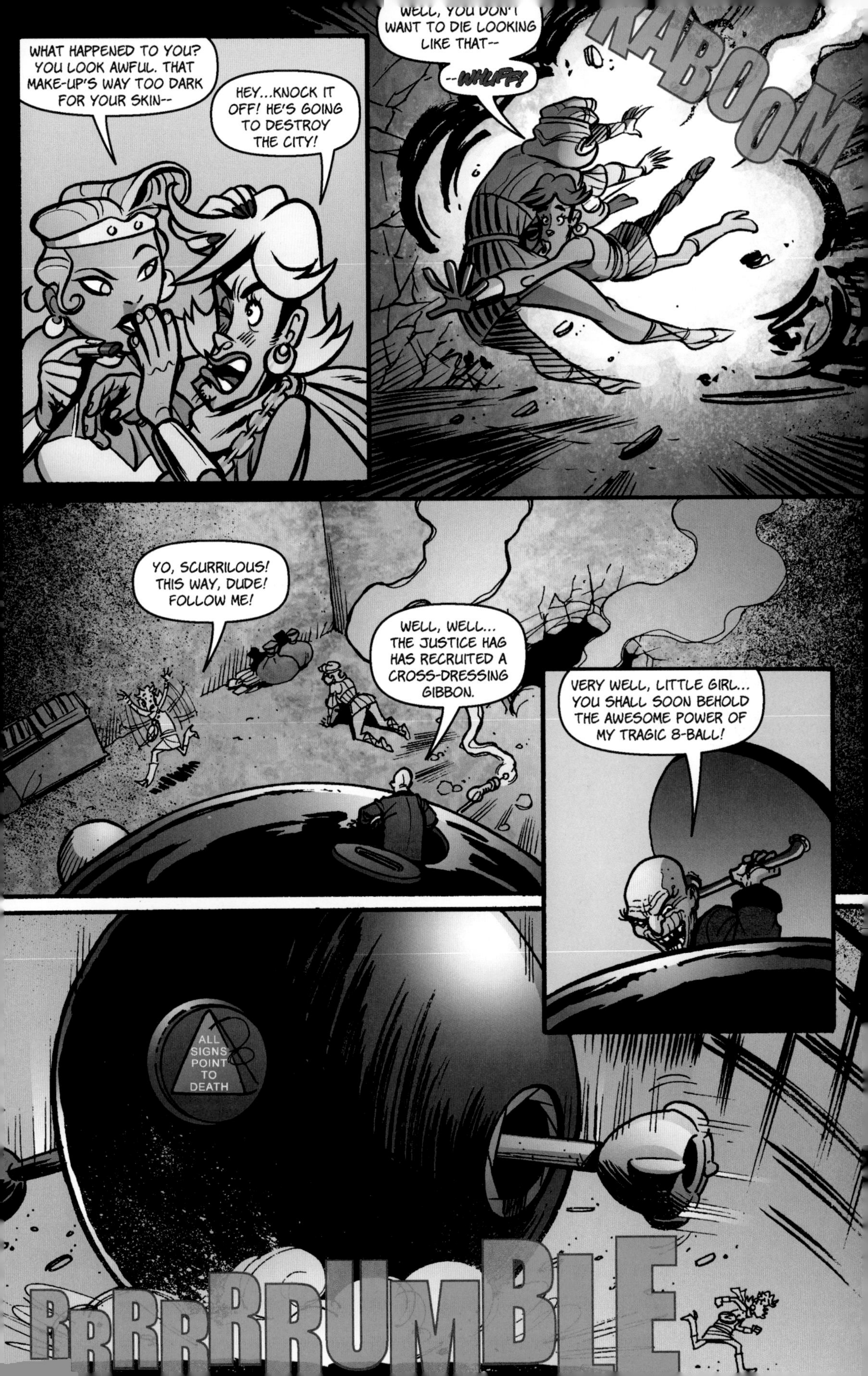
WHAT HAPPENED TO YOU? YOU LOOK AWFUL. THAT MAKE-UP'S WAY TOO DARK FOR YOUR SKIN--
HEY...KNOCK IT OFF! HE'S GOING TO DESTROY THE CITY!
WELL, YOU DON'T WANT TO DIE LOOKING LIKE THAT--
--WHUFF!
KABOOM
YO, SCURRILOUS! THIS WAY, DUDE! FOLLOW ME!
WELL, WELL... THE JUSTICE HAG HAS RECRUITED A CROSS-DRESSING GIBBON.
VERY WELL, LITTLE GIRL... YOU SHALL SOON BEHOLD THE AWESOME POWER OF MY TRAGIC 8-BALL!
ALL SIGNS POINT TO DEATH
BRRRRRUMBLE

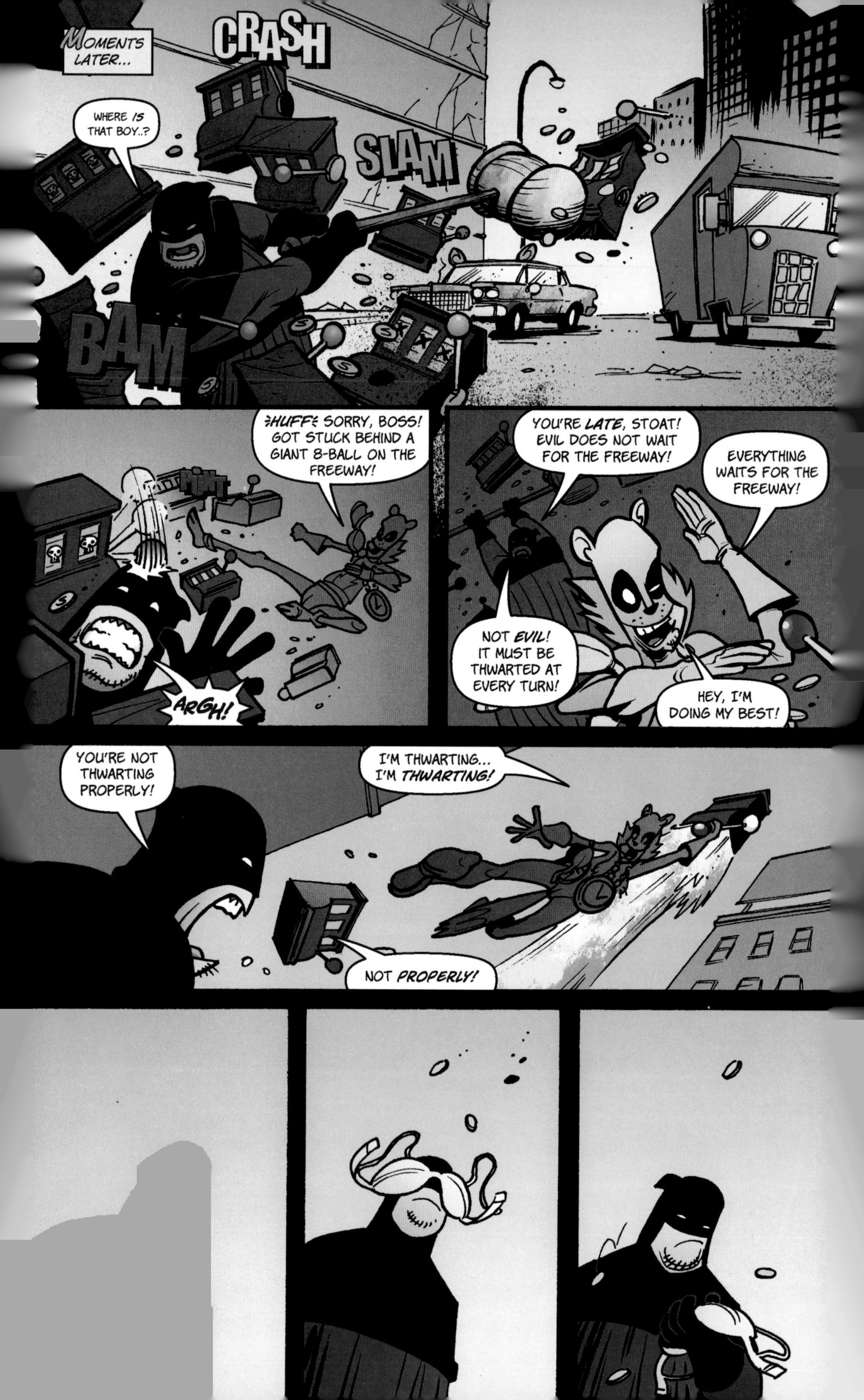

MOMENTS LATER...
CRASH
WHERE IS THAT BOY..?
SLAM
BAM
HUFF SORRY, BOSS! GOT STUCK BEHIND A GIANT 8-BALL ON THE FREEWAY!
PUNT
ARGH!
YOU'RE LATE, STOAT! EVIL DOES NOT WAIT FOR THE FREEWAY!
EVERYTHING WAITS FOR THE FREEWAY!
NOT EVIL! IT MUST BE THWARTED AT EVERY TURN!
HEY, I'M DOING MY BEST!
YOU'RE NOT THWARTING PROPERLY!
I'M THWARTING... I'M THWARTING!
NOT PROPERLY!

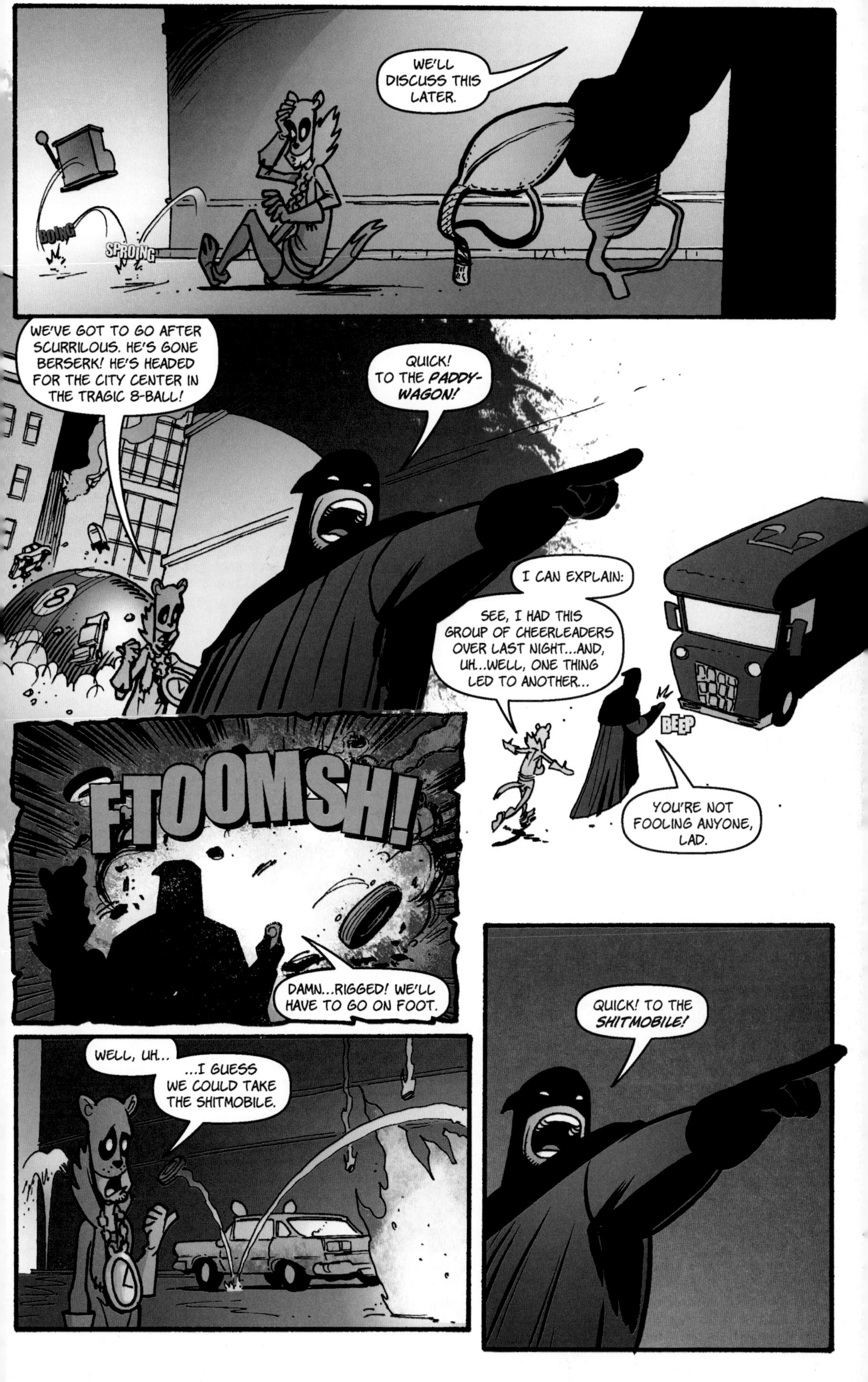
WE'LL DISCUSS THIS LATER.
BOING
SPROING
WE'VE GOT TO GO AFTER SCURRILOUS. HE'S GONE BERSERK! HE'S HEADED FOR THE CITY CENTER IN THE TRAGIC 8-BALL!
QUICK! TO THE *PADDY-WAGON!*
I CAN EXPLAIN:
SEE, I HAD THIS GROUP OF CHEERLEADERS OVER LAST NIGHT...AND, UH...WELL, ONE THING LED TO ANOTHER...
BEEP
YOU'RE NOT FOOLING ANYONE, LAD.
FTOOMSH!
DAMN...RIGGED! WE'LL HAVE TO GO ON FOOT.
WELL, UH...
...I GUESS WE COULD TAKE THE SHITMOBILE.
QUICK! TO THE *SHITMOBILE!*

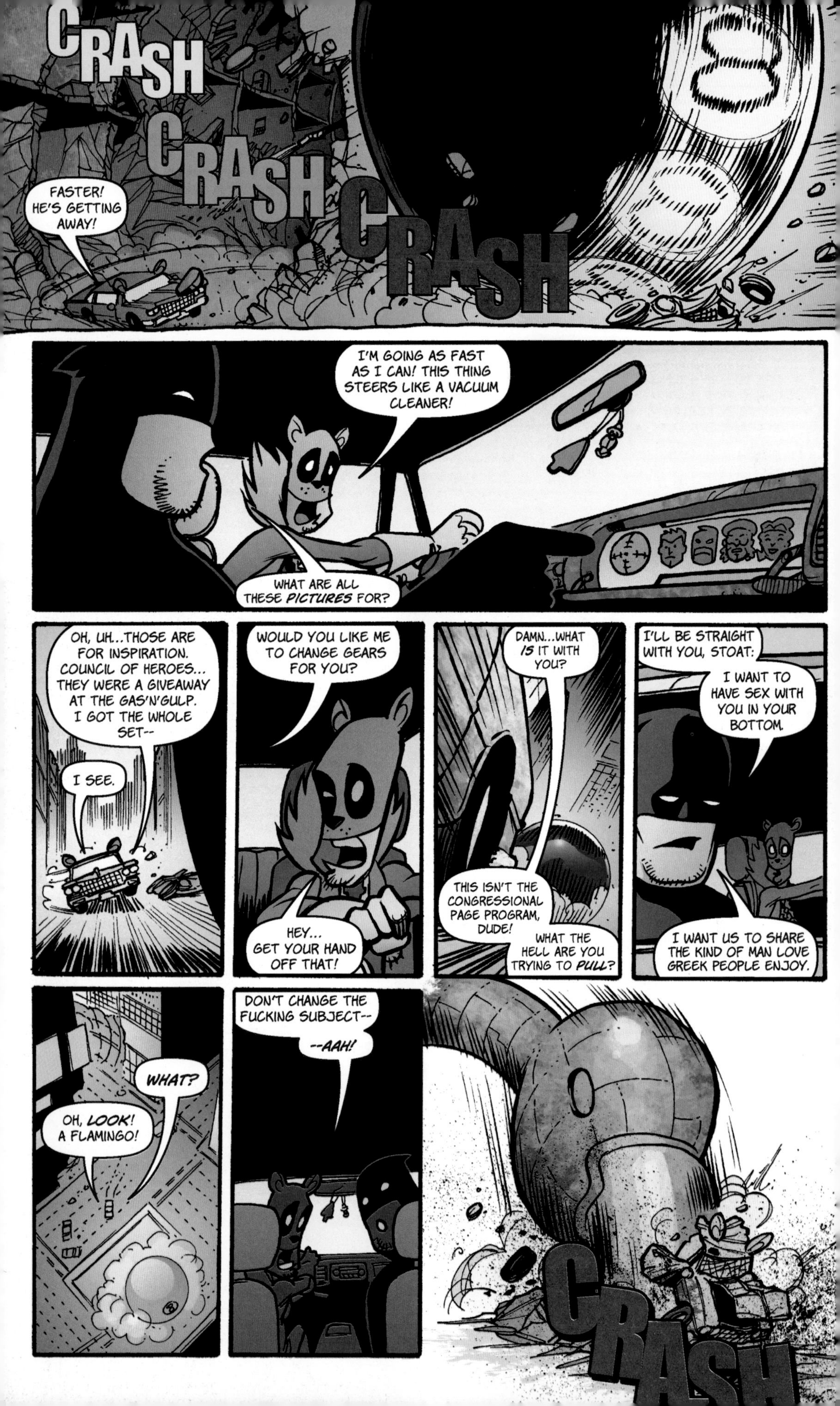
CRASH
CRASH
FASTER! HE'S GETTING AWAY!
CRASH
I'M GOING AS FAST AS I CAN! THIS THING STEERS LIKE A VACUUM CLEANER!
WHAT ARE ALL THESE PICTURES FOR?
OH, UH...THOSE ARE FOR INSPIRATION. COUNCIL OF HEROES... THEY WERE A GIVEAWAY AT THE GAS'N'GULP. I GOT THE WHOLE SET--
I SEE.
WOULD YOU LIKE ME TO CHANGE GEARS FOR YOU?
HEY... GET YOUR HAND OFF THAT!
DAMN...WHAT IS IT WITH YOU?
THIS ISN'T THE CONGRESSIONAL PAGE PROGRAM, DUDE!
WHAT THE HELL ARE YOU TRYING TO PULL?
I'LL BE STRAIGHT WITH YOU, STOAT:
I WANT TO HAVE SEX WITH YOU IN YOUR BOTTOM.
I WANT US TO SHARE THE KIND OF MAN LOVE GREEK PEOPLE ENJOY.
WHAT?
OH, LOOK! A FLAMINGO!
DON'T CHANGE THE FUCKING SUBJECT--
--AAH!
CRASH

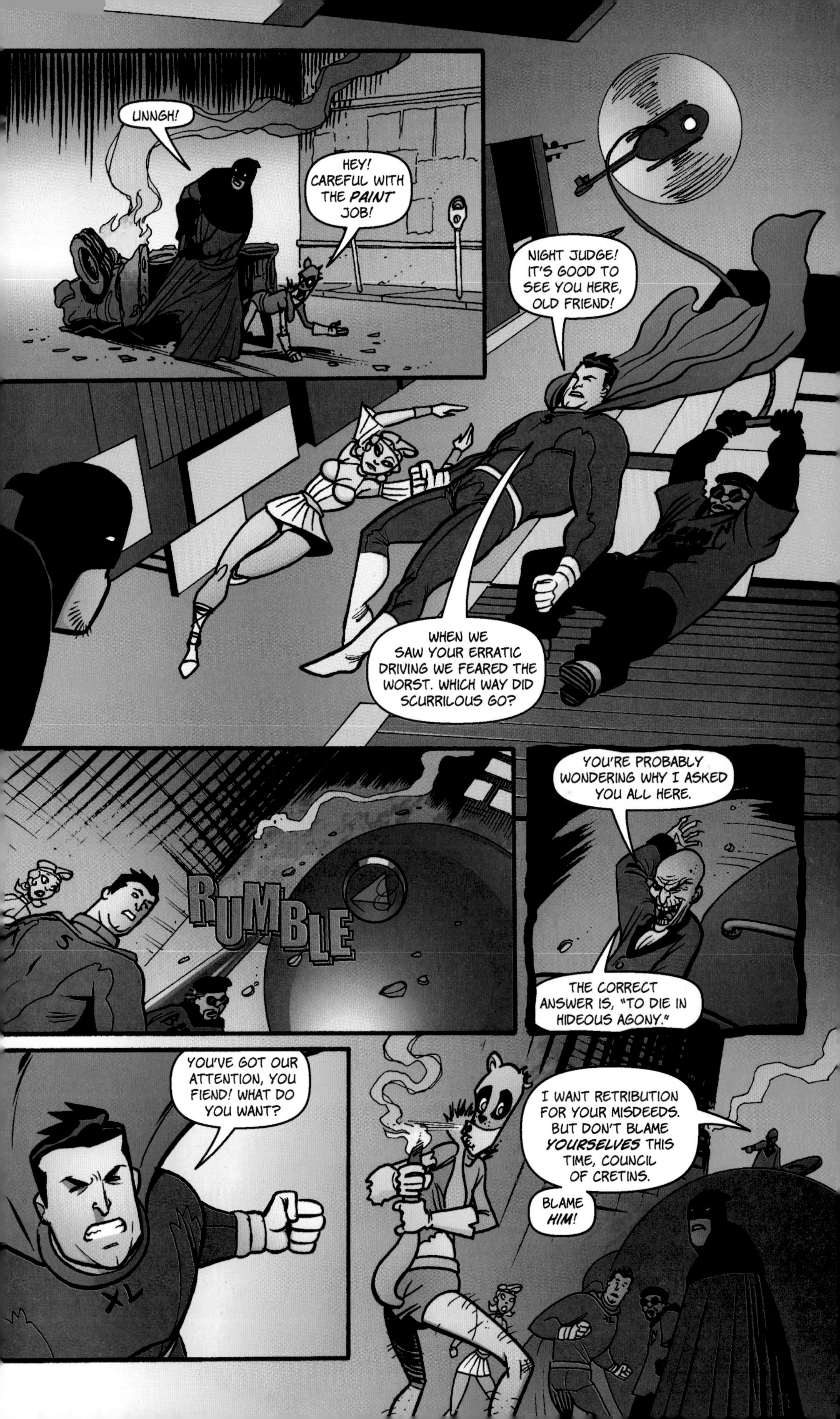
UNNGH!
HEY! CAREFUL WITH THE PAINT JOB!
NIGHT JUDGE! IT'S GOOD TO SEE YOU HERE, OLD FRIEND!
WHEN WE SAW YOUR ERRATIC DRIVING WE FEARED THE WORST. WHICH WAY DID SCURRILOUS GO?
RUMBLE
YOU'RE PROBABLY WONDERING WHY I ASKED YOU ALL HERE.
THE CORRECT ANSWER IS, "TO DIE IN HIDEOUS AGONY."
YOU'VE GOT OUR ATTENTION, YOU FIEND! WHAT DO YOU WANT?
I WANT RETRIBUTION FOR YOUR MISDEEDS. BUT DON'T BLAME YOURSELVES THIS TIME, COUNCIL OF CRETINS.
BLAME HIM!

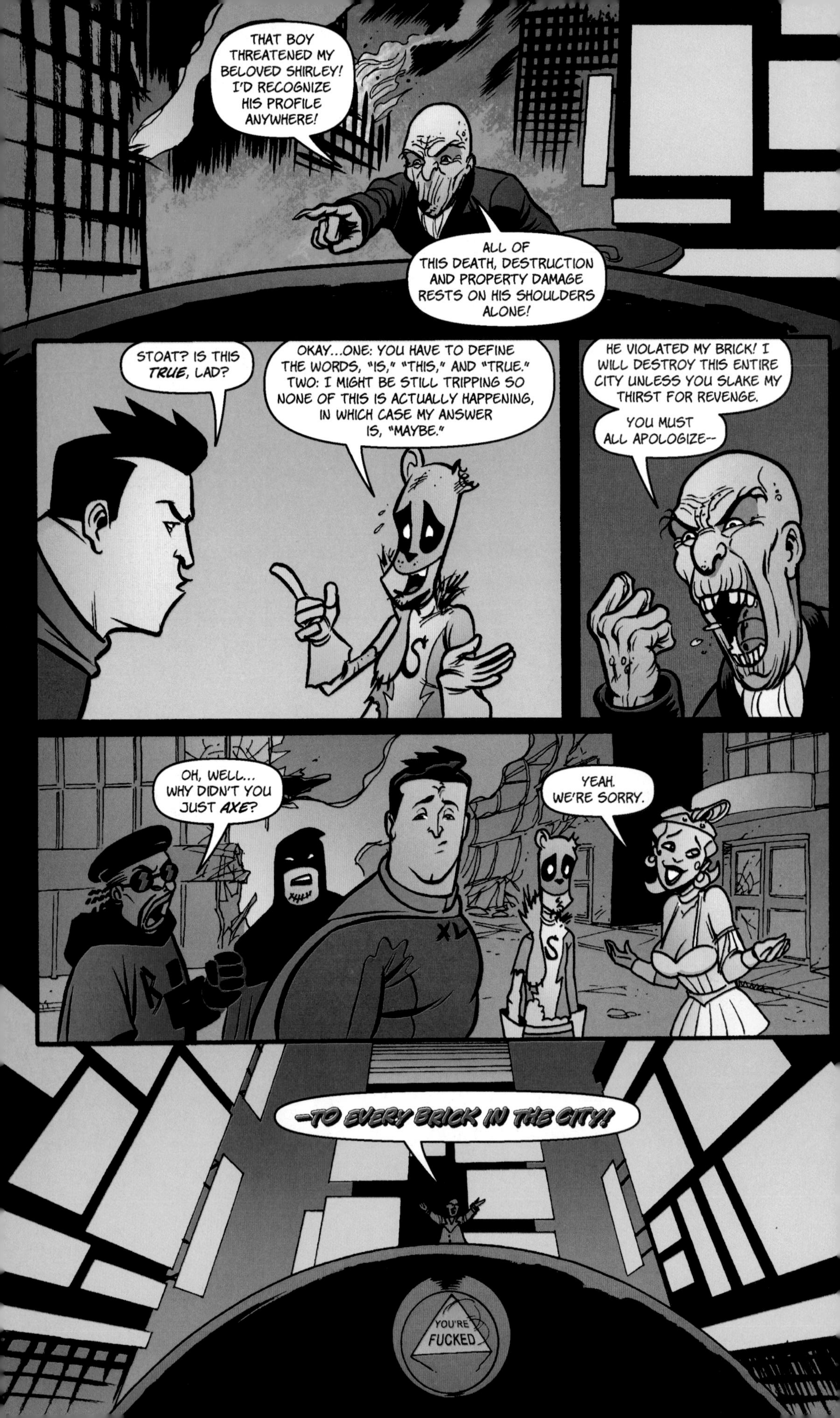
THAT BOY THREATENED MY BELOVED SHIRLEY! I'D RECOGNIZE HIS PROFILE ANYWHERE!
ALL OF THIS DEATH, DESTRUCTION AND PROPERTY DAMAGE RESTS ON HIS SHOULDERS ALONE!
STOAT? IS THIS *TRUE*, LAD?
OKAY...ONE: YOU HAVE TO DEFINE THE WORDS, "IS," "THIS," AND "TRUE." TWO: I MIGHT BE STILL TRIPPING SO NONE OF THIS IS ACTUALLY HAPPENING, IN WHICH CASE MY ANSWER IS, "MAYBE."
HE VIOLATED MY BRICK! I WILL DESTROY THIS ENTIRE CITY UNLESS YOU SLAKE MY THIRST FOR REVENGE.
YOU MUST ALL APOLOGIZE--
OH, WELL... WHY DIDN'T YOU JUST *AXE*?
YEAH. WE'RE SORRY.
--TO EVERY BRICK IN THE CITY!
YOU'RE FUCKED

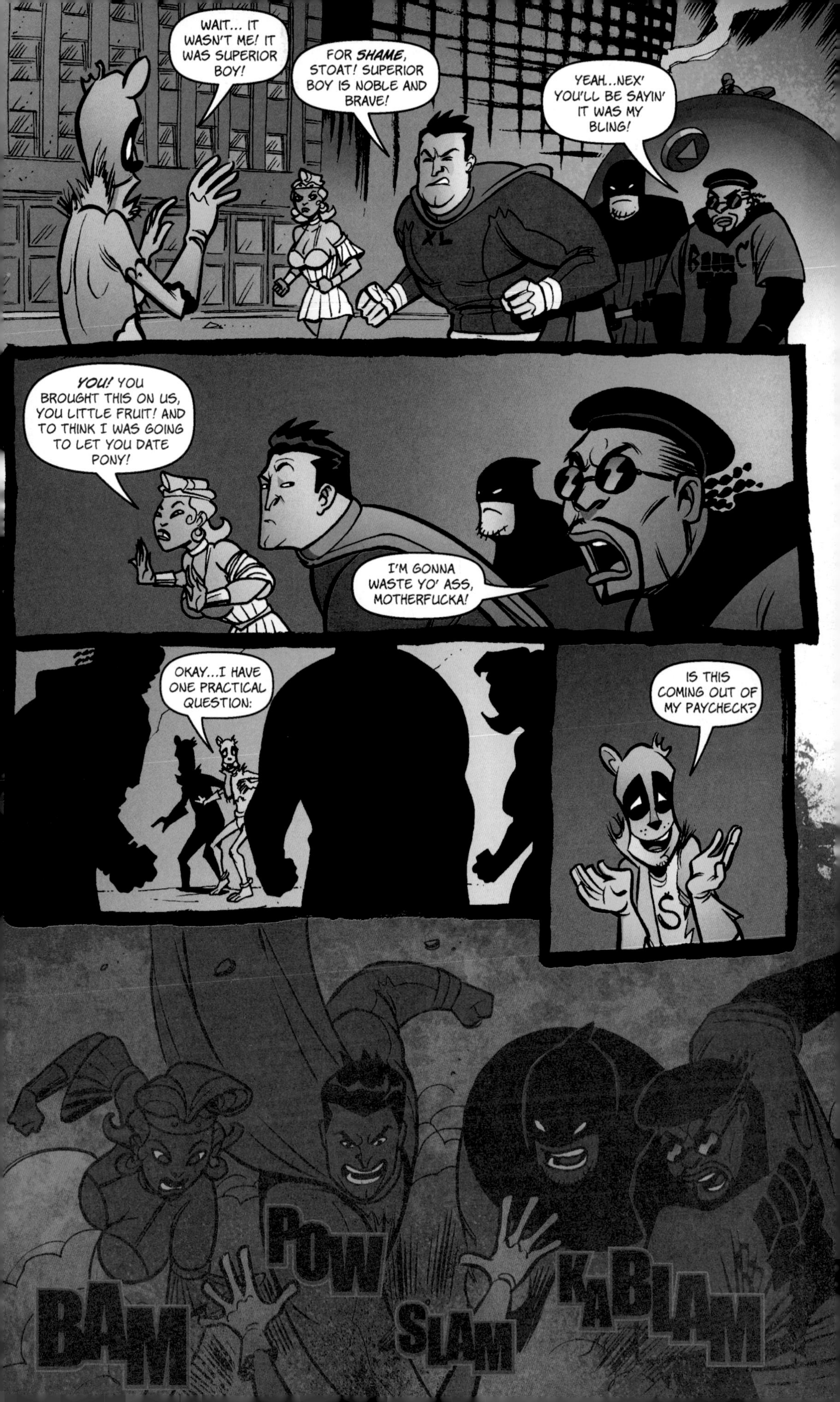

WAIT... IT WASN'T ME! IT WAS SUPERIOR BOY!
FOR *SHAME*, STOAT! SUPERIOR BOY IS NOBLE AND BRAVE!
YEAH...NEX' YOU'LL BE SAYIN' IT WAS MY BLING!
YOU! YOU BROUGHT THIS ON US, YOU LITTLE FRUIT! AND TO THINK I WAS GOING TO LET YOU DATE PONY!
I'M GONNA WASTE YO' ASS, MOTHERFUCKA!
OKAY...I HAVE ONE PRACTICAL QUESTION:
IS THIS COMING OUT OF MY PAYCHECK?
BAM
POW
SLAM
KABLAM

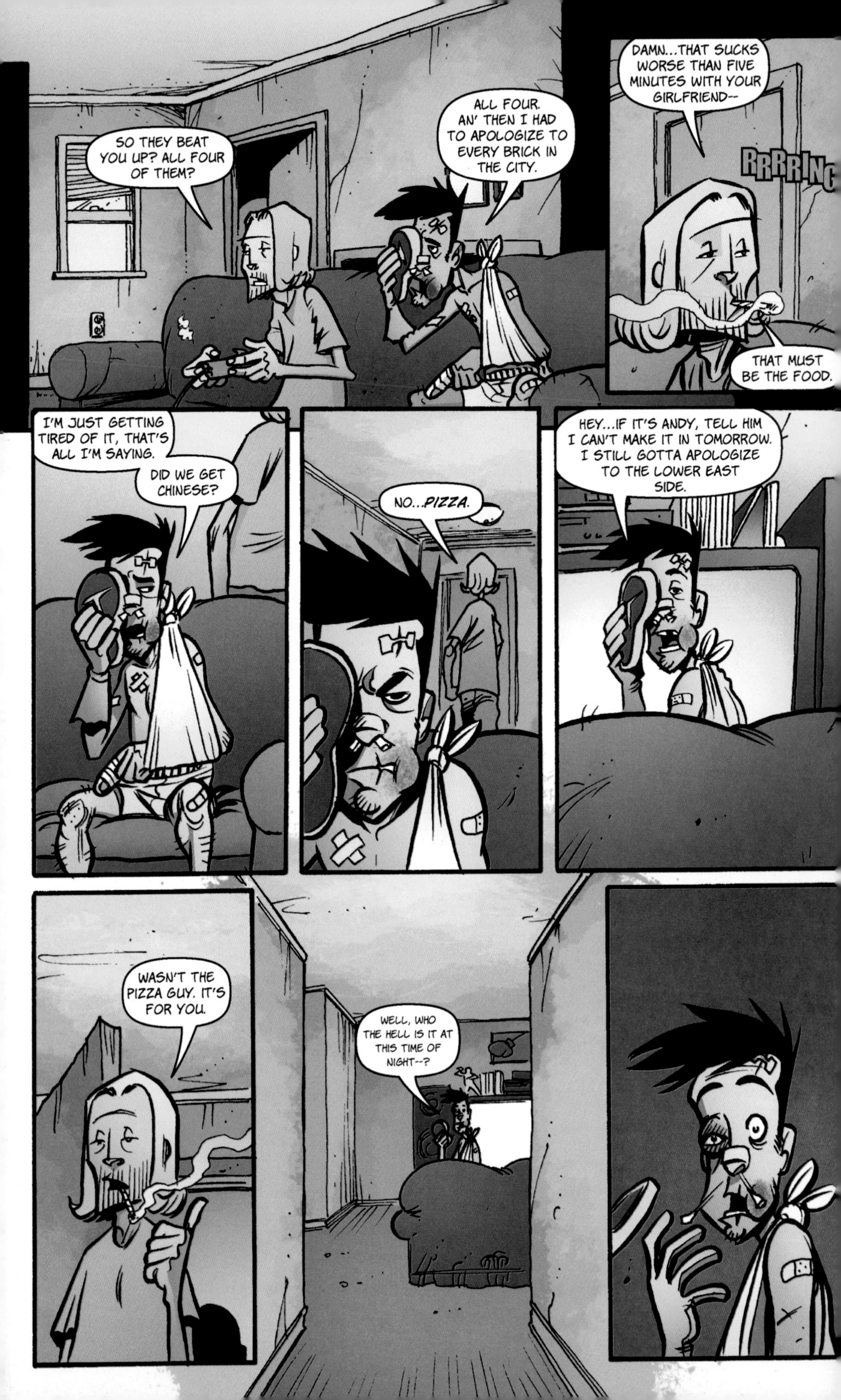
SO THEY BEAT YOU UP? ALL FOUR OF THEM?
ALL FOUR. AN' THEN I HAD TO APOLOGIZE TO EVERY BRICK IN THE CITY.
DAMN...THAT SUCKS WORSE THAN FIVE MINUTES WITH YOUR GIRLFRIEND--
RRRRING
THAT MUST BE THE FOOD.
I'M JUST GETTING TIRED OF IT, THAT'S ALL I'M SAYING.
DID WE GET CHINESE?
NO...PIZZA.
HEY...IF IT'S ANDY, TELL HIM I CAN'T MAKE IT IN TOMORROW. I STILL GOTTA APOLOGIZE TO THE LOWER EAST SIDE.
WASN'T THE PIZZA GUY. IT'S FOR YOU.
WELL, WHO THE HELL IS IT AT THIS TIME OF NIGHT--?

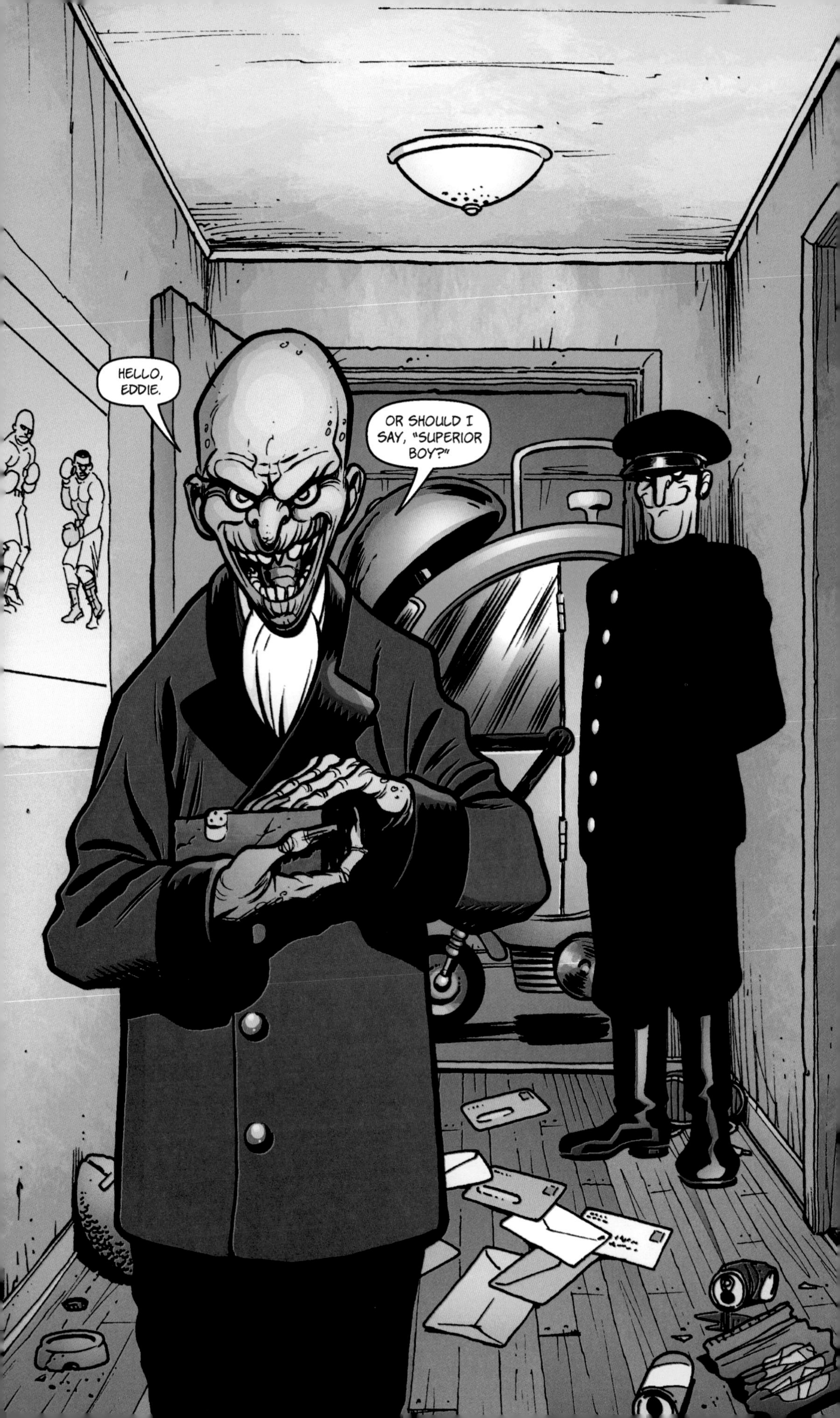
HELLO, EDDIE.
OR SHOULD I SAY, "SUPERIOR BOY?"

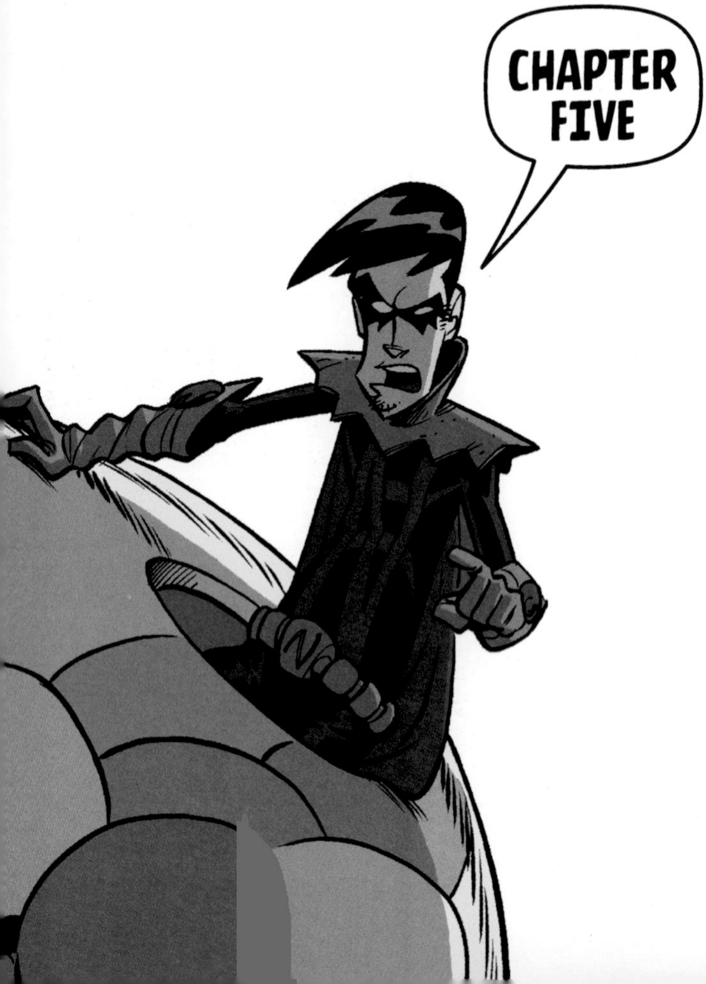
CHAPTER FIVE

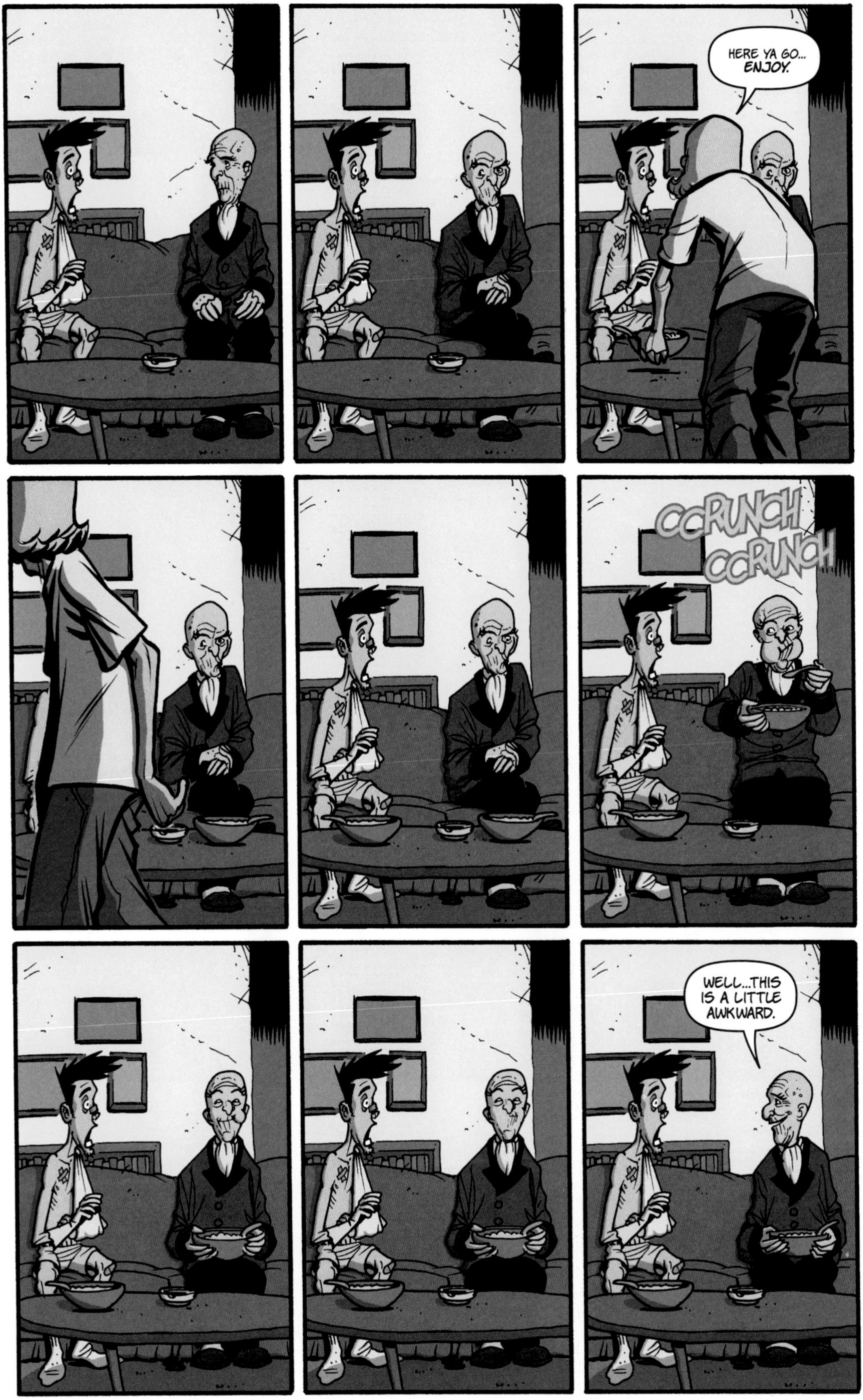
HERE YA GO... ENJOY.
CCRUNCH CCRUNCH
WELL...THIS IS A LITTLE AWKWARD.

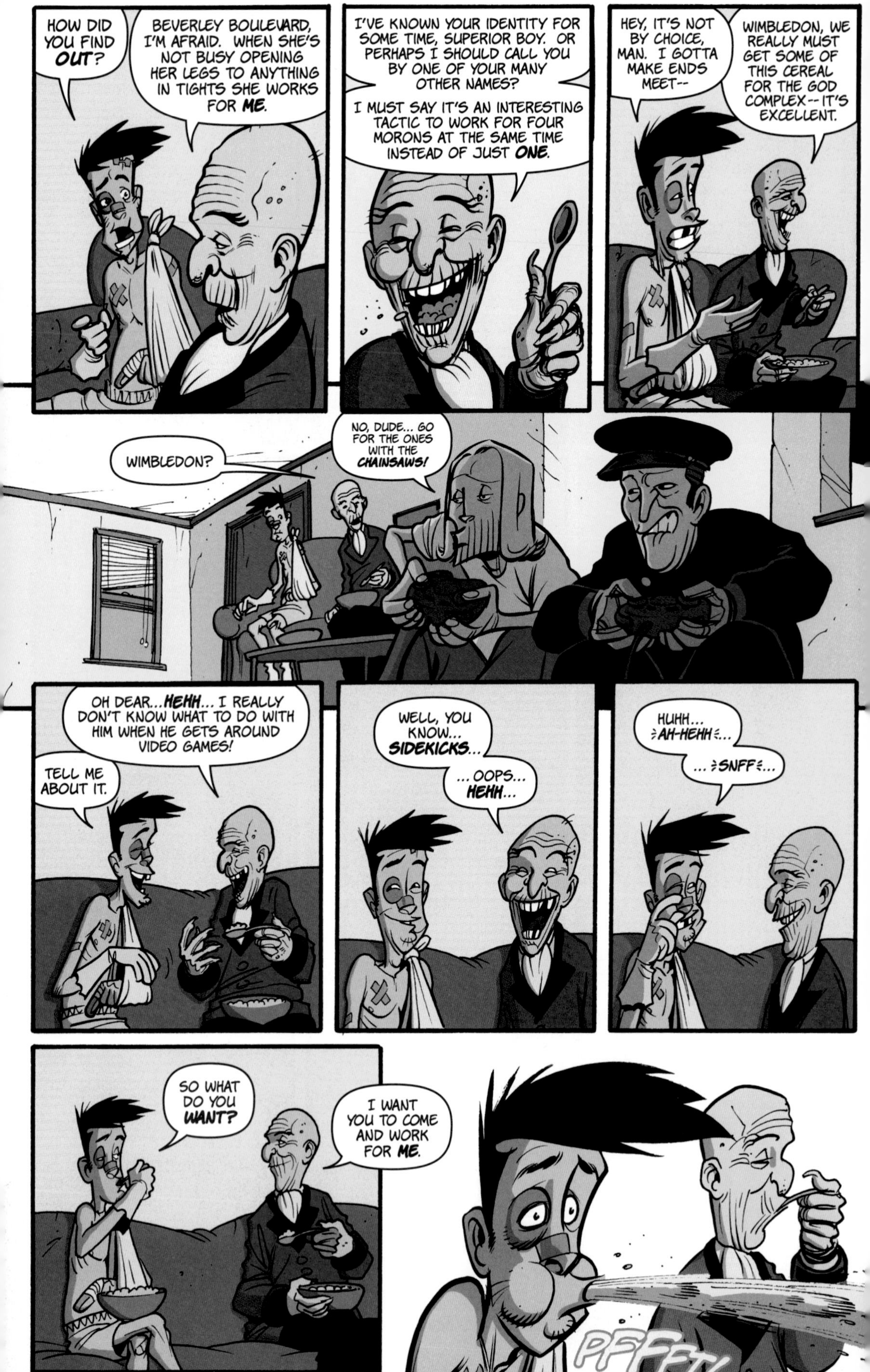
HOW DID YOU FIND OUT?
BEVERLEY BOULEVARD, I'M AFRAID. WHEN SHE'S NOT BUSY OPENING HER LEGS TO ANYTHING IN TIGHTS SHE WORKS FOR ME.
I'VE KNOWN YOUR IDENTITY FOR SOME TIME, SUPERIOR BOY. OR PERHAPS I SHOULD CALL YOU BY ONE OF YOUR MANY OTHER NAMES?
I MUST SAY IT'S AN INTERESTING TACTIC TO WORK FOR FOUR MORONS AT THE SAME TIME INSTEAD OF JUST ONE.
HEY, IT'S NOT BY CHOICE, MAN. I GOTTA MAKE ENDS MEET--
WIMBLEDON, WE REALLY MUST GET SOME OF THIS CEREAL FOR THE GOD COMPLEX--IT'S EXCELLENT.
WIMBLEDON?
NO, DUDE... GO FOR THE ONES WITH THE CHAINSAWS!
OH DEAR...HEHH... I REALLY DON'T KNOW WHAT TO DO WITH HIM WHEN HE GETS AROUND VIDEO GAMES!
TELL ME ABOUT IT.
WELL, YOU KNOW... SIDEKICKS...
...OOPS... HEHH...
HUHH... AH-HEHH...
...SNFF...
SO WHAT DO YOU WANT?
I WANT YOU TO COME AND WORK FOR ME.
PFFFFT!

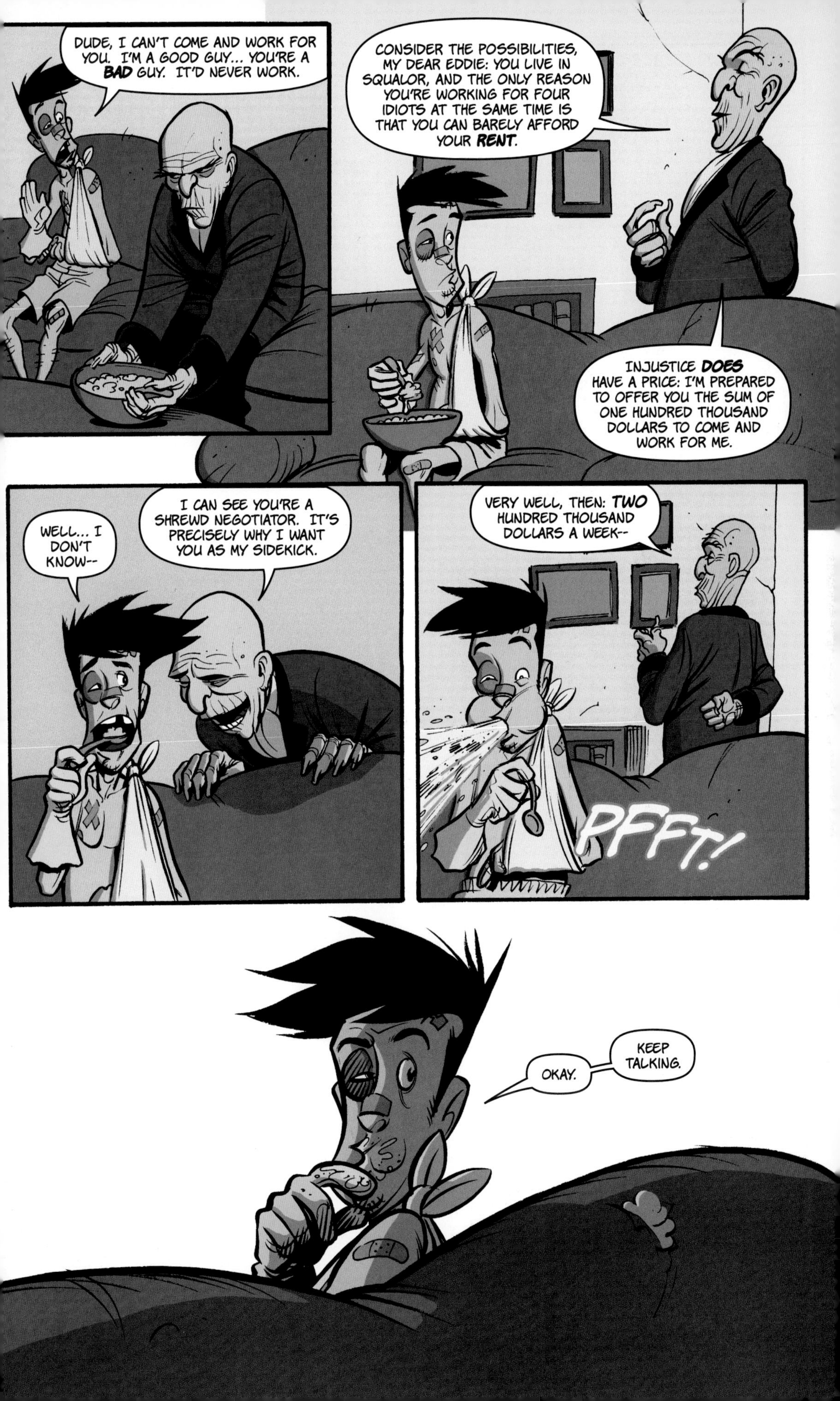

DUDE, I CAN'T COME AND WORK FOR YOU. I'M A GOOD GUY... YOU'RE A **BAD** GUY. IT'D NEVER WORK.
CONSIDER THE POSSIBILITIES, MY DEAR EDDIE: YOU LIVE IN SQUALOR, AND THE ONLY REASON YOU'RE WORKING FOR FOUR IDIOTS AT THE SAME TIME IS THAT YOU CAN BARELY AFFORD YOUR **RENT**.
INJUSTICE **DOES** HAVE A PRICE: I'M PREPARED TO OFFER YOU THE SUM OF ONE HUNDRED THOUSAND DOLLARS TO COME AND WORK FOR ME.
WELL... I DON'T KNOW--
I CAN SEE YOU'RE A SHREWD NEGOTIATOR. IT'S PRECISELY WHY I WANT YOU AS MY SIDEKICK.
VERY WELL, THEN: **TWO** HUNDRED THOUSAND DOLLARS A WEEK--
PFFT!
OKAY.
KEEP TALKING.

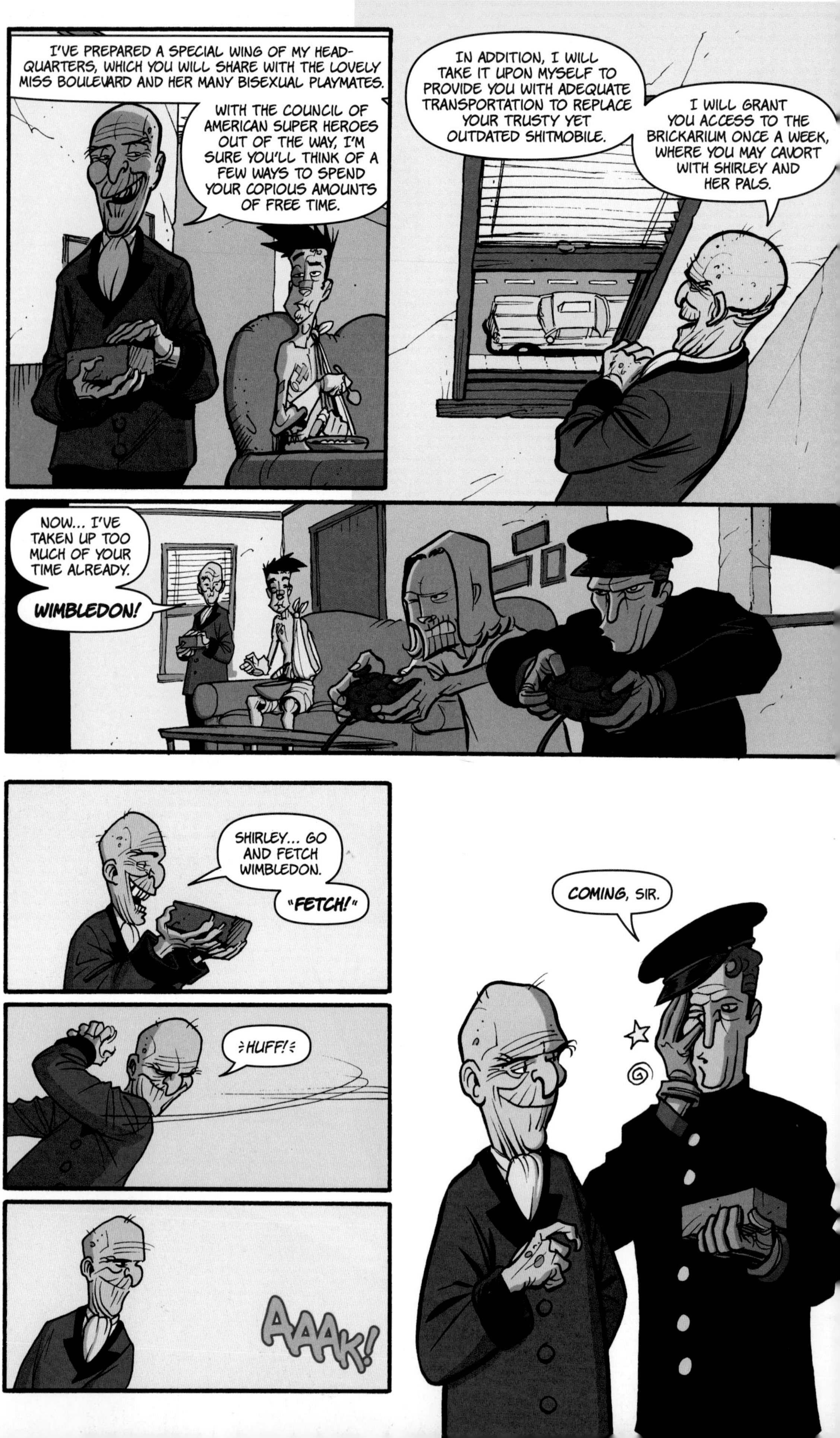
I'VE PREPARED A SPECIAL WING OF MY HEAD-QUARTERS, WHICH YOU WILL SHARE WITH THE LOVELY MISS BOULEVARD AND HER MANY BISEXUAL PLAYMATES.
WITH THE COUNCIL OF AMERICAN SUPER HEROES OUT OF THE WAY, I'M SURE YOU'LL THINK OF A FEW WAYS TO SPEND YOUR COPIOUS AMOUNTS OF FREE TIME.
IN ADDITION, I WILL TAKE IT UPON MYSELF TO PROVIDE YOU WITH ADEQUATE TRANSPORTATION TO REPLACE YOUR TRUSTY YET OUTDATED SHITMOBILE.
I WILL GRANT YOU ACCESS TO THE BRICKARIUM ONCE A WEEK, WHERE YOU MAY CAVORT WITH SHIRLEY AND HER PALS.
NOW... I'VE TAKEN UP TOO MUCH OF YOUR TIME ALREADY.
WIMBLEDON!
SHIRLEY... GO AND FETCH WIMBLEDON.
"FETCH!"
HUFF!
AAAK!
COMING, SIR.

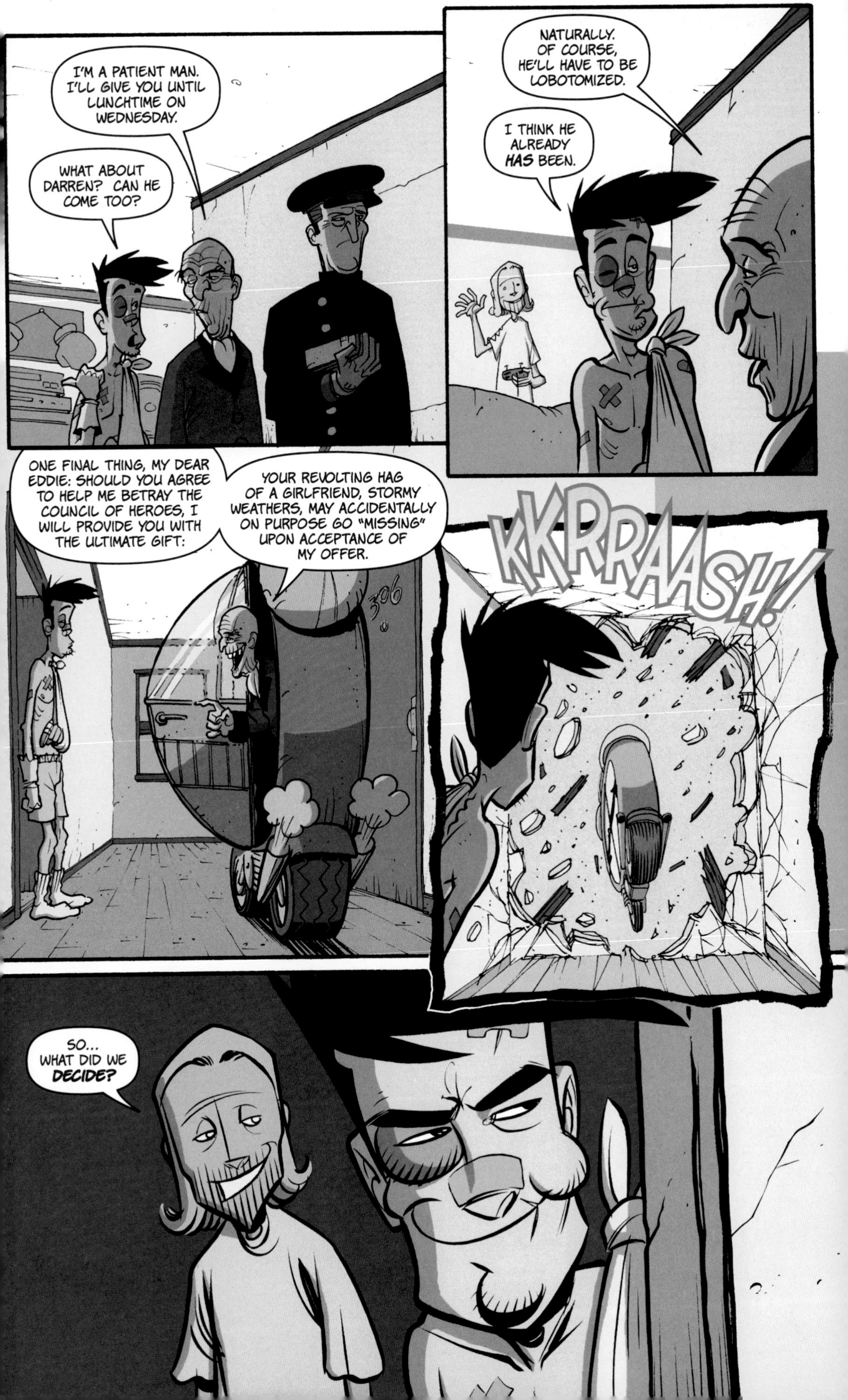
I'M A PATIENT MAN. I'LL GIVE YOU UNTIL LUNCHTIME ON WEDNESDAY.
WHAT ABOUT DARREN? CAN HE COME TOO?
NATURALLY. OF COURSE, HE'LL HAVE TO BE LOBOTOMIZED.
I THINK HE ALREADY **HAS** BEEN.
ONE FINAL THING, MY DEAR EDDIE: SHOULD YOU AGREE TO HELP ME BETRAY THE COUNCIL OF HEROES, I WILL PROVIDE YOU WITH THE ULTIMATE GIFT:
YOUR REVOLTING HAG OF A GIRLFRIEND, STORMY WEATHERS, MAY ACCIDENTALLY ON PURPOSE GO "MISSING" UPON ACCEPTANCE OF MY OFFER.
306
KKRRAASH!!
SO... WHAT DID WE **DECIDE?**

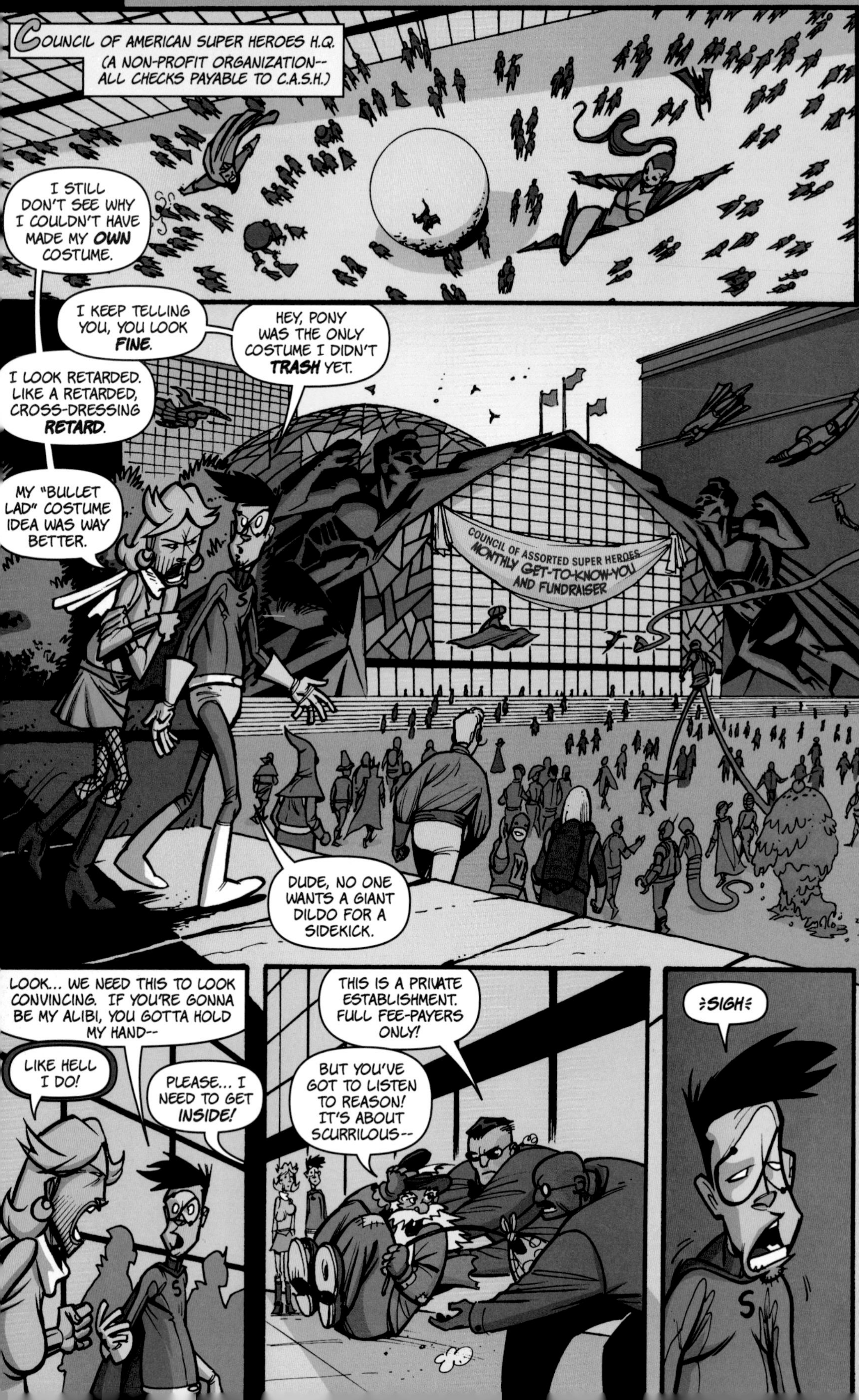
COUNCIL OF AMERICAN SUPER HEROES H.Q.
(A NON-PROFIT ORGANIZATION-- ALL CHECKS PAYABLE TO C.A.S.H.)
I STILL DON'T SEE WHY I COULDN'T HAVE MADE MY OWN COSTUME.
I KEEP TELLING YOU, YOU LOOK FINE.
HEY, PONY WAS THE ONLY COSTUME I DIDN'T TRASH YET.
I LOOK RETARDED. LIKE A RETARDED, CROSS-DRESSING RETARD.
MY "BULLET LAD" COSTUME IDEA WAS WAY BETTER.
COUNCIL OF ASSORTED SUPER HEROES MONTHLY GET-TO-KNOW-YOU AND FUNDRAISER
DUDE, NO ONE WANTS A GIANT DILDO FOR A SIDEKICK.
LOOK... WE NEED THIS TO LOOK CONVINCING. IF YOU'RE GONNA BE MY ALIBI, YOU GOTTA HOLD MY HAND--
LIKE HELL I DO!
PLEASE... I NEED TO GET INSIDE!
THIS IS A PRIVATE ESTABLISHMENT. FULL FEE-PAYERS ONLY!
BUT YOU'VE GOT TO LISTEN TO REASON! IT'S ABOUT SCURRILOUS--
SIGH

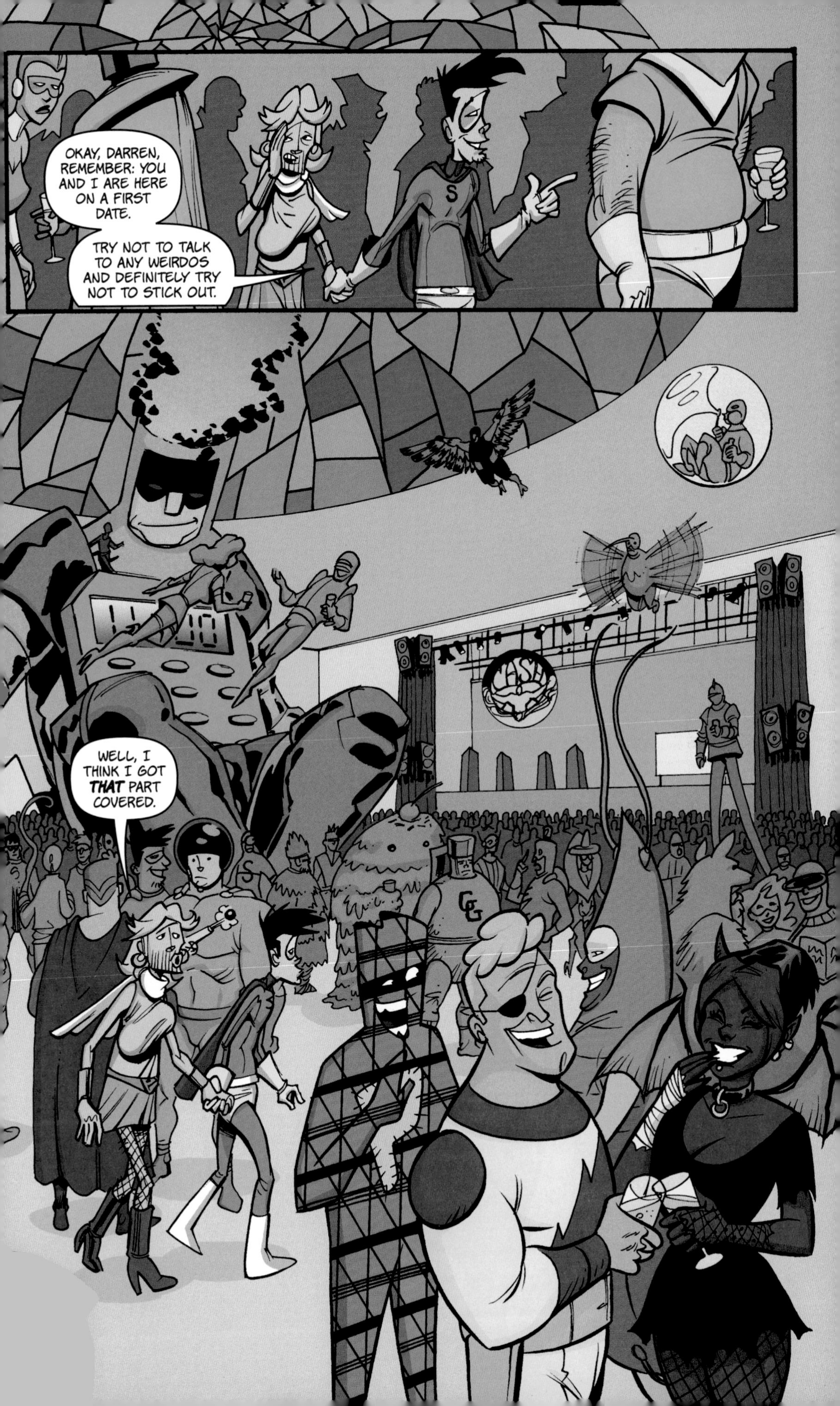
OKAY, DARREN, REMEMBER: YOU AND I ARE HERE ON A FIRST DATE.
TRY NOT TO TALK TO ANY WEIRDOS AND DEFINITELY TRY NOT TO STICK OUT.
WELL, I THINK I GOT **THAT** PART COVERED.

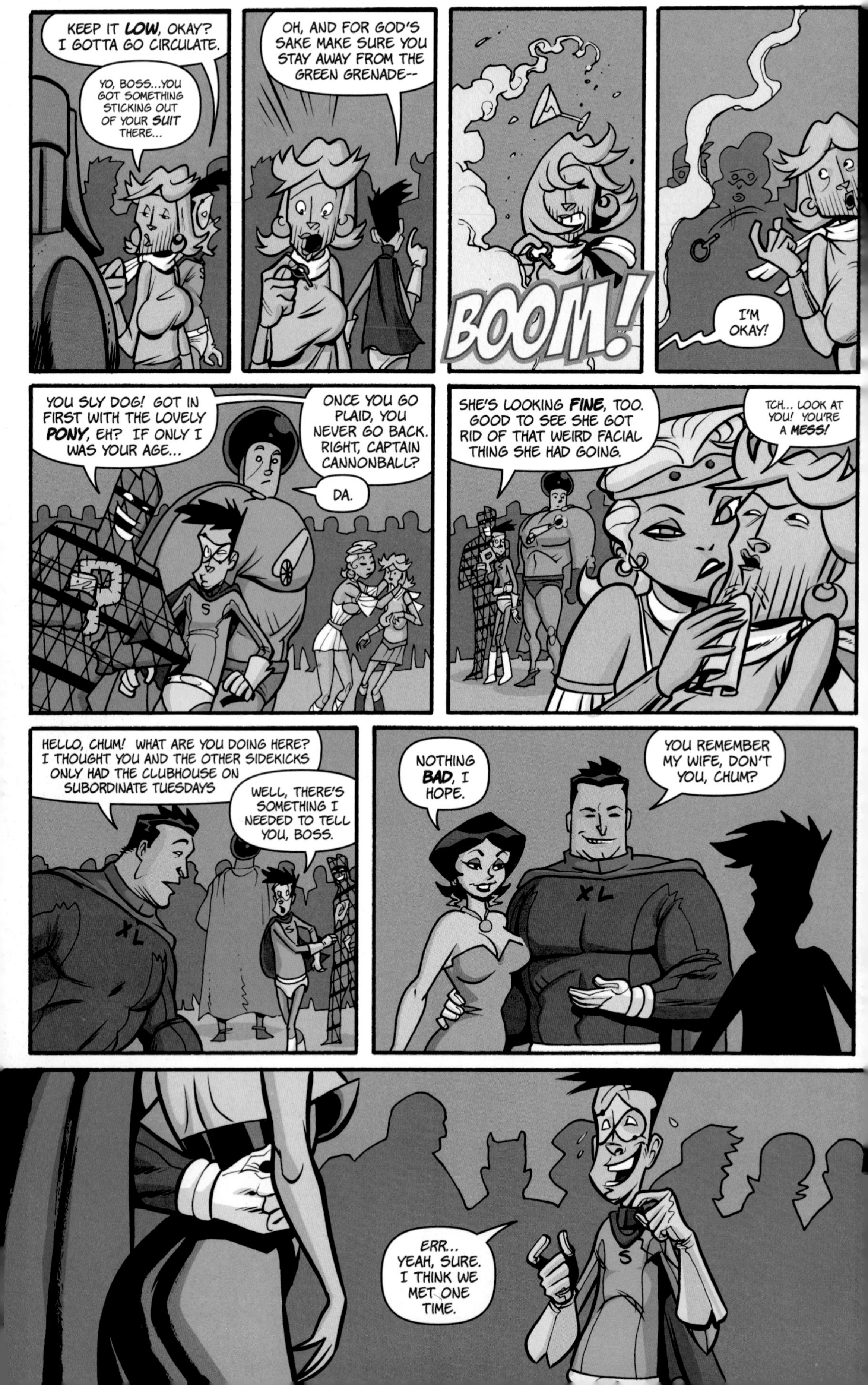

KEEP IT LOW, OKAY? I GOTTA GO CIRCULATE.
YO, BOSS...YOU GOT SOMETHING STICKING OUT OF YOUR SUIT THERE...
OH, AND FOR GOD'S SAKE MAKE SURE YOU STAY AWAY FROM THE GREEN GRENADE--
BOOM!
I'M OKAY!
YOU SLY DOG! GOT IN FIRST WITH THE LOVELY PONY, EH? IF ONLY I WAS YOUR AGE...
ONCE YOU GO PLAID, YOU NEVER GO BACK. RIGHT, CAPTAIN CANNONBALL?
DA.
SHE'S LOOKING FINE, TOO. GOOD TO SEE SHE GOT RID OF THAT WEIRD FACIAL THING SHE HAD GOING.
TCH... LOOK AT YOU! YOU'RE A MESS!
HELLO, CHUM! WHAT ARE YOU DOING HERE? I THOUGHT YOU AND THE OTHER SIDEKICKS ONLY HAD THE CLUBHOUSE ON SUBORDINATE TUESDAYS
WELL, THERE'S SOMETHING I NEEDED TO TELL YOU, BOSS.
NOTHING BAD, I HOPE.
YOU REMEMBER MY WIFE, DON'T YOU, CHUM?
ERR... YEAH, SURE. I THINK WE MET ONE TIME.

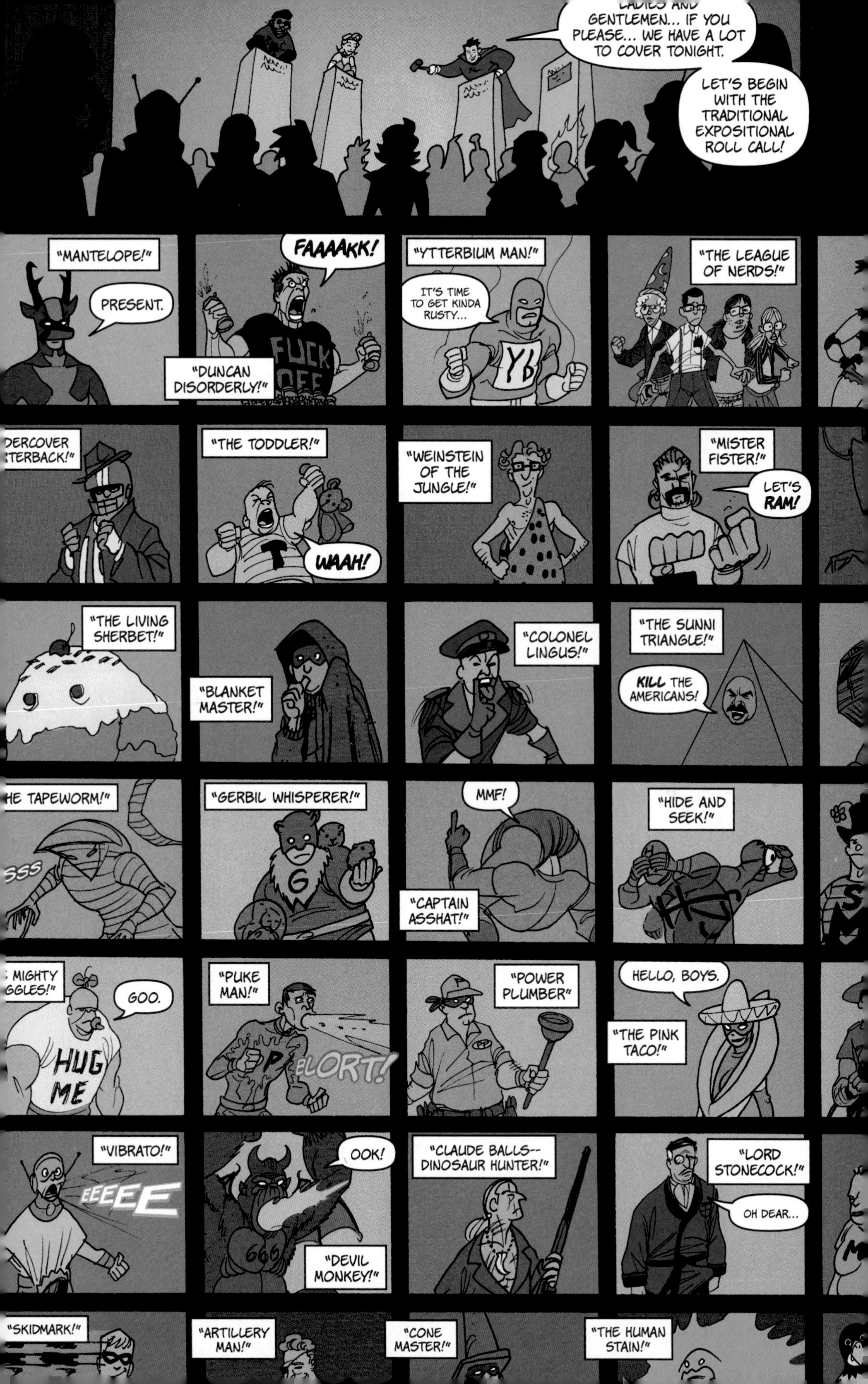
LADIES AND GENTLEMEN... IF YOU PLEASE... WE HAVE A LOT TO COVER TONIGHT.
LET'S BEGIN WITH THE TRADITIONAL EXPOSITIONAL ROLL CALL!
"MANTELOPE!"
PRESENT.
FAAAAKK!
"DUNCAN DISORDERLY!"
FUCK OFF
"YTTERBIUM MAN!"
IT'S TIME TO GET KINDA RUSTY...
Yb
"THE LEAGUE OF NERDS!"
DERCOVER TERBACK!"
"THE TODDLER!"
WAAH!
"WEINSTEIN OF THE JUNGLE!"
"MISTER FISTER!"
LET'S RAM!
"THE LIVING SHERBET!"
"BLANKET MASTER!"
"COLONEL LINGUS!"
"THE SUNNI TRIANGLE!"
KILL THE AMERICANS!
HE TAPEWORM!"
SSS
"GERBIL WHISPERER!"
MMF!
"CAPTAIN ASSHAT!"
"HIDE AND SEEK!"
MIGHTY GGLES!"
GOO.
HUG ME
"PUKE MAN!"
BLORT!
"POWER PLUMBER"
HELLO, BOYS.
"THE PINK TACO!"
"VIBRATO!"
EEEEE
OOK!
"DEVIL MONKEY!"
"CLAUDE BALLS-- DINOSAUR HUNTER!"
"LORD STONECOCK!"
OH DEAR...
"SKIDMARK!"
"ARTILLERY MAN!"
"CONE MASTER!"
"THE HUMAN STAIN!"

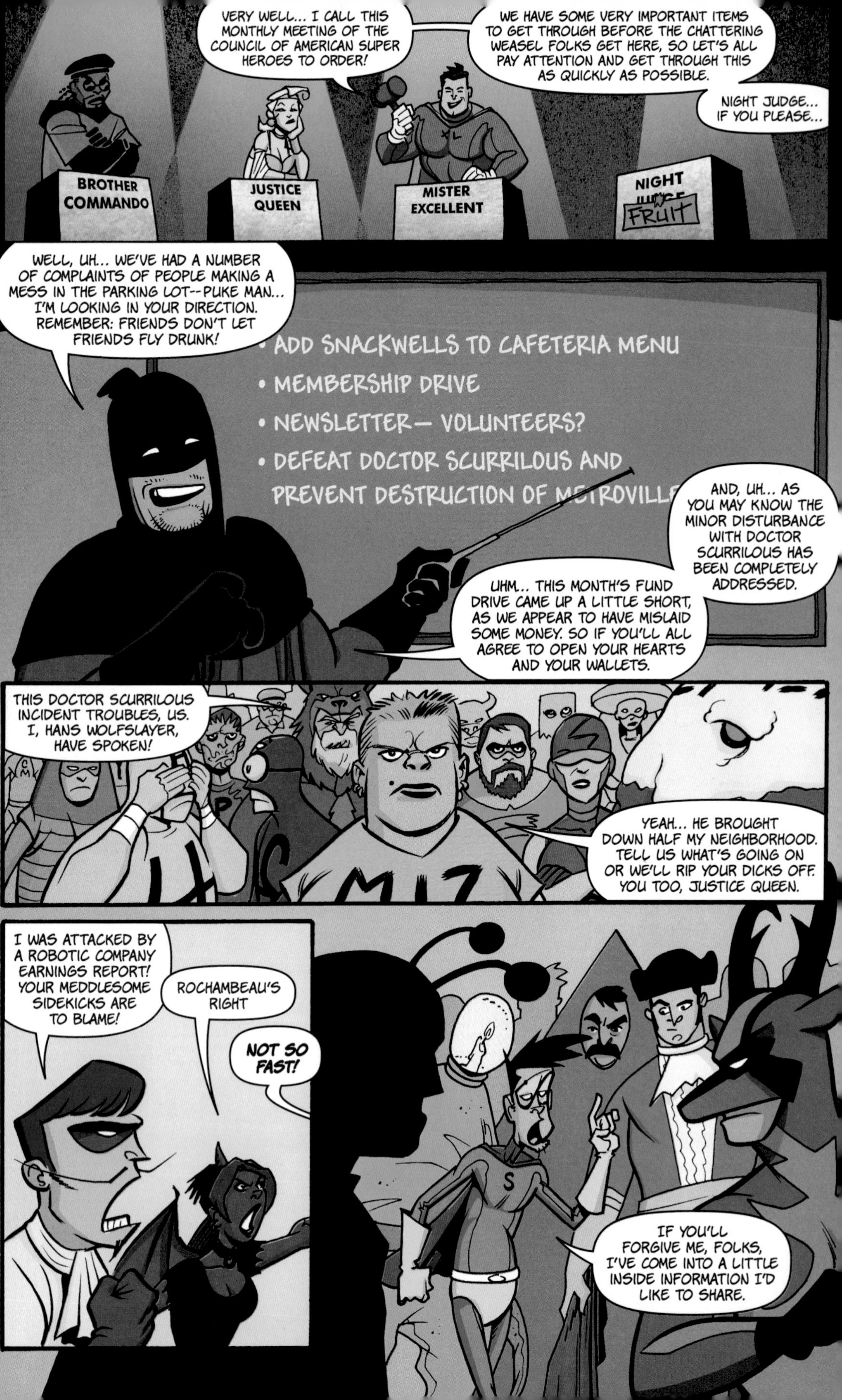
VERY WELL... I CALL THIS MONTHLY MEETING OF THE COUNCIL OF AMERICAN SUPER HEROES TO ORDER!
WE HAVE SOME VERY IMPORTANT ITEMS TO GET THROUGH BEFORE THE CHATTERING WEASEL FOLKS GET HERE, SO LET'S ALL PAY ATTENTION AND GET THROUGH THIS AS QUICKLY AS POSSIBLE.
NIGHT JUDGE... IF YOU PLEASE...
BROTHER COMMANDO
JUSTICE QUEEN
MISTER EXCELLENT
NIGHT FRUIT
WELL, UH... WE'VE HAD A NUMBER OF COMPLAINTS OF PEOPLE MAKING A MESS IN THE PARKING LOT--PUKE MAN... I'M LOOKING IN YOUR DIRECTION. REMEMBER: FRIENDS DON'T LET FRIENDS FLY DRUNK!
• ADD SNACKWELLS TO CAFETERIA MENU
• MEMBERSHIP DRIVE
• NEWSLETTER— VOLUNTEERS?
• DEFEAT DOCTOR SCURRILOUS AND PREVENT DESTRUCTION OF METROVILLE
UHM... THIS MONTH'S FUND DRIVE CAME UP A LITTLE SHORT, AS WE APPEAR TO HAVE MISLAID SOME MONEY. SO IF YOU'LL ALL AGREE TO OPEN YOUR HEARTS AND YOUR WALLETS.
AND, UH... AS YOU MAY KNOW THE MINOR DISTURBANCE WITH DOCTOR SCURRILOUS HAS BEEN COMPLETELY ADDRESSED.
THIS DOCTOR SCURRILOUS INCIDENT TROUBLES, US. I, HANS WOLFSLAYER, HAVE SPOKEN!
YEAH... HE BROUGHT DOWN HALF MY NEIGHBORHOOD. TELL US WHAT'S GOING ON OR WE'LL RIP YOUR DICKS OFF. YOU TOO, JUSTICE QUEEN.
I WAS ATTACKED BY A ROBOTIC COMPANY EARNINGS REPORT! YOUR MEDDLESOME SIDEKICKS ARE TO BLAME!
ROCHAMBEAU'S RIGHT
NOT SO FAST!
IF YOU'LL FORGIVE ME, FOLKS, I'VE COME INTO A LITTLE INSIDE INFORMATION I'D LIKE TO SHARE.

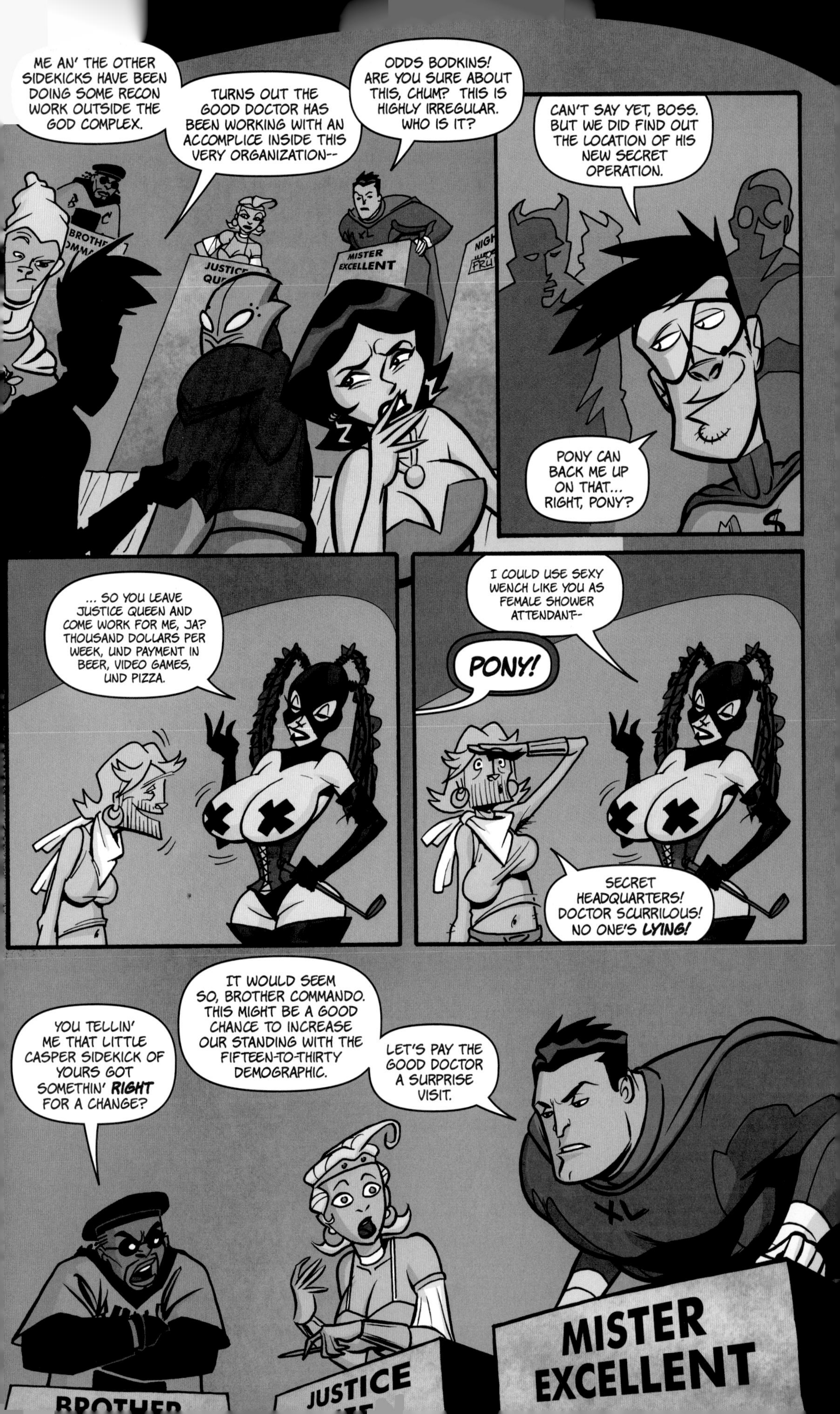
ME AN' THE OTHER SIDEKICKS HAVE BEEN DOING SOME RECON WORK OUTSIDE THE GOD COMPLEX.
TURNS OUT THE GOOD DOCTOR HAS BEEN WORKING WITH AN ACCOMPLICE INSIDE THIS VERY ORGANIZATION--
ODDS BODKINS! ARE YOU SURE ABOUT THIS, CHUM? THIS IS HIGHLY IRREGULAR. WHO IS IT?
BROTHER COMMANDO
JUSTICE QUEEN
MISTER EXCELLENT
CAN'T SAY YET, BOSS. BUT WE DID FIND OUT THE LOCATION OF HIS NEW SECRET OPERATION.
PONY CAN BACK ME UP ON THAT... RIGHT, PONY?
... SO YOU LEAVE JUSTICE QUEEN AND COME WORK FOR ME, JA? THOUSAND DOLLARS PER WEEK, UND PAYMENT IN BEER, VIDEO GAMES, UND PIZZA.
I COULD USE SEXY WENCH LIKE YOU AS FEMALE SHOWER ATTENDANT-
PONY!
SECRET HEADQUARTERS! DOCTOR SCURRILOUS! NO ONE'S LYING!
YOU TELLIN' ME THAT LITTLE CASPER SIDEKICK OF YOURS GOT SOMETHIN' RIGHT FOR A CHANGE?
IT WOULD SEEM SO, BROTHER COMMANDO. THIS MIGHT BE A GOOD CHANCE TO INCREASE OUR STANDING WITH THE FIFTEEN-TO-THIRTY DEMOGRAPHIC.
LET'S PAY THE GOOD DOCTOR A SURPRISE VISIT.
JUSTICE
MISTER EXCELLENT

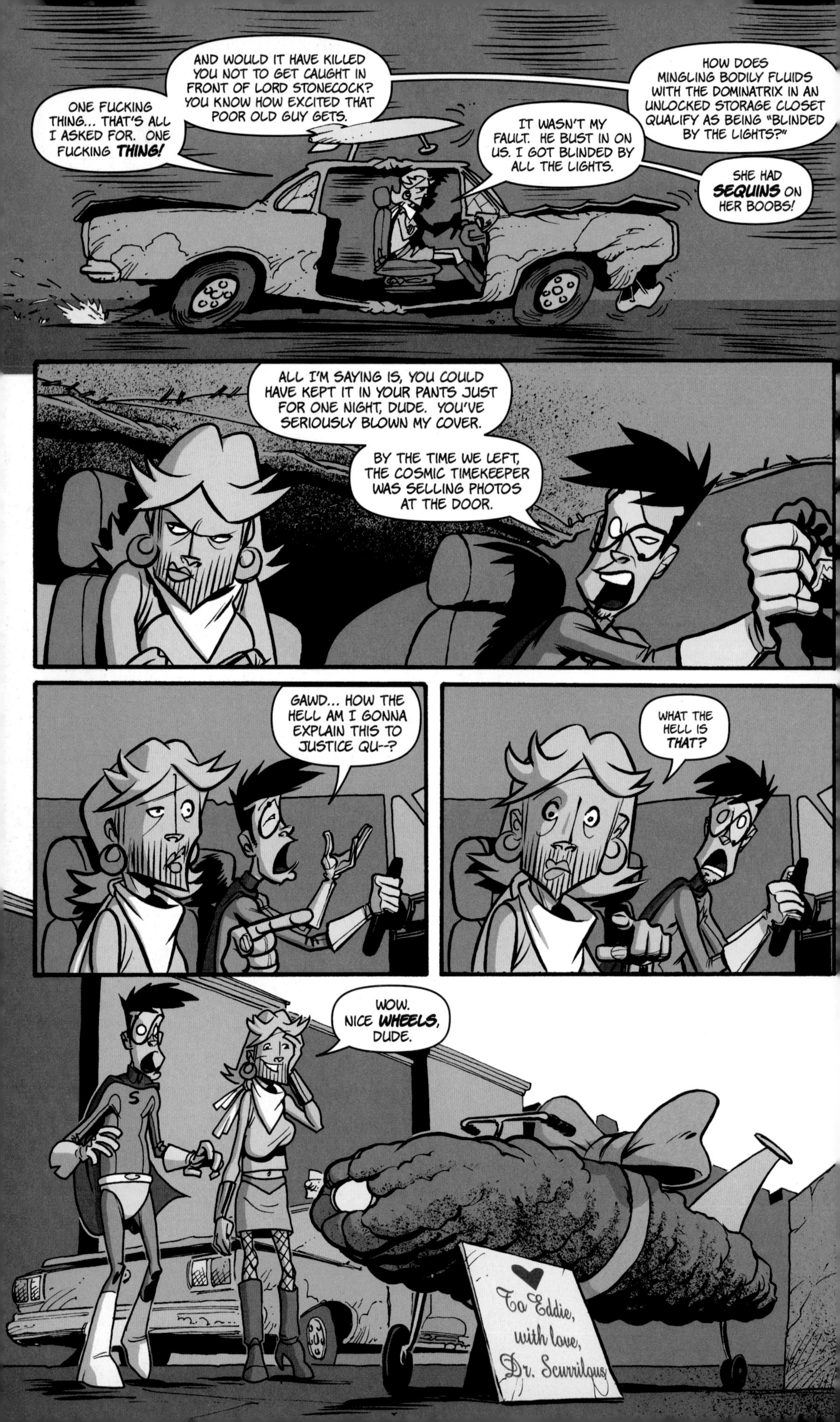
ONE FUCKING THING... THAT'S ALL I ASKED FOR. ONE FUCKING **THING!**
AND WOULD IT HAVE KILLED YOU NOT TO GET CAUGHT IN FRONT OF LORD STONECOCK? YOU KNOW HOW EXCITED THAT POOR OLD GUY GETS.
IT WASN'T MY FAULT. HE BUST IN ON US. I GOT BLINDED BY ALL THE LIGHTS.
HOW DOES MINGLING BODILY FLUIDS WITH THE DOMINATRIX IN AN UNLOCKED STORAGE CLOSET QUALIFY AS BEING "BLINDED BY THE LIGHTS?"
SHE HAD **SEQUINS** ON HER BOOBS!
ALL I'M SAYING IS, YOU COULD HAVE KEPT IT IN YOUR PANTS JUST FOR ONE NIGHT, DUDE. YOU'VE SERIOUSLY BLOWN MY COVER.
BY THE TIME WE LEFT, THE COSMIC TIMEKEEPER WAS SELLING PHOTOS AT THE DOOR.
GAWD... HOW THE HELL AM I GONNA EXPLAIN THIS TO JUSTICE QU--?
WHAT THE HELL IS **THAT?**
WOW. NICE **WHEELS**, DUDE.
To Eddie, with love, Dr. Scurrilous

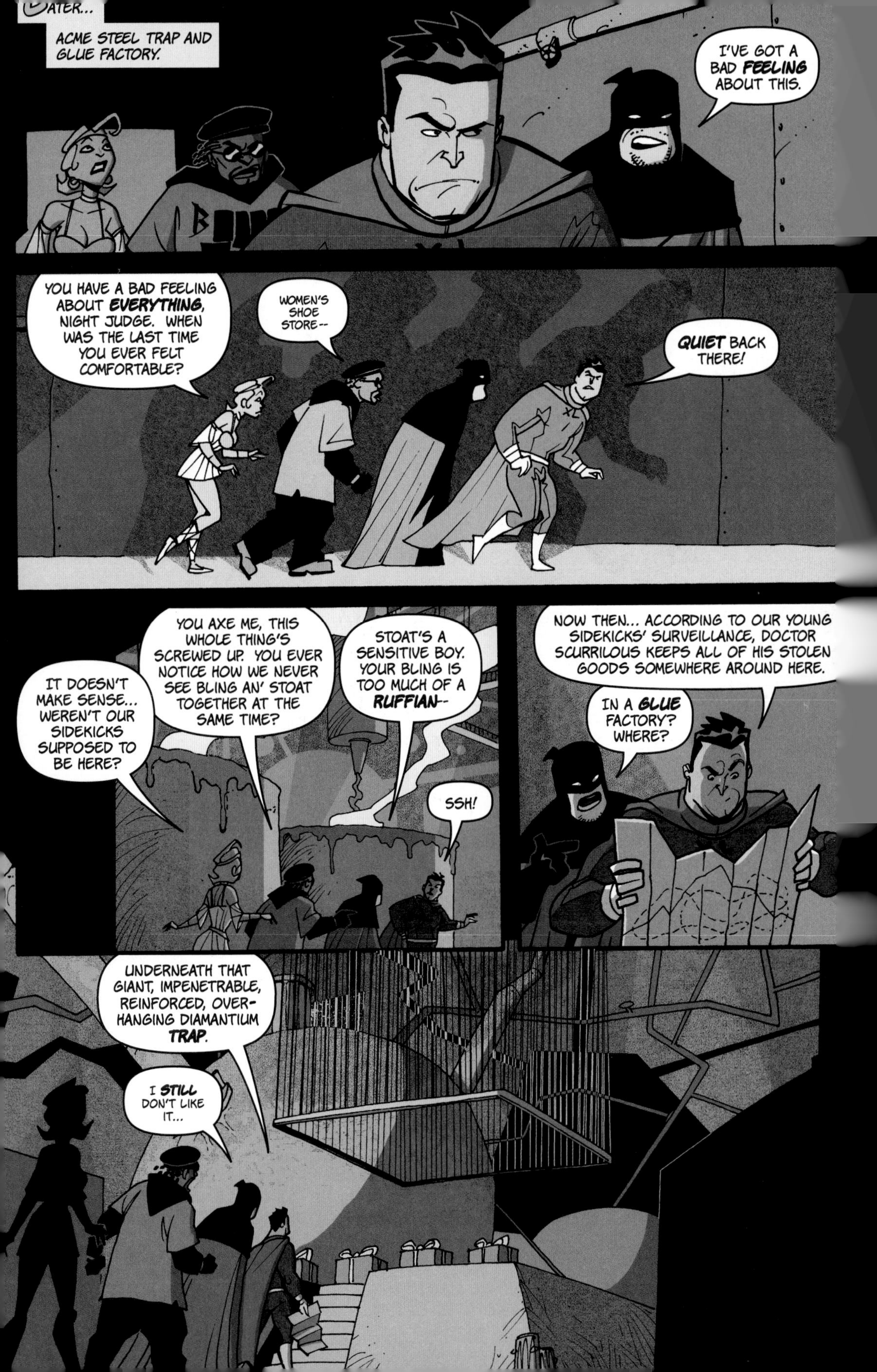
LATER...
ACME STEEL TRAP AND GLUE FACTORY.
I'VE GOT A BAD **FEELING** ABOUT THIS.
YOU HAVE A BAD FEELING ABOUT **EVERYTHING**, NIGHT JUDGE. WHEN WAS THE LAST TIME YOU EVER FELT COMFORTABLE?
WOMEN'S SHOE STORE--
QUIET BACK THERE!
IT DOESN'T MAKE SENSE... WEREN'T OUR SIDEKICKS SUPPOSED TO BE HERE?
YOU AXE ME, THIS WHOLE THING'S SCREWED UP. YOU EVER NOTICE HOW WE NEVER SEE BLING AN' STOAT TOGETHER AT THE SAME TIME?
STOAT'S A SENSITIVE BOY. YOUR BLING IS TOO MUCH OF A **RUFFIAN**--
SSH!
NOW THEN... ACCORDING TO OUR YOUNG SIDEKICKS' SURVEILLANCE, DOCTOR SCURRILOUS KEEPS ALL OF HIS STOLEN GOODS SOMEWHERE AROUND HERE.
IN A **GLUE** FACTORY? WHERE?
UNDERNEATH THAT GIANT, IMPENETRABLE, REINFORCED, OVER-HANGING DIAMANTIUM **TRAP**.
I **STILL** DON'T LIKE IT...

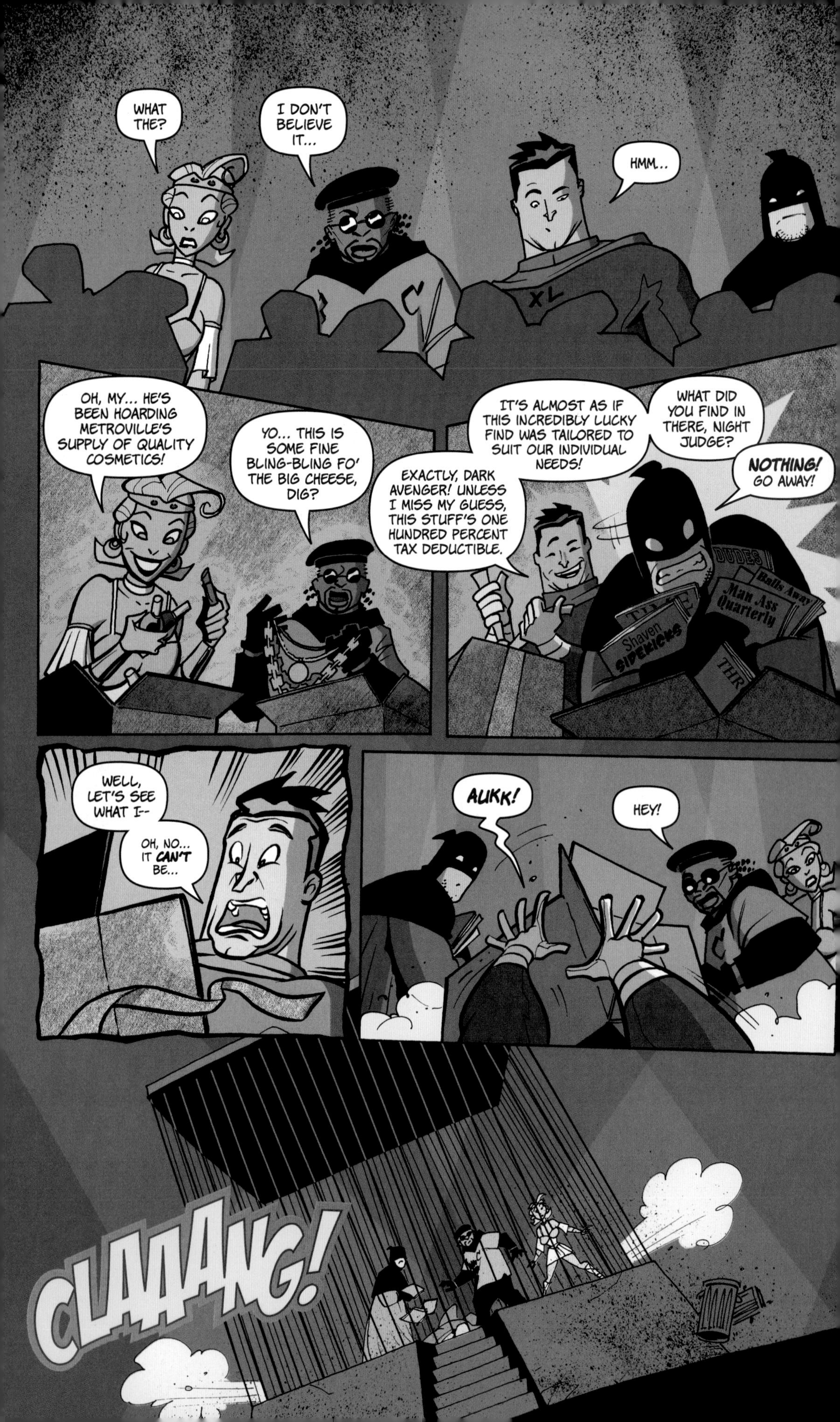
WHAT THE?
I DON'T BELIEVE IT...
HMM...
OH, MY... HE'S BEEN HOARDING METROVILLE'S SUPPLY OF QUALITY COSMETICS!
YO... THIS IS SOME FINE BLING-BLING FO' THE BIG CHEESE, DIG?
IT'S ALMOST AS IF THIS INCREDIBLY LUCKY FIND WAS TAILORED TO SUIT OUR INDIVIDUAL NEEDS!
EXACTLY, DARK AVENGER! UNLESS I MISS MY GUESS, THIS STUFF'S ONE HUNDRED PERCENT TAX DEDUCTIBLE.
WHAT DID YOU FIND IN THERE, NIGHT JUDGE?
NOTHING! GO AWAY!
DUDES
Balls Away
Man Ass Quarterly
Shaven SIDEKICKS
WELL, LET'S SEE WHAT I--
OH, NO... IT CAN'T BE...
AUKK!
HEY!
CLAAANG!

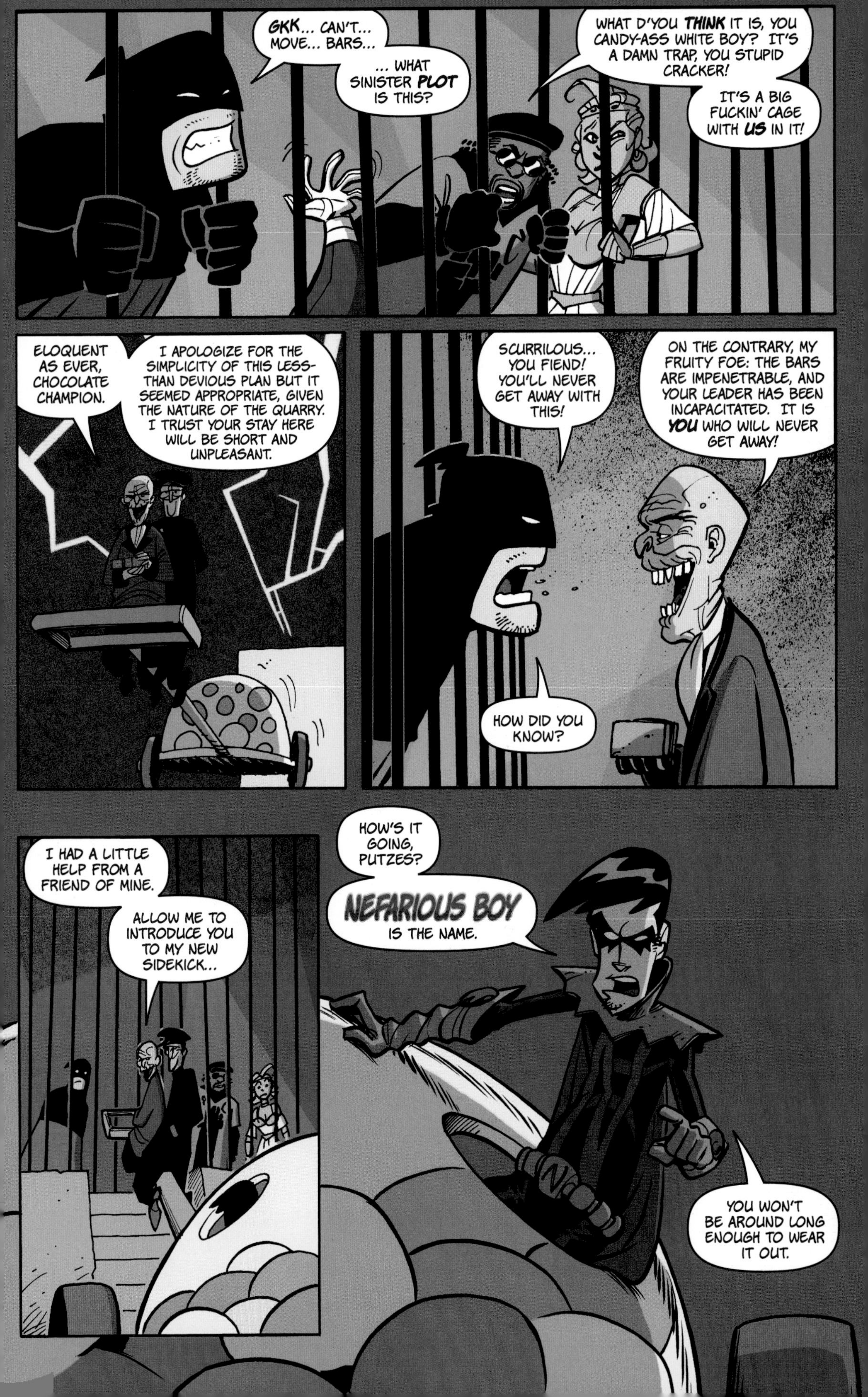
GKK... CAN'T... MOVE... BARS...
... WHAT SINISTER PLOT IS THIS?
WHAT D'YOU THINK IT IS, YOU CANDY-ASS WHITE BOY? IT'S A DAMN TRAP, YOU STUPID CRACKER!
IT'S A BIG FUCKIN' CAGE WITH US IN IT!
ELOQUENT AS EVER, CHOCOLATE CHAMPION.
I APOLOGIZE FOR THE SIMPLICITY OF THIS LESS-THAN DEVIOUS PLAN BUT IT SEEMED APPROPRIATE, GIVEN THE NATURE OF THE QUARRY. I TRUST YOUR STAY HERE WILL BE SHORT AND UNPLEASANT.
SCURRILOUS... YOU FIEND! YOU'LL NEVER GET AWAY WITH THIS!
ON THE CONTRARY, MY FRUITY FOE: THE BARS ARE IMPENETRABLE, AND YOUR LEADER HAS BEEN INCAPACITATED. IT IS YOU WHO WILL NEVER GET AWAY!
HOW DID YOU KNOW?
I HAD A LITTLE HELP FROM A FRIEND OF MINE.
ALLOW ME TO INTRODUCE YOU TO MY NEW SIDEKICK...
HOW'S IT GOING, PUTZES?
NEFARIOUS BOY IS THE NAME.
YOU WON'T BE AROUND LONG ENOUGH TO WEAR IT OUT.

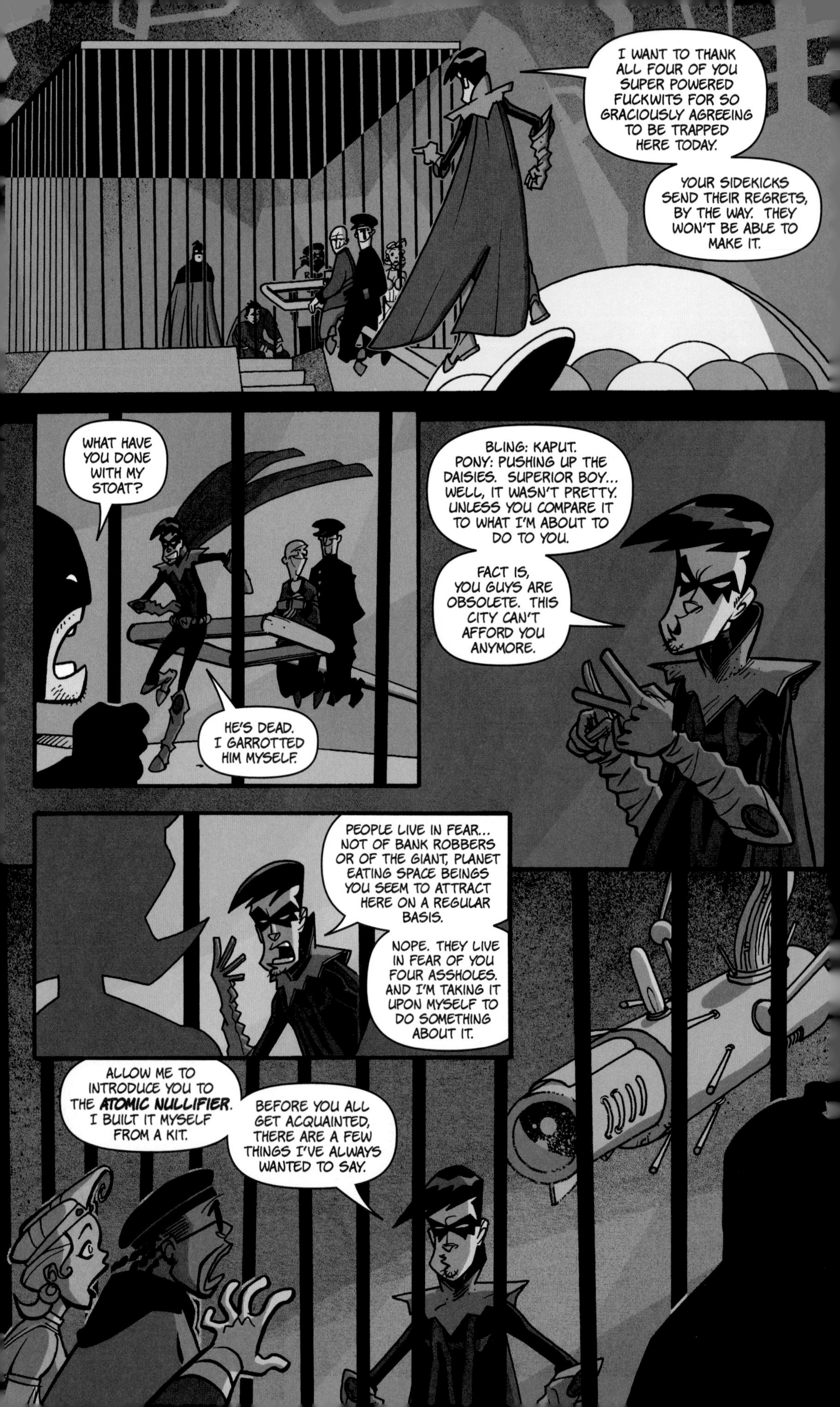
I WANT TO THANK ALL FOUR OF YOU SUPER POWERED FUCKWITS FOR SO GRACIOUSLY AGREEING TO BE TRAPPED HERE TODAY.
YOUR SIDEKICKS SEND THEIR REGRETS, BY THE WAY. THEY WON'T BE ABLE TO MAKE IT.
WHAT HAVE YOU DONE WITH MY STOAT?
HE'S DEAD. I GARROTTED HIM MYSELF.
BLING: KAPUT. PONY: PUSHING UP THE DAISIES. SUPERIOR BOY... WELL, IT WASN'T PRETTY. UNLESS YOU COMPARE IT TO WHAT I'M ABOUT TO DO TO YOU.
FACT IS, YOU GUYS ARE OBSOLETE. THIS CITY CAN'T AFFORD YOU ANYMORE.
PEOPLE LIVE IN FEAR... NOT OF BANK ROBBERS OR OF THE GIANT, PLANET EATING SPACE BEINGS YOU SEEM TO ATTRACT HERE ON A REGULAR BASIS.
NOPE. THEY LIVE IN FEAR OF YOU FOUR ASSHOLES. AND I'M TAKING IT UPON MYSELF TO DO SOMETHING ABOUT IT.
ALLOW ME TO INTRODUCE YOU TO THE ATOMIC NULLIFIER. I BUILT IT MYSELF FROM A KIT.
BEFORE YOU ALL GET ACQUAINTED, THERE ARE A FEW THINGS I'VE ALWAYS WANTED TO SAY.

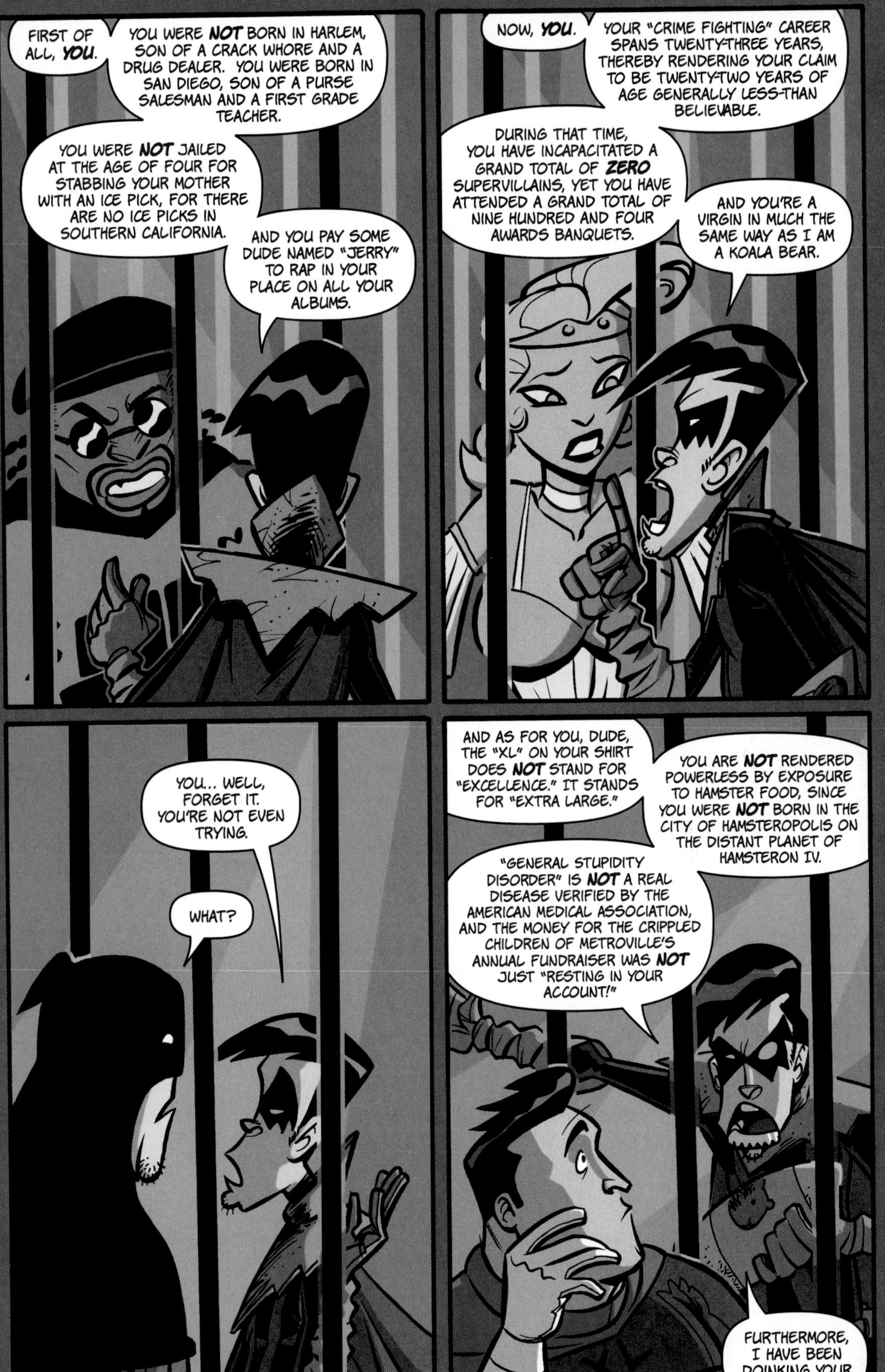
FIRST OF ALL, YOU.
YOU WERE NOT BORN IN HARLEM, SON OF A CRACK WHORE AND A DRUG DEALER. YOU WERE BORN IN SAN DIEGO, SON OF A PURSE SALESMAN AND A FIRST GRADE TEACHER.
YOU WERE NOT JAILED AT THE AGE OF FOUR FOR STABBING YOUR MOTHER WITH AN ICE PICK, FOR THERE ARE NO ICE PICKS IN SOUTHERN CALIFORNIA.
AND YOU PAY SOME DUDE NAMED "JERRY" TO RAP IN YOUR PLACE ON ALL YOUR ALBUMS.
NOW, YOU.
YOUR "CRIME FIGHTING" CAREER SPANS TWENTY-THREE YEARS, THEREBY RENDERING YOUR CLAIM TO BE TWENTY-TWO YEARS OF AGE GENERALLY LESS-THAN BELIEVABLE.
DURING THAT TIME, YOU HAVE INCAPACITATED A GRAND TOTAL OF ZERO SUPERVILLAINS, YET YOU HAVE ATTENDED A GRAND TOTAL OF NINE HUNDRED AND FOUR AWARDS BANQUETS.
AND YOU'RE A VIRGIN IN MUCH THE SAME WAY AS I AM A KOALA BEAR.
YOU... WELL, FORGET IT. YOU'RE NOT EVEN TRYING.
WHAT?
AND AS FOR YOU, DUDE, THE "XL" ON YOUR SHIRT DOES NOT STAND FOR "EXCELLENCE." IT STANDS FOR "EXTRA LARGE."
YOU ARE NOT RENDERED POWERLESS BY EXPOSURE TO HAMSTER FOOD, SINCE YOU WERE NOT BORN IN THE CITY OF HAMSTEROPOLIS ON THE DISTANT PLANET OF HAMSTERON IV.
"GENERAL STUPIDITY DISORDER" IS NOT A REAL DISEASE VERIFIED BY THE AMERICAN MEDICAL ASSOCIATION, AND THE MONEY FOR THE CRIPPLED CHILDREN OF METROVILLE'S ANNUAL FUNDRAISER WAS NOT JUST "RESTING IN YOUR ACCOUNT!"
FURTHERMORE, I HAVE BEEN DOINKING YOUR WIFE.
XL

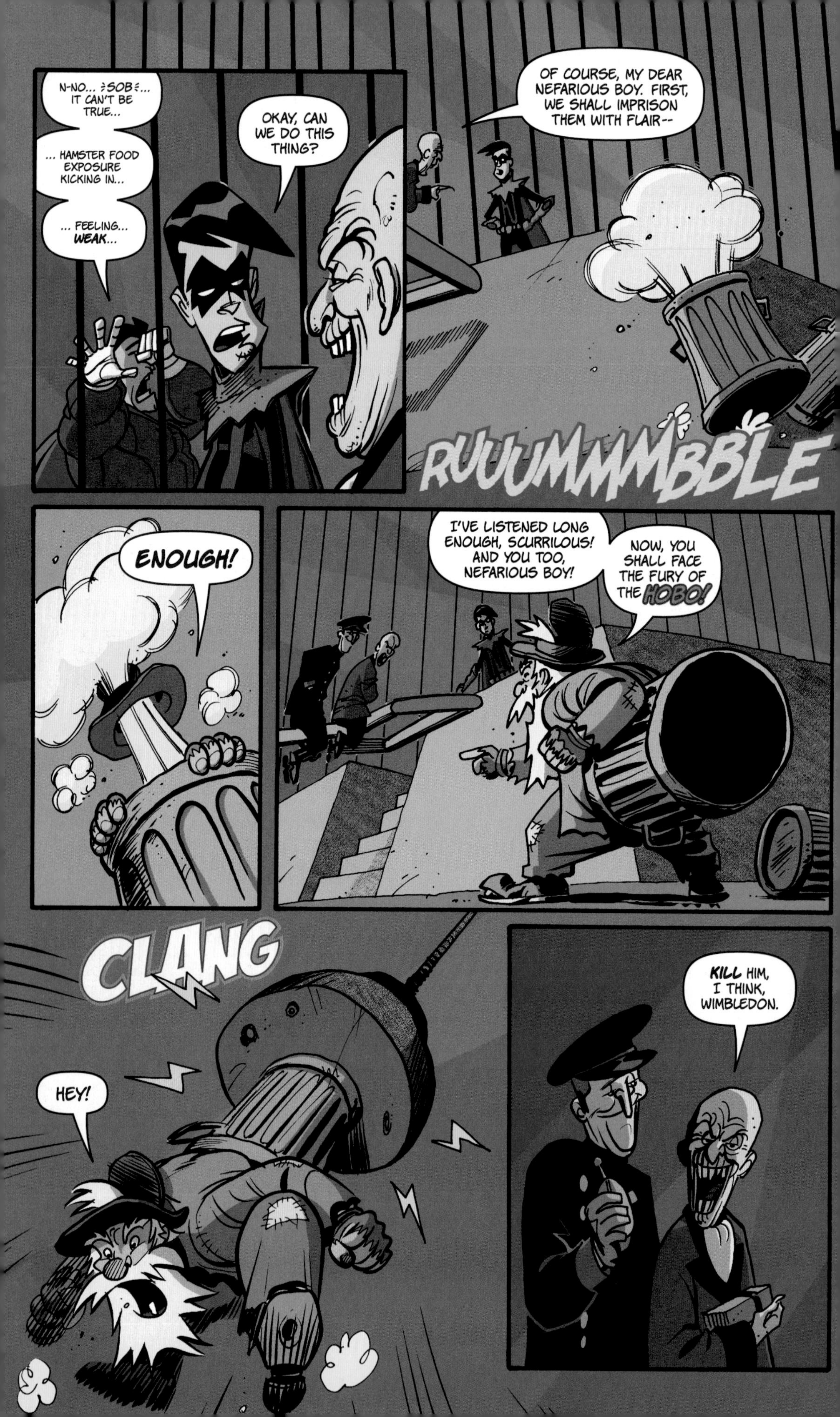
N-NO... ≷SOB≶... IT CAN'T BE TRUE...
... HAMSTER FOOD EXPOSURE KICKING IN...
... FEELING... **WEAK**...
OKAY, CAN WE DO THIS THING?
OF COURSE, MY DEAR NEFARIOUS BOY. FIRST, WE SHALL IMPRISON THEM WITH FLAIR--
RUUUMMMMBBLE
ENOUGH!
I'VE LISTENED LONG ENOUGH, SCURRILOUS! AND YOU TOO, NEFARIOUS BOY!
NOW, YOU SHALL FACE THE FURY OF THE HOBO!
CLANG
HEY!
KILL HIM, I THINK, WIMBLEDON.

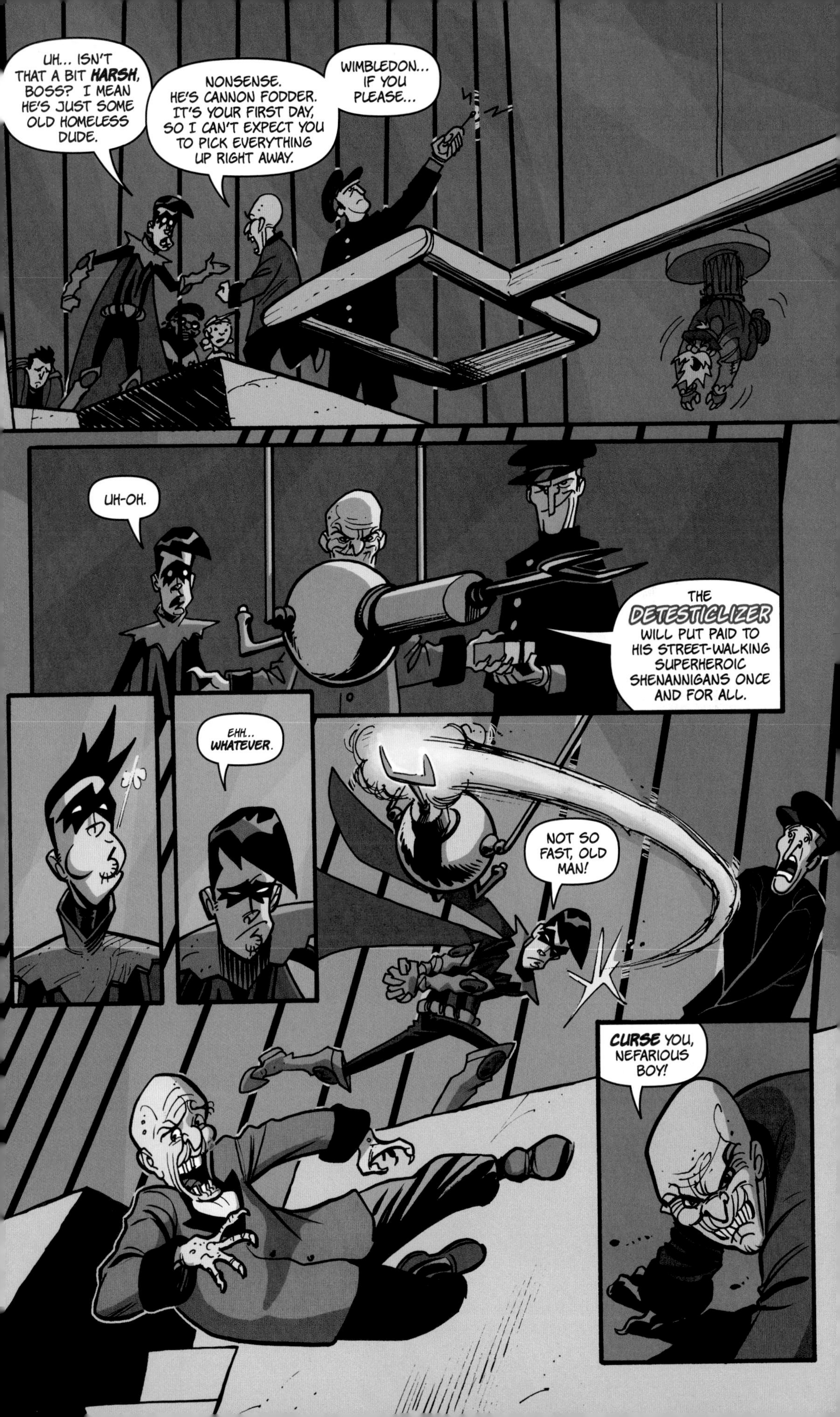
UH... ISN'T THAT A BIT HARSH, BOSS? I MEAN HE'S JUST SOME OLD HOMELESS DUDE.
NONSENSE. HE'S CANNON FODDER. IT'S YOUR FIRST DAY, SO I CAN'T EXPECT YOU TO PICK EVERYTHING UP RIGHT AWAY.
WIMBLEDON... IF YOU PLEASE...
UH-OH.
THE DETESTICLIZER WILL PUT PAID TO HIS STREET-WALKING SUPERHEROIC SHENANNIGANS ONCE AND FOR ALL.
EHH... WHATEVER.
NOT SO FAST, OLD MAN!
CURSE YOU, NEFARIOUS BOY!

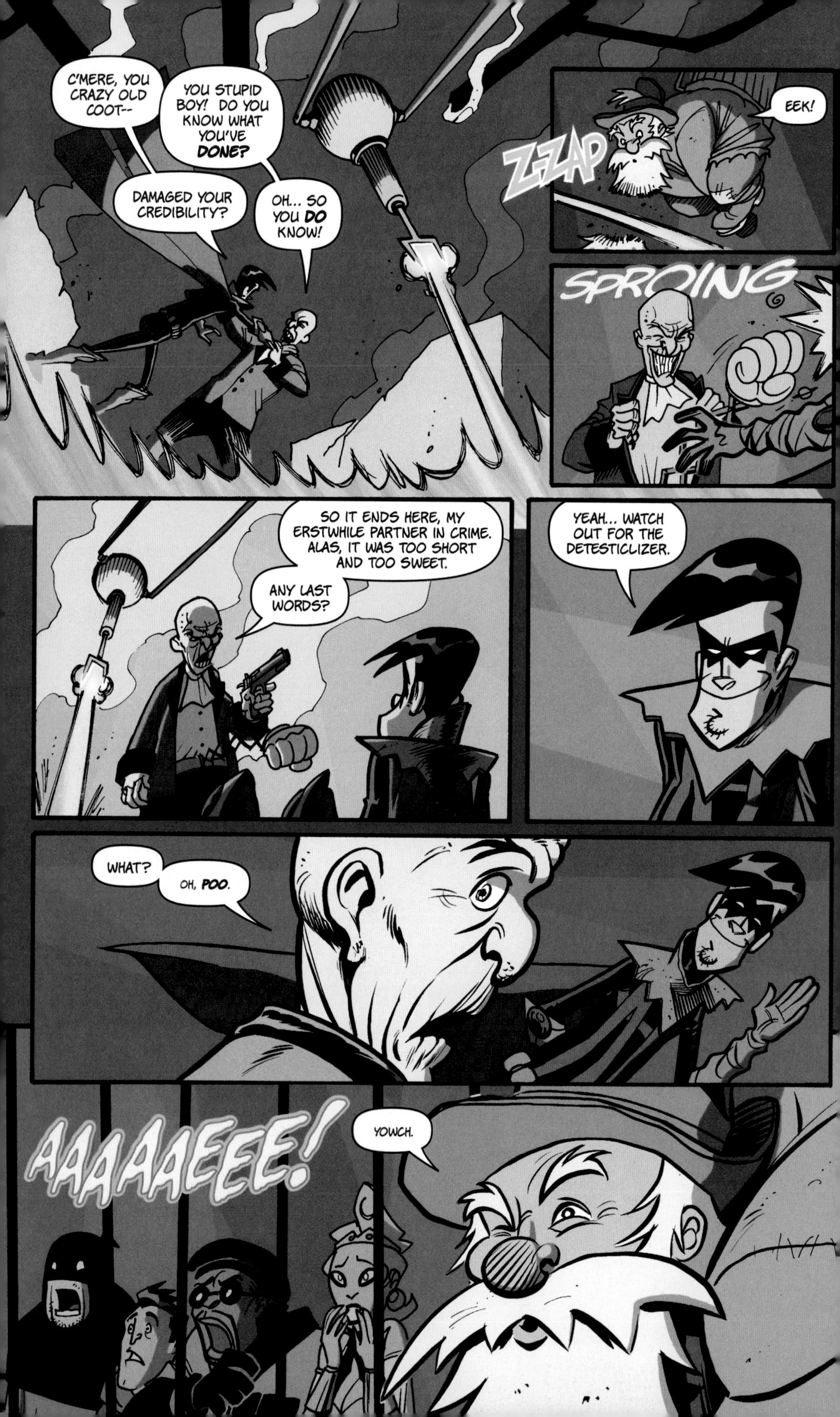
C'MERE, YOU CRAZY OLD COOT--
YOU STUPID BOY! DO YOU KNOW WHAT YOU'VE **DONE?**
DAMAGED YOUR CREDIBILITY?
OH... SO YOU **DO** KNOW!
Z-ZAP
EEK!
SPROING
SO IT ENDS HERE, MY ERSTWHILE PARTNER IN CRIME. ALAS, IT WAS TOO SHORT AND TOO SWEET.
ANY LAST WORDS?
YEAH... WATCH OUT FOR THE DETESTICLIZER.
WHAT?
OH, **POO**.
AAAAAEEE!
YOWCH.

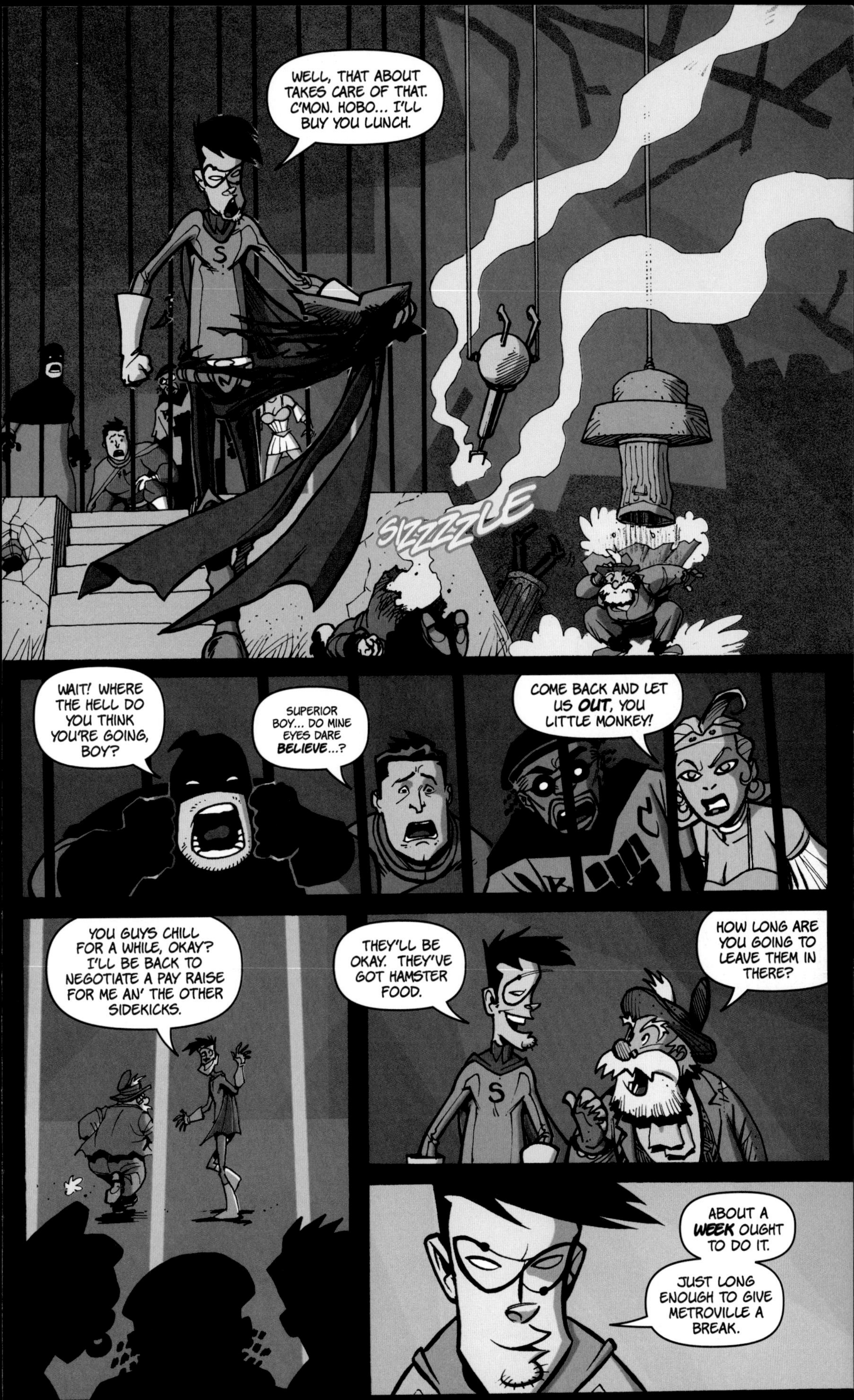
WELL, THAT ABOUT TAKES CARE OF THAT. C'MON. HOBO... I'LL BUY YOU LUNCH.
SIZZZZLE
WAIT! WHERE THE HELL DO YOU THINK YOU'RE GOING, BOY?
SUPERIOR BOY... DO MINE EYES DARE BELIEVE...?
COME BACK AND LET US OUT, YOU LITTLE MONKEY!
YOU GUYS CHILL FOR A WHILE, OKAY? I'LL BE BACK TO NEGOTIATE A PAY RAISE FOR ME AN' THE OTHER SIDEKICKS.
THEY'LL BE OKAY. THEY'VE GOT HAMSTER FOOD.
HOW LONG ARE YOU GOING TO LEAVE THEM IN THERE?
ABOUT A WEEK OUGHT TO DO IT.
JUST LONG ENOUGH TO GIVE METROVILLE A BREAK.

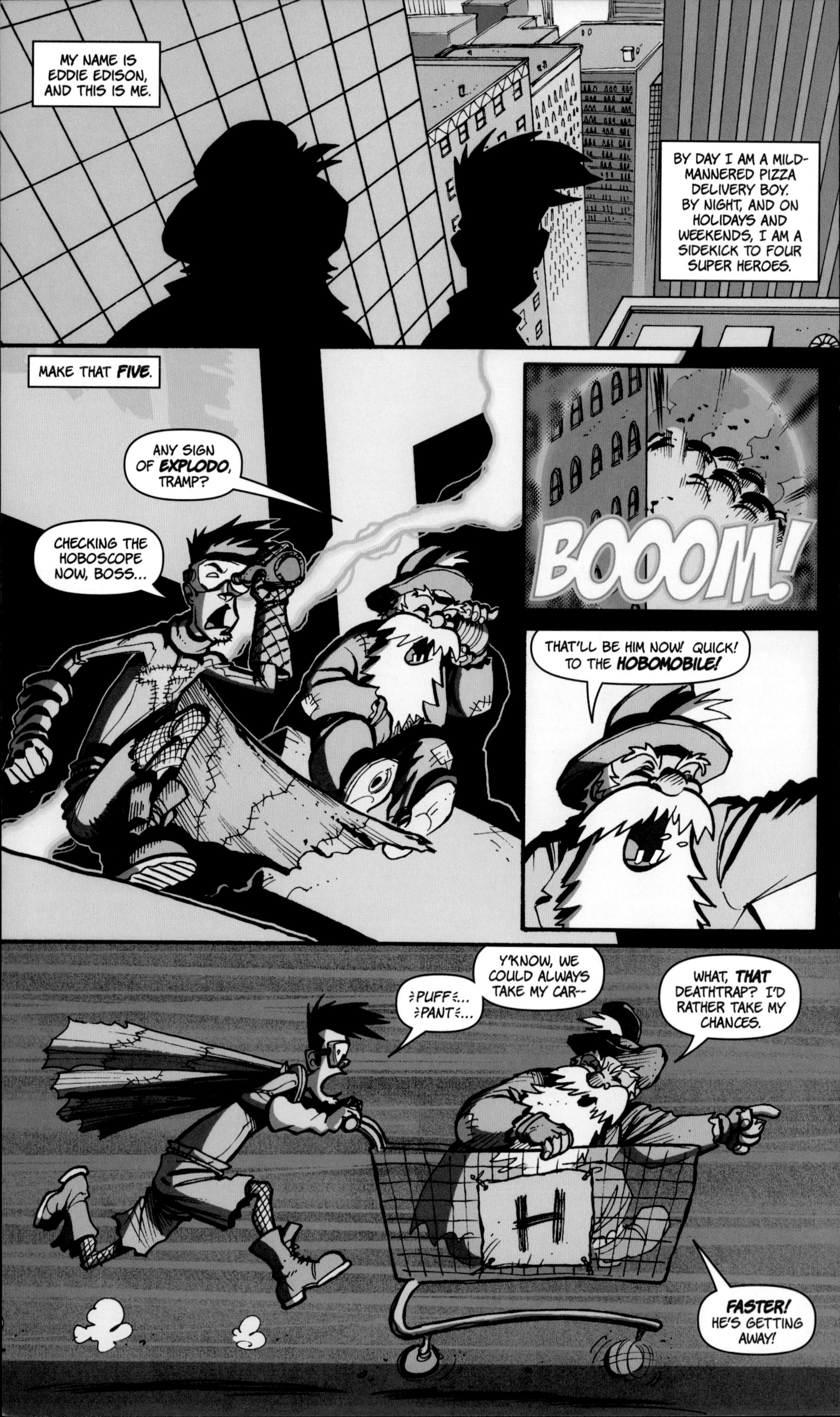
MY NAME IS EDDIE EDISON, AND THIS IS ME.
BY DAY I AM A MILD-MANNERED PIZZA DELIVERY BOY. BY NIGHT, AND ON HOLIDAYS AND WEEKENDS, I AM A SIDEKICK TO FOUR SUPER HEROES.
MAKE THAT FIVE.
ANY SIGN OF EXPLODO, TRAMP?
CHECKING THE HOBOSCOPE NOW, BOSS...
BOOOM!
THAT'LL BE HIM NOW! QUICK! TO THE HOBOMOBILE!
PUFF... PANT...
Y'KNOW, WE COULD ALWAYS TAKE MY CAR--
WHAT, THAT DEATHTRAP? I'D RATHER TAKE MY CHANCES.
H
FASTER! HE'S GETTING AWAY!

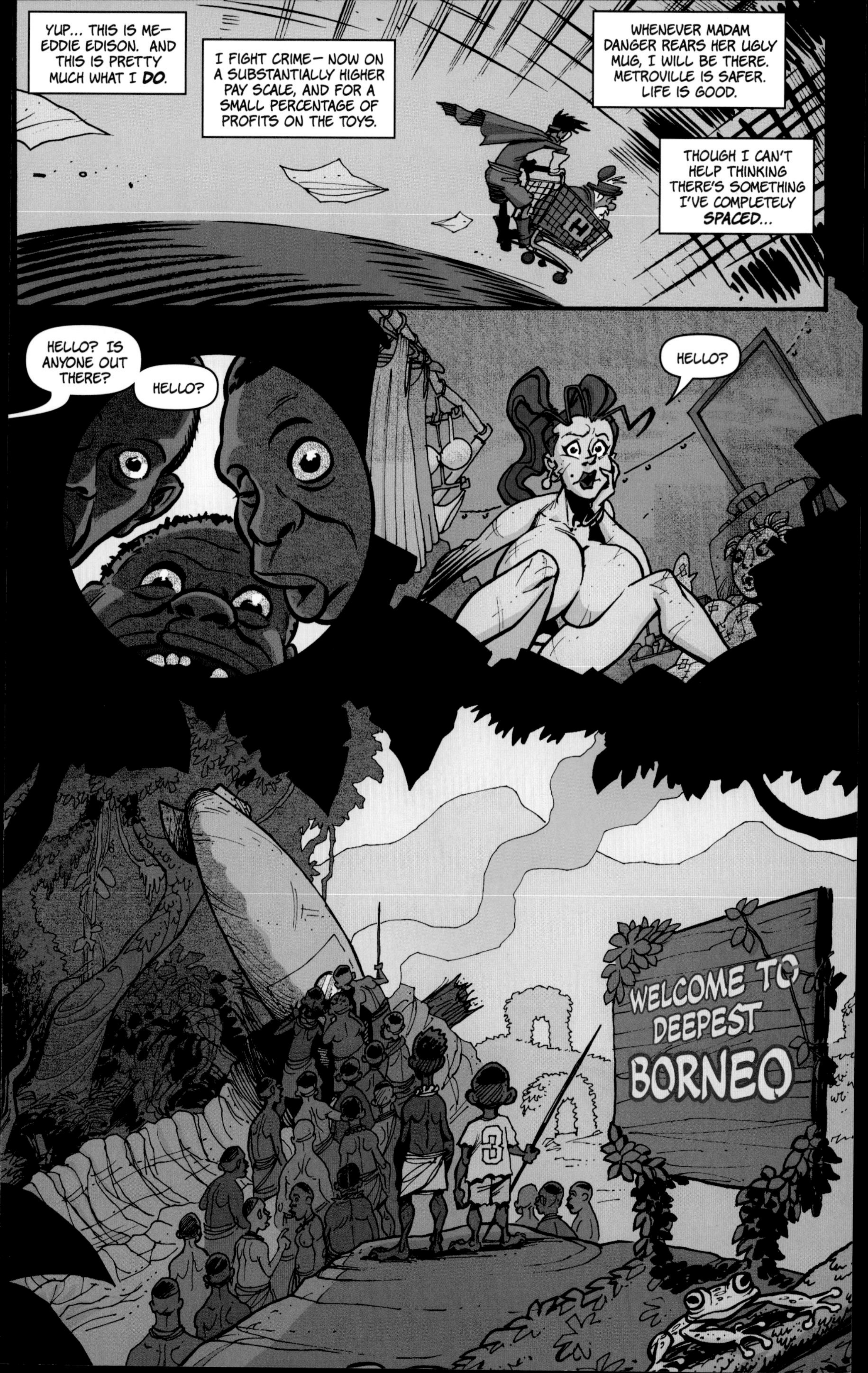
YUP... THIS IS ME— EDDIE EDISON. AND THIS IS PRETTY MUCH WHAT I DO.
I FIGHT CRIME— NOW ON A SUBSTANTIALLY HIGHER PAY SCALE, AND FOR A SMALL PERCENTAGE OF PROFITS ON THE TOYS.
WHENEVER MADAM DANGER REARS HER UGLY MUG, I WILL BE THERE. METROVILLE IS SAFER. LIFE IS GOOD.
THOUGH I CAN'T HELP THINKING THERE'S SOMETHING I'VE COMPLETELY SPACED...
H
HELLO? IS ANYONE OUT THERE?
HELLO?
HELLO?
WELCOME TO DEEPEST BORNEO
3

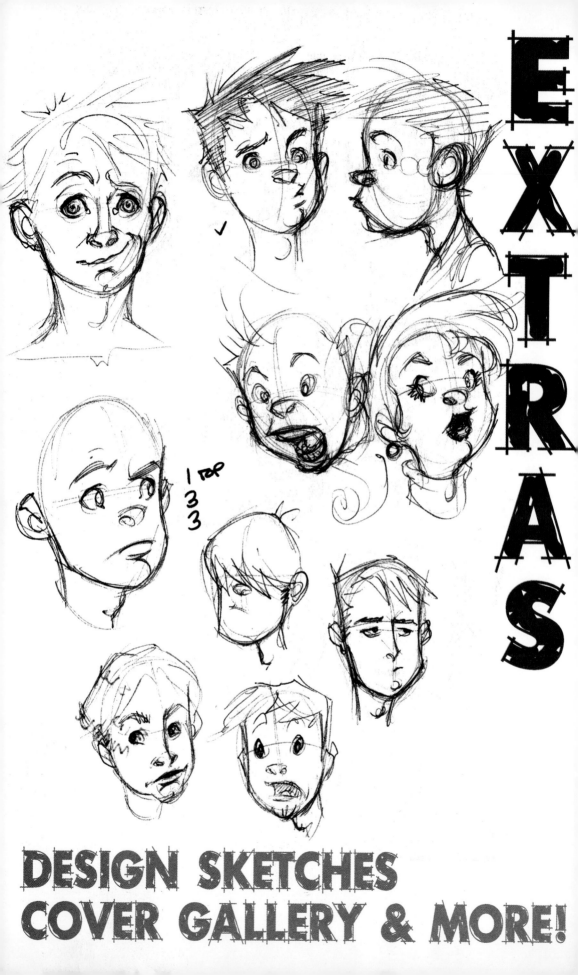

EXTRAS

DESIGN SKETCHES
COVER GALLERY & MORE!

EDDIE

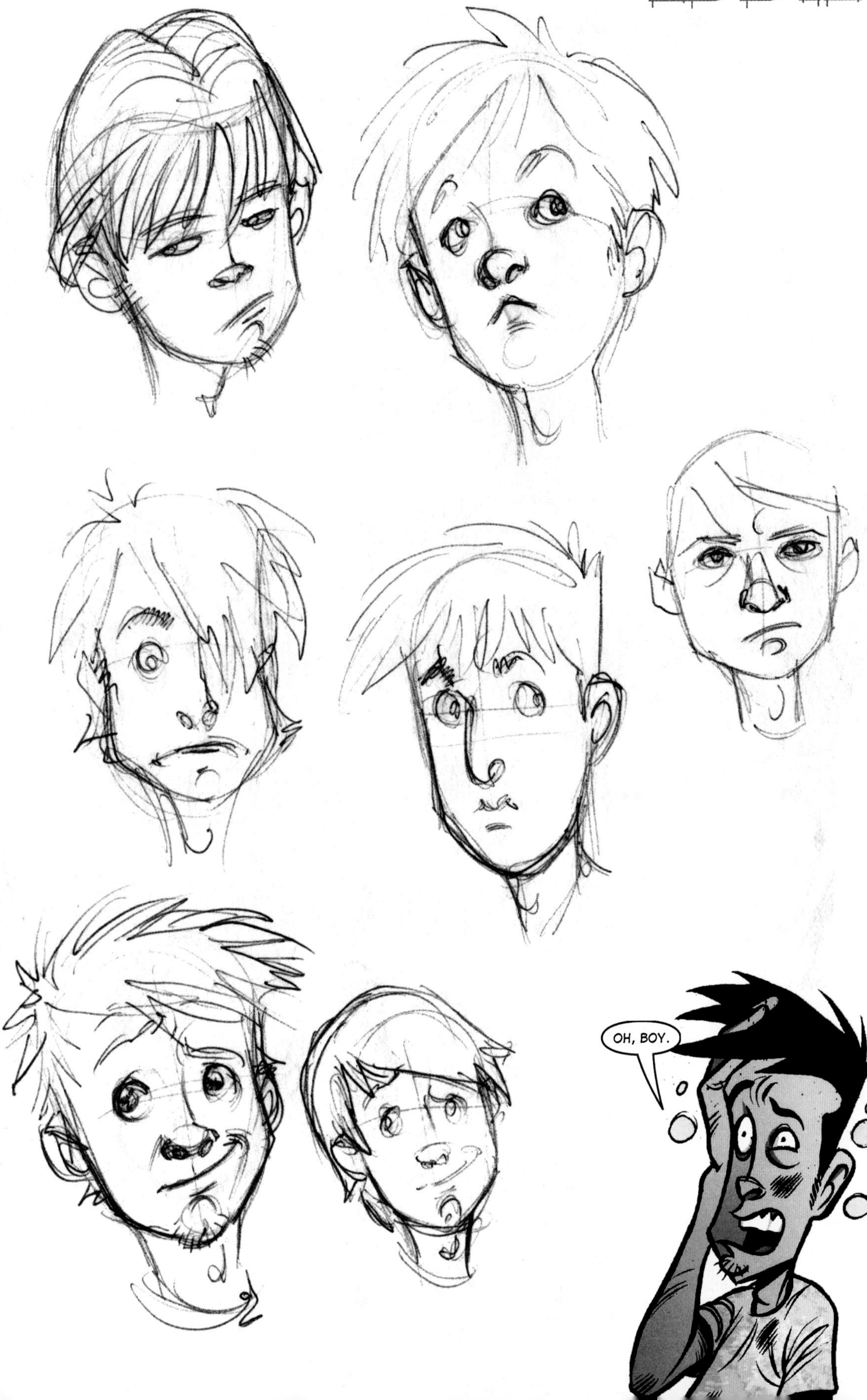
OH, BOY.

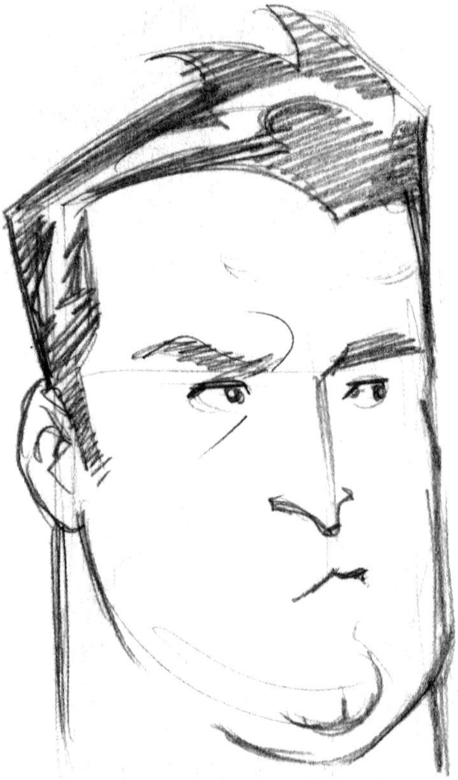

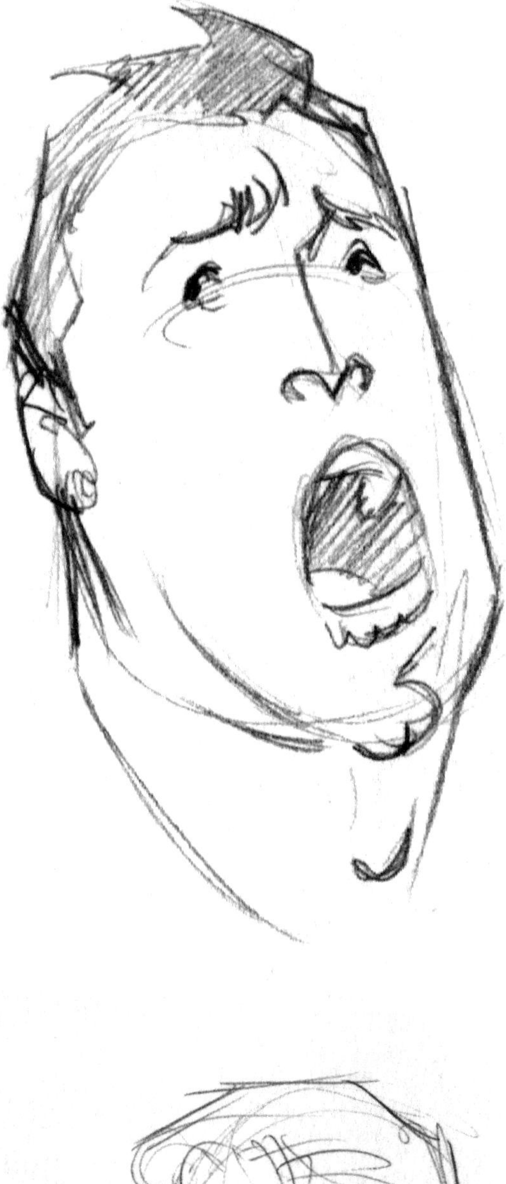

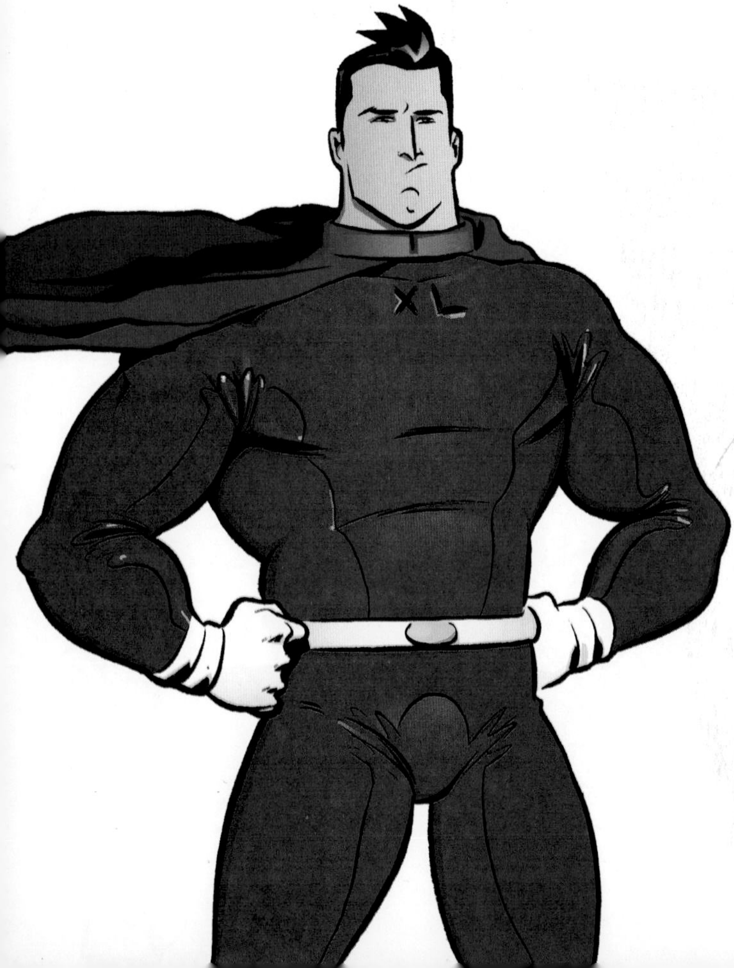
XL

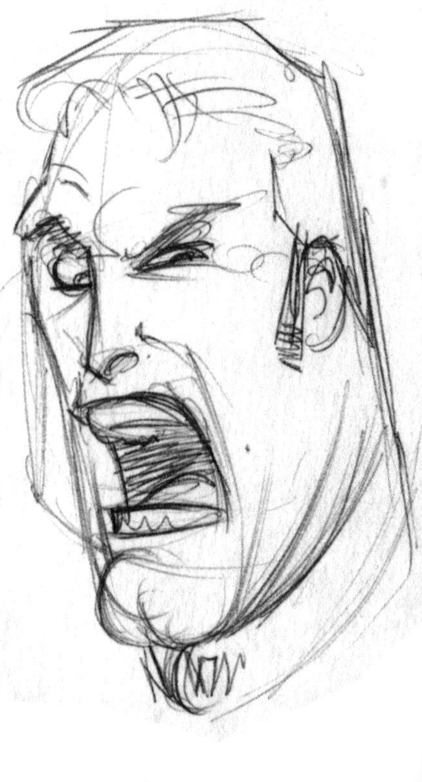

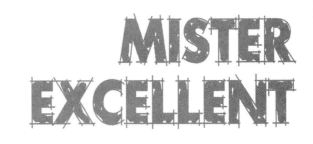

MISTER EXCELLENT

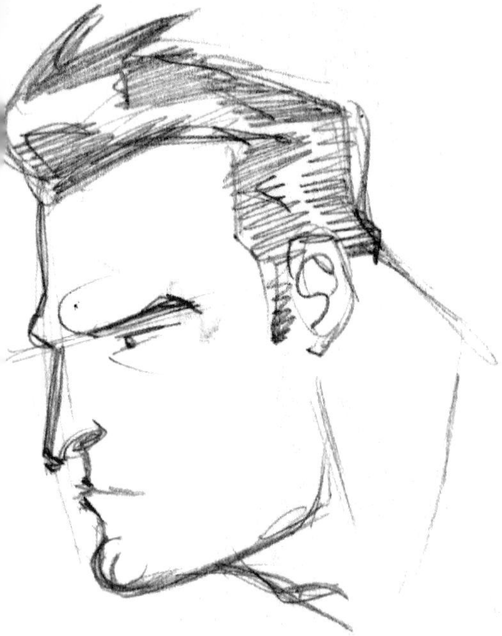

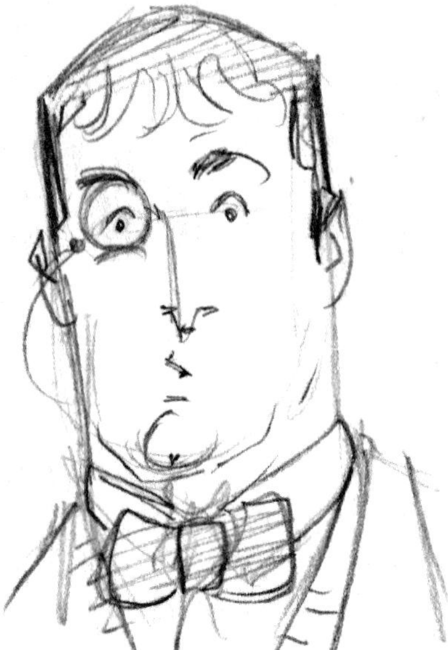

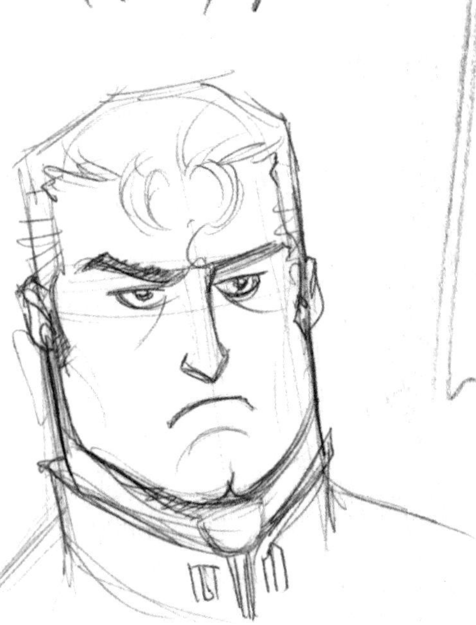

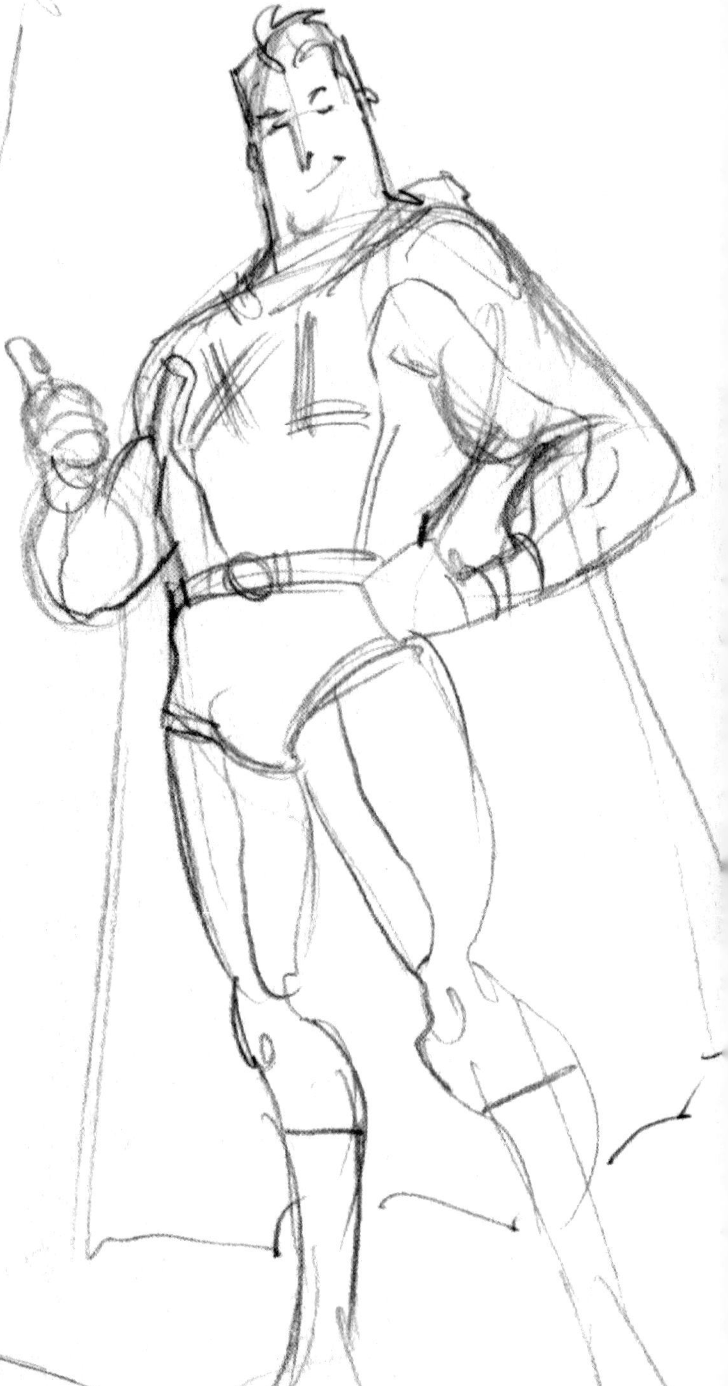

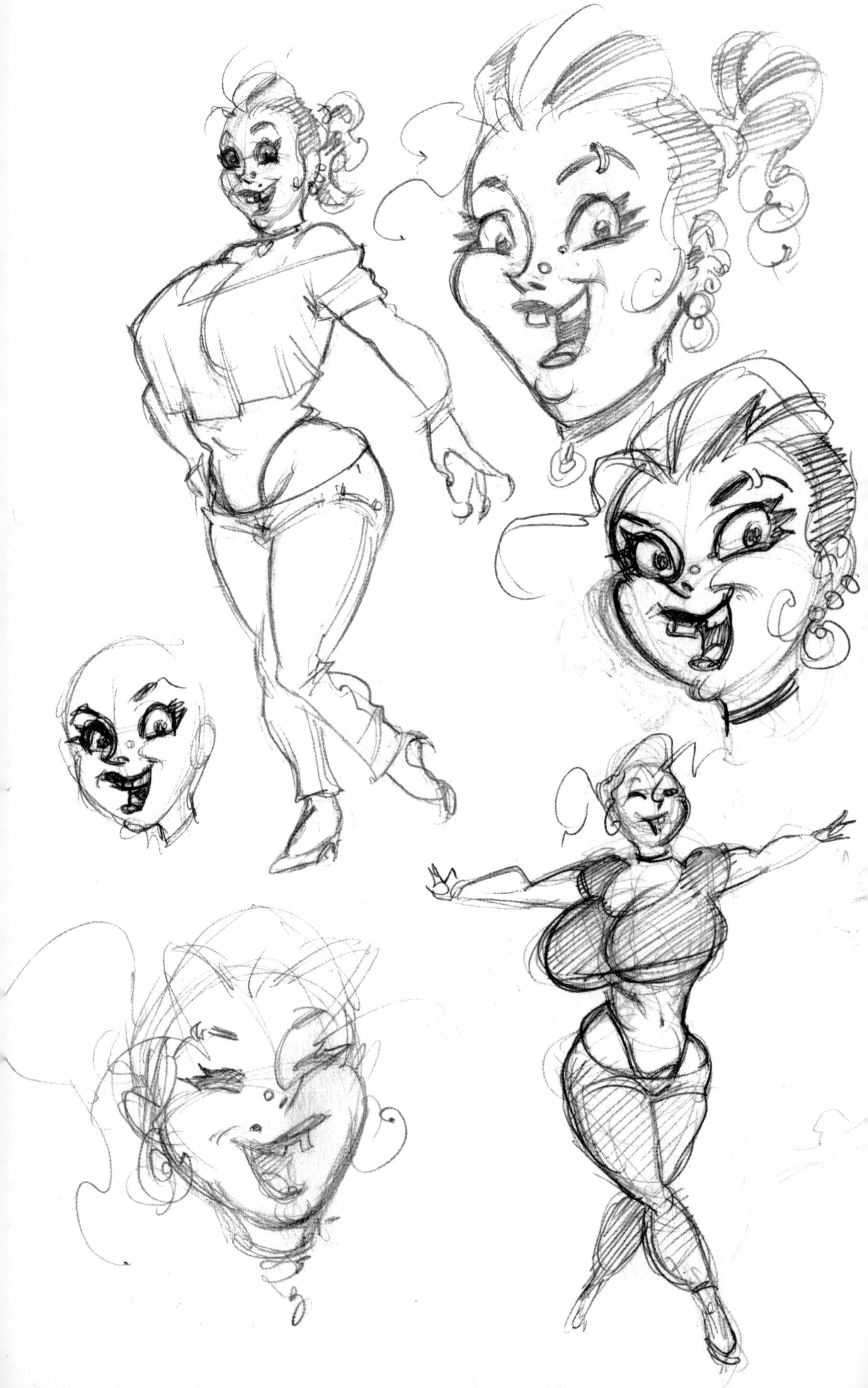

STORMY

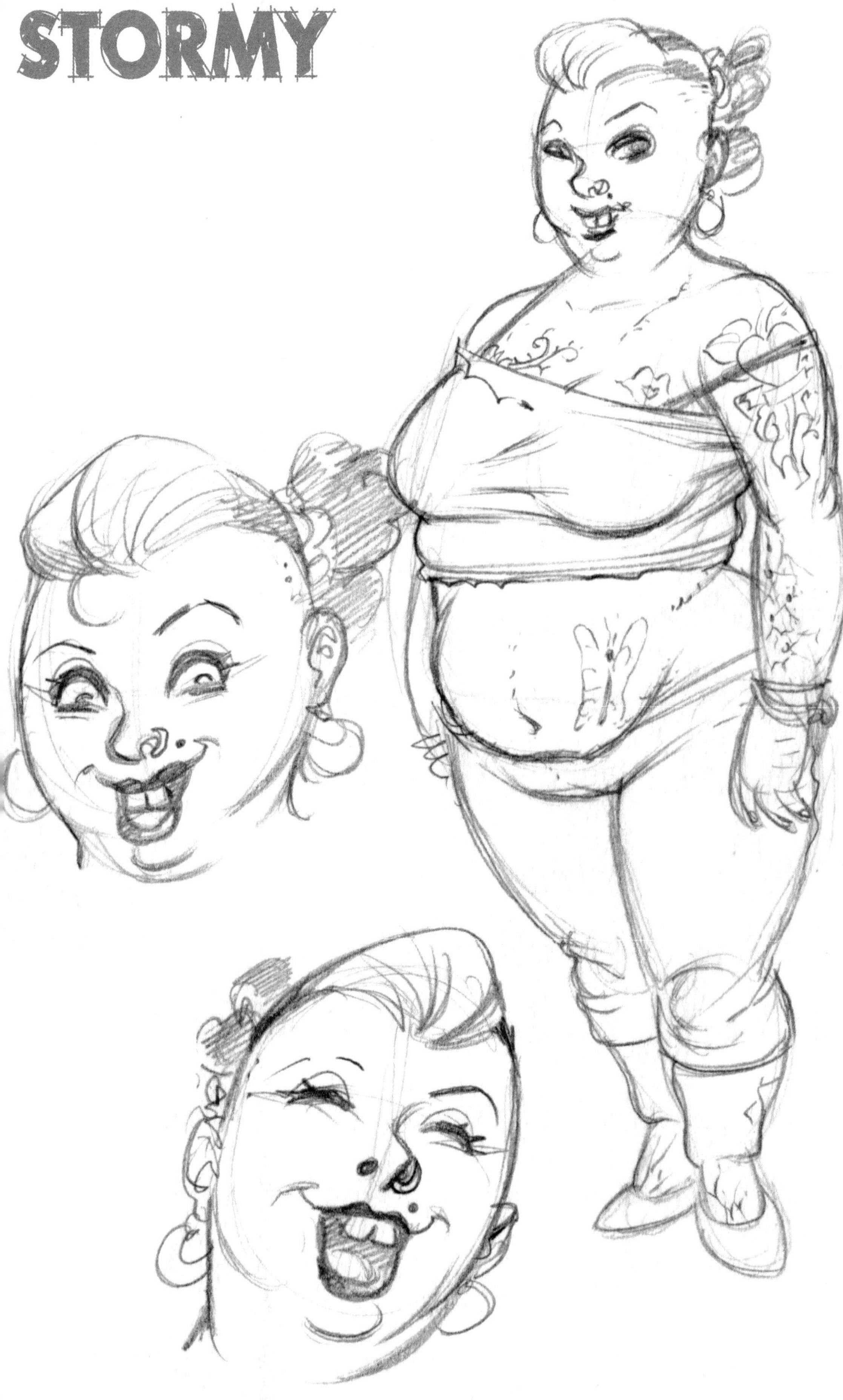

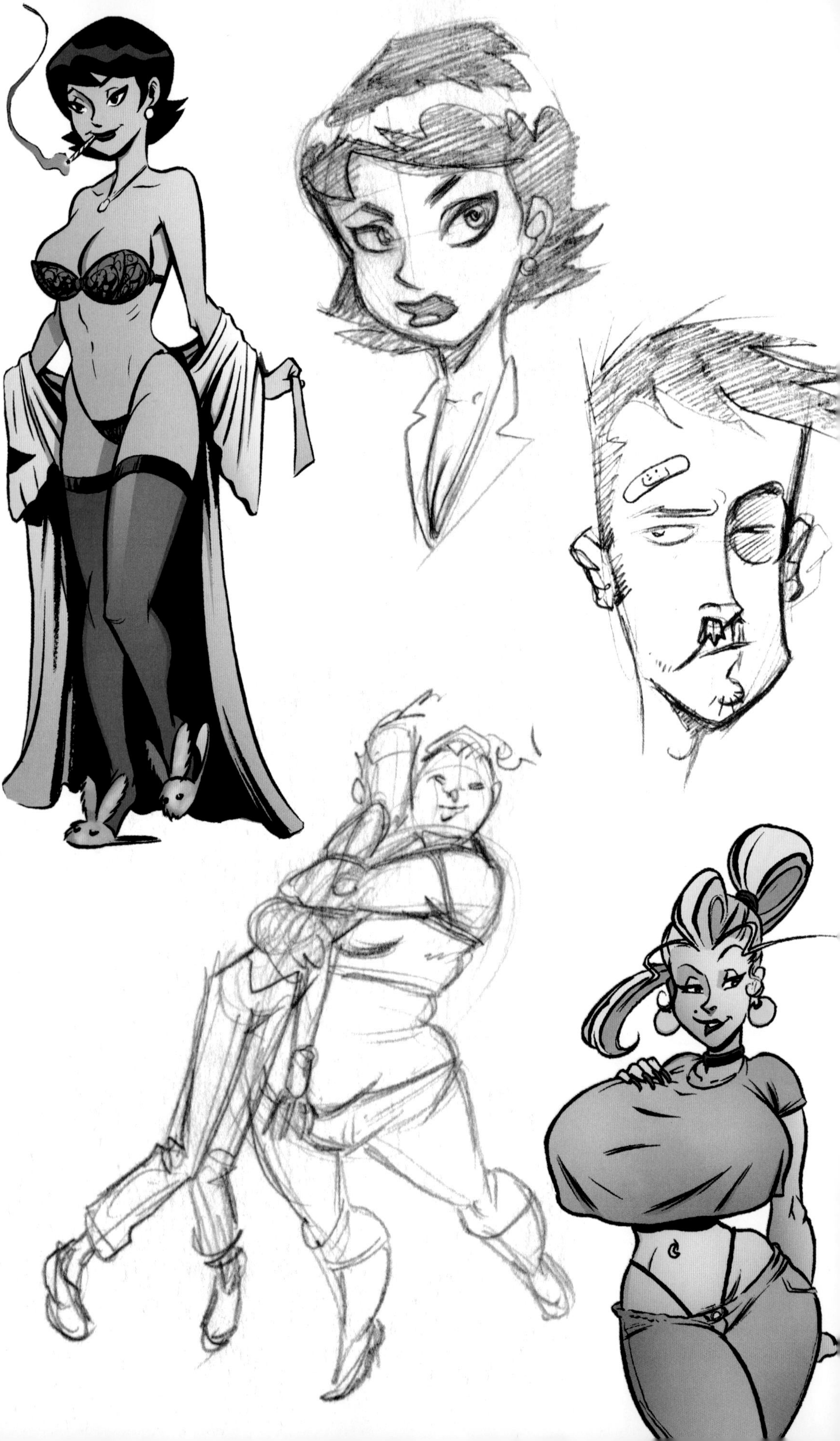

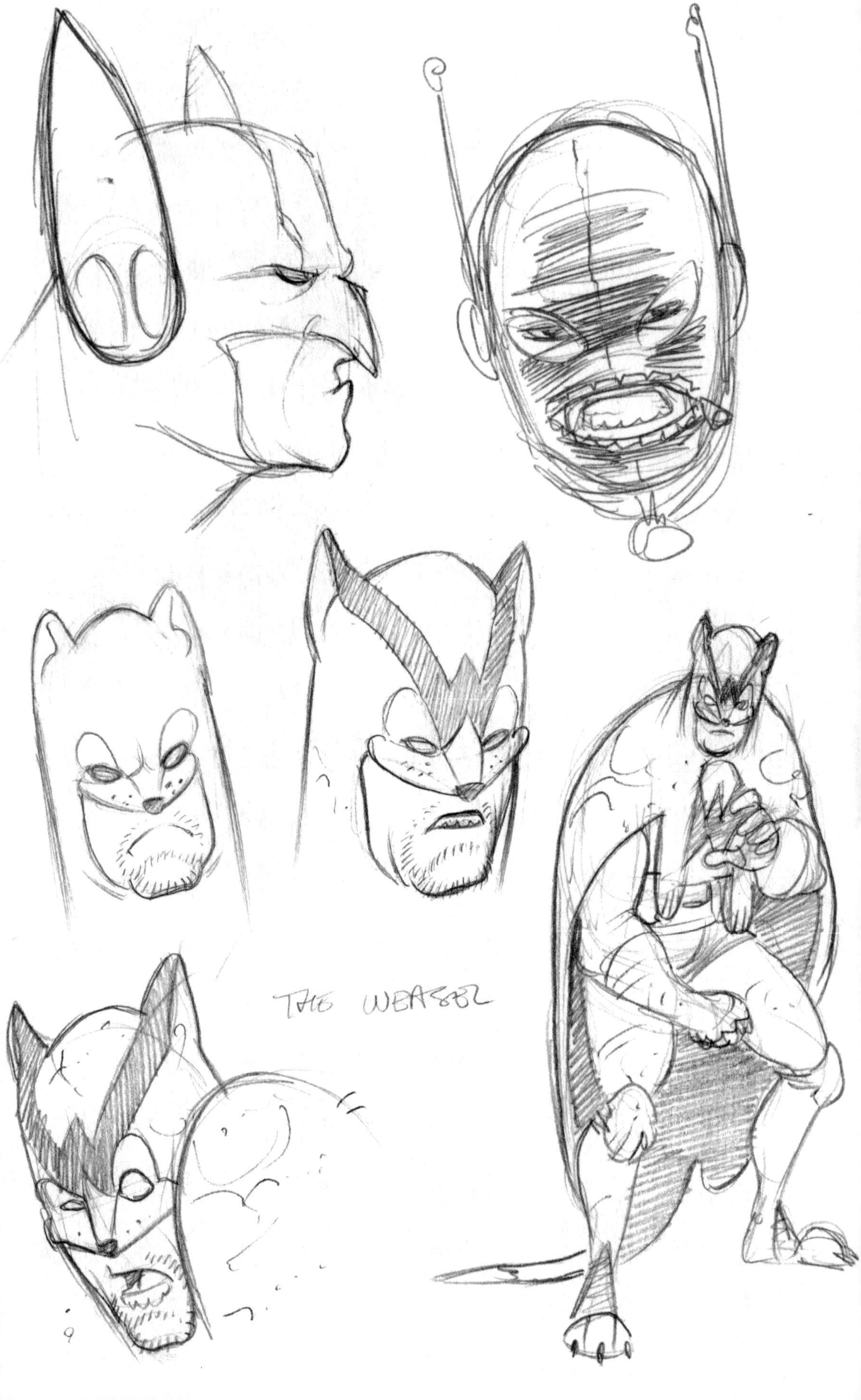
THE WEASEL

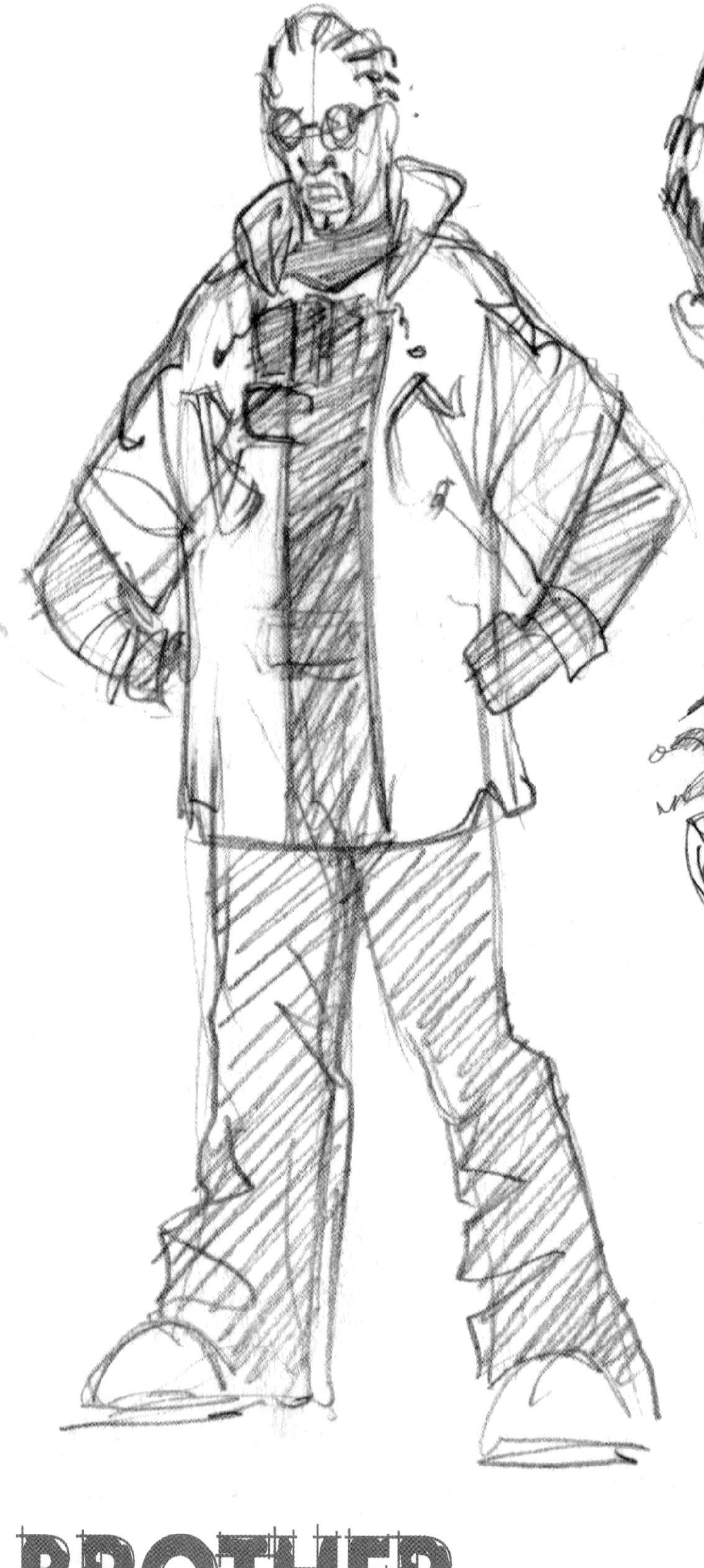

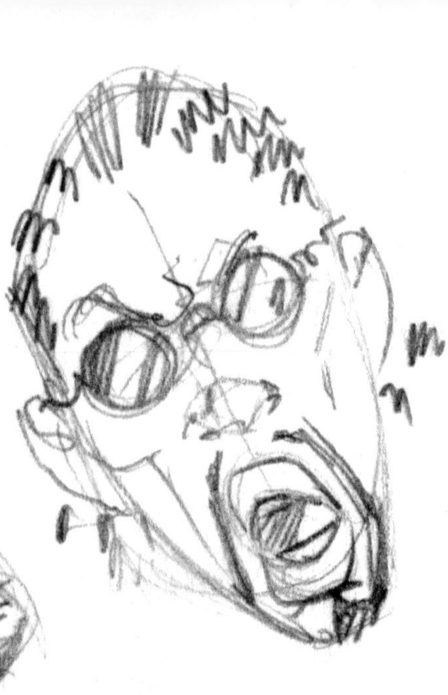

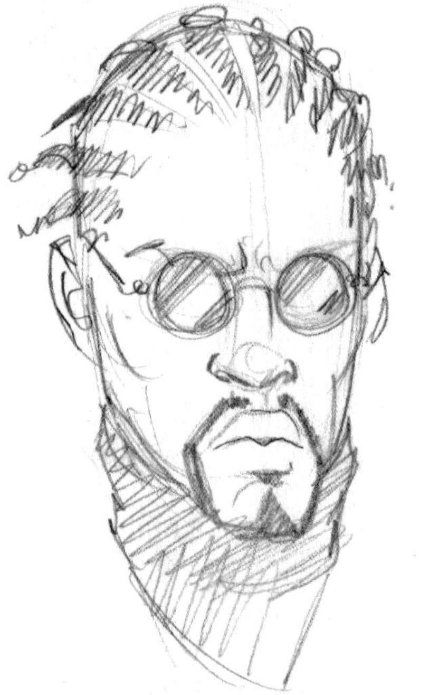

BROTHER COMMANDO

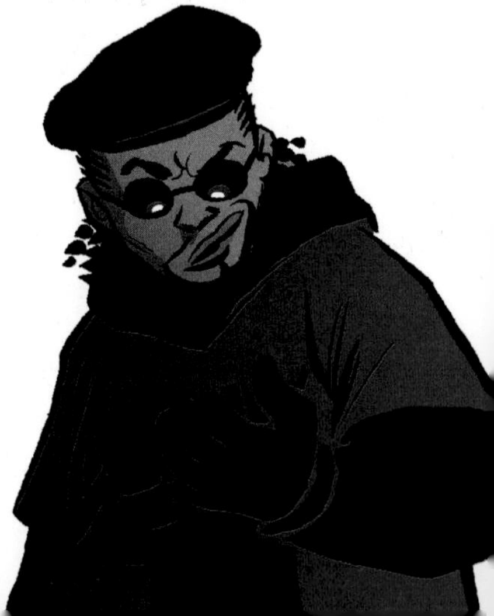

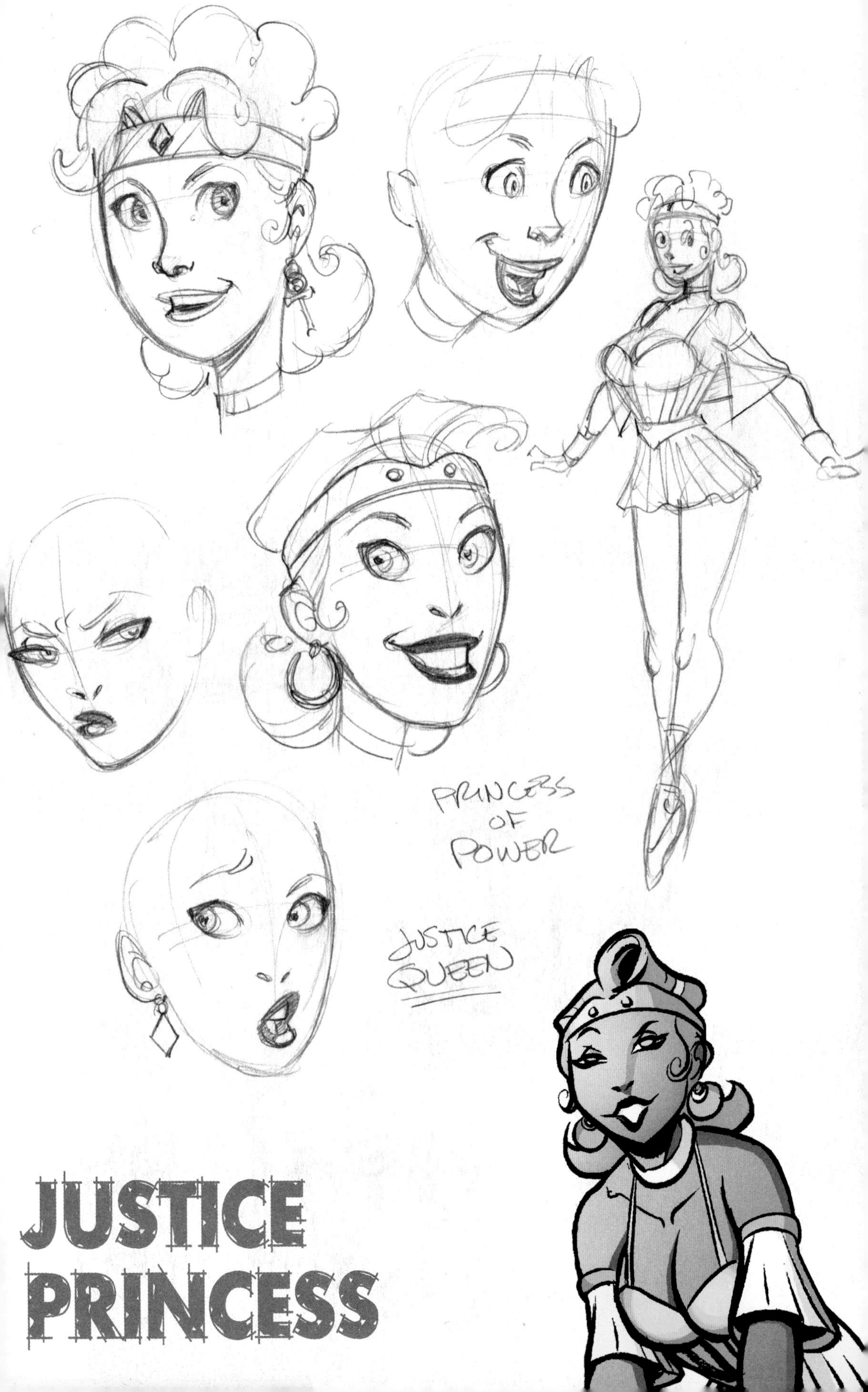
PRINCESS
OF
POWER
JUSTICE
QUEEN

JUSTICE PRINCESS

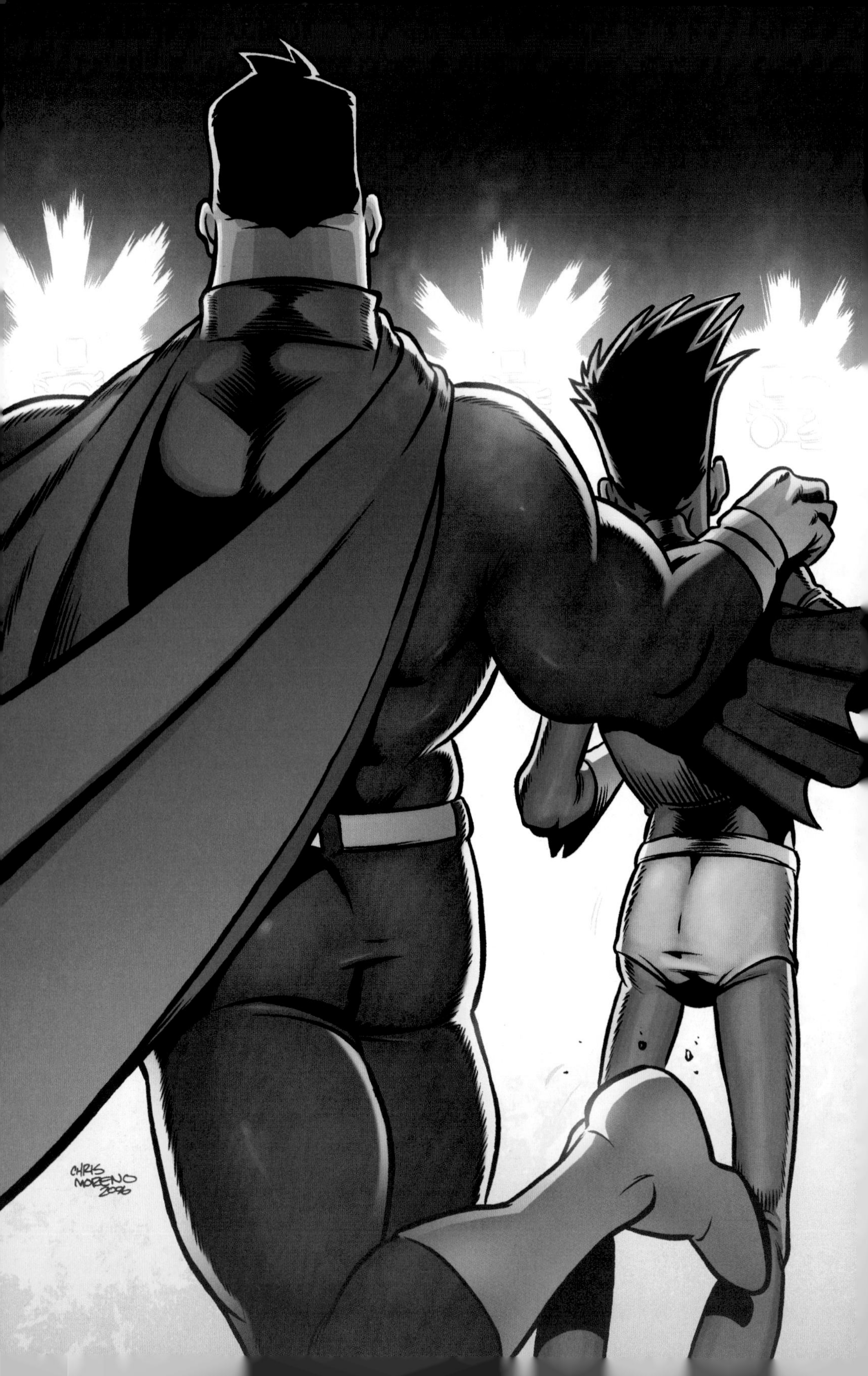
CHRIS
MORENO
2006

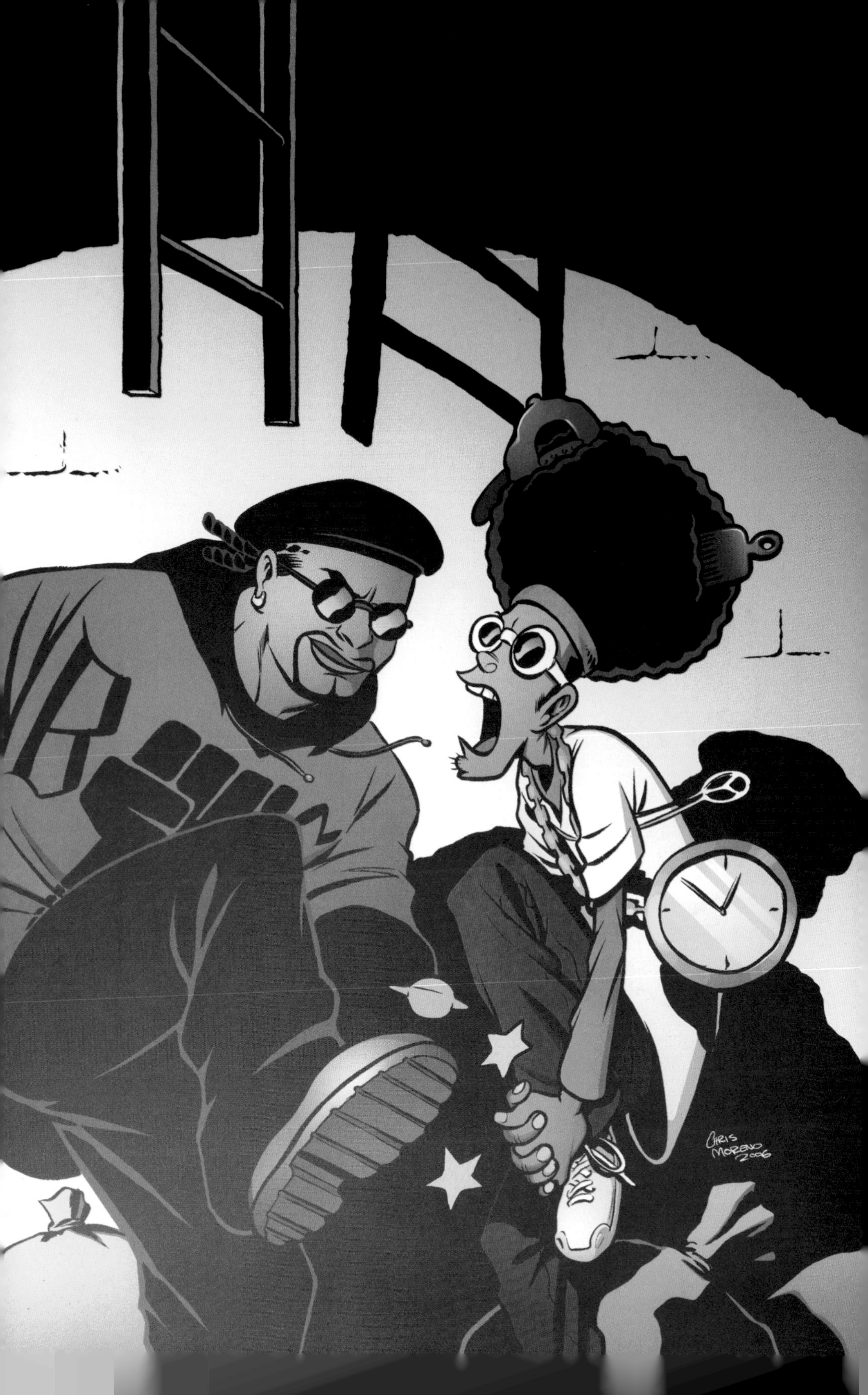
CHRIS MORENO 2006

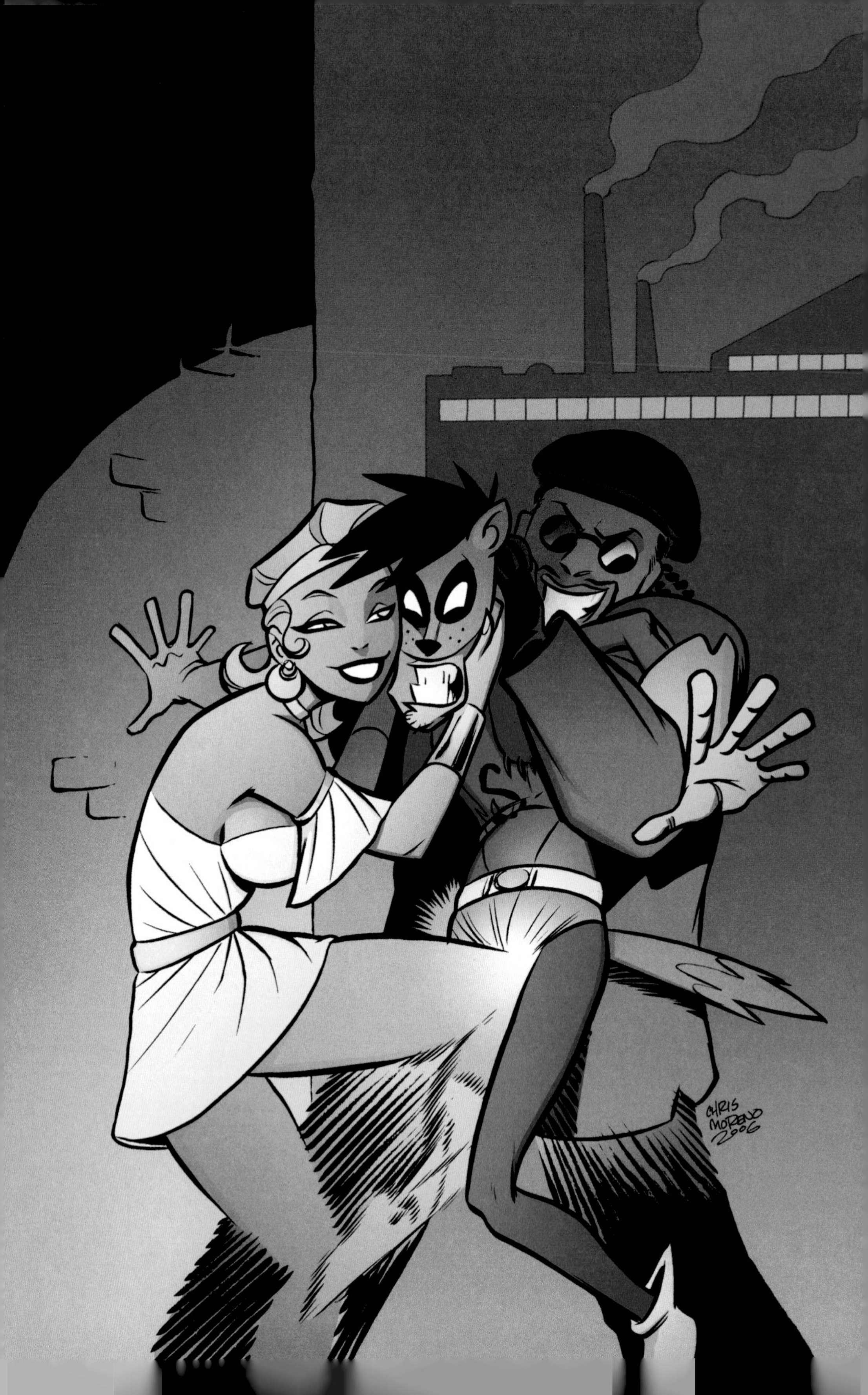
CHRIS
MORENO
2006

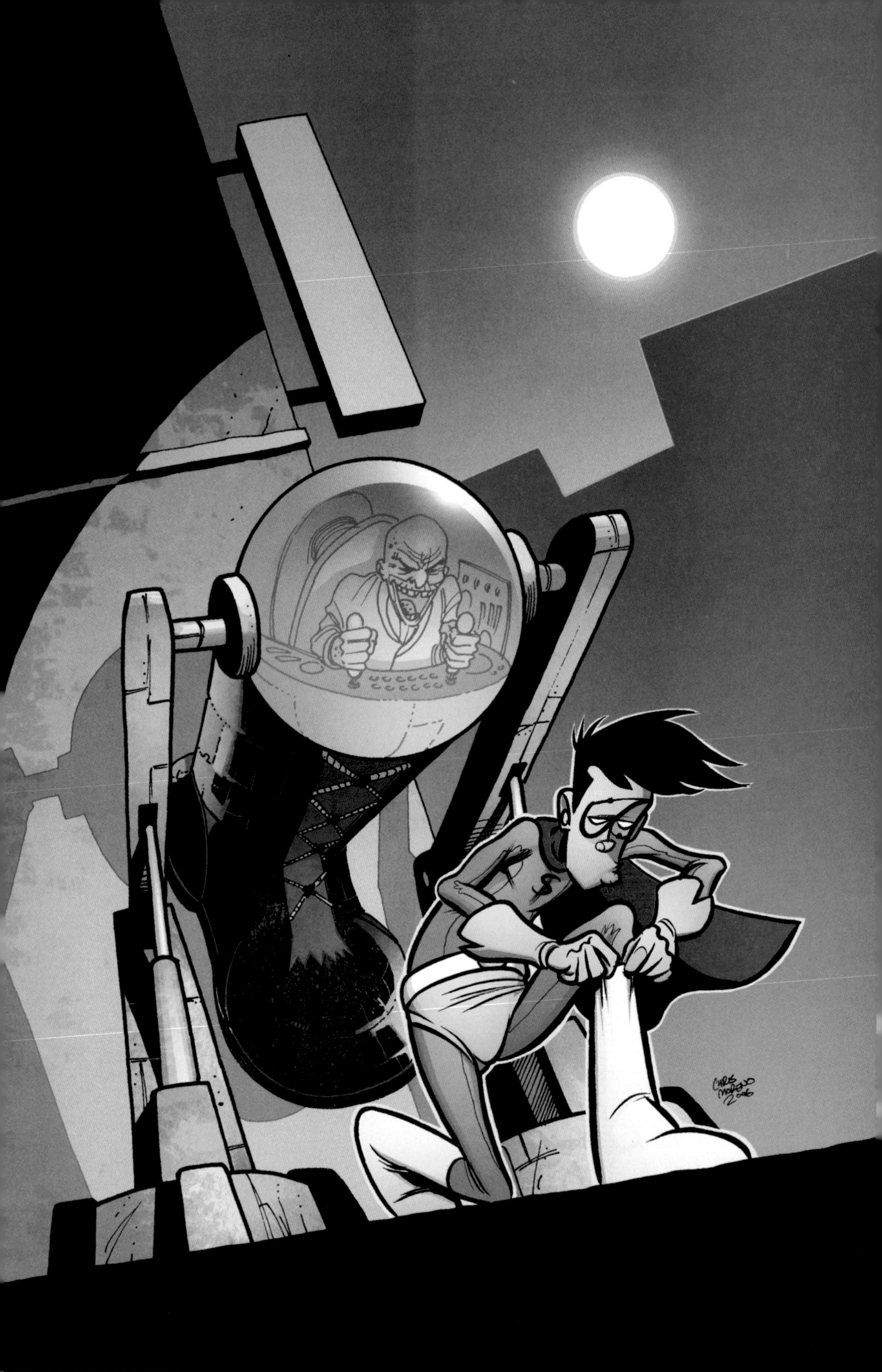
CHRIS MORENO 2006

SSUE #4 COVER

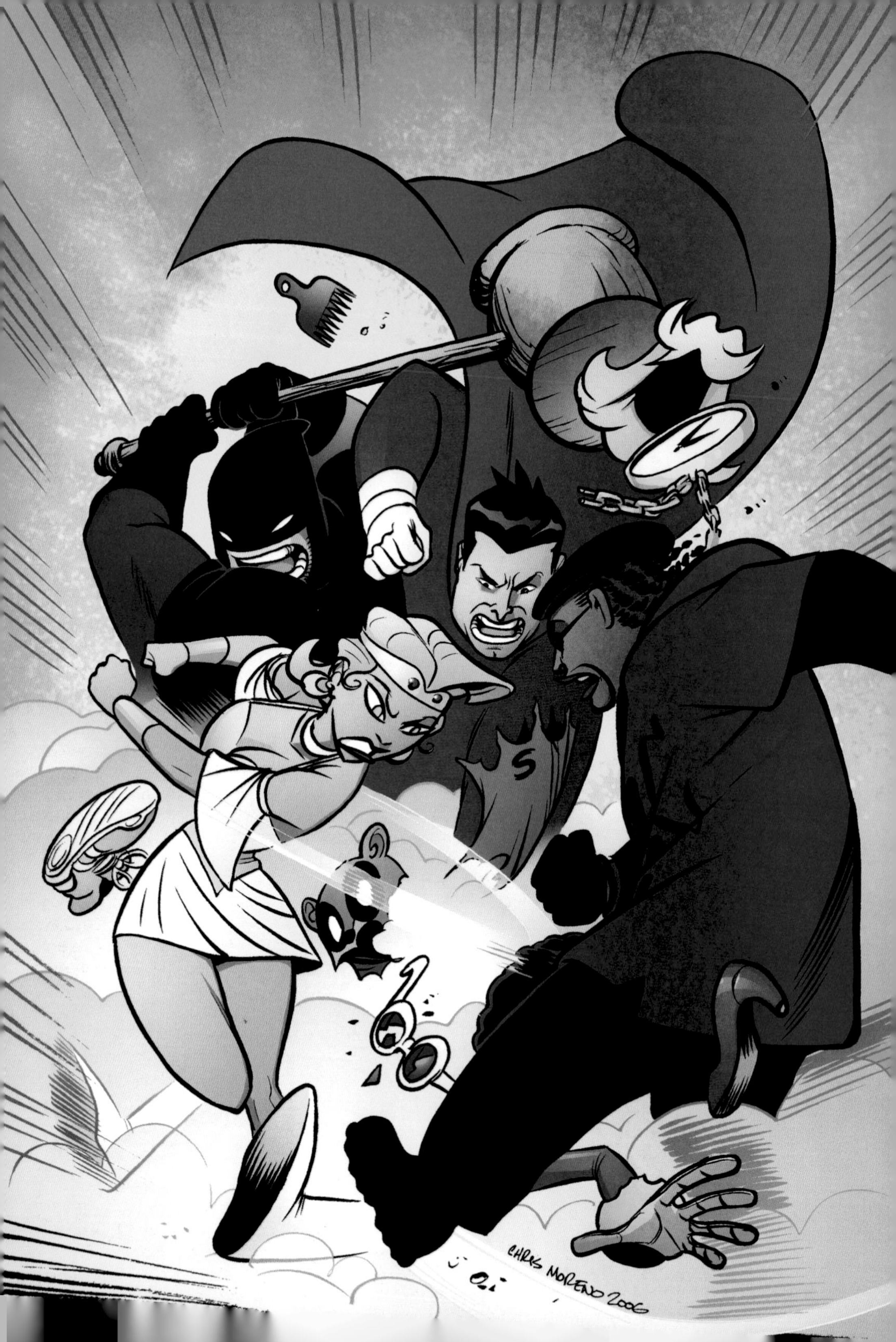
CHRIS MORENO 2006

WIZARD's Create-a-Sidekick Contest Shout Out

What's up, gang? Chris and Paul here with a shout-out to the depraved fans who frequent the so-called "Wizard" message boards (an obvious money laundering front).

Apparently, some of you sick bastards thought it would be a good idea to create a superhero of your own... like Metroville doesn't already have enough problems.

Thanks to "Hush" for sending, "The Lineman." You obviously have a fertile imagination. Please stop calling our houses. "j-Mac"... your Black Pearl idea proves that creativity is alive and well in cyberspace... encased in a black pearl indeed. You are clearly not well. "Comic Hound:" The restraining order is on its way. "tasq:" we definitely want some of what you are smoking. A superhero who does yoga is a lot like a serial killer who plays the bagpipes. "Spider-Dan"... your multiple entries fill us with a mixture of admiration and pure, unadulterated fear. If you see us at a convention, please make yourself known to security. "Ye Olde Iowa:" despite the confusing screen name, we were most impressed with your entry. But what the hell is that screen name all about? Seriously. "Gojira Toho:" remember that drugs are dangerous. Seek help at all costs. "Potatojoe:" It is quite possible you have spent too long in the sun. "Jerry Whitworth:" Chris thinks you spend too much time in strip clubs. Paul thinks it is internet porn. Either way, we salute you! More than one entry proves in a public forum that you are a freak. "Ninja:" just as a favor, we want to let you know that adding stuff like that on the internet is probably getting you a lot of attention from the FBI. "Argyle2001:" the correct medicine for your over-active imagination is spelled V-A-L-I-U-M. You can get it from Canada at half price. "dedred101:" please be careful, dude, as you may well be illegal in some states. We're telling you this for your own good. "drunken fire eater:" what is it with you people? Why are you so obsessed with pimps? Did your pimp beat you up? Let us know and we'll come kick his ass. "TonyM:" you have way too much time on your hands, my friend. We suggest some good, old-fashioned community service to set things straight. Nice job on the art, you sick fuck. "Joe Manic:" we hate you because you will clearly be doing or jobs by this time next year. What, did you spend like six weeks drawing those things? Someone call the police. "Pinkjoe03:" if you really want to get laid we can introduce you to girls... but that's as far as we can take it for legal reasons. "Rockcomics606:" uh... we're not one to criticize but have you ever actually been to Subway? 'Cause we think your superhero might be a real person. We met that guy once... he's pretty amazing. "lordwormm:" we want you to know that the power to control dried leaves was right up there with the power to become a pile of dirt. You almost won... but you didn't. So sue us. "lordosirisprime:" do you seriously expect us to believe you thought of that by yourself? It would take at least ten of our combined brains to think of something that odd. "Rocketboy13:" we loved the fact that you were so fucking lazy you just reprinted all of your Dungeons and Dragons characters. Come hang out with us at a convention. But not for too long. And bring beer. "eye1swuzlost:" frankly, you still are. Lost, that is. We applaud your stubborn desire to be silly in public. We could learn a lot from you. "hainted:" did you even realize all of your superheroes had some connection to food? What... did you have the munchies, or something, when you created those? 'Cause we're pretty certain you were at least mildly stoned. "Spellcheck Killa:" our guess is that you were kept back in Pre-K, and that you resent the American education system. So do we. "lex-man:" You're not fooling anyone, dude... you just want pictures of Goth Girls. In tight situations. Preferably naked. As is your right. "C. Tan:" Does this relate to your personal hygiene habits? "Callipoes Realm Comics:" don't you have a day job, or something? You're supposed to be a place of business. Jeez. "Comicbook13:" Paul considers himself taught a lesson. We bow in awe at your witty wordplay. You bizzaro freak. "anman4:" first of all, we want to know how you were forced to become anman4? What, were you behind three other people who wanted your screen name? As for your entry, while we are impressed, it's only because you are sicker than us. "Big Deb:" Uh... apparently you didn't post your hero properly... we couldn't see the jpeg. It was probably a winner. Hard luck. Nancy was disturbing, by the way. "Big Evil:" this whole thing you have with your character being a bachelor for life – now we're not implying anything but is this autobiographical work? Just asking... "Sammymack:" clearly, you also come from a distant planet. "jasinn:" we have days like that. It'll go away eventually. "jtwilber:" Fetch, the Wonder Stick? Seriously? Dude... you are one fucked up individual. We don't know whether to be afraid or impressed. Please tell us what to do. And frankly, that was the most benign of your many creations. We are in awe. Say hello to the other inpatients. "eliwingz:" stop making us look bad. "ronmolx:" stop making Western Civilization look bad. "The Combator:" it occurs to us that Gynaecology Lad is the single greatest hero of all time. The possibilities are endless. Well... maybe not endless but pretty close. "danielnjones:" sorry we couldn't help. We tried but it was too late. You are on your own. Let us know how it goes when you are released so we can hide under our beds. "quert:" Just say no to LSD, dude. 'Cause once you get started it's really hard to stop. "Martyr of the Cause:" your entry was both huge and terrifying. Our guess is that you probably sent it from Baghdad. If so, give our love to the other insurgents when the electricity comes back on. "stupidsite17:" we want to know how you knew your character was 5'3"? I mean how did you get that far into it, dude? Neither of us can concentrate that hard. Can we use you as a resource when someone asks us stuff like that? As far as we know, Mister Excellent weighs 200 pounds because it's easy to break into chunks of ten. "subpac9:" you know Kurt Cobain blew his brains out with a shotgun, right? We're just worried about you. It's not something to aspire to. "Kaileigh Blue:" At last – someone with intelligence. Someone with flair and creative ability. Someone with a future. We are, of course, talking about Frank Miller. You, on the other hand, are fucked. "Ernest Effort:" That is just, well... that's, uh. Wow. Damn. Since we know the meaning of the word "scat," we are apparently just as sick as you. But even so... dang. "Lyle:" did you also undergo art therapy? Sounds nice. "Buba Phatt:" We are confused, we'll admit it. How did you combine the two concepts of Monkey Feet and the name Jorge Congosa? Do you know someone with that name? Is it you? Do you have Monkey feet? "(.Y.):" Are you by any chance from Canada? What is it with you guys? Can you create a hero that is NOT Canadian? Weirdos. "Justin Hall:" You're not fooling anyone, dude. It's okay. Just let it out. We understand. "Fital:" You should have won. It was an accounting error. "donpobre: we hope that your character finds a home that is very far away on a different continent... preferably Antarctica. That way, we take care of the competition. "killianjdark:" you finished dead last in the voting. Congrats! "Ron G:" Do we know you? Aren't you the guy who gave us the idea for Sidekick in the first place? Call our lawyers. "cpr4life:" We shun you as we would shun a rabid badger. "frenzy:" we're pretty sure someone is spying on you over the internet. That would be us. We loved that Asian goat website. "batfan Sarah:" you get the final mention here, and that means you are dead last in our estimation. We have high hopes for Captain Ritalin. Good luck with that!

Best,

Paul and Chris

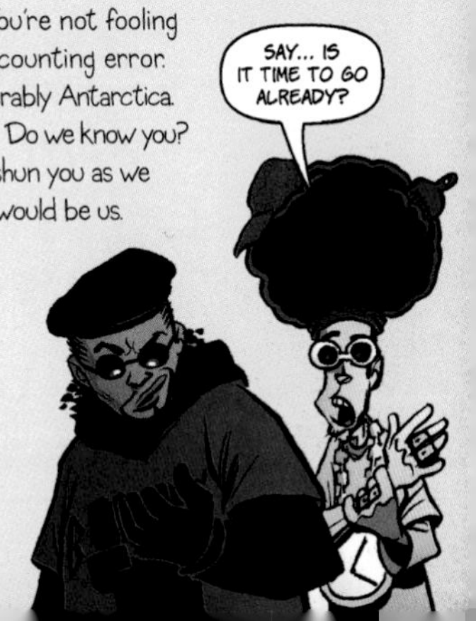
SAY... IS IT TIME TO GO ALREADY?

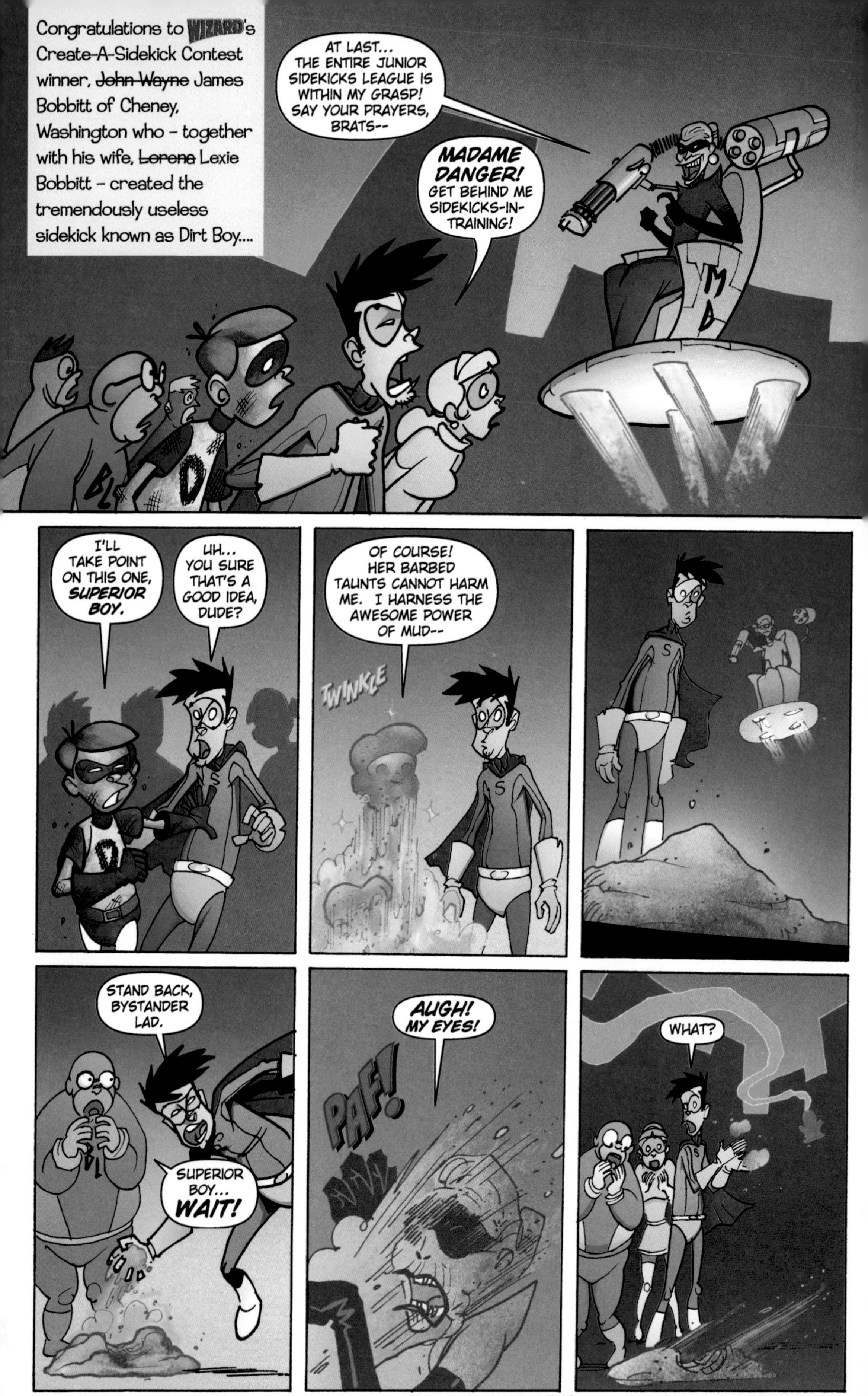
Congratulations to WIZARD's Create-A-Sidekick Contest winner, ~~John Wayne~~ James Bobbitt of Cheney, Washington who – together with his wife, ~~Lorena~~ Lexie Bobbitt – created the tremendously useless sidekick known as Dirt Boy....
AT LAST... THE ENTIRE JUNIOR SIDEKICKS LEAGUE IS WITHIN MY GRASP! SAY YOUR PRAYERS, BRATS--
MADAME DANGER! GET BEHIND ME SIDEKICKS-IN-TRAINING!
I'LL TAKE POINT ON THIS ONE, SUPERIOR BOY.
UH... YOU SURE THAT'S A GOOD IDEA, DUDE?
OF COURSE! HER BARBED TAUNTS CANNOT HARM ME. I HARNESS THE AWESOME POWER OF MUD--
TWINKLE
STAND BACK, BYSTANDER LAD.
SUPERIOR BOY... WAIT!
PAF!
AUGH! MY EYES!
WHAT?

...that we have just killed in print. And not a moment too soon.
- Paul and Chris

I would like to dedicate this book to the bipolar stripper on crack who stabbed me with a kitchen knife and then called the police trying to get me arrested. Thanks for the inspiration, bitch.

-*Paul*

This one goes out to all of us "Eddies" out there who've said "yes" too many times, "no" too few, and paid the price for it. If I had it to do all over again I wouldn't change a thing.

-*Chris*

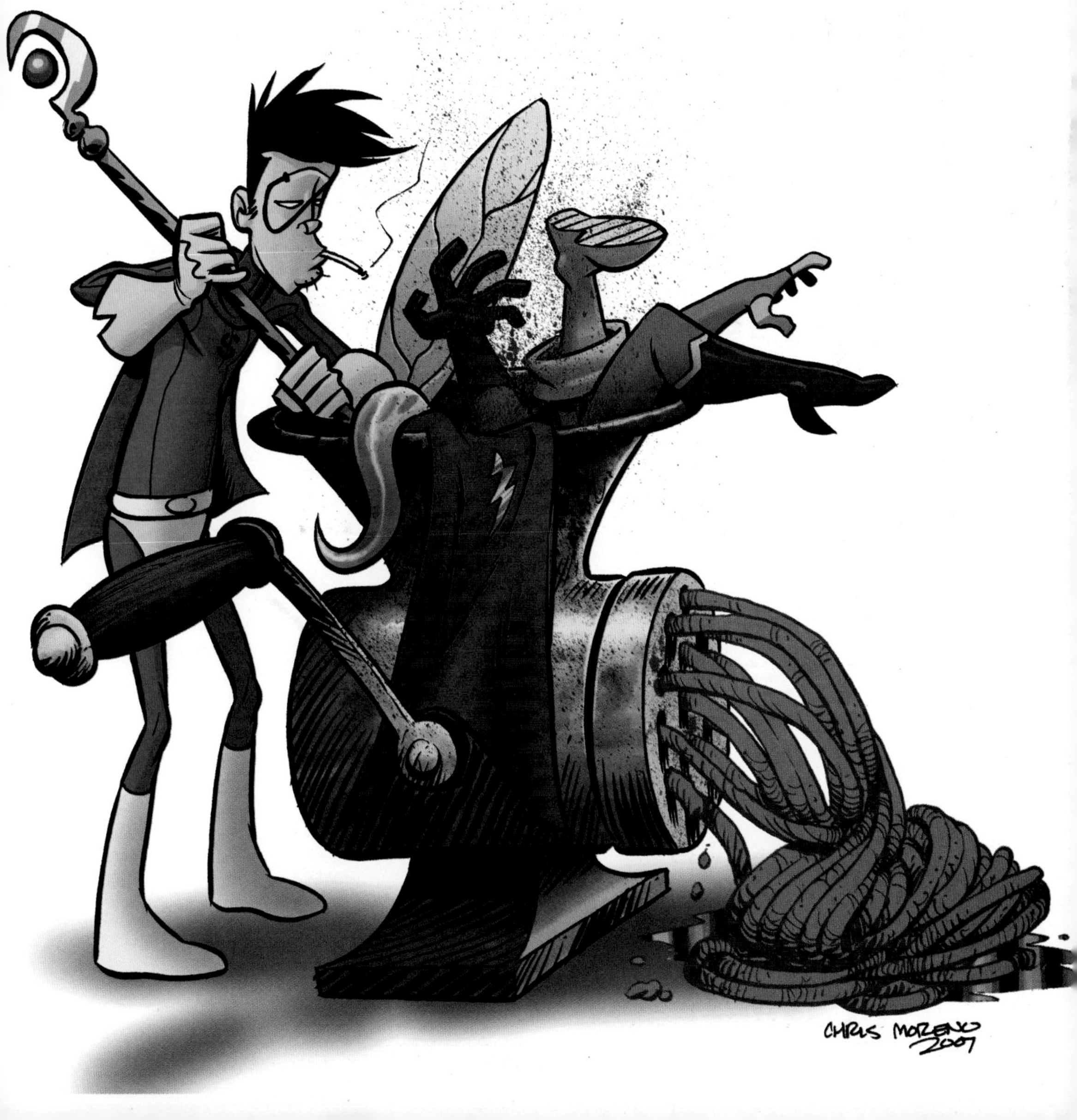
CHRIS MORENO 2007

the Ride

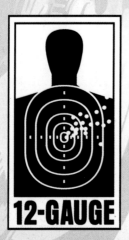

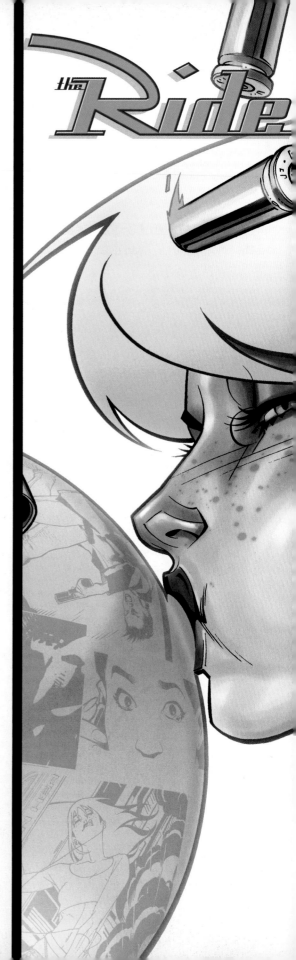

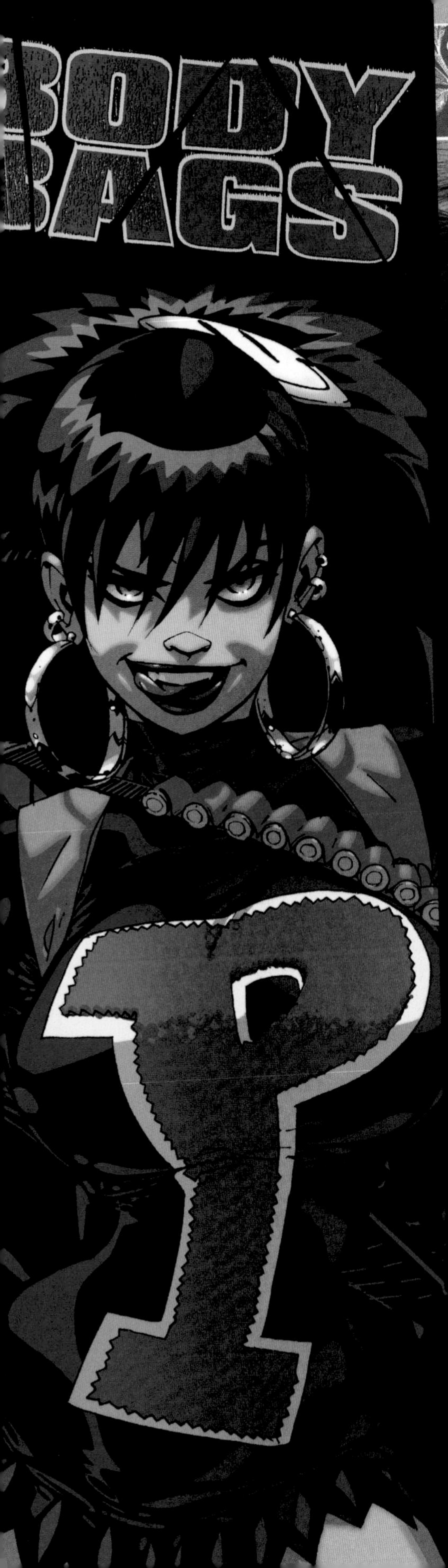
BODY
BAGS
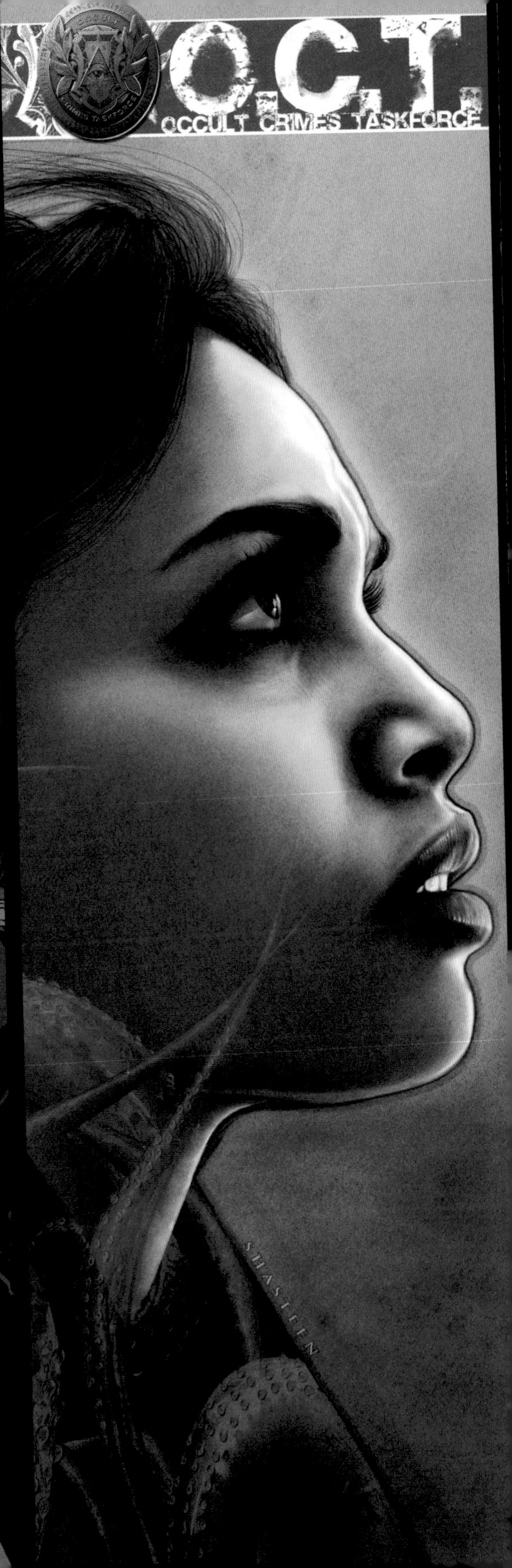
O.C.T.
OCCULT CRIMES TASKFORCE
SHASTEEN

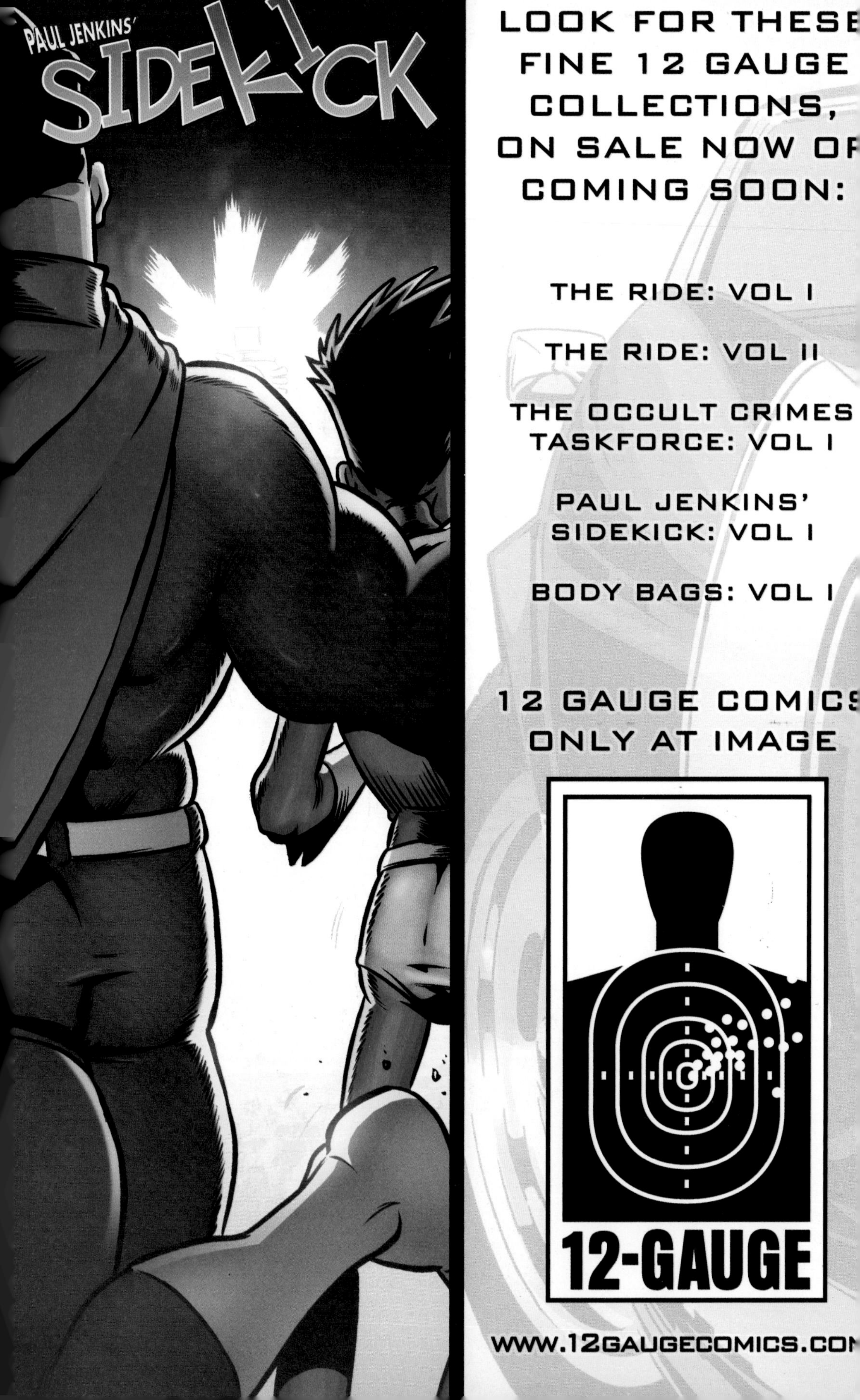
PAUL JENKINS'
SIDEKICK